PENGUIN BOOKS

Managing Without Profit

Praise for the first edition

'One of the best books of effective management I have seen'
Stuart Etherington, Chief Executive of the National Council of Voluntary Organizations

'An intelligent, thoughtful analysis' *David Green, Director of Voluntary Service Overseas*

'Thought provoking and reassuring' *Richard Eyre, former Director of the Royal National Theatre*

'An excellent practical and theoretical guide for those who have to manage' *Graham Collis, Managing Director of Two Castles Housing Association*

'Voted one of *Tomorrow*'s best ten books' Tomorrow
magazine

Mike Hudson is founder and senior partner of Compass Partnership, a firm of management consultants which works exclusively with not-for-profit organizations.

He studied Engineering Science at Durham University and then pursued his interest in protecting the environment by working for Friends of the Earth, latterly as Administrative Director. Following graduation as an MBA from London Business School, he worked for an international firm of consultants helping multinational firms in the UK and the USA resolve strategic management problems.

He has provided consultancy services to the not-for-profit sector for seventeen years in the course of which he has worked with over three hundred organizations, among them English National Ballet, Amnesty International, the World Wide Fund for Nature, Mencap, Guide Dogs for the Blind, the *Big Issue*, Oxfam, the Prince's Trust, Methodist Homes and the National Council for Voluntary Organizations. He has also worked for funding bodies such as the Arts Council, the Department of Health, the Home Office, Lloyds TSB Foundation and the National Lottery Charities Board. His overseas assignments have included work for organizations in Bangladesh, the Czech Republic, Nepal, Poland, South Africa, Switzerland, Uganda and Zimbabwe.

Mike Hudson has four children and lives near Marlow. He is chair of ACT, the Association of Consultants and Trainers working with not-for-profit organizations, a governor of a leading preparatory school and a Fellow of the Royal Society of Arts.

Managing Without Profit

The Art of Managing Third-sector Organizations

NEW EDITION

Mike Hudson

PENGUIN BOOKS
Published in association with the Directory of Social Change

PENGUIN BOOKS

Published by the Penguin Group
Penguin Books Ltd, 27 Wrights Lane, London w8 5tz, England
Penguin Putnam Inc., 375 Hudson Street, New York, New York 10014, USA
Penguin Books Australia Ltd, Ringwood, Victoria, Australia
Penguin Books Canada Ltd, 10 Alcorn Avenue, Toronto, Ontario, Canada m4v 3b2
Penguin Books (NZ) Ltd, Private Bag 102902, NSMC, Auckland, New Zealand

Penguin Books Ltd, Registered Offices: Harmondsworth, Middlesex, England

First published 1995
Second edition published 1999

10 9 8 7 6 5 4 3 2

Copyright © Mike Hudson, 1995, 1999

The moral right of the author has been asserted

Set in 9.5/12 pt Adobe Minion
Typeset by Rowland Phototypesetting Ltd, Bury St Edmunds, Suffolk
Made and printed in Great Britain by Clays Ltd, St Ives plc

Contents

Foreword ix

Acknowledgements xiii

Introduction xv

1 The Undiscovered Sector 1

1.1 A Historical Perspective 1
1.2 Boundaries of the Sector 8
1.3 The Sector is Significant and Growing 13
1.4 Managing Third-sector Organizations 15

2 Choosing an Appropriate Institutional Structure 23

2.1 The Meaning of Institutional Structure 23
2.2 The Options for Institutional Structures 24
2.3 The Special Circumstances of International Organizations 31
2.4 Governing Different Structures 32
2.5 Different Arrangements for Choosing Board Members 36

3 Concepts for Creating Boards that Govern 39

3.1 Boards Have Special Functions 39
3.2 Distinguishing Governance from Management 41
3.3 The Life Cycle of Boards 44
3.4 Key Roles of an Effective Board 47
3.5 Committees Do Board Work 54

4 Making Boards Govern 66

4.1 Strong Boards are Essential 66
4.2 Forces Driving Boards into Ineffectiveness 67
4.3 Attracting and Developing Board Members 69
4.4 The Special Role of the Chair 77
4.5 Increasing Board Effectiveness 80
4.6 Increasing Committee Effectiveness 89

5 Strengthening Strategic Management 93

5.1 The Strategic Management Process 93
5.2 Choosing Where to Start 97
5.3 The Concepts of Vision, Mission and Values 99
5.4 Creating and Refreshing Visions and Missions 105

6 Establishing Overall Objectives and Strategies 112

6.1 The Need for Objectives and Strategies 112
6.2 The Hierarchy of Objectives 113
6.3 Clarifying Strategic Objectives 120
6.4 Strategy Evolves 123
6.5 Strategic Reviews, Positions and Choices 125
6.6 Developing Strategic Plans 136
6.7 Common Strategic Dilemmas 148

7 Service Strategies and Operational Plans 157

7.1 Defining Services and Campaigns 157
7.2 Developing Service Strategies 160
7.3 Operational Plans 164

8 Managing Strategic Performance 171

8.1 Stakeholders Need Measurable Results 171
8.2 Concepts behind Performance Management 173
8.3 Performance Indicators 176
8.4 Strengthening Performance-Management Systems 181
8.5 Benchmarking Catalyses Performance Improvements 186
8.6 Continuous Improvement Through Quality Management 190
8.7 Ensuring Financial Information Supports Management 195

9	**Creating Flexible Management Structures**	205
9.1	Change by Continuous Adjustment	205
9.2	Options for Structuring Management	207
9.3	Design Dilemmas	214
9.4	Implementing Changes to the Structure	218
9.5	Strengthening Cross-departmental Working	225

10	**Managing Change**	233
10.1	Managing Change is an Essential Skill	233
10.2	Introduction to Organization Culture	235
10.3	Change Management Concepts	238
10.4	Characteristics of Change Processes	244
10.5	The Stages of a Change Management Initiative	246
10.6	Skills of the Change Management Leader	267

11	**Leading, Directing and Managing**	272
11.1	Management Jobs are Different	272
11.2	Special Characteristics of the Chief Executive's Job	273
11.3	Structuring the Chief Executive's Work	277
11.4	Chief Executives Provide Leadership	284
11.5	Divisional Directors Direct	291
11.6	Managers Must Manage	296

12	**Managing People**	303
12.1	Developing People is an Art	303
12.2	Managing Your Boss	304
12.3	Getting Performance from Teams	307
12.4	Delegating Work and Empowering People	319

13	**Creating a Learning Organization**	328
13.1	Encouraging Learning Throughout the Organization	328
13.2	Developing Individuals	330
13.3	Promoting Learning Through One-to-Ones and Performance Review	335
13.4	Encouraging Coaching, Mentoring and Shadowing	344

13.5	Encouraging Teams to Learn	348
13.6	Ensnaring Organization-wide Learning	351
14	**Managing Different Types of Organization**	**355**
14.1	Organization Life Cycles	355
14.2	Classifying Organizations	359
14.3	Putting the Classifications Together	366
14.4	Managing Service-providing Organizations	368
14.5	Managing Mutual-support Organizations	374
14.6	Managing Campaigning Organizations	378
15	**A Glimpse into the Future**	**383**
	Appendix: Compass Partnership	391
	Further Reading	392
	Index	403

Foreword

I started writing the first edition of this book five years ago; since then there have been many developments in the management of third-sector organizations:

- Organizations are changing more frequently and more rapidly as the pace of change in the external environment quickens.
- There is growing recognition that changes to management processes, relationships and culture are the keys to making organizations more efficient and effective.
- Funders have become increasingly demanding, expecting organizations to compete for funds, specify desired outcomes and report on results.
- There is now a core of highly experienced and sophisticated managers in senior positions in many organizations.
- Investment of time and resources into professional development is increasingly seen as critical to the long-term success of organizations.
- There is much greater interchange of people and ideas between the private, public and third sectors.
- Professional associations that support people working in the sector are stronger and are paying much greater attention to management development.
- Organizations have become more international in their orientation, setting up overseas offices and working with similar organizations in other countries.

These changes have occurred in all parts of the sector. They have been accompanied by a growing recognition that high-level management skills are essential, not just at the top of organizations but at all levels of management. It is increasingly acknowledged that regional, centre and service managers need to be as skilled in the art of management as people working at the corporate level. Consequently, there is growing demand for management skills to be further developed and strengthened at all levels of not-for-profit organizations.

During this period there has also been continued explosive growth in the use of new management methods in the world of business. Quality management, business process re-engineering, knowledge management, strategic performance management, benchmarking, de-layering, cost reduction, competencies, empowerment and organization transformation are just a few of the techniques that have become more widely used in the corporate sector. Criticized sometimes for their faddishness and sometimes for being ineffective, they are nevertheless the drivers of change in many business organizations.

Some of these methods have migrated to the third sector, most notably the use of quality-management systems and benchmarking. Both are now widely talked about, though the sector has yet to shape them to fit with its own culture and values. Some, such as strategic performance management and social audit, are just starting to generate significant interest and are likely to become more widely used as organizations face greater pressures to demonstrate their achievements to their funders and other stakeholders.

This movement of management ideas across sectors follows the pattern of the last twenty years, where management techniques were developed mainly in business schools, applied in the corporate sector and then transferred to the third sector. What has changed, however, is the time it takes for ideas to be applied. Whereas application in the third sector used to trail the business world by ten to twenty years, the lag is now nearer five to ten years.

Management methods have also started to flow in the opposite direction, from the third sector to the private and public sectors. Most third-sector organizations have a vision for making the world a better place. They are able to motivate people with a meaningful mission that relates their work to the organization's objectives. For many years they have involved users directly in the development and monitoring of services. They have been very successful at promoting and retaining women in senior management positions and they have much to teach the other sectors about equal opportunities practices. These skills are increasingly relevant in the private and public sectors.

Another change since starting work on the first edition is that a much wider range of learning opportunities and methods is available to managers. There are many more courses on offer and much more extensive use is made of on-the-job learning methods such as coaching, mentoring and shadowing.

There have also been developments within specific areas of management:

- In strategic planning much more attention is being given to implementation and improved management of performance.
- In governance it is widely accepted that boards need to focus on their special and distinctive role and that this takes effort and discipline.
- In linking governance and management, there is much greater awareness of the critical importance of the need for chairs and chief executives to have clearly delineated roles and to work closely together to maximize the effectiveness of their organizations.
- In decision-making the need for much greater user involvement has risen sharply up the agenda, with management exploring many different ways of enabling users to have greater influence on organizations.

Changes in this edition

The many changes I have made in this edition respond both to these developments and to the many constructive comments I received concerning the first edition. The main modifications are:

- three new chapters, one on managing change, one on managing strategic performance and one on creating a learning organization
- new sections on benchmarking, the importance of building a strong senior management team, the special role of the chair, cross-departmental working and empowering people
- integration of the concepts of organization culture into the new change management chapter
- consolidation of all the material on vision and mission, objectives and strategies and service planning into chapters of their own
- inclusion of many new examples in response to readers' requests for more cases

● descriptions of relevant books published since the last edition – which have been added to the appendix entitled Further Reading.

I have been heartened by the many positive responses to the first edition which I have received. Since it was published it has been reprinted twice and translated into three other languages. My aims in creating this new edition have been to make improvements where they were required and to bring the book up to date. The fundamental objective nevertheless remains the same: to provide busy managers with a handy reference book that fits into a briefcase and can be 'dipped into' every time you need an injection of new ideas or experience.

I hope you will find that this edition meets your needs, and I urge you to continue writing to me at Compass Partnership with your comments and feedback.

Mike Hudson
Seaview
Isle of Wight
August 1998

Acknowledgements

This second edition of *Managing Without Profit* is the result of a continuing collaboration with a large number of people who have provided me with immense support and guidance.

My thinking has been informed by British and American academics and authors who write about business management and increasingly about the management of third-sector organizations. They are too many to mention by name, but they deserve acknowledgement because their work continues to make a significant contribution to mine.

Particular thanks are due to all the clients of Compass Partnership who have invited my staff and me into their organizations and provided the crucial practical experience without which it would not have been possible to write a book that attempts to combine theory and practice.

Many readers of the first edition found the case studies to be among the most instructive parts of the book. Special thanks therefore go to all the chief executives who have updated case studies or allowed me to use their organizations as new case studies for this edition.

I would like to repeat my thanks to all the trustees, chief executives and managers who assisted with the first edition. You laid the foundations upon which this second edition has been built and I continue to be deeply grateful for your contributions.

This edition has been improved beyond recognition by the contributions of people who made constructive comments on the draft. Very many thanks for your time and effort: Lynne Berry (Chief Executive of the Charity Commission), Naomi Eisenstadt (Chief Executive of Family Service Units), David Green (Chief Executive of Voluntary Service Overseas), Dave Harker (Chief Executive of the National Association of

Citizens' Advice Bureaux), Jon Lane (Chief Executive of WaterAid), Geraldine Peacock (Chief Executive of Guide Dogs for the Blind), Richard Shaw (Deputy Chief Executive of English National Ballet) and Christopher Spence (Chief Executive of the National Centre for Volunteering).

Melinda Letts, until recently Chief Executive of the National Asthma Campaign, deserves very special thanks for working meticulously through the draft and making a large number of constructive and insightful comments.

Kate Sayer of Sayer Vincent and Keith Smith, until recently Chief Executive of Broadcasting Support Services, provided valuable comments on sections of the book.

This edition could not have been written without the generous support I have received from past and current colleagues at Compass Partner-ship. Thank you Allison Aldred, Joanna Buckingham, Lesley Ellarby, Joy MacKeith, Hilary Rowell, Irene Short and John Tierney. Roger Parry has to be singled out for particular support, both for his comments on the book and for taking responsibility for Compass Partnership while I was away from the office.

Debbie Emerson once again deserves particular thanks for her heroic effort, this time for taking a mass of inconsistently formatted diskettes and poorly prepared diagrams and converting them all into beautifully prepared manuscript. Claire Redfern also deserves special thanks for meticulously reading the proofs, improving the English and spotting many errors that slipped through the net.

Finally, my most grateful thanks are due to my wife Diana, who once again backed me throughout this venture, and to my children Jennifer, Timothy, Jessica and Katherine for providing loving support from the start to the finish of this project.

Introduction

Not-for-profit organizations exist throughout the world.

They prosper in industrialized economies and they are also a central part of the social fabric in developing economies. They thrive in free democratic societies and they play an important role in less democratic regimes. They flourish in urban areas and are equally important in rural areas. Not-for-profit organizations exist everywhere because of a human quality that brings people together to provide services for themselves and others and to campaign against abuse of fellow human beings, animals and the environment. People want health, welfare, educational, humanitarian, environmental and cultural services to improve the world we live in. They expect the organizations that provide them to be 'not-for-profit' and sometimes 'not-in-the-public-sector' as well.

This book is about managing not-for-profit organizations. It describes how to improve the performance of organizations that are part of the expanding 'third sector'.

DEFINING THE THIRD SECTOR

This sector consists of organizations whose primary objectives are social rather than economic. The core of the sector includes charities, religious organizations, arts organizations, community organizations, campaigning organizations, trade unions, trade and professional associations and other not-for-profit and civic society organizations.

The term 'third sector' distinguishes these organizations from the 'private sector' and the 'public sector'. The ethos that all these organizations share is that they are driven by a cause. They are established and managed by people who believe that changes are needed and who want to do something about it themselves. These organizations share two common characteristics. Unlike private-sector organizations, they do not distribute profits to their owners; and, unlike public-sector organizations, they are not subject to direct political control. These organizations have the independence to determine their own futures.

Around the periphery of these core third-sector organizations is a growing number of bodies that are semi-independent from the public sector. Examples include social housing organizations, education colleges, quasi-non-governmental organizations and, perhaps in the future, schools and hospital trusts. There is also a group of organizations such as independent schools, friendly societies and provident societies which sit on a periphery that overlaps with the private sector. These organizations share some management practices with the third sector.

Scope of the sector

Until relatively recently it was thought that this diverse range of organizations did not have much in common. All were seen as separate strands of social life, each with its unique history and role in society. Increasingly, these organizations are seen as part of one sector because they have a common heritage and the same motivation and desire to improve the world in which we live.

They are coalescing because they recognize that many have more in common with each other than with organizations in the public or private sectors. The process began in the USA some twenty years ago. In America the sector is much larger because many hospitals, colleges and universities have always been independent, not-for-profit organizations. There the state has tended to contract out the provision of a wider range of services. In the UK many of these organizations were independent until the twentieth century, when they increasingly became part of the welfare state. Some are now starting to move back from the public sector into the third sector.

The third sector is enormously influential. Many of the greatest social changes and innovations have been brought to fruition through the creation of a third-sector organization. Hospital services, education, services for disadvantaged groups and people with disabilities, research into disease, spiritual development, benevolent funds for industry employees, social services, international development and, more recently, environmental protection and most human rights campaigns emanated from third-sector organizations.

This sector is currently growing in confidence. At a time when many public-sector organizations are perceived to be inadequate at dealing efficiently with the social problems of today, the third sector sees itself as having the potential to play an expanded role. It has the unique ability to combine entrepreneurialism with a social conscience – the very characteristics that are needed to address some of the most deeply rooted social problems facing both industrialized and non-industrialized countries.

The marriage of mission and management

These organizations are driven by a desire to improve the world in which we live. Most of the people who manage, work and volunteer for them believe in the creation of a fairer, more caring, better-educated and more healthy world.

The mission often pervades all aspects of these organizations. Board members volunteer their time because they support the mission; staff often work long hours for no extra financial reward; and funders give money to demonstrate their solidarity with the mission.

However, management is equally important to the success of these organizations. Until the middle of the 1970s management was not a word many people used when talking about third-sector organizations. Management was seen to be part of the culture of business and was not felt to be appropriate in third-sector organizations.

The dramatic growth and the increasingly professional and skilled approach of these organizations have completely changed that view. Nowadays management is being colonized for third-sector organizations and its language and concepts trip off people's tongues as easily as eloquent speeches about the cause.

But management cannot be imported unchanged and imposed on third-sector organizations. There are subtle and critical differences that are rooted in the different ethos that underlies these organizations. All too often people from both the private and public sectors believe or make the implicit assumption that their management theories should be applied to third-sector organizations to make them more effective. 'If only this charity were more business-like' is a common sentiment. However, while these theories can bring benefits, they are of limited value unless they are crafted to address the critical features of third-sector organizations.

In order to understand how to manage these organizations effectively, theories which are sometimes implicit need to be made more explicit. Approaches by managers that are currently based on experience need to be better understood and better documented to provide a body of knowledge that can be taught and shared among people with less experience. The third sector needs management theories that have been adapted to suit its own needs.

This book is an overview of the management of third-sector organizations. It sets out the essential elements of management that are needed to make organizations more successful. It is based on a series of propositions about management; in summary these are:

- boards need to take responsibility for 'governing' organizations. They need to delegate 'management' to chief executives and their paid staff
- the process of strategic management is a powerful way of focusing the diverse constituencies of these organizations on to their purpose
- managing performance is now a critical ingredient of an effective organization
- management structures need to become increasingly flexible, responding with frequent small adjustments rather than once-in-a-lifetime reviews
- improvements in management skills are critical to enable organizations to grow and develop
- chief executives have both to manage their organizations and provide them with leadership – creating a sense of mission, inspiring people and focusing the organization on the achievement of ambitious objectives
- managers have to manage their boss, work as part of a team, and learn the subtle skills of delegating work and empowering people
- organizations need to use every available opportunity to maximize learning.

In schematic form the chapters have been grouped together as follows:

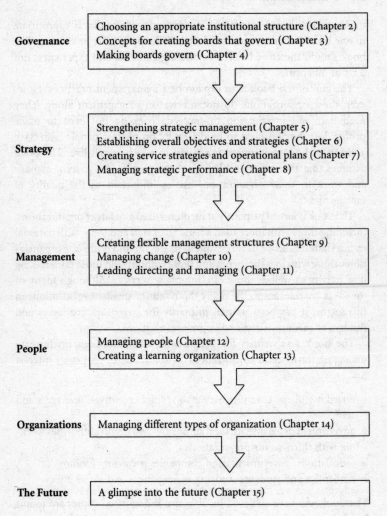

Governance
- Choosing an appropriate institutional structure (Chapter 2)
- Concepts for creating boards that govern (Chapter 3)
- Making boards govern (Chapter 4)

Strategy
- Strengthening strategic management (Chapter 5)
- Establishing overall objectives and strategies (Chapter 6)
- Creating service strategies and operational plans (Chapter 7)
- Managing strategic performance (Chapter 8)

Management
- Creating flexible management structures (Chapter 9)
- Managing change (Chapter 10)
- Leading directing and managing (Chapter 11)

People
- Managing people (Chapter 12)
- Creating a learning organization (Chapter 13)

Organizations
- Managing different types of organization (Chapter 14)

The Future
- A glimpse into the future (Chapter 15)

The book is prescriptive. It demonstrates ways to improve the management of organizations. It is, however, based on the premise that third-sector organizations are full of contradictions and ambiguities. There are no right or wrong prescriptions for many situations. These organizations are complex and messy. They have many stakeholders with different values and they attract an extraordinarily diverse range of people as volunteers, managers and board members. Consequently, advice that is appropriate in one set of circumstances may be totally inappropriate in another. The book should therefore be seen as offering guidance and experience, not a set of blueprints.

The aim of the book is to explain best management practices. However, these organizations do not survive on management alone. They need flair and imagination to succeed. They do not exist to make profits, but they do need to be driven by prophets – people who have a vision of how to improve the world in which we all live. The book assumes that the values and beliefs of the people who govern, manage and work in these organizations are as important as the quality of management.

The book is aimed primarily at medium-sized and larger organizations, including those with more than a handful of staff and those with national or international scope. It is relevant to single-site and multi-site organizations, those with local branches and those without, and those undertaking one activity as well as those offering many services. Although many of the ideas are relevant to the many thousands of smaller organizations in this sector, it has been written primarily for governors, managers and funders of medium-sized and larger organizations.

The book was written for people who want thorough briefing on managing third-sector organizations. It should be of particular interest to:

- board members, committee members, chief executives, managers and staff
- government departments, local authorities and health authorities working with third-sector organizations
- foundations, governments and companies providing funding
- academics and students studying management and social policy.

The book will have achieved its objective if dog-eared copies are found in all these people's briefcases.

The book is based on the experience that my colleagues at Compass Partnership and I have gained while working and consulting in the sector. Since starting to undertake consulting assignments in 1982 we have helped organizations of almost every type and size. We have assisted with the establishment of new strategies, the development of management processes, restructuring of management, development of boards and senior management teams, and many other challenges.

I could have written many books from the mountain of material I have collected from my consultancy work and the literature I have gathered from the UK and the USA in my research for this book. However, my aim was to distil it all down into a practical overview for busy managers who need to learn a lot in a short space of time. People who want more detail should therefore refer to the Further Reading chapter.

Finally, this is the second edition. The first edition encouraged readers to send me comments, feedback and examples of good practice. Many people wrote to me, and some of their experiences and cases have been included in this edition. Continuing that spirit of co-operation and the desire to do better that pervades the sector, further comments and cases would be most welcome. They should be sent to me at: Compass Partnership, 203–209 North Gower Street, London NW1 2NJ (Tel.: 0171-391 9911; E-mail: mhudson@compassnet.co.uk).

OVERCOMING LANGUAGE PROBLEMS

The diverse histories of third-sector organizations mean that different organizations often use very different language to describe the same idea. To maintain clarity and avoid repetition, the following terms are used consistently throughout the book.

Organization The body that is providing services or organizing campaigns, whether it be a voluntary body, a charity, a trust, a trade union, a registered social landlord, a professional institution, a school, a college, etc.

Stakeholders People or other organizations who have an acknowledged interest in the organization, including members, funders, service users, board and committee members, managers, staff, volunteers and branches.

Service users The people who benefit from a service provided by a third-sector organization, whether students, trade union members, patients, clients, people with disabilities, church-goers or members of an audience. Although somewhat prosaic, this term is better than beneficiary, which is condescending, or customer, which implies that people pay for the service.

The board The body that is legally responsible and accountable for governing and controlling the organization, sometimes called Council, Management Committee, Board of Directors, Board of Trustees, Executive or Governing Body.

Board members People who sit on the board and are legally accountable for all the organization's work and are usually unpaid. Sometimes called Council Members, Management Committee Members, Trustees, Directors, or Members of a Governing Board.

Officers People who are elected to specific positions on the board and are usually unpaid (including the Chair, Vice Chair, Treasurer and Secretary to the Board).

Committees Small groups who are delegated responsibilities by the board, sometimes called sub-committees, advisory panels or working groups.

Chief Executive The senior paid member of staff who reports to the board. Sometimes called the Director, the Head, the Principal, the General Secretary, the Director General and other similar terms.

Divisional Directors The paid managers (usually in large organizations) who report to the chief executive and who have managers reporting to them.

Senior Management Team The chief executive and the divisional directors or senior managers who together have overall responsibility for the day-to-day management of the organization.

Department The level of organization below the senior management team. In smaller organizations it may be called a region, a team or a project. In larger organizations it may be called a division.

Service The benefit the service user receives, irrespective of whether it is a conventional service, a performance, an education, spiritual development, some information or another desired benefit.

Service Delivery Unit The lowest level of the organization at which human and financial resources are brought together by a manager to deliver a service with specific objectives, a budget and performance measures (see section 7.1 for a full description).

Branches Field outposts of the organization, including national branches of international organizations, local groups and church dioceses, and autonomous branches of federal organizations that have come together as part of a movement.

1   The Undiscovered Sector

1.1   A HISTORICAL PERSPECTIVE

The central philosophy that permeates virtually every part of the third sector is the human desire to assist other people without gaining personal benefit. Most people think of it in terms of charity and assume that it is a modern phenomenon. Some suggest it goes back to Elizabethan times or, at most, to Roman times. Indeed, fear of voluntary associations as a locus for political dissent is well documented in imperial Rome; for example, Trajan refused a provincial governor's request to form a fire brigade, saying it would become a political pressure group.

In fact the word 'charity' has Greek origins – χαρις (charis) – which originally meant grace and subsequently came to mean favour, kindness and goodwill towards another. Another related meaning in Greek was thankfulness or gratitude. The word 'philanthropy' also has a Greek origin – meaning love of people.

However, the philosophy of charity goes back much further. People say, 'Charity begins at home' – and so it did. From earliest times it was the extended family that looked after its young, sick, disabled, elderly, widowed and orphaned members. With the growth of the first towns and cities and the movement of people away from their families, new forms of social provision were needed. Early Egyptian civilizations developed a strong moral code founded on social justice. This code encouraged people to help others in relation to their need, for example, by ferrying a poor person across the river without charging. The Pharaoh himself contributed by giving shelter, bread and clothing to the poor almost 5,000 years ago.

In ancient India, the Buddhist Emperor Asoka (c. 274–232 BC) provided medical facilities, ordered wells to be dug and, in an early environmental initiative, planted trees for people's enjoyment. In early Greek society, wayfarers were either given food and shelter in the houses of wealthy people or they would share the hospitality of peasants. The Jewish prophets were the forerunners of the modern campaigning organization. They worked tirelessly for social, economic and political justice and put pressure on their governments to change both policies and administrative practices. The idea of alms-giving was also widely recognized. In Roman times the right to free or cheap corn was dependent on citizenship and was hereditary – passing from father to son. Trusts also date back to Roman times, as people established schemes to maintain control over the fate of an economic asset after their death. A good example of self-help that originated in Imperial Rome was the establishment of burial societies, which were created to ensure that people of modest means received a decent burial. They ran as co-operatives, involved a monthly payment and were also a focus for social events.

Throughout history, charity has also been closely interwoven with the growth of religious organizations. Jewish teaching promoted the view that the poor had rights and the rich had duties. Early Christian churches established funds to support widows, orphans, the sick, the infirm, the poor, the disabled and prisoners. Church-goers were expected to bring gifts which were laid on the Lord's table so the recipients obtained them from the hands of God. The first legacies were authorized by Emperor Constantine I in AD 231, enabling endowments to be established for charity.

In the Islamic world, philanthropy was used to establish many great hospitals. Early examples of 'hardship funds' also come from Islam, when indigent patients were given five pieces of gold on their discharge. In short, the charitable sector has been around for a long time, always playing a significant role.

Management problems have a long history

The issues facing these organizations also have a long history. Many of the dilemmas which perplex organizations today also confounded their predecessors. Medieval monasteries in Britain tended to be indiscriminate in their alms-giving. They consequently fostered a class of professional beggars which in time contributed to the breakdown of this system of relief. Similar problems occurred when hospitals, designed for use by the poor, were placed at the service of rich people. The issue of means testing clearly concerned these organizations as much as it troubles modern charities.

Arguments about the conflicting roles of the public and charitable sectors raged during the sixteenth century when Henry VIII and Edward VI confiscated hospital and guild property. During this time, the Reformation undermined the church-centred welfare system and the gap was filled by greater state intervention funded by increased taxes. This included money given to almshouses, hospitals and university colleges, loan schemes to help people start businesses, and for capital works such as building bridges and repairing roads. Indeed, the boundary with the state was just as much an issue then as it is today. For example, in 1572 Elizabeth I passed a law that allowed parishes to levy a poor rate to pay for the upkeep of almshouses and workhouses, effectively subsidizing charitable provision with state money.

Abuse by charities is also an old phenomenon. In 1601 Elizabeth I passed the Charitable Uses Act, which gave the Chancellor power to investigate the misuse of charitable funds. The Act provides an interesting perspective on the history of the third sector. Charitable endowments could only be given for:

relief of aged, impotent and poor people, maintenance of sick and maimed soldiers and mariners, schools of learning, free schools and scholars in universities, repair of bridges, ports, havens, causeways, churches, sea banks and highways, education and preferment of orphans, relief, stock or maintenance of houses for correction, marriages of poor maids, supportation, aid and help of young tradesmen, handicrafts-men and persons decayed, relief or redemption of prisoners or captives and aid or ease of poor inhabitants concerning payment of taxes.

The beginning of a more strategic approach

For much of the period up to the middle of the nineteenth century, charity in Britain was characterized by a large number of often jealous organizations pursuing activities without any real understanding of the extent of the underlying causes of poverty. Organizations worked with little knowledge of what others were doing and with little examination of the circumstances of individual beneficiaries. However, during the second half of the nineteenth century, charities began adopting a more coherent approach. The Poor Law Amendment Act of 1834 had drastically reduced relief for the poor. Paralleling government action, charities wanted to distinguish between the poorest people with no resources and less deserving people who could rely on workhouses.

The emerging sector took a great leap forward with the formation of the Charity Organization Society in 1869. It is an example of how many of the great innovations in human welfare have led to the creation of third-sector organizations and have subsequently become an accepted part of civil society. Founded after Henry Solly read a paper to the Society of Arts, it aimed to encourage responsible spending on the poor and avoid welfare dependency. Henry Solly became its first General Secretary and remained in that position for forty years. This organization, today called the Family Welfare Association, was among the first to put into place what would now be called a strategic approach to meeting people's needs. It strove to:

- prevent indiscriminate giving of relief
- promote careful inquiries into individual cases
- discover the causes of an individual's distress
- remove the causes of distress
- co-ordinate charitable activities to prevent excessive help being given to particular people.

In addition to taking a more strategic approach, which is now a central part of managing third-sector organizations, it also combined service delivery with a sharp and effective campaigning role. It fought against the state and against voluntary organizations because it believed both approached welfare in ways that encouraged dependency.

WHEN WERE THEY ESTABLISHED?

Providing housing, hospital care, services for disabled people, protecting the environment and campaigning for social change all had or have a venerable history, illustrated by the establishment of the following organizations:

1123 St Bartholomew's Hospital
1215 St Thomas's Hospital

1697	Oxford Hospital, Ampthill
1698	Society for Promoting Christian Knowledge
1702	Hospital for Fishermen, Yarmouth
1707	Almshouses at Abingdon
1823	Anti-Slavery International
1824	Royal National Lifeboat Institution
1824	Royal Society for the Prevention of Cruelty to Animals
1830	Society for the Improvement of the Condition of Labouring Classes
1854	Oxford Economic and Sanitary Association
1862	Peabody Trust
1865	Salvation Army
1866	Barnardo's
1868	Royal National Institute for the Blind
1869	Family Welfare Association
1870	British Red Cross
1881	Children's Society
1884	National Society for the Prevention of Cruelty to Children
1886	Octavia Hill Housing Trust
1889	Guinness Trust
1895	National Trust
1902	Imperial Cancer Research Fund
1908	Scout Association
1910	Guide Association
1918	National Council for One Parent Families
1919	Save The Children Fund
1921	Royal British Legion
1923	Cancer Research Campaign
1924	Wellcome Trust
1930	Youth Hostels Association
1931	Guide Dogs for the Blind Association
1937	Nuffield College, Oxford
1938	RELATE
1939	Glyndebourne Arts Trust
1942	Age Concern
1942	Oxfam
1946	MENCAP – Royal Society for Mentally Handicapped Children and Adults

1948 Leonard Cheshire Foundation
1950 Queen Elizabeth's Hospital, Bristol
1953 Samaritans
1956 Abbeyfield Society
1958 Voluntary Service Overseas
1961 National Institute for Social Work
1966 SHELTER
1967 St Christopher's Hospice
1971 Greenpeace
1976 Stonham Housing Association
1979 Victim Support
1981 Business in the Community
1983 Terrence Higgins Trust
1984 Charity Projects/Comic Relief
1994 National Lottery Charities Board
1997 The Diana, Princess of Wales Memorial Fund

Organizations are referred to by their latest name.

State intervention increases

The trend towards a more strategic approach occurred simultaneously with increased state intervention in social affairs. As a result, many of the innovative schemes for meeting people's needs that were established by the third sector over the last 150 years have gradually been adopted by government. This started when government began playing a greater role in education in the 1840s. As a result, one of the basic principles of state provision, that of ensuring minimum standards, was established and later extended to many services, including pensions, school meals, unemployment and health insurance.

Nevertheless, until 1948 the voluntary and charitable organizations remained major providers of direct services. Voluntary hospitals were part of the sector, and services for children and people with disabilities relied heavily on voluntary organizations. However, voluntary providers were increasingly criticized for rivalry among themselves and for their inability to provide universal services available to everyone without payment at the point of delivery. As state provision expanded, the role of the voluntary sector was seen as supplementary to state provision and not as the parallel system that had been envisaged earlier.

In the period immediately after the Second World War, the role of the voluntary sector was further reduced as the state took over hospitals and other services and offered more comprehensive provision through local social services departments. For a period the third sector played second fiddle.

Revival of the sector

However, from the beginning of the 1960s the voluntary sector began to re-exert its influence as new needs were identified and new means of raising income were established. It has not looked back since that date. In particular:

- large service-providing organizations have focused on services not provided by the state
- specialist organizations have been established for almost every conceivable cause (the National Council for Voluntary Organizations' directory alone lists over 2,500 national voluntary organizations)
- government and local authority funding has grown dramatically.

More significantly, the separation of purchasers from providers of services has presented many new opportunities for third-sector organizations. Some are now returning to their previous role as mainstream providers of services. They are competing – often with considerable success – for the growing number of contracts that government, local and health authorities are putting out to tender.

These new opportunities, combined with the break-up of monolithic health, education and welfare providers into smaller, more independent organizations, are fuelling the growth of the sector. Many institutions that until a few years ago were indisputably part of the public sector are becoming indistinguishable from state-funded voluntary organizations. Colleges of education, schools and hospital trusts are beginning to see themselves as semi-independent organizations rather than part of the public sector. There is consequently a need to define and explain the boundaries between the public, private and third sector in a little more detail.

1.2 BOUNDARIES OF THE SECTOR

The sector consists of an extraordinarily diverse range of organizations: some are charitable (Oxfam), some are not (the Automobile Association), some are based on vast membership (the National Trust), some are not (English National Ballet), some are primarily government funded (Victim Support), some eschew government funding (Amnesty International), some are politically left of centre (the Transport and General Workers' Union), some right (the Adam Smith Institute), some are large (Nuffield Nursing Homes Trust) and many are small (the British Hedgehog Preservation Society).

There are many names which broadly cover the notion of this sector. Each establishes different boundaries, but they all overlap:

- the **charitable sector** includes all organizations which meet the strict conditions required for charity registration
- the **voluntary sector** includes charities and many other organizations with social and political aims that have not registered as charities or do not meet the criteria
- the **NGO sector** (an acronym for Non-Governmental Organizations that is widely used in the international development field) refers to voluntary or charitable organizations
- the **not-for-profit sector** is a wider term which emanates from the USA and includes independent not-for-profit universities and hospitals, trade unions, professional associations and other organizations which can make profits but do not distribute them
- **civil society organizations** is a term used to refer to all the non-profit institutions that are necessary in modern democratic societies. It has become more common following the re-emergence of voluntary organizations in Eastern Europe
- *économie sociale* is a term increasingly used in the European Union; it includes not-for-profit organizations and many business-type organizations such as mutual insurance companies, savings banks, co-operatives and agricultural marketing organizations whose profits are used to benefit their members or customers.

None of these definitions suits the purposes of this book. The charitable and voluntary sectors are too narrow; many of the propositions about management have much wider application. The not-for-profit sector is a negative definition which emphasizes the intention not to make profits – when in practice many of these organizations need to make a financial surplus to replace their capital and to fund new activities. The *économie sociale* is a little too wide. Many of the additional organizations captured in this definition have a better fit with private-sector management theories.

This book therefore adopts the term **third sector** and includes within it all organizations that:

- exist primarily for a **social purpose** rather than having a profit-making objective
- are **independent of the state** because they are governed by an independent group of people and are not part of a government department or a local or health authority
- **re-invest all their financial surpluses** in the services they offer or the organization itself.

The boundaries are fuzzy

The boundaries between the private, public and third sectors are not clear-cut. Some organizations are widely agreed to be at the heart of the sector; other organizations sit on its periphery. Many share the values of the sector but also have characteristics in common with either the public or the private sector.

A useful way, therefore, to think of the third sector is as a core of pure third-sector organizations and peripheries which overlap with both the private and public sectors. Many of these, such as museums, housing associations and education colleges, can use third-sector management skills but are ultimately subject to some control by the government.

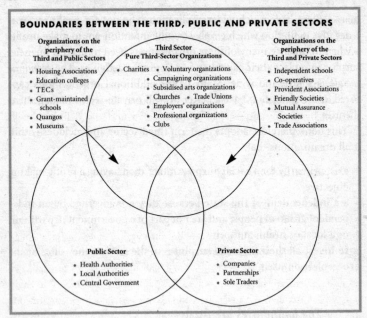

BOUNDARIES BETWEEN THE THIRD, PUBLIC AND PRIVATE SECTORS

Organizations on the periphery of the Third and Public Sectors
- Housing Associations
- Education colleges
- TECs
- Grant-maintained schools
- Quangos
- Museums

Third Sector Pure Third-Sector Organizations
- Charities
- Voluntary organizations
- Campaigning organizations
- Subsidised arts organizations
- Churches
- Trade Unions
- Employers' organizations
- Professional organizations
- Clubs

Organizations on the periphery of the Third and Private Sectors
- Independent schools
- Co-operatives
- Provident Associations
- Friendly Societies
- Mutual Assurance Societies
- Trade Associations

Public Sector
- Health Authorities
- Local Authorities
- Central Government

Private Sector
- Companies
- Partnerships
- Sole Traders

Examples of pure third-sector organizations include voluntary organizations, campaigning organizations and clubs. Other types of organizations such as trade unions, churches, trade and professional associations and employers' organizations are less commonly seen as part of the third sector but are equally part of the core.

While the core accounts for the majority of the sector, many organizations sit on the peripheries. These include organizations on the periphery of:

- the **third** and **public** sectors, such as further and higher education colleges, which have been given greater independence and are currently migrating into the third sector. It also includes Training and Enterprise Councils and other quasi-non-governmental organizations (known as quangos) such as the Arts Council, which are heavily government-funded but operate with a degree of managerial independence

- the **third** and **private** sectors, such as friendly societies and co-operatives, which do not distribute profits, but in most other respects operate like commercial companies.

Other writers and academics have adopted slightly different definitions (for a UK model see, for example, D. Billis, *A Theory of the Voluntary Sector*, Working Paper 5, LSE, 1989, and for an international perspective see L. Salamon and H. Anheier, *In Search of the Non-profit Sector*, Voluntas, 1992). Debates about the definition of the sector have continued for many years and are unlikely to be resolved by one book. The spirit of the sector is driven by its diversity, so the boundaries around any definition will always be fuzzy.

Organizations move across the boundaries

Over the years there has been considerable movement of organizations across the boundaries of the sectors. Movement across the third–private boundary has been mainly one-way. Building societies and mutual societies now see themselves as part of the private sector, operating in competition with profit-distributing businesses. The Abbey National, for example, began when twelve building workers formed a society to save money for purchasing houses. It gradually grew into a huge institution that had to operate in a competitive market and consequently lost its third-sector roots.

Historically, movement across the third–public boundary has been dominated by the state taking responsibility for services that are needed by the majority of people. Starting with the maintenance of bridges (a common charitable purpose of monastic foundations), through the care of prisoners (originally a charitable activity) to the more recent case of hospitals taken over to create the NHS, the movement has been towards the public sector.

That trend is now being reversed. The perceived limitations of the public sector as an efficient supplier of services are persuading governments around the world to delegate responsibility for the management of services. Schools, hospitals, colleges, youth and other services are increasingly being required to operate more like independent non-profit-distributing organizations than under the rules of public service. These organizations are finding that they have to compete against each other for funds and service users and have to diversify their funding sources to top up their government grants. When this happens they begin to behave like independent not-for-profit organizations and consequently move into the third sector.

This flood of organizations moving from the public to the periphery of the third sector is being driven by:

- a political philosophy that believes state-run organizations are neither efficient nor responsive to people's changing needs, and the consequent separation of the functions of the *purchaser* (to specify standards, and desired outcomes) and the *provider* (to deliver services efficiently and effectively, responding quickly to changes in the external environment)
- a desire to give local managers greater control over the management of their organizations
- tighter control over public expenditure coinciding with increased social need
- a belief that competition between suppliers can lead to efficiency gains, even though the notion of competition in the provision of basic services is often deeply uncomfortable, particularly to professionals in these services
- a desire by citizens to participate in society and have choice.

This trend will continue because the political philosophy that favours independence from the state has become well established. Indeed, as providers are given greater independence, they are becoming more sophisticated managerially, require less support from centralized bureaucracies and place increasing value on their independence.

In summary, even before these new organizations joined the third sector, it was a significant part of the social fabric in the UK and many other countries. Today it is becoming increasingly responsible for the provision of a huge range of essential services.

1.3   THE SECTOR IS SIGNIFICANT AND GROWING

The scope and scale of the third sector is now so huge that it affects virtually everyone. People volunteer, they join professional associations, attend college or an artistic event, worship, join a trade union, support a campaign, donate to charity or join a club or society. They are all engaging in civic society.

Many of our lives are touched by the third sector more than once a week and some more than once a day, as we:

* seek advice from a Citizens' Advice Bureau (nearly 5.5 million people do every year)
* volunteer (22 million people do every year)
* visit a sports club (there are 150,000 in the UK)
* call a charity help line (35,000 people do every day)
* attend a trade union meeting
* call a motoring organization (the AA is non-profit distributing)
* read the *Guardian* or the *Observer* (they are both owned by the not-for-profit Scott Trust).

The sector is not only diverse, it is also very influential. In 1948 William Beveridge wrote, 'the strength of voluntary action is the distinguishing mark of a free society'. More recently, Professor Ken Young has argued in his essay entitled *Meeting the Needs of Strangers* (Gresham College, 1991) that the voluntary sector makes three crucial contributions to society:

Representation   Voluntary action in today's changed circumstances has a wider role – and is of greater social and political significance – than that of an adjunct provider of social services alongside mainstream state provision. It contributes to the representative process, to the development of public policy and to the processes of social integration and cohesion.

Innovation   The creativity of voluntary bodies is a source of innovation. Governments today address issues that are often formulated and shaped by those outside the central departments. The history of social policy in Britain is largely one in which the agenda for action has been set by voluntary bodies turning hitherto tolerated conditions into problems and claims to action.

Citizenship
The effectiveness of voluntary bodies as advocates of change owes much to their informal nature. Whether or not people are excluded from effective citizenship rests in no small measure upon the strength of the local voluntary sector.

In short, the third sector is the social glue that helps to create a cohesive society, and no significant governmental decision is usually taken in a sophisticated democracy without many third-sector interest groups being consulted or making their case.

THE THIRD SECTOR AFFECTS EVERY STAGE OF OUR LIVES

Most of the 500,000 third-sector organizations in Britain are small. This is how some of the medium-sized and larger ones affect our lives:

Before Conception	During Pregnancy and Birth	Early Childhood
Sex Education Forum	National Childbirth Trust	Pre-school Play Groups Association
Family Planning Association	Baby Life Support Systems	National Toy Libraries Association
Birth Control Campaign	Active Birth Centre	Child Accident Prevention Trust

During Education	In Adolescence	In Further Education
Nuffield Foundation	Childline	London Business School
Barnardos	National Children's Home	Workers Educational Association
The Scouts and Guides	YWCA	

In Employment	In Leisure	In Sport	In Housing
Confederation of British Industry	National Trust	British Olympic Association	Anchor Housing
UNISON	Royal Opera	British Blind Sport	Abbeyfield Society
			Guinness Trust

In Campaigning	In Sickness	In Health	In Relationships
Amnesty International	Stroke Association	Royal Society for the Promotion of Health	RELATE
Greenpeace	National Asthma Campaign		Westminster Pastoral Foundation
Shelter	MIND		

In Disability	In Emergencies	In Research
Royal National Institute for Deaf People	Royal National Lifeboat Institution	Cancer Research Campaign
Leonard Cheshire Foundation	Women's Royal Voluntary Service	Cambridge University British Heart Foundation
MENCAP	British Red Cross	
	Victim Support	

In Poverty	In Retirement	In Old Age	At Death
Family Welfare Association	REACH	Age Concern	Voluntary Euthanasia Society
Salvation Army	Pensioners Link	Help the Aged	
Family Service Units	University of the Third Age		Natural Death Centre
			St Christopher's Hospice

After Death
Cruse – Bereavement care
Compassionate Friends
Stillbirth Society

1.4 MANAGING THIRD-SECTOR ORGANIZATIONS

There are many similarities in managing organizations in all sectors of the economy. All rely on skilled managers who need to have objectives, control resources, work in teams, have professional development and be praised and criticized. The third sector has particular parallels with the private sector because organizations which sell services, sometimes at subsidized prices, need some of the theories of the market place. Likewise, many organizations are providing public services in situations where there is little connection between the recipient of the service and payment for that service. This inevitably leads to limitless demand which can be managed only by turning people away.

Indeed, it is fair to say that the similarities between all sectors are growing. Greater use of contracts, which link funding to levels of service and outcomes, requires skills that have been well understood in the private sector for many years. Equally, private- and public-sector organizations are increasing their effectiveness by building staff commitment to missions and core values, activities that are taken for granted in the third sector.

Partnerships between organizations in different sectors are also increasing, partly as a result of encouragement from central government. Organizations are discovering that working together can be a very effective way of tackling some of the most intractable social problems that society faces.

The crucial differences between the sectors

Nevertheless, a central theme of this book is the proposition that managing third-sector organizations is subtly different from managing in the private or public sectors. Managers who have transferred from either the public or the private sector to the third sector quickly discover that there is something intrinsically different about making things happen in a not-for-profit context. It is difficult to spot the relevant differences and distinguish them from the superficial ones. The symbols of informal dress, cramped offices and seemingly endless meetings hide more deep-seated differences in people's values and beliefs. Yet it is these values and beliefs that are at the root of the differences.

Some senior managers in the third sector are recruited from the public and private sectors and not from the third sector itself. Those from the private sector usually bring the economic logic of the market place and the values of shareholders, customers and profits. Those from the public sector bring the political perspective and the public service values which influence that sector.

Most third-sector organizations can recount experiences of recruiting talented people from the private and public sectors who came to grief in the third sector. Examples abound of the talented military commander who decides to continue in public service by directing a charity, or the high-flying business executive who takes responsibility in a church or hospital trust. Those who come to grief have usually failed to make the necessary changes in their implicit assumptions about the differences between the sectors.

In the private sector there is a relatively straightforward relationship between suppliers and customers. Suppliers offer goods and services to customers, and in return customers pay a market price. In the public sector, government and local authorities supply public services, and in return the voters choose the government which they believe offers the most appropriate programme of taxation and public services.

In the third sector a different model of transactions applies. In the straightforward case of an organization funded purely by donors, money is given and used to fund projects, supply services or carry out research. Oxfam, the Royal National Lifeboat Institution and the Cancer Research Campaign are typical examples. A variation of this model is where money comes from contracts, a source that continues to grow rapidly. Although widely believed to be a relatively new source of funds, contracts were used extensively in the early part of this century when the Liberal Government of 1905 funded friendly societies and councils for voluntary service to deliver its reforms.

Yet another variation is where services are part funded by the service user and part funded by grants, contracts and donations. This happens in housing associations, disability organizations, arts organizations and education colleges. Nevertheless, in all these cases the key difference between the third and the other two sectors is that there is only a weak link between the service users and the funders of the service. The feedback which companies get from their customers (or lack of them) and

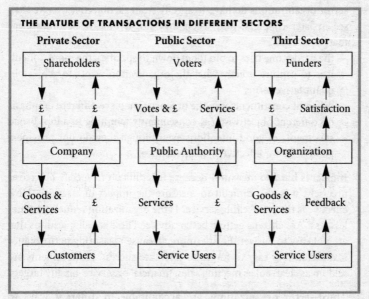

THE NATURE OF TRANSACTIONS IN DIFFERENT SECTORS

Private Sector	Public Sector	Third Sector
Shareholders	Voters	Funders
£ — £	Votes & £ — Services	£ — Satisfaction
Company	Public Authority	Organization
Goods & Services — £	Services — £	Goods & Services — Feedback
Customers	Service Users	Service Users

which the public sector gets from the ballot box is very weak in the third sector.

This crucial difference in the nature of transactions means organizations have to manage the problems of:

- demand for their service being limitless or contained only by minimizing the marketing and promotion of the service
- being caught between the different expectations of funders and users
- minimal automatic feedback from service users.

The case of the pure charity funded by donors is made more complicated when donors, volunteers or service users are elected to the board or appointed to the staff. This creates even more unusual sets of relationships, all of which require careful and special attention.

In addition to the different nature of the transactions, there are eight other characteristics of third-sector organizations which, although not exclusive to the sector, combine to make management a challenging occupation:

- **It is easy to have vague objectives.** Social, health, educational, environmental and spiritual objectives are difficult to specify precisely. Third-sector organizations do have to specify strategic objectives, as we shall see in later chapters, but, when they do, it quickly becomes clear that:
  — the harder one tries to pin them down to specifics, the more difficult it is to capture exactly what the organization wants to achieve in quantitative terms
  — different constituencies in the organization place different emphasis on different objectives; it is consequently tempting to adopt broad statements of good intentions even though they do not provide a good basis for effective management.

- **Impact is hard to measure.** Because it is difficult to specify objectives precisely, it is also difficult to measure the impact of a service. How effective is the counselling service? Is the organization reducing homelessness? Are citizens getting better advice? These are all questions that are not easy to answer. Furthermore, because measuring performance is difficult, it is easy to forget to celebrate success. Achievements are seldom as clear-cut as meeting sales, financial or service-quality targets.

- **Third-sector organizations are accountable in different ways to**

many stakeholders. Members, funding bodies, individual donors, staff, volunteers and service users all have different claims on a third-sector organization. They are often in a position to have a powerful influence on the organization, yet they invariably have different views of priorities and sometimes on the style and culture of the organization as well.

● **Management structures are intricate.** The need to keep the interests of different stakeholders in a delicate balance results in complex structures of governing bodies, committees, user-groups and funder-groups, each of which has a legitimate position in the structure. Taken together, this requirement creates a complex machine which has to be consulted, co-ordinated and managed in order to get things done. Even organizations that have streamlined their structures often have much more intricate arrangements than organizations of equivalent size in the private sector.

● **Voluntarism is an essential ingredient.** The majority of third-sector organizations have unpaid voluntary governing boards whose members may or may not have governance experience. Many rely on voluntary labour and the 'voluntary' commitment of employees, giving extra time for no financial reward. This coalition of voluntary interests has to be held together without using financial incentives. In return for their voluntary commitment people often expect to have their views listened to and to be actively involved in decision-making.

● **Purpose has a powerful impact on approaches to management.** The ideology that lies behind the organization can strongly influence people's assumptions about the way the organization should be managed. For example, people in campaigning organizations tend to take a highly political approach to management; they build coalitions among people with common views rather than using formal decision-making structures; they lobby decision-makers and challenge authority. In contrast people in therapeutic organizations tend to take very conciliatory approaches to management; they see all sides of an issue and find it difficult to reach decisions quickly.

● **Values have to be cherished.** Third-sector organizations are at their most effective when the people involved share common values and assumptions about the organization's purpose and its style of operation. Insensitive trampling on cherished values quickly results in demotivation and lengthy argument. The point is not that organizations in other sectors do not have values, but that people contributing to third-sector organizations are motivated by values that are crucial to achieving the aim and are therefore important to everyone.

● **The financial 'bottom line' is not the main determinant of priorities.** Third-sector managers can seldom use a financial bottom line of profit or a discounted cash-flow projection to guide their choice of future priorities and investments. These organizations have to rely more heavily on complex negotiation to agree priorities. Unfortunately there is no standard methodology or template for this. Every organization has to develop its own criteria for allocating resources that suit its circumstances at a particular time.

People have multiple motives

Beyond these explicit characteristics, there is a human perspective that needs to be understood in order to gain a complete picture of the challenges of managing these organizations. This issue is seldom discussed openly but nevertheless is central to an understanding of their management.

Virtually everyone who contributes time and effort to these organizations has well-founded altruistic and philanthropic motives. Indeed, without these values the sector could not exist. However, people often have other – and self-serving – motives for contributing to these organizations:

● They join governing boards, particularly of larger and more prestigious organizations, because of the recognition, esteem and status that are attached to board membership. Such membership frequently leads to contacts with other people in powerful positions, to increased influence and to a greater sense of self-worth.

● Some donors give money in order to gain national recognition, for public-relations benefits, to salve their consciences and (sometimes) to gain greater influence over the organization's affairs.

● Some volunteers give their time because of their need for friendship and social activity, to gain useful skills, to enhance their employment prospects and to give them a role in the broader community.

● Some people seek employment in third-sector organizations because they would not find it comfortable working within the ideology of the private sector or the constraints of the public sector.

This is not to argue that altruism does not exist. It does and it is present in most third-sector organizations. But people have multiple motives, and the hidden ones have a significant impact on management. At their most extreme, these motives can combine to make the survival of the organization a greater priority than the services it gives to users.

Fortunately, not all these explicit and implicit characteristics apply to all organizations simultaneously! However, they do create a special set of circumstances, and this explains why managing these organizations needs to be based on an understanding of their special nature. They illustrate why the management tools and styles that work in the other sectors are only partially applicable to this sector. Finally, they explain why theories about management need to start from a set of propositions that are derived specifically to help managers of third-sector organizations.

SUMMARY OF KEY POINTS

Historical perspective
- The history of the third sector goes back to the earliest civilizations.
- The special problems of managing these organizations have an equally long history.
- Following rapid growth in the nineteenth and early twentieth centuries, the sector in Britain was eclipsed by the welfare state.
- It has re-emerged with the entrepreneurial skills and social conscience needed to address today's social, educational and environmental problems.

Boundaries of the sector
- The third sector includes organizations that:
  — exist primarily for a social purpose
  — are independent of the state
  — reinvest financial surpluses in their services.
- The boundaries with the public and private sectors are not clear-cut.
- Over time, organizations move across the boundaries.

Growth of the sector
- The number and size of organizations are both growing.
- The crucial contributions of the sector are its ability to represent people's views, to innovate and to provide people with a sense of citizenship.

Managing third-sector organizations
- The central difference between the third and the other sectors is that there is only a weak link between providers of funds and service users.
- Eight other distinguishing factors are that:
  — it is easy to have vague objectives
  — impact is hard to measure
  — organizations are accountable to many stakeholders
  — management structures are intricate
  — voluntarism is an essential ingredient
  — purpose has a powerful impact on approaches to management
  — values have to be cherished
  — the financial 'bottom line' is not the main determinant of priorities.
- Management is complicated by the fact that people who contribute to third-sector organizations have a pot-pourri of motives which may be both philanthropic and self-serving.

2 Choosing an Appropriate Institutional Structure

2.1 THE MEANING OF INSTITUTIONAL STRUCTURE

Many third-sector organizations have a straightforward institutional structure of a board that is either elected by a membership or that appoints itself. This arrangement is ideal for organizations based essentially in one location, that do not have branches and that control most of their own resources.

However, as organizations grow many conclude that they can raise more funds, attract more volunteers and achieve greater results by developing new parts to the organization that have a degree of autonomy from the original body. They may create offices in other countries and local branches in their home country, and they may establish new organizations that subsequently wish to seek funds from other sources. All of these actions have implications for the institutional structure of the organization.

This chapter is about the fundamental constitutional arrangements that third-sector organizations adopt in order to enable different parts of multi-faceted organizations to relate to each other. It is concerned with the arrangements that enable local, national and international parts of an organization to work together. It avoids the many legal issues that board members will have to consider (for example, company and charitable status) since they are a matter for legal books rather than a management book.

The chapter covers:

● the different types of institutional structure that organizations can adopt

- the special circumstances of international organizations
- the different tasks that board members should focus on in the different structures
- the different methods of choosing board members.

2.2 THE OPTIONS FOR INSTITUTIONAL STRUCTURES

The options for the institutional structures of third-sector organizations are best seen as existing on a continuum with at one end a 'linear' structure and, at the other end, a 'federal' structure.

Organizations at the **linear** end operate in what might be termed a straight-line structure. In this structure members (or the government or another external body) appoint a board to govern the organization. In some cases the board appoints its own members, so the membership and the board are just one group. They in turn appoint a staff, who run the organization on a day-to-day basis. Sometimes the organization also creates regional offices or local branches to support its work. The linear structure is 'top-down'.

Organizations at the **federal** end of the continuum are circular in nature. The board is responsible for governing the organization but it is appointed by the branches and is accountable to them. This situation usually arises from historic circumstances when independent branches of an organization have seen the need for national co-ordination. They establish the centre in order to provide branches with advice and support. In other circumstances a national organization may encourage the establishment of local branches, believing that the organization would be most effective if the branches had some real power within the institutional structure. In both, the resulting structure is a federation in which the branches both appoint the board and recognize its authority. Many international organizations have federal structures that allow each country organization to operate relatively autonomously within a shared mission. Well-known examples of national voluntary organizations with a federal structure include the Samaritans, RELATE, Family Service Units and the Citizens' Advice Bureaux.

The critical determinant of these two institutional structures is the role of branches. In the linear structure the centre ultimately controls the branches and retains the power to open and close them and to control their behaviour. In the federal structure the branches control the centre.

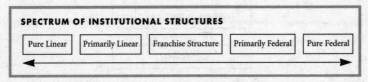

SPECTRUM OF INSTITUTIONAL STRUCTURES

| Pure Linear | Primarily Linear | Franchise Structure | Primarily Federal | Pure Federal |

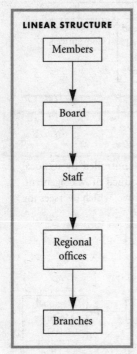

LINEAR STRUCTURE

Members → Board → Staff → Regional offices → Branches

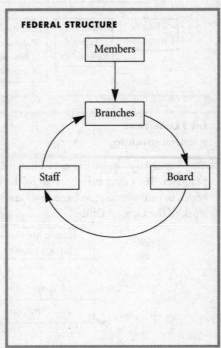

FEDERAL STRUCTURE

Members → Branches → Board → Staff → Branches

CANCER RESEARCH CAMPAIGN
A linear structure

The Cancer Research Campaign used to be a federal structure but, over the years, all but two of the original branches have been absorbed into the national campaign. It now has a linear structure consisting of approximately 123 members who elect a council of seventeen people to govern the organization. Local committees work with area fund-raisers, who are part of the paid staff. In summary its institutional structure is:

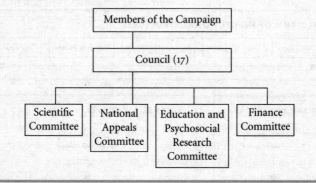

THE SAMARITANS
A federal structure

The Samaritans organization is ultimately controlled by its local branches. They elect members on to the Council of Management, which in turn appoints an Executive Committee, which oversees the work of the General Office.

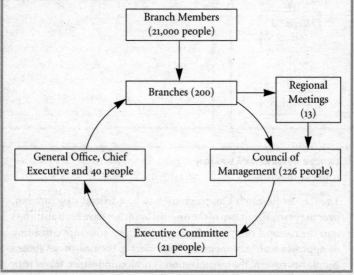

Between these two ends of the spectrum many organizations have institutional structures that are either more linear or more federal in orientation. Some organizations with linear structures reserve a number of board places for people elected from the branches. Some establish consultative councils in order to provide branches with a constitutionally agreed way to put their views to the board. Some have places on the board for regional representatives. All these mechanisms are designed to create an appropriate balance of power between the centre and the field.

Linear structures are appropriate where the local outposts of the organization neither want nor need to have significant influence in the overall management of the organization. This structure is common in fund-raising charities where fund-raising groups want to raise money but do not wish to have a greater involvement in the organization.

Federal structures are appropriate where the success of the whole organization is dependent on the work of the voluntary branches. Where volunteers are the major provider of a service, they want to have significant influence on how the service is run. This is achieved by having the power to elect members of the board and consequently control the management of the organization.

Federal structures have the advantage of allowing independent local branches the freedom to manage themselves in ways that suit local circumstances. However, large federal structures are cumbersome to manage and, because major changes have to be agreed by a majority of branches, these organizations do not respond quickly to changes in their environment. The centre has to devote significant resources to keeping all the people on the local committees informed about the organization's national situation. Consequently, some federal organizations are considering changing their structure to make them more responsive and to put more resources into services and fewer into management of the organization.

For many organizations the main determinant of their institutional structure will have been whether they started as a series of local initiatives that set up a national co-ordinating body or whether they started as a national organization that subsequently established local outposts.

Organizations should make periodic reviews to establish whether their institutional structure is appropriate. The critical questions to ask are:

● **Are the flows of funds broadly aligned with the sources of power in the organization?** If most of the funds for local work are raised locally, then the local outpost should have significant influence over their affairs. If the funds for local work are raised nationally, then the centre needs to have greater influence.

● **Do the advantages of the current structure outweigh the disadvantages?** If commitment to decisions is important, then the discipline of having to consult members of the federation may be an essential ingredient of the organization's success. If speed of response and low cost management is critical, then a linear structure may be more appropriate.

CHANGING THE INSTITUTIONAL STRUCTURE
OF THE BRITISH RED CROSS

The British Red Cross provides caring and emergency services to those most in need in their local communities and raises funds to support international work. It is supported by over 100,000 volunteers.

A major review of strategy led the organization to focus its UK activities on emergency response. At that time it was a federal organization with 86 local branches, each with its own trustees, finances and staff. Differences in the activities of branches, their ability to respond to emergencies, their financial resources and in the pay and conditions of staff were widespread.

A major review of the institutional structure led the organization to conclude that it should restructure itself as one organization. The primary aim was to improve the service it offered. In addition, the reorganization aimed to:

● encourage greater co-operation between branches
● reduce administrative costs by £4 million per year
● introduce clear accountability through the Director General to a new Board of Trustees
● create an organization that could develop a career structure for the workforce.

It set out to achieve these aims by creating one national society and de-registering branches as charities so that they were no longer independent societies. The organization also introduced a new regional structure, headed up by Regional Directors reporting to National Headquarters. Regional and branch councils were reconstituted as advisory bodies. The resultant structure was as follows:

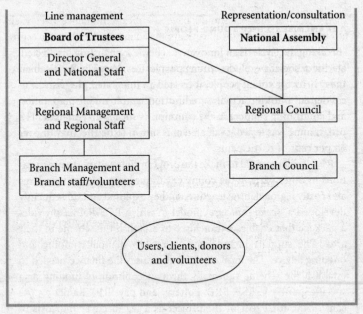

One structure in the middle of the linear–federal continuum that has emerged more recently is the **franchise** arrangement. This structure is useful when an organization has been established around a new idea and it wishes to roll out the service across the country as quickly as possible. Modelled on the idea of a business franchise, the franchiser grants independent local organizations (franchisees) the right to run the service and to use the franchiser's name on condition that it operates within the terms of a franchise agreement.

The critical difference between this structure and the federal structure is that the franchisers and franchisees do not ultimately control each other; their relationship is controlled by the terms of the franchise agreement. The agreement gives local organizations freedom to deliver the service in ways that are appropriate for their circumstances, provided they operate within the nationally prescribed terms. The arrangement allows franchisers to roll out a new service across the country more rapidly than if they tried to do it alone.

A FRANCHISE TO HELP YOUNG PEOPLE

'Breaking the Cycle' is an innovative scheme for assisting disaffected, at-risk or socially excluded young people. Developed by RPS Rainer, the charity for young people, it created an integrated programme of residential outdoor activities, education, employment preparation and continuing support in the community for 15–21-year-olds. The programme was tested, evaluated and shown to be effective for over 90 per cent of participants.

RPS Rainer wanted to make the programme available to organizations in other parts of the country without having to set up a large and costly regional infrastructure, so they explored and subsequently developed a '*social franchise*' model in which RPS Rainer provides a package that enables a franchisee to establish the scheme in their area. The support includes an operations manual, training and ongoing advice. The local organization raises the finance needed to establish the scheme (normally through community funding or a specific grant, e.g. ESF, SRB, Lottery) and pays RPS Rainer 7.5 per cent of the total cost of the project as a fee to cover the costs of administering the scheme nationally, continuing support and future project research and development. The franchise agreement sets out the obligations of both parties, the training required, the 'all stakeholder monitoring system', the terms of renewal and the costings.

The great advantage of the scheme is that RPS Rainer's expertise in selecting scheme leaders, establishing performance benchmarks and providing experienced advice is focused on those activities where it can offer greatest 'value added', while local organizations remain responsible for the success of the scheme in their area.

The scheme works because there are mutual benefits to both parties remaining in the franchise relationship. RPS Rainer has designed its scheme to be delivered nationally as rapidly as possible while maintaining the elements of quality delivery, without having to create a national infrastructure. Local organizations want a tested way of setting up a scheme to help some of the most disadvantaged people in society, the availability of continuing support and the freedom to tailor the scheme to their local circumstances. Through '*social franchising*' all this can be achieved without the problems and cost associated with new project development.

Organizations seldom change from one type of structure to the other. However, some are starting to ask whether their institutional structure is appropriate for their current circumstances. A few are changing their structures to create simpler and more streamlined arrangements that put more resources into service delivery and fewer into managing and co-ordinating structures that are seen as inefficient in today's competitive working environment.

2.3 THE SPECIAL CIRCUMSTANCES OF INTERNATIONAL ORGANIZATIONS

Organizations generally start in one country and their cause then spreads to other countries. When this happens, the board has to choose an institutional structure that best suits the organization's circumstances.

The spectrum of options from linear to federal is still appropriate. Essentially there are four options:

1. The board can set up offices in other countries that are line-managed by the centre (usually the country of origin). Examples of this approach include Intermediate Technology and the International Union for the Conservation of Nature. They raised funds to establish these regional offices and appointed staff, who report to the centre. This arrangement works well until the country office starts to raise a significant proportion of its resources directly from funders. It is then likely to claim that a degree of independence from the founding organization is appropriate. If, as often happens, the founding office had established a local advisory board to ground their work in that country, that board is likely to begin operating as a governing board rather than as an advisory board.

2. The board can set up a country organization with the same name, but grant it independence to operate within agreed boundaries. It would be expected to raise its own funds and manage its own affairs. Oxfam has sister organizations in some countries that work on this basis. The key is to anticipate both the opportunities this offers and the problems that will occur if things go wrong in a country office, since the reputation of the founder could be at risk. Organizations taking this option sometimes also form a federal body to represent the views of all the

country offices and to regulate the affairs of the organization as a whole.
3. Established organizations can decide to form relationships with similar bodies in other countries by forming an organization that enables them to work together on matters of mutual interest. The World Blind Union is an example of this arrangement.
4. The board can establish, fund and manage a new agency with the specific intention of growing it to the point when it can become self-sustaining and independent. WaterAid established Nepal Water for Health in this way.

The critical issues for the board to consider in these situations are:

● the extent to which it wishes to control the use of the organization's name
● the cost and management effort required to manage the country organization from a distance
● the controls that are required to ensure that no single part of the organization can put the other parts at unnecessary risk
● the need to acknowledge that an ability to raise funds independently leads organizations to expect greater freedom in managing their affairs.

2.4 GOVERNING DIFFERENT STRUCTURES

Different institutional structures require subtly different approaches to governance. Although the tasks of governing each type of structure appear at first sight to be common, the critical difference lies in the importance attached to each of the governance roles.

Governing linear structures

In a linear structure the board has considerable freedom, and in those organizations without a separate membership it has great freedom. Linear organization boards need to pay particular attention to:

● **surveying the external environment** and bringing a range of perspectives into the organization from their experiences as:
— members of the organization
— members of branches

— individuals with particular skills and specialisms
- **setting policy, strategy and objectives**, so that the organization is given a clear sense of direction by those people who have authority to drive the organization
- **monitoring performance**, since the board is ultimately accountable for the achievements of the organization
- **proposing entrepreneurial initiatives**, because the board is responsible for the renewal and development of the organization.

Although boards of organizations with linear structures are not directly accountable to their branches, the views of the latter cannot be ignored. Organizations with branches are dependent on voluntary support and goodwill. Managers who are tempted to push through changes that are not supported by the field will face loss of morale, lack of commitment and opposition by stealth. They need to listen to their branches, respond to their concerns and keep them informed of plans and decisions.

Governing federal structures

In federal structures, power ultimately lies with the branches or the field units of the organization as they elect the board; and in many charities these people are also the trustees of the organization. These boards also have to survey the external environment, set policy and strategy and monitor performance. But these are secondary to the critical functions of:

- **setting standards** that all members of the federation will agree to adhere to (for example, over the quality of professional work, and accreditation of workers)
- **establishing policies** that can be agreed throughout the federation (for example, on forestry in an environmental organization)
- **co-ordinating decision-making**, because many parts of the organization need to be involved
- **control of the name and logo**, since independent local branches create many variations if their use is not controlled
- **promotion of the cause** through public speaking and publishing materials on behalf of the federation when a national voice is required to promote common interests

- **strategic planning** to give the whole federation a sense of direction and national purpose.

The board has to do all of this with the consent of the field, because branch representatives can elect new board members if they do not agree with the actions the board has taken. This means that change can be slow. In particular, those organizations lacking external pressures to force changes through cannot keep themselves up to date because no one part of the organization has the authority to drive them through.

Governing federal organizations presents a special set of challenges. Representatives of the members of the federation have two separate interests to balance. As board members they have legally prescribed duties, and they are responsible for the overall management and development of the institution, for example meeting funders' requirements, or for collaborating with other agencies. These objectives may conflict with their roles as representative of the local branches, who may have encouraged or mandated them to vote in particular ways on contentious issues.

Board members of federal organizations also face practical problems. Members often wish to be consulted on more issues than is consistent with quick, decisive action. Both the freedom and the boundaries on the centre need to be very clear in order to avoid unnecessary arguments. Another common issue is poor performance by one part of the federation. Since branches are often predominantly voluntary, achieving improvements requires skill to encourage recognition of the problem and action to overcome it. These problems are often exacerbated by the different perspectives of the centre (often London-based, cosmopolitan, influenced by the media, parliament and the civil service) and the field (usually urban or rural and influenced by local people and community values).

One of the foundations of a successful relationship between the centre and the field is total clarity as to the roles of each party. Many organizations document the relationship in a charter or agreement. This sets out the rights and obligations of both the centre and the field. It creates an appropriate set of expectations and enables both to see that they have responsibilities to each other and to hold each other accountable. The key is to clarify what each party will do for the other. The centre might protect the use of the organization's name, establish and monitor overall standards, agree policy and provide leadership. The branches should have a mechanism for holding the centre accountable for these functions. The branches themselves might raise funds, deliver services and run campaigns, and the centre should be able to hold them accountable for these functions.

The relationship needs to be well understood and regularly reinforced. If a new or changed agreement is to be established, it will have to involve representatives of the centre and the field and there must be widespread consultation to ensure that the resulting arrangements have everyone's strong support.

Boards have three main mechanisms to bring about change in federations:

- They can **bring about change through leadership**. By charismatic appeal and the logic of their proposals, the centre can command the authority needed to make things happen.
- They can **bargain with the branches** by offering additional support in return for changes in branch priorities. For example, by offering additional services or agreeing to consult more frequently, managers can encourage branches to accept new national standards on the quality of services or the income to be remitted to the head office.
- They can **use existing rules and procedures** to enforce change. In the final analysis this can be used to force changes through.

The key is to choose the most appropriate combination of mechanisms for the circumstances. Leadership is a powerful influence, but it may be insufficient to achieve the required changes. Bargaining may be required to ensure a fair arrangement among all parties. If changes still cannot be agreed, application of the rules and procedures may be unavoidable.

In successful federations, managers work hard to establish realistic expectations. They establish many communication channels (e.g. meetings, newsletters, induction workshops) between different levels of the organization and continuously clarify what each can expect of the others. They make certain that the relationship is well documented and, more importantly, they ensure that there is consistency in the behaviour of the centre. In this way the field becomes clear about what it can reasonably expect from the centre, and the centre becomes committed to providing the field with the highest-quality services.

2.5 DIFFERENT ARRANGEMENTS FOR CHOOSING BOARD MEMBERS

The arrangements for choosing members are an essential part of the institutional structure of organizations. Four structures are common:

1. **The Elected Board**

   Most federal and many linear organizations have this arrangement. The board is chosen by a large membership, which elects from among themselves individuals to serve on the board. Most membership organizations such as trade unions and some service delivery organizations such as the National Trust and the Consumers' Association have this model. This structure is appropriate for boards that need to take account of members' views. Members vote their representatives on to the board. They also influence the board's agenda by passing motions at AGMs requiring action by the board.

2. **The Self-Perpetuating Board**

   In this type, board members themselves are responsible for choosing their successors. When an entrepreneurial or individual group establishes a new trust, charity or campaigning organization, this may be the most appropriate board structure.

3. **The Selected Board**

   In this model a small membership, usually of fewer than a hundred people, is responsible for selecting people (often without elections) to be members of the board. These 'guardians' may be past members of the board or individuals who have made a significant contribution to the organization. These people tend to have relatively little influence on the board. They act only when the board is divided or when serious problems occur. Arts organizations, some national charities and some housing associations have this type of board when they do not have a membership and do not want a self-perpetuating board.

4. **The Appointed Board**

   On these boards a third party, such as a government minister or the organization which established the body, appoints members. This model is suitable for quasi non-governmental organizations and co-ordinating bodies that represent the interests of other organizations. These organizations appoint their representative to the board. They may require their representative to take action on an issue or vote in a particular way.

Within these structures, many boards have the power to co-opt members. This is a particularly useful way of filling gaps in competencies and skills. A review of skills after an election can point to specific requirements which the board can use to guide its search for people who will bring the required experience.

Difficulties sometimes arise when boards have a mixture of these electoral arrangements. A common example is where some members are elected and others are appointed by nominating organizations. On these boards different members may expect the board to play different roles. In these circumstances, discussing the role of the board openly and encouraging members to understand their different but equally legitimate roles is vital. Difficulties that are sometimes put down to 'difficult personalities' may well be due to the different roles board members are expected to perform for their different constituencies.

Another difficulty occurs in charities when the trustees of the charity are not the same people as the board members. Sometimes the trustees are a sub-group of the board. Trustees have special duties and there are legal responsibilities that they have to discharge, in particular in relation to the Charity Commission. Giving some members of the board these extra responsibilities tends to be divisive. It is generally better for all board members to share the responsibilities of trusteeship.

SUMMARY OF KEY POINTS

The meaning of institutional structure

- Organizations working from one location, without branches and controlling their own resources have a straightforward institutional structure.
- More complex organizations require arrangements that enable their different parts to work together effectively.

Options for institutional structures

- Structural options exist on a continuum from pure 'linear' to pure 'federal'.
- The critical determinant of the structure is the extent to which branches and the centre control each other.

- As organizations develop, directors should review whether:
  - the flow of funds is aligned with the sources of power in the organization
  - the institutional structure provides the best arrangement for delivering effective services.
- A social franchise is a new institutional arrangement that allows a new service to expand across the country through existing organizations.

The special circumstances of international organizations

- There are four options for national organizations wishing to expand internationally.
- The choice of option depends on:
  - control of the organization's name
  - the cost of managing from a distance
  - the controls required to protect the organization's reputation
  - the ability of the local office to raise its own funds.

Governing different structures

- The critical tasks of governing each type of structure are different.
- Federal organizations present particular challenges because their boards have to overcome lack of authority through strong leadership, bargaining and the use of agreed rules.

Different arrangements for choosing board members

- There are four different ways to choose board members. Each leads to a different type of board.
- Boards that include members chosen by different ways need to allow time to discuss the different roles members need to play.

3   Concepts for Creating Boards that Govern

3.1   BOARDS HAVE SPECIAL FUNCTIONS

Boards of third-sector organizations are a coalition of people, often from different backgrounds and with different motives, who join together to provide organizations with governance. They have to work as a group to deliver the special functions that only a board can provide.

Boards have to perform a leadership function. They have to add value to the organization by steering, anticipating and providing wisdom and good judgement. They have to concern themselves with the vision of the organization, its values and culture and its achievements. They have to pay close attention to the systematic development of a strong board that not only plans succession but strives to increase the calibre of the people it attracts. Effective boards recognize the essential contribution that they make in the very limited time that members give to the organization.

Effective board members recognize that the task of running a board is a complex and subtle activity. Boards have to fulfil the very different functions of:

- agreeing policy and strategy
- performing a representation function
- providing accountability for the organization
- resolving tensions between different stakeholder groups
- giving advice to management.

Consequently, the simple view that the board has a totally clear-cut function of setting policy and strategy and that the staff's function is purely to implement policy is not entirely applicable in practice.

This chapter sets out some fundamental concepts about the roles and structures of boards. It:

- makes the distinction between governance and management
- introduces the idea of the life cycle of boards
- identifies the critical roles of boards that govern effectively
- describes different board and committee structures.

It assumes that there is no single solution to the structure and role of boards. Every organization has to define both according to its needs. However, there are some powerful propositions about governance that apply in most circumstances. In a nutshell these are that:

Effective governance is best provided by a small group of people:

- This makes it possible to hold management to account.
- A group of this size can meet with the necessary frequency.
- Members of the group feel a personal sense of responsibility.
- It is easier to make significant progress at meetings.

Representation can involve more people; it has to be open, transparent and well communicated in both directions:

- This requires effective management of the processes of governance.
- Representatives have to be accountable primarily for the organization as a whole and secondarily to their electorate.

A workable structure is essential, but well-managed processes and communications are the real essence of good governance:

- This means that managers and board members need to have a deep understanding of the distinct roles of governance and management.
- It means that managers are responsible for managing the processes and keeping board members well informed.
- Chairs have to ensure that committees stick to their agreed roles.
- Committees have to be clearly designated as advisory or decision-taking.

Regular review of the board's performance needs to be an integral part of the board's work:

- Boards and committees must always invest time in their own development.

● They should review their performance briefly at the end of every meeting, and thoroughly at the end of the year.

This chapter describes the concepts of good governance. The next chapter describes application of the concepts and the actions needed to create strong and effective boards.

3.2 DISTINGUISHING GOVERNANCE FROM MANAGEMENT

Boards have many functions. First, they have overall responsibility for deciding the **policy and strategy** of the organization. They are responsible for agreeing the policies that the organization adopts on matters relating to its fundamental purpose and on the standards it adopts on the way it works (for example, over investments or employment matters). They also have to approve the mission, objectives and strategies pursued by the organization and they have to monitor its performance against the agreed plans. They have to be aware of the changing external environment and ensure that the organization is geared up to respond to new circumstances.

Secondly, the board has a **representation** function. Board members have to listen to the voices of all the organization's stakeholders, including users, funders and staff, and often the general public, who, because of the high profile of these organizations, take a great interest in their work. The board has to tune in to their concerns and take decisions that reflect their interests.

Many boards are elected by a membership. These board members have to represent the views of the people who elected them on to the board. They have to keep themselves informed about members' ambitions for the organization and their concerns about the way it is run. Frequently they will have been either a member themselves or part of a branch that elected them to the board. Their continuing involvement with grass-roots members will be critical to discharging their representation function.

Thirdly, the board is ultimately **accountable** for the organization. It is responsible for overseeing all the organization's work, for appointing the chief executive and for setting up the necessary reporting procedures to ensure it knows and understands what the organization is doing. Depending on the nature of the organization, it may be directly accountable to members, funders, regulatory bodies and the general public.

Fourthly, the board has a function of **resolving tensions** within the organization. Since these organizations are coalitions of people with different interests, such as service users, funders, staff and volunteers, the board has to arbitrate between competing demands placed on the organization.

In the limited time that board members devote to the organization they have to focus their efforts sharply on those critical functions no one else can discharge. The most common mistake boards make is to spend time on activities that should be delegated to paid staff. To separate the roles of the board and staff, it is useful to think in terms of the discrete functions of governance and management.

There is no clear-cut distinction between governance and management. Unfortunately, the roles of the board and of paid management cannot be neatly separated. But neither do they need to overlap entirely. They need to be distinct but complementary. The critical functions of the board are different from the tasks of paid staff.

Governance is the board's responsibility. It is about ensuring that the organization has a clear mission and strategy, but not necessarily about developing it. It is about ensuring that the organization is well managed, but not about managing it. It is about giving guidance on the overall allocation of resources, but is less concerned with the precise numbers. Governance is about taking responsibility for the organization's performance, but not involving the board in the detail of the performance measurement system. Governance is ultimately concerned with providing insight, wisdom and good judgement.

Management is a staff responsibility. Staff are responsible for supporting the process of developing strategy and for implementing it once it is agreed by the board. They are responsible for turning the board's intentions into action and for administering the systems and procedures needed to get results. They also help to ensure that the mechanics of the governance process run smoothly.

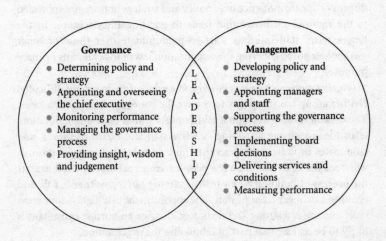

Governance	LEADERSHIP	Management
● Determining policy and strategy ● Appointing and overseeing the chief executive ● Monitoring performance ● Managing the governance process ● Providing insight, wisdom and judgement		● Developing policy and strategy ● Appointing managers and staff ● Supporting the governance process ● Implementing board decisions ● Delivering services and conditions ● Measuring performance

Balancing governance and management

The balance of responsibility between the board and management depends on circumstances. Organizations where the staff are effective and share a common set of values require less intervention from the board. In this situation, it is easier for the board to stick closely to its governance role.

Organizations with a strong board but a weak or divided staff will find the board intervening in detail more often and crossing the boundary between governance and management. This is common in smaller organizations with few staff but with board members willing to work voluntarily. Indeed, even larger organizations have to acknowledge that, for many people, it is the actual work of the organization that motivates board members to give their time voluntarily to the organization. Few people join an organization's board because they are motivated by an interest in governance!

Organizations with a strong staff and a weak board are taking a long-term risk, because management will not be held accountable. To ensure that the organization continues to function, staff have to take on duties that should really be carried out by the board. They have a disproportionate influence over policy and strategy and are not subjected to the rigorous challenge that leads to good-quality decisions. In the longer term, staff interests start to predominate over those of other stakeholder groups, leaving the organization less fit to achieve its primary purpose.

Organizations with a weak board and weak staff are in serious difficulty. Neither group has the ability to resolve the issues the organization faces. The organization is in a spiral which starts with a declining reputation, leads to difficulty in attracting effective staff and board members, and culminates in deteriorating services and a further fall in reputation. It will need the dedication of a few people over an extended period to start the process of building a new board, carving out a governance role and creating a stronger team of staff. The appointment of a highly competent chief executive, a strong and dedicated chair or an outside consultant is likely to be an essential part of rebuilding the organization.

3.3 THE LIFE CYCLE OF BOARDS

One way of developing insights into the work of the board and its changing relationship with staff is to think in terms of a life cycle, which many boards follow. The detail of the cycle varies from one organization to the next, but the pattern is so common that it helps boards to understand the way their work has to evolve in line with the development of the organization.

The founding phase

Many organizations are established by a charismatic founder who has the vision and personality to define a social, cultural or environmental problem and to create an organization to address it. The founder gathers together a group of people who share the same views, and an organization is created. The founder is sometimes the first, unpaid, chief executive or chair and may hold on to that position when other staff are hired.

The appointment of staff frequently leads to the first crisis. Board members find that their role as both doers and deciders is usurped. The board goes through its first transformation and has to distinguish its role more clearly from that of the staff. In well-established organizations this will have happened many years ago.

The youthful phase

When new roles are agreed upon, often implicitly, the board settles down into the second stage of the cycle. The organization grows, more staff are appointed and soon the chief executive has a senior management team who take responsibility for most of the work of the organization. As time passes, the board begins to take a back seat and meetings become routinized, attendance falls, discussions become less sharp and respect for the board declines. Suddenly a crisis jerks it out of its complacency; this may be the fact that the organization has outgrown the capabilities of its chief executive, or a dispute with staff, or a difference of opinion over a policy issue. Whatever the trigger, the board is forced to reassess its role and, usually, revise its membership as well.

The adult phase

When the board reassesses its role, it will frequently conclude that it needs people with a wider range of skills. Once found, these people generally bring a different set of assumptions and, after a period of difficult relationships, many of the founding members may leave. The organization settles into the third stage of the cycle. The new board brings the rational mindset of setting objectives, monitoring performance and managing the budget. They risk, however, losing the original sense of mission that inspired the organization in the first place.

Because members are often new to the role, this new board feels the need to grasp the detail of the organization. It meets more often and establishes sub-committees. Board papers become thicker, and before long it is accused by staff of meddling in the detail.

Eventually another crisis precipitates a review, which concludes that the board's role of establishing policy and the staff role of implementation need to be adhered to more rigorously. Committees are streamlined, new operating procedures are written and the role of the board is again transformed. Members heave a sigh of relief, start to meet less frequently and give the staff greater freedom within agreed boundaries.

The mature phase

As the years pass, the board takes a more hands-off role. The well-established organization finds it easier to recruit new members, who are often leading figures in their own fields and who will have less time to devote to the board. Some attract 'big names', who are willing to lend the respect that goes with their name but unwilling to get involved in the detail of the organization's work. Some boards become dominated by establishment figures and members who are unwilling to challenge accepted views about the organization and its work. Meetings become ritualized and membership stagnates. Eventually the board slips back into its old bad habits and a crisis erupts; some members leave and the board returns to a previous stage of development.

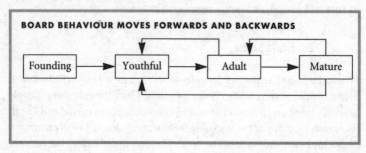

BOARD BEHAVIOUR MOVES FORWARDS AND BACKWARDS

Founding → Youthful → Adult → Mature

The life cycle varies widely from one organization to another, with some organizations remaining at one stage for many years. However, the pattern is sufficiently common to be helpful in describing dispassionately why a board may be in the middle of a series of difficulties that no one can really understand. Having a picture of an old stage and a new one is a powerful tool in helping people relate to the problem and find ways forward that are acceptable to the majority.

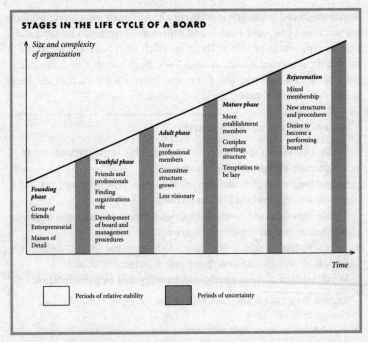

STAGES IN THE LIFE CYCLE OF A BOARD

Size and complexity of organization

Founding phase

Group of friends

Entrepreneurial

Masses of Detail

Youthful phase

Friends and professionals

Finding organizations role

Development of board and management procedures

Adult phase

More professional members

Committee structure grows

Less visionary

Mature phase

More establishment members

Complex meetings structure

Temptation to be lazy

Rejuvenation

Mixed membership

New structures and procedures

Desire to become a performing board

Time

☐ Periods of relative stability   ▨ Periods of uncertainty

A similar cycle has been reported in the USA (see 'Is Governing Board Behaviour Cyclical?', *Non-profit Management and Leadership*, Winter 1992).

3.4 KEY ROLES OF AN EFFECTIVE BOARD

Irrespective of their stage of development, the best boards strive to give high value to their organization, creating policy when needed and involving themselves in detail only when the board has a significant contribution to make. These boards ask for information about achievements and for figures that enable members to make judgements about value for money. They work hard on developing the role of the board and regularly take time to assess their own performance and to initiate actions to improve board procedures.

The effective governing board sees its role as a **partnership** with the chief executive and the senior management team. It is a partnership in which the board is the first among equals. Although some organizations are dominated by their boards and others are dominated by their staff, neither type works as well as those in which both have distinctive roles to play in achieving common objectives. Both the staff and the board need to work at carving out distinctive functions for each other. Each needs to avoid duplicating the other's work.

THE ROLE OF THE BOARD IS SUBTLE

'What exactly is the role of the board in this organization?' asked the recently appointed chief executive.

'We have a simple rule,' replied the chair. 'The board agrees the overall strategy and the staff implements it.'

'But how does the board distinguish between strategy and implementation?' asked the chief executive.

'It's simple,' replied the chair. 'Whatever the board wants to discuss is strategy and everything else is implementation.'

Work seldom divides neatly into strategy and implementation.

Adapted from *Govern More and Manage Less*, R. Chait, National Centre for Non-profit Boards, USA.

In defining its role, the board needs to **add value** to the organization. The key question to ask is: what is different as a result of the board's work? In some cases the board is a critical ingredient of the organization's success and effectiveness. In others it will not be clear that the board has added value to the organization. It can be a significant drain on the staff, who have to prepare for and attend meetings, and it can cost substantial amounts in travel and accommodation expenses. In the worst cases the board and its sub-groups can be a net drain on the organization's resources, costing more than it is worth.

Effective boards usually take few decisions; they have a much more sophisticated role. The critical ingredient of an effective board is to **anticipate decisions**. Boards that anticipate are in command of the organization's affairs. Boards that fail to anticipate find that events run out of control and they are driven by circumstances into crisis management. All too soon the board finds itself repeating the work of the staff, dragged into the detail and unable to raise itself into a more strategic role.

When a board has a commanding view of what it is trying to do and how it is going about the task, the following require active anticipation:

- significant changes in the funding environment
- significant changes in the size and needs of the user group or campaign priorities
- the need to change the overall structure of the organization or the senior management structure
- succession of the chair
- review of the chief executive's contract and personal performance and, when necessary, replacement of an under-performing chief executive.
- establishing processes for determining the organization's strategy and monitoring its overall performance

With good anticipation, the effective board finds that **shaping decisions** is just as important as taking them. It creates the context within which the organization functions. It influences the organization by asking the right questions at the right time. It guides with wisdom and good judgement rather than by making decisions on matters of detail.

A key role of the board is to **balance** different stakeholders' interests in the organization. Members, staff, funders, service users and the general public have an interest in the organization. These interests are seldom the same. Each group therefore attempts to influence the organization towards its own priorities. Funders may place unnecessarily burdensome conditions on their grants, members can make unreasonable demands on staff, service users can develop expectations beyond the organization's resources, and staff may put their own interests before those of the organization. The board is morally **accountable** to all these groups and legally accountable to some. It has to act as **mediator** between their competing interests.

DILEMMAS OF THE BOARD'S ROLE

'This board shouldn't be involved in setting the prices of our services,' said the recently recruited board member who was also a company chief executive. 'Pricing decisions are an operational matter for our talented team of staff.'

'But they do have critical impact on our overall success,' replied a long-standing board member and respected member of the local community. 'If we increase our prices, fewer people will be able to afford our service – and our aim is to reach as many people as possible.'

'I know that,' replied the company chief, 'but if we meddle with the prices, we will get drawn into a discussion about the type of service we offer, the quality of the service and even how it is promoted. Before long we will be doing management's job.'

'I'm not suggesting we should get into that detail, but I do think that as representatives of the community we have a responsibility to ensure that we keep our prices as low as possible,' retorted the slightly angry community leader. 'We can't do that if we just let staff put the prices up without discussion by this board.'

Boards need to discuss and agree their roles, and periodically review them.

The practical roles which an effective board needs to discharge fall into two categories: those concerned with the organization's work and those concerned with the work of the board itself.

Roles concerning the work of the organization

Roles in which the effective board can legitimately involve itself include:

- shaping and periodically redefining the mission
- agreeing long-term objectives and strategic plans
- influencing the overall allocation of resources to different purposes or user groups (usually through the strategic planning and budget-setting processes)
- establishing performance measures for the organization as a whole and monitoring against these measures
- ensuring the financial security of the organization and establishing effective financial management systems
- appointing, supporting, supervising and monitoring the performance of the chief executive (sometimes by delegating this to a sub-group)
- establishing broad policies about the way the organization should work (e.g. financial policy, personnel policy and policies on ethical issues such as special support for people with disabilities and ethical investments)
- agreeing a list of matters that are reserved for board decisions.

Roles concerning the work of the board

The key roles of the board in determining its own work programme include:

- defining the ideal size and composition of the board
- structuring committees and working groups to anticipate the future needs of the organization
- recruiting and inducting new members to meet present and future requirements of the organization
- ensuring board members are clear about the board's responsibilities and how they are discharged
- providing training and support to meet members' development needs
- determining its own agenda and priorities
- monitoring its own performance and that of its committees.

For many boards this will sound good on paper and be difficult in practice. The most common reason for this is that the board is investing insufficient time in discussing and agreeing its own roles and the operational procedures needed to discharge those roles. As a result it steps on to the slippery slope which leads inexorably to excessive involvement in detailed operational matters.

An effective board can anticipate spending a significant proportion of its time discussing and agreeing its own role, structure and ways of working. This investment pays handsome dividends. When complex issues arise, there is an agreement and a framework within which they can be discussed and resolved. It takes time to agree roles and procedures but, once it has been done, meetings run more smoothly and decision-taking is easier.

Defining the board's role is a never-ending task. Over time external circumstances will change, new members will join the board, and a new chief executive will bring different assumptions. These changes should all encourage the board once again to spend more time redefining its own role and the requirements it places on its staff to enable it to discharge its role.

SIX BOARD COMPETENCIES

Research by Richard Chait, a well-known American guru on non-profit board performance, has correlated the competencies of boards with the effectiveness of the non-profit organizations they manage. These are described in six dimensions.

Competency	Definition
1. Contextual dimension	The board understands and takes into account the values and beliefs of the organization it governs.
2. Educational dimension	The board ensures that board members are well informed about the organization, the profession and the board's role, responsibilities and performance.
3. Inter-personal dimension	The board nurtures the development of members as a group and fosters a sense of cohesiveness.
4. Analytical dimension	The board recognizes complexities in the issues it faces and draws upon different perspectives to find appropriate solutions.
5. Political dimension	The board accepts the need to develop healthy relationships with key constituencies.
6. The strategic dimension	The board helps ensure a strategic approach to the organization's future.

His research concluded that organizations which had boards that exhibited all six competencies performed significantly better than those lacking one or more of these competencies.

Size of the board

The size of the board also influences its role. There are three fundamentally different models, each of which can accommodate a different number of members. In all three cases they are the governing body of the organization, accountable in law for its work and decisions. The sizes shown below are broad guidelines. Precise numbers depend on circumstances. In practice the number of people who attend meetings is often more important than agreed limits.

The **hands-on board** usually has between seven and twelve members. It can meet regularly, and members can all participate equally in the governance of the organization. These boards do not necessarily have to delegate much to committees. Boards of fewer than seven members can seldom represent all the constituencies (e.g. geographical regions) of the organization. They also risk having insufficient breadth of specialist skills and expertise to discharge their responsibilities. Hands-on boards of more than twelve members become increasingly cumbersome to manage; members have less 'air time' in meetings and each feels less personally responsible for the decisions the board takes.

The **representative board** has between twelve and thirty-five members. It ensures that a wide range of views is presented. Its meetings have to concentrate on fewer critical issues because it is less efficient at taking decisions. Boards at the larger end of this spectrum need to appoint an executive committee to perform some of the hands-on functions of governance. This type of board is suitable in situations where representation of different constituencies is a paramount priority.

The **policy-making board** has more than thirty-five members. It functions as the organization's parliament, debating broad policy issues but remaining distanced from month-by-month decisions. These boards meet less frequently, so delegating decision-making and most of the practical functions of governance to an executive committee is essential. It is most useful where many disparate viewpoints need to be taken into account in decision-making and where representation of many constituencies is necessary.

Every so often, the size of the board becomes a hot topic in an organization. The advantages and disadvantages of larger or smaller boards are fiercely debated because everyone has strongly held views on this issue! However, these debates frequently fail to recognize that the appropriate size depends on the need for representation of different constituencies and the role the board is designed to perform. There is consequently no right or wrong size. In the 1990s many organizations with large boards reduced their size and created non-executive fora to provide mechanisms for representation and consultation.

DIFFERENT BOARDS TO SUIT DIFFERENT CIRCUMSTANCES

The board of LEWISHAM HOSPITAL TRUST has ten members and meets twelve times a year. It has separate Remuneration and Audit Sub-Committees. Its roles include shaping issues with a time horizon of more than one year, taking capital expenditure decisions, managing the interface with the local community and resolving major strategic and organizational issues. It is a **hands-on board.**

The board of RSPCA has twenty-five members, consisting of ten regional representatives elected by the branches and fifteen members elected by the national membership. It meets six to eight times a year and is supported by seven standing committees. It is a **representative board.**

The governing body of the SAMARITANS, called the Council of Management, consists of 200 people, each representing a branch or a region of the organization. It formulates policy for the movement, approves the annual budget and elects an executive to govern the organization. The executive meets five times a year and the Council meets once a year. It is a **policy-making board.**

3.5 COMMITTEES DO BOARD WORK

When organizations grow beyond a certain size or degree of complexity, most boards find they need to create groups such as sub-committees, advisory panels or task groups to take responsibility for some of the board's work. Organizations use different words to describe these sub-groups, so clarification of the language used in this book is required.

The term **committee** is used as a generic word to cover sub-committees, advisory panels and task groups. The term **sub-committee** refers to a permanent committee of the board to which specific, ongoing functions are delegated. Sub-committees take decisions and are accountable to the board for their actions.

The term **advisory panel** refers to a group established to advise the board on an ongoing basis. This group has no decision-making power, though in some cases, such as medical research advisory panels, they can be very influential. The term **task group** refers to a group established to carry out a specific job in a given timescale and then report back to the board. The task may require either actions (e.g. to co-ordinate preparation of the strategic plan) or investigation (e.g. to propose improvements to governance procedures).

Functions of committees

There are many reasons for establishing committees. Boards have limited time and need to delegate some board work. They may need specialist advice from groups of people with expertise in a particular area of work. They may have specific problems that require detailed investigation in preparation for a board decision. These are legitimate roles for committees.

While there are undoubted advantages of committees, there are also many dangers:

- establishing a committee can delay decision-taking or lead to decisions not being taken
- having too many committees can dilute the board's overview of the organization
- boards can abrogate their responsibilities and accept committee recommendations without challenge.

There is a tendency for boards to create committees as problems arise. In some organizations these groups in turn create another layer of sub-groups. They grow incrementally until sometimes the structure is of labyrinthine complexity. As the number grows, the work required to recruit people, service and support them increases proportionately. Before long, there is a risk that the annual cycle of meetings will become the dominant management process in the organization.

Committees are nevertheless important to the functioning of organizations. When working effectively they:

- increase the efficiency of the board by taking responsibility for defined areas of work
- allow representatives of different stakeholder groups (e.g. parents, musicians, special interest groups, major donors) to present their views in a coherent way
- help the organization keep more closely in touch with service users. Members of the committee are the antennae of the organization, able to listen to the views at the front line and report directly back to the centre
- are an effective means of representing and consulting on people's views. They perform an important role in keeping people in different parts of the organization (for example, regions and branches) in touch with plans and current activities
- provide support, guidance and wisdom to staff responsible for delivering the services.

However, many problems can arise when an organization does not keep a tight grip on the structure and roles of its committees:

- their precise role and purpose easily become confused
- they are sometimes given roles (for example, press relations, membership or information) that are inappropriate and should be a staff responsibility
- the total number grows inexorably because there are always reasons to establish more of them. Sometimes people are averse to cutting them because this implies that their members are not doing a useful job
- committees expand their remits beyond their stated responsibilities and cause confusion about who is responsible for what
- over time, sub-committees in particular grow larger, their deliberations grow longer but each member feels less personal accountability for the performance of their sub-committee
- committees can blur the direct line of accountability of the staff to the chief executive and then to the board
- the cost of committees can exceed the value of the contribution they make to the organization in terms of the demands they make on staff to prepare reports and attend meetings.

The objective of committees should be to add value to the organization in the same way as the board should add value. They need to be able to define their unique contribution to the enterprise. They need to be able to convince themselves and the board that the benefits which come from their committee are significant and are worth the costs of servicing it.

Structure of committees

The overall structure of committees is a critical board issue. It has to be considered at two levels: first, the need for a co-ordinating executive committee and, second, the structure and functions of specialist committees.

Large boards that meet relatively infrequently usually appoint an **executive committee** (sometimes known as the management committee or by the rather quaint term, 'finance and general purposes committee'). The board delegates specified responsibilities to this group to govern the organization in between its meetings. The executive committee may, in turn, appoint committees to delegate some of its work.

In this common arrangement the board needs to clarify:

- whether both groups should have a common chair (two chairs can lead to confusion and misunderstanding, but doing both jobs is a time-consuming task for one person and limits the number of people who will stand for the job)
- whether all the members of the executive committee should be members of the board (common membership simplifies matters, but it limits the opportunity for the executive committee to co-opt people with skills it requires)
- whether the chief executive reports to the board or to the executive committee (it is usually a mixture of both, but it is worth clarifying where the buck stops to avoid problems)
- whether committees report to the board or to the executive committee (it is often a mixture, with some reporting to the board and some to the executive committee).

One arrangement that has attracted increased interest in recent years is a structure that draws a clear distinction between the functions of governance and those of representation. This structure is particularly applicable to membership organizations that make complex demands on their board and also require a large amount of representation. In this circumstance, boards often become large and unwieldy and do not necessarily attract people with the skills needed to provide strong and effective governance.

One way to address this is to focus the work of a '**representative board**' exclusively on representation. Its job is to listen systematically and closely to the views of the members and to ensure that the board is kept continuously abreast of these opinions. Its only other function is to appoint a board to govern the organization. It delegates to a '**governing board**' full responsibility for governance and retains the power to sack the governing board only if it believes the board is taking actions which are not in the organization's long-term interest. The board in return agrees to take into account the views of the representative board. It ignores them at its peril!

This structure allows each group to focus sharply on the task that it is best placed to deliver. Representatives concentrate on the job of listening to members of their constituency and reporting views systematically to the board. Governing board members can then devote their skills and expertise to delivering top-quality governance.

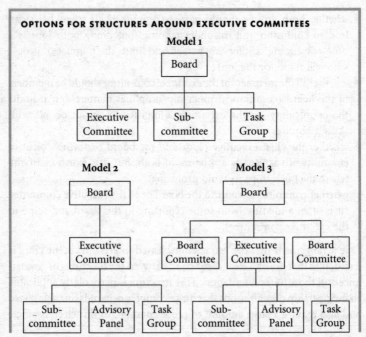

OPTIONS FOR STRUCTURES AROUND EXECUTIVE COMMITTEES

Model 1

Board

Executive Committee — Sub-committee — Task Group

Model 2

Board

Executive Committee

Sub-committee — Advisory Panel — Task Group

Model 3

Board

Board Committee — Executive Committee — Board Committee

Sub-committee — Advisory Panel — Task Group

Model 4

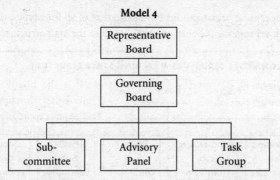

Model 1 is suitable for a medium-sized organization that needs to delegate month-by-month work to an executive committee but also needs, for example, a specialist committee on professional standards or a working group on the training of board members.

Model 2 would suit an organization with a large board that wishes to delegate most of its month-by-month work to an executive committee.

Model 3 would be more appropriate for the largest and most complex organizations that have specialist problems at board level (e.g. managing the election process) and need an executive committee which in turn finds it necessary to delegate part of its work to other committees.

Model 4 would suit an organization that needs the views of its members to be strongly represented but that also delivers a wide range of services to different groups of people.

The next issue to consider is the structure of **sub-committees**. The theoretical options include structuring:

By function	By service	By geography	By task
● finance	● education	● Latin America	● capital appeals
● fund-raising	● social services	● Africa	● audit committee
● personnel	● research	● Asia	● board recruitment

In practice, most organizations have a mixture of all four types, the most common arrangement being one that matches the staff structure.

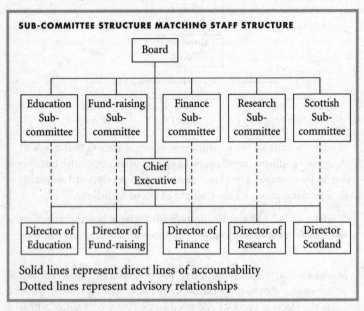

SUB-COMMITTEE STRUCTURE MATCHING STAFF STRUCTURE

Board

Education Sub-committee · Fund-raising Sub-committee · Finance Sub-committee · Research Sub-committee · Scottish Sub-committee

Chief Executive

Director of Education · Director of Fund-raising · Director of Finance · Director of Research · Director Scotland

Solid lines represent direct lines of accountability
Dotted lines represent advisory relationships

In geographically dispersed organizations there may be sub-committees for each geographical area (e.g. the north-west, Scotland, or Latin America). They will often have a direct relationship with the director for that territory.

This type of sub-committee structure can lead to many problems if it is not carefully managed. Members of the board and the sub-committee need to be totally clear about the different lines of accountability of committee members and senior managers. Sub-committees are delegated governance tasks by the board and they report back to the board. Managers may advise sub-committees, but they remain accountable to the chief executive.

Problems arise when:

● there is a legitimate disagreement between the manager and the sub-committee
● roles are not clearly understood by everyone involved.

Legitimate disagreements need to be passed up the line by the chair of the sub-committee and the manager as soon as they are identified. The chair of the board and the chief executive should then resolve the issue, since they are responsible respectively for governance and management.

A recent development has been the establishment of audit committees. Mirroring developments in the corporate sector, these have been established to oversee the organization's financial affairs, and in particular to ensure that proper financial controls are in place. Some boards have widened this definition to include 'audit' of the organization's overall performance. This includes looking at the service outputs (or the campaigns) so that the board can make better assessments of the value for money that the organization is delivering.

Another development has been the establishment of remuneration committees to advise the board on salaries and other remuneration of all employees.

Definition of the roles of committees needs to go beyond drawing lines on a chart. These lines always oversimplify a complex and subtle relationship. What is needed is a written description of the role and a thorough debate by members of the board and the sub-committee to ensure that all aspects of their roles are clearly understood by everyone involved. This is particularly important when new managers are appointed and new committee members are elected.

The best way to develop the committee structure is to pinpoint specific governance or representational roles that the board needs to delegate. Too often the committee structure is built on the 'wouldn't-it-be-a-good-idea-if' approach. Carefully defining responsibilities, relationships and tasks ensures that sub-committees are clear about their roles.

Advisory panels

Advisory panels are essentially sub-committees without decision-making powers. They are useful when a board needs expert advice but does not wish to delegate responsibility for taking final decisions. Examples include medical research panels which advise boards on spending research funds, and standards panels which advise on professional or technical standards.

It is most common for advisory panels to be created to give advice to the board. However, some organizations have created advisory panels whose primary function is to give advice to management; and some organizations have both types. One advantage of advisory panels is that they bring wisdom, expertise and good judgement into the organization without becoming an alternative decision-making mechanism. This avoids the risk of a committee structure that mirrors the management structure.

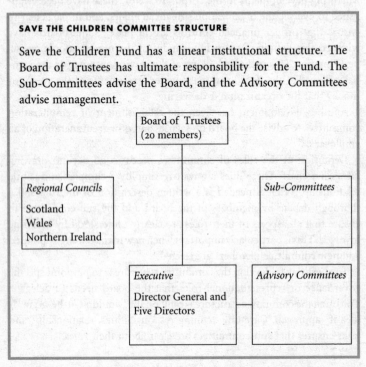

SAVE THE CHILDREN COMMITTEE STRUCTURE

Save the Children Fund has a linear institutional structure. The Board of Trustees has ultimate responsibility for the Fund. The Sub-Committees advise the Board, and the Advisory Committees advise management.

Board of Trustees
(20 members)

Regional Councils
Scotland
Wales
Northern Ireland

Sub-Committees

Executive
Director General and
Five Directors

Advisory Committees

Advisory panels are generally a permanent part of a structure, so they are appropriate when the board needs ongoing advice over a period of years from a group that builds its experience over time. Boards and senior management need to be seen to listen closely to their advisory panels. Members give their time voluntarily and have no real power in the organization, so they need to give top-quality advice and to be heard if they are to feel a valued part of the decision-making process.

A special type of advisory panel is the **advisory board**, sometimes referred to as an assembly. This is created to give the board advice on the overall direction of the organization. Advisory boards are often established when a large board is being reduced in size and the organization wishes to retain departing members' skills and experience. This group sits on top of the board in the organization chart, but it does not have any constitutional powers. It often consists of the organization's elder statesmen and other people whose experience and expertise the organization wishes to draw upon on a regular basis. Appointments are made by the board, and it is perceived as being an honour to join such a group. It may meet once or twice a year, receive presentations of the organization's work and discuss policy and progress at the most general level.

Task groups

Task groups are teams of people established to resolve a well-defined problem within a given time-frame. They are most effective at resolving very specific board-level problems. The board can set the group a brief, agree its membership and delegate the problem. Examples include purchasing new property, merging with another organization, recruiting a new chief executive, setting standards for work and overseeing a consultancy.

Task groups have the great advantage of flexibility. They can be created when required and disbanded when they have completed their work. Members are motivated by having a clearly specified task to undertake within an agreed time-frame. They get the satisfaction of completing specified tasks.

SUMMARY OF KEY POINTS

Boards have special functions

- The critical functions of boards are agreeing policy and strategy, representing members' views, providing accountability and resolving tensions between stakeholders.
- Effective governance is best provided by a small group of people
- Representation can involve more people, has to be open, transparent and well communicated in both directions
- A workable structure is essential, but well-managed processes and communications are the real essence of good governance
- Regular review of performance needs to be an integral part of the board's work.

Distinguishing governance from management

- The concepts of governance and management are useful in separating the roles of the board and of management, but the boundaries between the two ideas are often blurred in practice.
- Governance is concerned with the critical functions of clarifying the mission, setting objectives and strategy, monitoring overall performance, appointing the chief executive, approving the senior staff structure, managing the election process, inducting board members and establishing processes to enable the board to discharge those responsibilities.
- Management is concerned with supporting the board in carrying out those tasks and taking initiatives to ensure the board can discharge its responsibilities.
- The balance between the governance and management roles depends on circumstances.

Life cycle of boards

- Boards go through phases of development, characterized as founding, youthful, adult and maturity.
- They behave in different ways at each stage of their development.

Key roles of an effective board

- An effective board is one that works in partnership with the chief executive. It adds value to the organization, anticipates and shapes decisions and balances stakeholders' interests.
- Boards have roles concerning the work of the organization and roles concerning the board itself.
- The appropriate size of a board depends on the role it is required to perform.

Committees do board work

- Boards establish committees so that they can delegate board work. Committees should not do management tasks.
- Sub-committees, advisory panels and task groups each have different roles.
- Committee structures are best considered at different levels:
  - the need for and functions of an executive committee
  - the need to separate representation and governance
  - the functions and reporting lines of other committees.

- Committees can be an encumbrance. The board should regularly evaluate their effectiveness and abolish them if they are not adding value.

4 **Making Boards Govern**

4.1 **STRONG BOARDS ARE ESSENTIAL**

In the past, board membership was sometimes treated as an honour or a duty. People saw it as something they did for the good of the organization and the wider community. Some viewed it as a hobby, others as light relief from the pressures of the office or an alternative to the chores of domestic life. Skills weren't seen as necessary – common sense and commitment were all that the job required.

Nowadays, however, the task of governing third-sector organizations is increasingly demanding. Many organizations are large and complex and deliver a wide range of services. As they become more influential, the public expects to see higher standards from the people who are ultimately responsible for these organizations.

Organizations need strong boards because:

1. They are **legally responsible** for the organization. Boards that understand their duties and responsibilities are better placed to carry them out efficiently.
2. They **provide security and continuity** to the organization, particularly at critical times such as when a new chief executive is appointed or when strategy and direction are re-evaluated.
3. A group of people is required to **hold the chief executive accountable** for his or her actions, to agree performance targets and to conduct an annual performance review.
4. A group of people is required to **stand back from day-to-day operations** and take a dispassionate view on the critical issues of:
   - the mission

- the objectives
- the allocation of resources to different purposes
- the long-term financial security of the organization.

5. A body is needed to **monitor the organization's performance**. In business, falling sales quickly tell managers that services are not meeting customers' requirements. Third-sector organizations either operate in the 'muted market' or have no paying customers at all. They need the board to keep staff alert to quality problems and ensure that the needs of service users are always paramount.

However, there is no single model of an ideal board. The way a board governs depends on circumstances and the purpose of the organization. Organizations that have one purpose or work in one location or with one group of people are considerably more straightforward to govern than those that both provide services and campaign, those with many outposts and those supporting different user groups.

The complexity of the board's work also depends on the diversity of its funding sources. Organizations funded by a mixture of donations, grants and contracts are more complicated to govern than those that are primarily dependent on one source.

This chapter:

- explains the many pressures that lure boards into ineffectiveness
- describes how to attract people to board membership and develop their skills
- highlights the special role of the chair .
- suggests actions to improve the operational effectiveness of boards
- demonstrates actions to increase committee effectiveness.

4.2 FORCES DRIVING BOARDS INTO INEFFECTIVENESS

Despite the pressing need for strong boards, the reality is that many boards are surrounded by pressures that lure them away from their essential tasks. Some of these pressures come from the board and its members:

- Board members are volunteers and are not necessarily chosen for their skills and experience in governing organizations.

- Boards are required by their constitution or by law to take decisions on a wide range of essentially managerial issues, such as agreeing contracts and leases, approving the annual report, setting staff terms and conditions, disciplinary actions, and so on.
- Strong chairs have their own views of the board's role and can sometimes dominate proceedings.
- Board members with specific interests raise issues of detail at board meetings when other fora would be more appropriate.
- Cliques form around a particular issue and incrementally take over board meetings.

Other forces that can make boards less effective emanate from the staff:

- Chief executives need the security of knowing that they have the board's support on certain issues, even though they may not really be board issues.
- Chief executives and senior managers do not service the board well, so it becomes increasingly difficult to provide good governance.
- Staff avoid difficult decisions and take too many decisions to the board.
- Chief executives under-perform so the board is obliged to intervene in ever-increasing detail.
- Genuine lack of understanding exists about what the board's role ought to be.
- The function of supporting the board is under-resourced so planning, paperwork and maintenance of board functions fall below the required standard.
- The values and beliefs of the staff and board gradually move in different directions, to the point where they interfere with practical management of the organization.

Boards that can stand up to these pressures face yet more potential difficulties. Chief executives are seldom given training in the task of professionally managing a board. It is assumed that they will be able to master the intricacies of a complex relationship without any support. People in their first chief executive position face particular difficulties as they no longer have their own chief executive to guide and support them with the many judgements that they have to make when dealing with the governance–management relationship. In other circumstances the chief executive has the skills, but the people on the board do not fit the task in hand. Chairs may not have had previous experience of that role and may require support. Board members of organizations that have grown rapidly or diversified into a number of different activities may not have the skills needed in the new circumstances.

Recently, some boards have attempted to overcome skill shortages by bringing in expertise from other sectors on to their governing body. With the right calibre of people, this has many advantages. It is not, however, without its own pitfalls:

● Some talented individuals fear that the third sector is so different that their normally confident approach becomes weak and half-hearted.
● Some have such passion about the issue that it overrides their normally cool-headed approach.
● Others preach business or public sector gospel, only to discover that their assumptions and, more often, their underlying beliefs are different from those of the third sector.

The unique characteristic of third-sector boards is that they bring together people from a wide variety of backgrounds and different professions. Third-sector boards can include service users, politicians and business people, as well as people from other professions such as medicine, social services, accountancy, science and the law. Each member brings with him or her a mass of assumptions about how a board should work and about the nature and purpose of the organization. These assumptions can be very different, so a great deal of time has to be spent understanding one another. This is in contrast to a business board, where the majority of members are likely to be managers who come with broadly similar assumptions.

Faced with these compelling pressures, it is easy to see why some boards find it difficult to lift themselves above the purely managerial role and become boards that govern organizations.

4.3 ATTRACTING AND DEVELOPING BOARD MEMBERS

Organizations need to attract people who can make a contribution to the future of the organization. This section explains good practices in:

- finding and recruiting board members
- involving service users on boards
- recruiting people to different types of board
- developing board member skills.

Talented people, particularly those with board skills, are a scarce resource. They are in a position to choose which organizations they are willing to help. This choice will depend on whether the organization can satisfy their particular motives for joining a board. Boards therefore need to present themselves as being well organized. They need to understand the motives of the people they want to persuade to join the board and be able to meet their needs. At the end of the day, talented people are more likely to join the board if they respect the organization, believe that the board is well managed and that their contribution will make a significant difference to the organization.

In searching for the most able people that the board thinks it can attract, the potential relationship can be seen as a trade in which individuals give their time in return for rewards that meet their needs. These needs will be a balance of their desires to:

- see the organization succeed (often born out of personal convictions or personal circumstances)
- know that their skills and experience are being put to good use
- make new contacts
- have the prestige that is attached to board membership
- develop skills and enhance their career prospects
- find an additional role in their life.

Finding and recruiting board members

Boards can be strengthened if they take a systematic and energetic approach to recruiting new members. Boards that put little effort into this issue can end up with weak members, unable to contribute effectively to governance. The recruitment, selection and election process should be just as professional as the procedures that are used to appoint staff.

A series of actions can be taken to recruit new members. Application of these depends on the type of board (elected, self-perpetuating, selected or appointed – see above) but the principles are similar for all types. Effective boards:

- agree the balance of skill and representation required (e.g. financial, legal, educational, service users, donors, political)
- prepare job descriptions setting out what the board expects of members filling different 'posts' on the board. This ensures that potential candidates have clear expectations of the duties of board members and the time commitment required. It deters inappropriate people from standing
- require staff and board members or nominating organizations to make a concentrated effort to seek people with the requisite skills and motives. Current board members meet them informally to explain what is expected of board members and give them a briefing paper on the expectations desired of people standing for board positions
- advertise for members when an injection of new people is needed
- expect people who stand for election to meet the criteria set out in the job description.

Effective boards develop a structure which allows people to join the board in stages. For example, they may be expected to join a committee in order to learn about the organization before they can stand for election to the board. They may be co-opted on to the board for a limited period before deciding whether to stand for election, or they may sit in on meetings to gain a better understanding of the organization.

Next, effective boards make all appointments time-limited. This avoids the board going stale, and it allows people to leave the organization with dignity. For most organizations, three years should be a minimum time to serve. Six to nine years should be a maximum time to serve before members are required to have a break of one year and then, if appropriate, rejoin the board.

A final consideration is to create a group of people who can work together effectively as a team. A board can have all the skills required and represent all constituencies but be so diverse that members are unable to work together. Requiring people to attend a number of board meetings as an observer and to meet board members informally helps ensure that the board gets people who can both challenge the *status quo* and also work as part of a team.

Involving service users on boards

In some organizations, boards consist of members and service users (often known as organizations 'of' a particular group of people). In others, the board consists of professionals and people with an interest in its work (often known as organizations 'for' a group of people). A third group has boards that are a mixture of users and professionals.

Service users can make an important contribution to the effective governance of organizations. Many organizations have strengthened the representation of users on their boards. However, this has proved to be a much more complicated and sensitive issue than some people imagined.

Addressing the issue of user involvement frequently starts with the suggestion that users should be represented on the board. However, their contribution is likely to be much more pervasive when organizations start by developing a broadly based strategy for involving service users throughout the organization. This may involve recruiting users on to the staff, working as volunteers, assisting with fund-raising and joining user groups, as well as being represented on the board. Indeed, the obvious starting place is to include users in the development of the user involvement strategy. Part of that strategy can include user representation on the board and its committees.

There are many advantages to involving users in governance:

- They may have skills and experiences that the board requires, in addition to being service users.
- They bring first-hand experience of services to the board.
- They ensure that users' views are heard.
- They are 'empowered' through their commitment to the organization.

THE DILEMMA OF SKILL AND REPRESENTATION

'People with disabilities should be better represented on this board,' argued a board member of an organization established many years ago 'for' people with disabilities. 'We need to empower disabled people to determine their own future; at present we only have token representation on this board.'

'But the organization is financially complex, now we offer six different services and have contracts with twenty-two authorities,' said the chair. 'We need people with marketing, strategic planning, financial and legal skills if we are to have a chance of surviving in the competitive market.'

'We may succeed in getting more contracts, but if we lose our authority as the voice of disabled people the contracts won't be worth the paper they are written on,' said the disabled board member. 'Already there is one organization challenging our authority to represent our service users. More of our members will join them unless we make a clear commitment to having a majority of people with disabilities on this board.'

'You know we tried before, but we just couldn't find enough people with disabilities who were willing to serve and who had the business skills,' retorted the chair.

'But we didn't organize a systematic initiative to define what we are looking for, actively seek out the people with the skills we require and sell membership of this board as an opportunity not to be missed,' said the member. 'We all know there are people with disabilities who have more skills than some of us. We just need to be more proactive in making the transition to an organization of people with disabilities.'

Organizations need to balance representation and specialist skills when appointing board members.

However, there are also a number of pitfalls to avoid:

- Board members draw on their own experience. Their involvement is not a substitute for other methods of consulting users and seeking their many and varied contributions to the organization.
- Members of the board who are not users may feel disempowered by those who are users. Non-users may feel unable to challenge users, even when challenge is required. This problem is particularly acute in organizations concerned with health and disabilities.
- The title 'users' can become a pejorative term, implying people who have no 'professional' contribution to make because they are 'only' users.
- Users and non-users may assume that 'pure' users may be the only people with legitimate views, forgetting that members of their families,

work colleagues, neighbours and friends of users have a different, but none the less valid, perspective to contribute.

This topic of user involvement therefore needs to be discussed openly and thoroughly before initiatives are taken. It needs to be managed carefully to ensure that the board gets maximum benefit from non-users, people connected to users and users themselves.

USER INVOLVEMENT AT ARTHRITIS CARE

Arthritis Care exists to work with people with arthritis and to promote their health, quality of life and independence through services, support, self-help, information and influence. It has 630 branches throughout the country. Its new mission statement is: 'Putting people with arthritis in control of their arthritis, their lives and their organization.'

Arthritis Care recently reduced the size of its board from fifty to eighteen people, and at the same time agreed a policy that it was desirable for a majority of the board to be people with personal experience of having arthritis. This has been achieved. A number of staff posts are also designated specifically for people with arthritis, for example, counsellors on the help line, Young Arthritis Care development officers, and trainers. Many of its volunteers are also people with arthritis.

According to the Chief Executive, 'the changes will mean Arthritis Care becomes a more user-led charity, more vociferous and more visible. New services will be developed in line with the needs of people with arthritis and we believe we will be more attractive to funders because we are seen as empowering people with arthritis.'

Recruiting people to different types of board

For boards that are **elected** by a mass membership or **selected** by a smaller group, the democratic process has to be allowed to prevail. However, this does not mean leaving the choice of board membership purely to an election. Quite the reverse, it means that the democratic process needs to be professionally organized to ensure that:

- the membership ultimately has the freedom to choose the board they want
- nominees are advised on the organization's expectations of board members
- the board ensures that the organization is governed by a group of people who have an appropriate balance of skills, experience, values and knowledge.

In this 'managed democracy', action can be taken to ensure that a strong board is elected. Details of the roles that board members are expected to discharge should be widely publicized. Current skill and experience gaps that the board wishes to fill should be announced. Existing members should positively seek out people with the necessary skills and time, and persuade them to stand. Similarly, on **appointed boards**, the chair can give details of the skills and commitment required to the funding bodies or government departments that appoint members, to ensure that the organization gets the people it needs and not people who happen to be available.

On **self-perpetuating boards** there is a tendency to appoint friends and contacts rather than to engage in a systematic search and selection process. These boards need to be aware of the risk of becoming stagnant. They need to put extra energy into the search and selection process. They should look particularly for people who will challenge the *status quo*. This may be uncomfortable, but it will often provide a more robust board, better able to anticipate the future demands of the organization and to seek new opportunities that were not seen by existing members.

Whether a board has been elected or appointed, it can carry out an audit of the skills of its members and compare this with an agreed list of skills needed by that board at that particular time. If there are gaps, then they can be filled by co-opting people to join the board. The chair or the key officers of the board should carry out this exercise.

Boards that take actions to strengthen their own membership are in a much better position to govern than those that leave membership to the luck of the electoral draw.

Developing board member skills

Once board members have been chosen, actions should be taken to strengthen people's skills. New members need:

- **induction** – they should receive a briefing on the organization's work and be given descriptions and reports on current strategies and plans. They should be given written information on their role and responsibilities, the way the board and its sub-committee work, the board's code of conduct and the organization's expectations of its board members
- **orientation** – they should be expected to acclimatize themselves to the values and vision of the organization by reading past papers, visiting services, meeting users and sitting in management meetings as an observer.
- **a mentor** – they should be linked to an experienced member who can answer questions
- **training** – they should be given opportunities to attend the growing number of training courses offered to board members

---

THE SEVEN PRINCIPLES OF PUBLIC LIFE

The seven principles of public life created by the Nolan Committee can be applied to board members of third-sector organizations. The following advice is based on the National Council for Voluntary Organizations' interpretation of Nolan:

Selflessness
Board members have a duty to act in the best interest of the organization as a whole. They should not do so in order to gain financial or other material benefits for themselves, their family, their friends or the organizations they come from or represent.

Integrity
Board members should not place themselves under any financial or other obligation to outside individuals or organizations that might influence them in the performance of their duties.

Objectivity
In carrying out their duties, including making appointments, award-

ing contracts, or recommending individuals for rewards and benefits, board members should make choices on merit.

Accountability

Board members are accountable for their decisions and actions to the public, funders and service users. They must submit themselves to whatever scrutiny is appropriate to their role.

Openness

Board members should be as open as possible about all decisions and actions they take. They should give reasons for their decisions and restrict information only when the wider interest clearly demands.

Honesty

Board members have a duty to declare any interests relating to their role and to take steps to resolve any conflicts arising in favour of their trustee role.

Leadership

Board members should promote and support these principles by leadership and example.

4.4 THE SPECIAL ROLE OF THE CHAIR

The chair of a third-sector organization has a unique and special role. Discharging the role effectively is a critical ingredient in the long-term success of the organization.

There are five activities for which they should see themselves accountable:

1. **The chair is responsible for the performance of the board.** Although this duty is discharged in conjunction with the chief executive, the chair is ultimately accountable for the quality of governance of the organization.

   Discharging this responsibility centres around the quality of board meetings; preparation for meetings is therefore a critical activity. This requires advance planning of agendas and, most importantly, making good judgements about what a meeting can achieve in the time available. This ensures that board members feel satisfied with their achievements rather than feeling frustrated that meetings end without completing the agenda.

It also requires the chair to hold the chief executive accountable for the quality of board papers and for ensuring that board papers clearly identify items for decision.

The chair should take the initiative to ensure that once a year the board carries out or commissions a review of its own performance. In addition, the chair may wish to improve performance of the board on a continuous basis by taking five minutes at the end of each meeting to ask:

- What went well?
- What did not go so well?
- How could the board's performance be improved in future?

2. **The chair is the chief executive's line manager.** Chief executives have a particularly challenging role and require a great deal of wise counsel and good advice. Chief executives need the chair to act as a sounding-board, to evaluate their work and to provide them with support. They need guidance about priorities and assistance in dealing with difficult management issues (e.g. under-performing managers). Good chairs will be the primary source of this support.

3. **Chairs manage the boundary between governance and management.** The chair is responsible for keeping board members focused on their governance role, and for avoiding incremental slippage into the management role. The chair therefore has a duty to protect staff from over-enthusiastic board members who become too involved in detailed managerial issues. While this boundary is never clear-cut, and staff may require assistance from board members with special skills and experience, the chair should act swiftly when any board member begins to interfere in management issues. Chairs should remind board members that their job is to hold management accountable for the organization's work and not be tempted into doing managers' jobs.

4. **Chairs are responsible for succession planning.** The chair is responsible for ensuring that board member succession is planned well in advance of anticipated departures and that people with the necessary skills are selected or put forward for election.

They have a particular responsibility for developing people with the potential to succeed them in the chair. The best way to ensure that all the work that chairs put in during their time in office is continued into the future is to leave the organization in the hands of someone who can take the organization on to its next stage of development. This often requires effort over an extended period of time. It may involve other board members and the chief executive, but ultimately it is the responsibility of the chair.

5. **The chair is the figurehead.** The chair represents the organization on key public occasions.

Making the chair–chief executive relationship work

A constructive working relationship between the chair and the chief executive is essential. Both are responsible for creating and nurturing it.

The relationship is the critical link between management by the staff and governance by the board. A strong link ensures that both the board and the staff can be provided with effective leadership. A weak link leads to growing confusion over the distinctive roles of the staff and the board.

Experience demonstrates that there is no clear dividing line between the functions of the chair and the chief executive. Sometimes one will represent the organization and sometimes the other; sometimes one will play a greater role in managing the board and sometimes the other. The best partnerships build upon the strengths of each individual. Both parties agree how the areas of overlap should be divided between them, whenever possible playing to each other's strengths.

Chairs and chief executives should invest time in developing their relationship. They should:

- meet regularly
- talk openly
- agree expectations of each other
- plan the board's annual programme together
- prepare for meetings together.

Chairs who visit the organization's offices frequently or unannounced or who have an office at the organization's headquarters can cause unintended problems. The chair's efforts are often entirely well meant, but being 'in the office' almost always blurs the roles of the chair and the chief executive. It can be very frustrating for the chief executive to have the chair too involved in the detail, and it can result in the chair not being able to retain a detached overview of the organization. It should almost always be avoided.

Another common problem arises when a weak and ineffective board appoints a new chief executive. The board may not have the resources to improve its own performance but the chief executive will not have earned the authority to take an initiative on this issue. In this circumstance, chief executives should bide their time, working in a series of calculated steps to strengthen the membership of the board and consequently develop a board that can govern the organization effectively. Catalysing the appointment of a strong chair is undoubtedly a good starting point.

A SUCCESSFUL RELATIONSHIP

Watching the chair and chief executive of a national housing association working together, I noticed:

- The chief executive went out of her way to ensure that the chair was always kept informed of major developments, copying papers and talking regularly on the phone.
- The chair always defended the chief executive in meetings, and had a private discussion if problems needed to be resolved.
- They met before the quarterly board meetings to agree the agenda and the papers needed at the meeting.
- They had regular one-to-one meetings to discuss progress and problems.
- The annual performance review was a two-way discussion in which each reviewed the performance of the other.
- They had dinner together at least twice a year to review progress and problems in an informal setting.

4.5   INCREASING BOARD EFFECTIVENESS

Boards can increase their effectiveness by improving their working methods. Responsibility for improving board effectiveness ultimately lies with the chair. The chair is better placed than anyone else in the organization to ensure that the board is governing. However, it is a time-consuming task, particularly if board practices have become sloppy. Since chairs seldom have time, increasing board effectiveness is often a joint effort between the chair and the chief executive. This joint effort is similar to the work done by the chief executive and the senior management team to develop the skills of paid management.

In most organizations today, management development is receiving more attention and larger budget allocations. Governance development is equally important and needs to be given similar attention.

RESEARCH INTO BOARD EFFECTIVENESS

Researchers have striven for many years to discover correlations between different structures and roles of boards and the effectiveness of the organizations they govern. This is extremely difficult because of the need for criteria to measure that elusive quality called effectiveness. Results from America, which should be treated with some caution, suggest:

- either the proportion of business people on boards was not significantly related to organizational performance, or the relationship was negative (based on research in the YMCA; Siciliano, 1990)
- there is a positive relationship between board involvement in strategic planning and the organization's performance (Bradshaw et al., 1992)
- ratings of organizational effectiveness are positively related to the extent to which board members felt informed about their responsibilities and duties (Herman and Tulipana, 1985)
- chief executives who emphasize working with and through their board are more likely to be seen as effective (Herman and Heimovics, 1987)
- board structure accounts for only a small proportion of the variations between the performance of different organizations (Bradshaw et al., 1992)
- boards are largely risk-averse and play a limiting role, mostly as trustees rather than entrepreneurs (Austin, 1991).

Involve the chief executive

Since chief executives will play a significant role in governance development, they need to be given a clear mandate by the board to assist with this task. The board needs to put governance development on its agenda, establish the priorities for action and agree an annual programme of work, setting out what has to be achieved and by when. This encourages and legitimizes the role of chief executives when they are reluctant to become involved in governance development.

When the board is unaware that its performance is an impediment to the success of the organization, the chief executive will have to take the initiative in close co-operation with the chair. The conventional notion that the chief executive only follows the board's instructions is not appropriate in this circumstance. Chief executives cannot give their best performance when the board is weak. Sometimes they have to challenge the board about its own behaviour in order to strengthen the organization's governance.

Plan an annual meeting cycle

Most boards need an annual cycle of meetings. This plan should set out:

- the timetable of board and sub-committee meetings throughout the year
- specific items that need to be done at particular times of the year. Such items include:
  — an annual review of achievements
  — review of the strategic plan
  — agreement to budget-setting guidelines
  — approval of the budget
  — induction of new members.

Ideally the cycle should include at least one overnight meeting away from the office, where board members and the senior management team can review past performance and agree future strategy. These meetings are particularly good for building personal relationships and creating team spirit between the two groups, and may prove critical to the organization's success.

Another action to improve the overall effectiveness of the board is to focus each meeting on an in-depth resolution of a small number of critical issues, rather than attempting to consider briefly a wide range of issues. Sometimes board meetings may briefly touch on many aspects of the organization's work. This should not squeeze out thorough discussion, debate and resolution of the few critical issues that require board attention at that point in time.

Establish the right agenda

One of the quickest ways of increasing board effectiveness is to gain control over the agenda. Sometimes items arrive on the agenda from many different sources, and no one scrutinizes the resulting agenda before it is distributed. This usually leads to a managerially driven agenda rather than one set by the priorities of governance.

The agenda and preparation for meetings should not be based on regular reports from each department. It needs to start with governance issues. These might include:

- specific achievements of the service user group in the last period
- the overall allocation of resources to different service user groups
- new policies that the organization needs to adopt
- political and campaigning initiatives required to raise the profile of the service user group
- review of the chief executive's contract
- succession of the chair
- improvement of board procedures and board information systems.

Gaining a grip on the agenda means that every item that is a contender for board attention needs to pass through a fine sieve in which the chair and chief executive ask:

- Is this a fundamental issue for the organization?
- Does it have policy implications?
- Is it a priority for board time?

Small actions can stop the board unintentionally embroiling itself in detail. Items for information only can be distributed separately from board meeting papers or on different-coloured paper. Matters that require legal approval from the board can be grouped and taken together as one item. The board can require that all papers initiated by members themselves are cleared through the chair before being circulated. It can agree that amendments to minutes be submitted two weeks before the meeting, to avoid time-wasting at the start of the meeting. These may sound trivial matters but they are critical. They avoid well-intentioned board members raising unimportant issues and taking valuable board time. Every minute spent discussing a minor item is a minute not spent on the crucial activities of governance.

Boards should also avoid falling into the trap of repeating committee discussions and rendering their work somewhat redundant. This is best managed by ensuring that the board agenda and papers report on the conclusions, recommendations and decisions of committees and allow issues to be re-opened only when members have alerted the chair in advance that they have an important disagreement with the committee's work. This should not be allowed to happen too often, otherwise members of the committee begin to feel disempowered and complain that their effort was wasted. If the board has to re-open issues frequently, it should consider whether the committee has the skill and experience required to discharge the responsibilities it has been given.

Clarify the staff's role

Staff play an important role in an effective board. They inform, guide and make recommendations to the board. But they need to be careful not to step over the boundary and infringe upon the board's legitimate role. This is common when the staff are themselves the inspiration and, sometimes, the founders of the organization. In these situations the board needs to take extra care in defining and clarifying its relationship with the staff.

The role of the staff is to support the chief executive in managing the organization and servicing the board. They need to do this without inadvertently taking over the governance role or involving board members in matters of management.

One critical issue is whether the senior management team attends board meetings. There are three models which can be followed:

ATTEND BY INVITATION

In this model, the chief executive attends board meetings and invites colleagues to join the meeting when their expertise and advice are required. This makes it easier to retain the boundary between governance and management, but it means that senior managers and board members are less likely to have a good understanding of each other. It also means the chief executive has to be particularly thorough in reporting back to the senior management team.

ATTEND AS EQUALS

Although in law board members have tightly specified responsibilities, managers attend and participate in all the discussions. This model is the equivalent of company boards and National Health Service Trusts that have executive and non-executive members. It requires the board itself to be comparatively small (otherwise meetings become very cumbersome) and that board members and managers are skilled and experienced at maintaining the distinction between governance and management. If members – and in particular the chair – are not vigilant about keeping the board focused on the governance task, it is very easy for the board to slip into management tasks. In this model there should be a procedure for board members to meet in private to discuss confidential staff matters and the performance of the senior management team.

ATTEND AS OBSERVERS

In this model, members of the senior management team attend, but they are there solely to give advice when required. Where appropriate, this can be emphasized by seating them away from the main table. They are asked to leave when private discussions are required.

Each model has its advantages and disadvantages. The key to ensuring that everyone is clear about their role is to agree which model best suits the organization at a particular point in time. The most common problem occurs when different people are operating on different models in the same meeting. This should be avoided by discussing which model is being used and by the chair and chief executive talking to board members and managers when they inadvertently slip off the governance task.

THE ROLE SWAP GAME

This is a powerful exercise which board members and senior staff can undertake together to clarify roles. It takes about an hour and can be both illuminating and entertaining.

The board and the senior management team meet together in one room. The board gathers at one end of the room and imagines that it is the staff. It has twenty minutes to address the question: 'What do we expect of an effective board?'

The staff meet at the other end of the room and imagine that they are the board. They address the question: 'What do we expect of an effective senior management team?'

The two groups then meet together and report on their deliberations for twenty minutes. The final twenty minutes should be spent agreeing the changes that need to take place for each to meet the expectations of the other.

It is remarkable what high expectations can be established when one group stands in the shoes of the other.

Communicate extensively

Board members need to keep in touch with all levels of the organization so that they see the work, gauge staff and users' feelings and listen to concerns. This does not imply interfering in management, but it does mean visiting services, attending joint staff–board events and meeting users.

Similarly staff and managers need to have confidence in the board. This can be strengthened by:

● communicating board decisions to staff quickly and honestly

- inviting staff to sit in as observers in board meetings
- establishing joint board–staff task groups to address specific issues
- holding joint social events.

Document the board's procedures

Documenting the board's procedures ensures that members of the organization, staff, candidates for election, other stakeholders and board members themselves can understand the policies and processes of the organization's governance.

The policies that should be documented include:

- the board's structure, role and responsibilities
- the processes for electing and inducting members
- the processes for choosing officers and committee members
- terms of reference of all committees
- the processes for arranging and administering meetings
- its conflict-of-interest policy
- its equal opportunities policy
- the role of the chair.

This is particularly important in large organizations where there is much scope for confusion about the roles and responsibilities of the board and its committees. There are a number of models which provide a good starting point (see ACENVO in Further Reading).

In addition, there should always be up-to-date lists of members of the board and its committees, preferably with details of their relevant experience.

Resource the board support function

Providing proper support for the board takes time and effort from staff. While the chief executive is responsible for ensuring that the board receives proper support, much of the routine work is best delegated to one member of staff. Management of paperwork, minute-taking and meeting arrangements can then all be tightly co-ordinated by someone who might be called the Executive Assistant to the Board. This person needs to ensure that the board's processes run smoothly, to avoid engaging in the substance of board decision-making and to be totally loyal to the chief executive.

The danger of not providing sufficient support in this area is that the chief executive ends up doing work that should be delegated. So, in large and complex organizations, this work can be a full-time position, reporting to the chief executive. In smaller organizations and more straightforward circumstances, this person can also be responsible for providing similar support to the senior management team.

Review the board's performance

At least once a year the board should review its own performance. Boards are often embarrassed to engage in such discussion; there is sometimes an implicit assumption that the board's performance is something that shouldn't be discussed. However, reviews provide a structured setting for evaluating successes and problems and setting an agenda of actions to improve board performance in the future. An annual away-day provides an appropriate setting for such discussion. It should:

● review the performance of the board and its committees against agreed lists of governance responsibilities:
— for the work of the organization
— for the work of the board
● review the structure and role of the board and its committees
● review its composition to check that the governance structure has people with the skills and abilities to take the organization on to the next stage in its development
● check that two-way communication between management and the board has been effective
● confirm that members have attended the agreed minimum number of meetings to qualify for continued membership of the board
● identify areas for improvement in all the above
● agree a package of actions needed to implement changes and the criteria for monitoring those improvements at the next annual review.

External assistance can be helpful when reviewing board performance.

Research has shown that, when groups review their own performance without external input, they are less rigorous with themselves than other people involved in the organization or independent external consultants believe they should be. An independent input from someone who is not a member of the board encourages consideration of difficult issues, such as the performance of the chair or of other officers. A third party is also invaluable when board members have different views on the way it should operate. If these difficult matters are left to fester unresolved, the resulting tensions often spill over into other board discussions. The independent person can be used to see different views in a dispassionate way and to develop new perspectives on the problems. Members unite around a new solution – or at least they release some of the tension through open discussion.

To get to a position where the board is in command but not involved in the detail takes time and effort. It requires that members are in agreement both on the mission and objectives of the organization and on the way the board should work. On the most effective boards, members will challenge and question enthusiastically and persistently in appropriate ways, at pertinent times and within a broad understanding of the way the board works.

4.6   INCREASING COMMITTEE EFFECTIVENESS

Actions needed to increase committee effectiveness are similar to those required to increase board effectiveness. However, committees are even more prone to falling into bad habits. Three common problems are: lack of leadership by the committee chair, excessively large committees and poor-quality paperwork. This section shows how they can be overcome.

Leadership by committee chairs is essential to effective committees. People respond to committee chairs who take the initiative to define the committee's work programme, agree relevant agendas for meetings with the staff member responsible for the committee, and ensure that staff write top-quality papers.

Good chairs involve everyone in the discussion but take the initiative themselves when the time comes for decisions. They delegate work to members to free up their own time for the leadership function. They are totally clear about the committee's role and strive to ensure that it makes a significant contribution to the work of the organization and, in particular, of the board.

The **size of committees** is the second determinant of committee effectiveness. If a committee is too small, it may have insufficient expertise to be effective. If it is too large, meetings become protracted and each member feels less personally responsible for the committee's effectiveness.

The precise size depends on the function of the committee. A committee that exists to advise the board on medical research may need to have more members to reflect different disciplines. The audit committee, in comparison, may need fewer members to check that proper financial management and audit procedures are in place.

There are many pressures that push boards into creating committees that are too large:

- people would like to be involved
- some feel they will miss out on important decisions if they are not members
- there is always a good justification for bringing someone extra on to the committee
- no one likes to say 'no' when members volunteer to give their time to a committee.

These pressures need to be resisted. When committees grow too large, their effectiveness falls. Meetings take longer, more staff time is consumed and members become frustrated at the lack of progress.

The third component of an effective committee is the **quality of the paperwork**. Effective committees have agendas that are short and prioritized and that maintain the boundaries of committee and staff responsibilities. Chairs plan agendas ahead and do not allow the committee to slip unintentionally into the management task. They are always aware that the primary role of committees of the board is to undertake governance tasks.

They also expect high-quality paperwork from staff. The chair can play an important role here by insisting that papers are short, focused, dated, labelled 'for decision', 'for discussion' or 'for information', and include a succinct summary and a clear articulation of options. Anticipation is once again essential, since a committee faced with a poor paper feels obliged to untangle the issues rather than send it back for improvement. The chair should agree the agenda before it is distributed and, when paperwork is a problem, should ask to see draft papers as well.

Minutes should be short and succinct, highlighting action points and when they are to be achieved. Minutes should be circulated within a week or two of the meeting.

The outside world often sees third-sector committees as cumbersome, inefficient, an opportunity to reward time-serving members and as expenses-paid trips for people who have nothing better to do with their time. While there is sometimes more than a grain of truth in this perception, there is no doubt that third-sector organizations need more committees than their private-sector counterparts. Committees do solve problems; they bring free expertise into the organization, they provide a training ground for potential board members, they represent user views, they are a valuable way of promoting consensus, they provide funders with confidence and they can be a source of good judgement for the organization.

When they are not well managed, they delay decisions, are inefficient, consume valuable staff time and make effective governance virtually impossible. When they work well, they embody the very essence of third-sector organizations: people working together voluntarily to achieve an important mission.

SUMMARY OF KEY POINTS

Strong boards are essential
- Board membership used to be an honour. Today it is a demanding task, requiring specific competencies and skills.
- Strong boards are needed:
  — to provide the organization with security and continuity
  — to hold the chief executive accountable
  — to provide a long-term perspective
  — to monitor overall performance.

Forces driving boards into ineffectiveness
- Boards are surrounded by forces that lure them into ineffectiveness and need to be resisted.
- Chairs and chief executives may need help to learn how to manage board matters professionally.

Attracting and developing board members
- Talented board members are a scarce resource, so boards need to be energetic and systematic in searching for people.

- Procedures for recruiting and electing potential board members should be as rigorous as those for recruiting staff.
- Users can make a significant contribution to effective governance. Bringing users into governance should be within an overall strategy for user involvement and should avoid the many (often unanticipated) pitfalls.
- The processes and priorities are different for elected, self-perpetuating, selected and appointed boards.
- Board member skills should be systematically developed.

Special role of the chair

- The chair has special responsibilities for the performance of the board, managing the chief executive, maintaining the boundary between governance and management, managing succession and being a figurehead.
- Creating a strong relationship with the chief executive is critical.

Increasing board effectiveness

- Effectiveness is the chair's responsibility, often discharged jointly with the chief executive.
- Together, they need to ensure that the board has:
  — an annual meeting cycle
  — the right agendas
  — clarity about the staff's role
  — documented procedures
  — an annual review of its own performance.
- Boards should avoid repeating committee discussions.

Increasing committee effectiveness

- Committee effectiveness is enhanced by:
  — leadership from the committee chair
  — making the size of the committee appropriate for the task
  — ensuring that staff produce top-quality paperwork.

5   Strengthening Strategic Management

5.1   THE STRATEGIC MANAGEMENT PROCESS

The next four chapters are all about the management of third-sector organizations. They describe functions that are driven primarily by paid management, within boundaries and policies prescribed by the board. This chapter introduces the concept of strategic management and explains how missions and visions are created, renewed and reinvigorated. The next three chapters demonstrate:

- how objectives and corporate strategies are created and used
- how service strategies and operational plans are devised
- how performance is measured and managed.

Strategy is particularly important in third-sector organizations because they are coalitions of people with different aspirations that need to be integrated to enable the organization to thrive. In recent years a bewildering number of ideas have been developed by management gurus to help people understand organizations and manage them more effectively. Management by objectives, critical success factors, zero-base budgeting, scenario planning, total quality management, corporate culture, business process re-engineering and even catastrophe theory are among almost 200 strategic management concepts recognized by the Strategic Planning Society. In practice, a coherent philosophy for managing strategy in third-sector organizations can be derived from the core concepts of:

- **the vision** – the organization's view of the desired future
- **the mission** – the fundamental purpose of the organization

- **the objectives** – statements about what the organization wishes to achieve in a given time-frame
- **the strategies** – descriptions of how human and financial resources will be applied to achieve the stated objectives
- **performance management** – the feedback loop that informs trustees, managers and staff how the organization is performing.

These concepts can be linked together into an overview of strategic management.

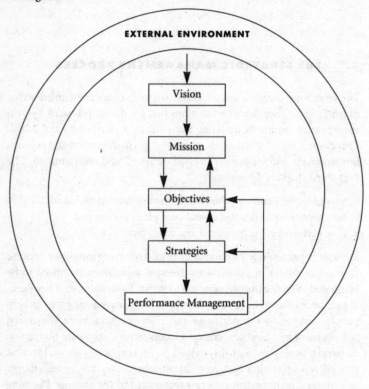

At first sight this looks straightforward. The idea of mission, objectives and strategy have been used by the military for thousands of years, by business for the last thirty years, and more recently by the public sector as well. However, large and complex third-sector organizations are a comparatively new phenomenon. The need to get hundreds – and, more recently, thousands – of people working together towards common object-ives has arisen for many organizations only in the last fifteen years. Given that it took from five to ten years for similarly complex businesses to give their managers sufficient skill and experience to manage strategically, it is hardly surprising that the third sector is finding this challenge equally time-consuming.

The daily pressures on managers attempting to undertake complex tasks with limited resources can combine together to put strategic man-agement at the bottom of their agenda. The sheer volume and variety of tasks people are expected to undertake can be enormous: requests to meet funders, responding to press inquiries, politicians needing briefs, co-ordinating with other agencies, motivating volunteers, manage-ment meetings, regional conferences. These can divert managers' atten-tion from critical strategic questions that need to be at the top of their minds:

● What specifically does our organization want to achieve in the next few years?
● How should we allocate resources among different objectives?
● What quality standards should we aim to achieve?
● What have we learned from past experiences?
● What improvements are required to enable us to make better use of our resources?

According to Johnson and Scholes (*Exploring Corporate Strategy*, Prentice Hall, 1993), the characteristic that distinguishes strategic management from other aspects of management is that it is complex in nature. Three facets contribute to this complexity. Strategic management:

● usually involves a **high degree of uncertainty** – it requires people to make judgements about the future when information is only partial
● requires an **integrated** approach – thinking has to cross the functional boundaries (such as fund-raising, service delivery, personnel)
● involves **major change** – it invariably challenges the values and power of particular groups in the organization.

Strategic management links funders and service users

Strategic management is a powerful tool because it provides an **intellectual connection** between funders and service users. In the private sector the competitive pressures of the market place drive organizations to think strategically in order to survive. This pressure is weak in third-sector organizations because funders have only partial information about the service or the campaign. Strategic management provides the discipline to assess users' needs, orchestrate resources to meet those needs and monitor the outcomes.

Strategic management is also a **mechanism for building coalitions** around new priorities. The process of analysing needs, setting new objectives and agreeing new strategies can be both motivating and unifying. Strategic management provides a structure within which disparate views can be brought together into a shared vision of the future of the organization.

Some organizations are currently being given greater strategic freedom than they had in the past. Schools have more control over their budgets and are seeing opportunities to use their buildings, facilities and staff during the evenings and in vacation time; universities are engaging in joint ventures with businesses to exploit new research findings; arts organizations are seeking contracts with health authorities to exploit the therapeutic effects of music and the visual arts. Such diversification increases the need for organizations to **develop new conceptions of themselves** and to revise their own view of their purpose.

Other organizations are losing strategic freedom as the proportion of their funds coming from contracts and other statutory sources continues to grow. Moreover, these funders are specifying the services they want in ever-increasing detail. These organizations need to grasp strategic management in order to help find ways to **maintain or increase their independence and their strategic freedom**.

The benefits resulting from improved strategic management are immense:

- Everyone becomes clearer about his or her objectives and how they fit into the wider task of the organization as a whole.

- It leads to more effective use of resources.
- It is an ideal way of building commitment and motivation.
- Diverse constituencies can be brought together around a common purpose.

5.2 CHOOSING WHERE TO START

Before starting to work on an organization's strategy, the board, chief executive and senior management need to consider where their overall priorities lie. The essential components of the overall management of organizations includes:

- the governing arrangements (Chapters 3 and 4)
- strategic management (described here and in Chapters 6, 7 and 8)
- the management structure (Chapter 9)
- the process of managing change (Chapter 10)
- managing people (Chapters 11 and 12)
- the creation of a learning organization (Chapter 13).

Although improvements could doubtless be made in all these areas, choices have to be made as to where to focus people's efforts. In many situations it can be counter-productive to attempt to make fundamental changes in more than one area at any one time. Major changes in the management structure can result in work on the strategy going seriously off course because people become more interested in their position within the organization than in a dispassionate debate about strategy. Changing both the governing structure and the management structure at the same time may open potentially difficult alliances among board and staff members threatened by changes. Promoting learning and organization development is difficult if a significant number of management posts remain unfilled.

Making explicit choices about these alternatives is a critical role of the board and senior management, and of the chief executive in particular. Judgements have to be made about where effort is most required to take the organization into its next stage of development. This will depend on a high-level assessment of the overall strengths and weaknesses of the organization and about the sequencing of change. Sometimes a weak team may need to be strengthened before a new strategy can be developed.

In other circumstances, a new strategy may be needed before it is possible to decide upon the future shape of the management team.

The role of the chief executive in strategic management is crucial. Choosing which issues to work on, why to work on them and how to approach them are central tasks for her or him. A common mistake chief executives make is to initiate change on too many fronts at the same time. From their vantage point it is easy to see all the changes that need to be made and, being experienced managers, they can usually see most of the solutions required. However, the critical judgement they have to make concerns the number of changes that can be initiated, debated, resolved and embedded into the organization culture simultaneously. Some enthusiastic chief executives allow their ambitions to exceed the organization's capacity to cope with change.

Most books, including this one, present strategic management as a top-down process, starting with the mission and moving down through objectives to strategy to action, and finally closing the loop with performance monitoring. It is easy to think of it in this way, but in practice all the elements are changing simultaneously. Before starting to work on strategic management it is therefore necessary to decide whether to focus time and effort on:

- vision and mission
- corporate objectives and strategy
- service strategies and operational plans
- the performance-management process.

The choice depends on which will produce the most beneficial results from the investment of management time and effort.

Sometimes the overall strategy is well established, but departments do not have straightforward annual plans to encourage clear thinking about the specific activities that require time and attention. Sometimes the plans are well established, but there is no explicit process for reviewing achievements against the original intentions. In yet other circumstances, strategies and plans are well developed but management processes need attention.

Having made decisions concerning where to start, it is worth remembering that strategic management is one of the most satisfying aspects of management. People find it motivating to be involved in setting the organization's mission, strategic plans and priorities. They enjoy seeing more clearly how the organization fits into its environment. At the end of each stage of the work people are likely to be fired up and will endeavour to achieve more ambitious targets and work together in ways that are more effective.

5.3 THE CONCEPTS OF VISION, MISSION AND VALUES

Three ideas sit at the top of the strategic management hierarchy, each of which deserves definition. Organizations find that they need one or more of these to clarify their understanding of themselves and to promote their organization to the wider world.

VISION

The most useful way to think about the idea of vision is to see it as a description of a **desirable future situation** for the organization's users and for the world at large. Visions are likely to be articulated with language such as 'We want a world in which . . .'. They express a view of what the organization ultimately wants to achieve, knowing that it is unlikely to achieve it on its own.

VISIONS

British Epilepsy Association
We want to live in a society where everyone understands epilepsy and where attitudes towards people with the condition are based on fact, not fiction.

The National Asthma Campaign
The National Asthma Campaign's vision is of a world without asthma.

WaterAid
WaterAid's vision is of a world in which all people have access to safe water and sanitation.

> ### Royal National Institute for the Blind
> RNIB wants a world in which people with a visual impairment
> enjoy the same rights, freedoms, responsibilities and quality of life
> as people who are fully sighted.

Third-sector organizations need to have visions of the way they want
the world to be. Visions are a powerful motivating influence on people.
Founders and leaders often bring the vision, and they need to ensure that
it is sustained.

Visions change only when they have been achieved and the organization
needs to move on to a new and often more broadly defined cause.

MISSION

Missions are concerned with answering the question **'what does the
organization exist for?'** They tend to take the form of statements using
language such as 'Our mission is to . . .'.

People who work in third-sector organizations are usually motivated
by a deeply held desire to change society; consequently, most third-sector
organizations have a strong sense of mission. Christian churches use the
word 'mission' to describe their work and people working in charities
often talk about 'our mission'.

As a result, the missions of some organizations are implicit. They are
part of the accepted beliefs that often are not discussed or written down.
Most third-sector organizations begin with a missionary zeal that doesn't
need to be made explicit. For example, at the end of the first national
meeting of parents who had children with cerebral palsy, the chairman
slapped a £5 note down on the table and said dramatically, 'I want
this to be five million pounds within five years.' The mission was clear:
parents wanted a significant increase in services and they were going
to raise the money to establish new services. The Spastics Society, now
called SCOPE, was created, and this first mission was successfully
achieved.

Third-sector organizations often have a much stronger sense of mission
than their counterparts in the private and public sectors. Campaigning
organizations and membership organizations that are championing a
cause have a particularly strong sense of mission. Service-giving organiza-

tions that were set up by people with a disease or disability maintain a strong sense of mission for many years.

Missions change infrequently, and then usually when an organization wishes to redefine its scope, either more broadly or more narrowly.

In short, while vision is concerned with the organization's view of an ideal world for its beneficiaries, mission is specifically what the organization thinks it can do to help create that ideal world.

MISSIONS

WaterAid
WaterAid aims to work through partner organizations to help poor people in developing countries achieve sustainable improvements in the quality of their life by improving domestic water supply, sanitation and associated hygiene practices.

The Royal National Institute for the Blind
Our mission is to challenge blindness. We challenge the disabling effects of blindness by providing services to help people determine their own lives. We challenge society's actions, attitudes and assumptions. Many barriers are put in the path of people with a visual impairment – our task is to help dismantle those barriers. And we challenge the underlying causes of blindness by helping to prevent, cure or alleviate it.

The Leadership Trust
To be the premier provider of leadership development to industry, commerce and society.

London Business School
To be a world leader in helping individuals and organizations enhance their managerial effectiveness.

The Prince's Youth Business Trust
To help young people who would not otherwise have the opportunity to develop their self-confidence, achieve economic independence, fulfil their ambitions and contribute to the community through the medium of self-employment.

PURPOSE

Some organizations have found the concept of purpose useful as an alternative to a mission, which sounds a little ecclesiastical. Statements of purpose tend to describe why the organization exists and what it does.

STATEMENTS OF PURPOSE

National Asthma Campaign
National Asthma Campaign is the UK charity working to conquer asthma in partnership with people with asthma and all who share their concern, through a combination of research, education and support.

The Guide Association
Our purpose is to enable girls to mature into confident, capable and caring women, determined, as individuals, to realize their potential in their career, home and personal life, and willing, as citizens, to contribute to their community and the wider world.

Voluntary Service Overseas
VSO enables men and women to work alongside people in poorer countries in order to share skills, build capabilities and promote international understanding and action, in the pursuit of a more equitable world.

VALUES

Values are critically important to people who work for and support third-sector organizations. Most people join an organization because they believe in the cause that it champions. Values describe the underlying beliefs that the organization holds and that inform board members and staff when they are establishing policies and making decisions.

Some organizations have found it useful to articulate their core values. This process can lead to a much deeper understanding of the beliefs that hold the organization's board, staff and supporters together as one group.

VALUES

London Lighthouse

London Lighthouse was set up to tackle the challenges faced by people affected by HIV and AIDS. Its aims are supported by values, which it calls its commitments:

- to make sure that people living with HIV and AIDS are central in the organization, so they can influence policies, develop services and actively contribute to the decision-making process
- to create safe and welcoming environments which offer time and space to meet the needs of service users, carers, paid and unpaid staff and visitors
- to challenge the denial of death – to bring the issue of death into the open and recognize that it is part of life and living
- to challenge oppression, discrimination and prejudice, promote equal opportunities and to speak up for social justice.

These commitments are set out every year in their annual plan and in their annual report as a way of reinforcing their beliefs and communicating them to their stakeholders.

Voluntary Service Overseas

- VSO values the individual and believes in the equal right of all to realize their potential.
- VSO believes in countering disadvantage by practical action, person to person.
- VSO values action motivated by and responding to the needs of others, both through their work abroad and through voluntary activity by supporters at home.
- VSO values and respects diversity of culture.
- VSO values two-way partnership which openly shares costs and benefits.
- VSO values the learning and friendship which result from people living and working alongside each other, in pursuit of shared goals.

Barnardo's
- Respecting the unique worth of every person
- Encouraging people to fulfil their potential
- Working with hope
- Exercising responsible stewardship.

The concepts of vision, mission and purpose have been brought together in a model developed at Ashridge Strategic Management Centre. Although it uses the words in a slightly different way, the underlying ideas are very similar. The Centre argues that mission is concerned with both **hearts** and **minds**: the beliefs that come from the heart and the rationale that comes from the mind.

THE ASHRIDGE MODEL

Research at Ashridge Strategic Management Centre led to the development of the idea that organizations need a 'sense of mission'. This notion of mission has four components.

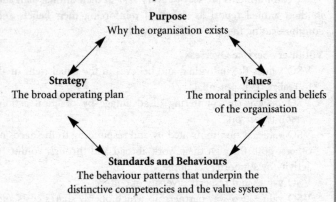

Purpose
Why the organisation exists

Strategy
The broad operating plan

Values
The moral principles and beliefs
of the organisation

Standards and Behaviours
The behaviour patterns that underpin the
distinctive competencies and the value system

Adapted from *A Sense of Mission*, A. Campbell *et al.*, Hutchinson Business Books, 1990

5.4 CREATING AND REFRESHING VISIONS AND MISSIONS

Organizations are more effective when they have a clear vision and a strong sense of mission. These are powerful motivators and help people to make sense of the organization. They ensure that people are clear in an abstract way about the overall direction of the organization and they encourage people to strive to achieve the organization's purpose. In organizations with clear vision and mission there is consistency between people's beliefs and the organization's strategy.

The vision and mission therefore need to be worked on:

● when the organization's purpose and *raison d'être* have become woolly and unfocused
● when the organization has become directionless and lacks a sense of its own distinctive competencies
● when the motivation of the board, staff and other supporters is low.

An essential prerequisite for creating a strong sense of vision and mission is having a group of people, on the board and among the staff, who share similar aspirations and are willing to work together to make things happen.

Another prerequisite to creating a sense of mission is continuity of the key decision-makers. It takes time to understand the fundamental beliefs of an organization and to see the varied ways in which the beliefs connect with the strategy. Particularly in larger organizations, it takes time for key individuals, such as the chair, the chief executive and members of the senior management team, to become known in the organization and to be seen to be acting in ways that are consistent with the mission.

THE MISSION OF THE MEDICAL CHARITY

This organization existed to help people with a terminal neuromuscular disorder. It aimed both to raise funds for medical research and to provide care and support for people with the disease. The board included eminent medical researchers, senior social workers and people with the disorder.

One third of the board believed that the organization existed primarily to fund medical research, and they grudgingly agreed to fund care for people with the disorder. One third believed that the organization should focus on helping social services departments to provide better care, and they felt that medical research was expensive and making little progress. One third felt that the organization should provide direct care itself, because it knew best the particular problems people with the disability and their families faced.

Not surprisingly, staff were very confused about the organization's purpose. Morale was low and a great deal of time and effort were wasted arguing about the allocation of resources to different activities.

To overcome the problem, the board and senior staff held two special workshops, at a neutral venue and with an outside consultant, to clarify the organization's mission. They began to find common ground when it was agreed that, above everything else, they shared a common desire to help people with the disorder. They acknowledged to each other that the medical professionals, the social-work professionals and the volunteers all had distinctive contributions to make. They also agreed that close co-operation among these groups would yield more benefit for people with the disorder than working separately for the same cause. Finally, they agreed a formula for allocating resources to different activities.

The mission was clarified, enthusiasm began to grow, arguments declined and the organization began to thrive again.

The board is ultimately responsible for managing the mission, but it needs to involve staff, members and sometimes service users as well, in a joint effort to agree and strengthen the mission.

Management needs to construct a process, which may last for two months for a small organization and up to six months for a larger body. Relevant stakeholders need to know when and how they can make their contribution. The process may start with a board discussion, or it may start in lots of places and culminate with a board session that draws together the various strands needed to renew the organization's sense of mission.

Although it is tempting for the chief executive or senior management to draft a mission statement, 'to give people something to chew on,' this focuses the process on the wording of the mission statement rather than on creating a deeper understanding of the values and beliefs that underpin the organization's mission.

Debates about the future vision and mission of the organization should aim to:

1. Define the purpose of the organization at the most fundamental and general level. This can involve asking seemingly simple questions about why the organization exists, who it exists for and what (at the most basic level) it aims to achieve.
2. Identify the core values and beliefs upon which the future of the organization can be built. Asking questions about what the organization stands for, what its philosophy is and what position it takes on the central issues of concern can help to clarify values and beliefs.
3. Clarify distinctive features and competencies. Identification of those characteristics that distinguish the organization from others in the same field can help to develop a better understanding of an organization's distinctiveness. Similarly, looking at specific competencies can provide a useful perspective.

Developing the vision and mission can be undertaken as part of a strategic planning process or it can be a separate management initiative. It often results in sets of words which sound worthy and about which it is easy to be cynical. However, organizations that have ironed out common misunderstandings among people on the fundamental issues are undoubtedly more effective and more satisfying to work for than those that leave those issues unresolved.

Once the mission has been clarified, continuous effort is required to keep it alive and relevant to everyone's work. The larger the organization, the greater is the effort required. Annual general meetings can be turned into workshops that celebrate achievements and plan future developments. Regional meetings can be actively supported by senior staff from headquarters. Branch chairs and directors can be encouraged to communicate regularly with the central office, and they can be brought together once a year to seek their views and discuss future developments. Managers can draw the attention of staff to the links between the mission and the daily grind of activities; they can also remind people how their work is a part of achieving the mission. Volunteers can be invited in to be thanked for their support and be briefed and consulted on future plans. These are the actions that give an organization vibrancy, clarity of purpose and a sense of mission.

STRENGTHENING THE MISSION OF THE GUINNESS TRUST

Guinness Trust is one of Britain's largest housing associations, with 17,000 homes all over the country. Established over 100 years ago, the Trust had recently reorganized itself into four decentralized regions, with each regional director also holding responsibility for a national function (such as housing development or maintenance).

The senior management team decided that the 'command and control' culture of the organization was no longer appropriate. They wanted to empower managers and free them up to be more entrepreneurial within a broad mission for the future of the organization. To achieve this required that some 70 managers be involved in a process of defining a mission that they all felt they owned and believed in.

They embarked on a twelve-month programme of activities including:

- Two senior-management team away-days to diagnose the problem, establish the precise objectives of the work and define a programme of activities that would eventually involve almost all 700 staff.
- Two conferences for the top 70 managers, to allow them to develop their views on the mission and on the obstacles that got in the way of their contributing effectively to that mission. This included training in facilitating group discussions for the next event.
- A conference, with half the staff attending on one day, half the next, and all staying overnight, designed to engage everyone in the process of developing the new mission.
- Further away-days for the senior management team to distil all they had learned from the staff and to create a new mission which reflected the debate over the preceding months.
- An action plan which identified how the obstacles of the 'command and control' culture would be removed so that everyone could take the organization forward with a new mission and a new culture.

Preparing vision, mission and values statements

Mission, vision and values statements all document the outcome of an organization's work in this area. They are also a way of communicating the organization's purpose to staff, volunteers, funders and the outside world.

However, it is important to recognize that the greatest value of these statements accrues to those people who have been involved in their development. Management teams sometimes go into their bunker and spend countless hours arguing about each word in these statements in the belief that they will be a powerful tool for improving organization effectiveness. They are usually disappointed. The carefully crafted copy sent down with a memorandum from the chief executive usually has the opposite effect to the one desired. Unless statements have been developed through a process of discussion and debate through the organization, they are likely to promote cynicism and encourage the view that senior management doesn't know how to make good use of its time.

Organizations must make their own choices about which types of statements will best suit their needs. The resulting package should tell the reader:

● who the organization exists for
● what its ultimate purpose is
● what it stands for
● how, at the broadest level, it will go about achieving its purpose
● where it operates.

The statements should be:

● **short** and easy to communicate
● **understood** throughout the organization
● **broad** enough to last for a long time
● **specific** enough to differentiate the organization from others.

THE BRITISH RED CROSS

Vision   The certain sign of hope in crisis

Mission   To be the leading voluntary provider of emergency help to people in most need, anywhere in the world

Pledge   *To the vulnerable in crisis:* help without discrimination or question

To Red Cross volunteers and staff: the fulfilment that comes from a job done professionally and well

To our supporters: respect for, and efficient use of, your vital assistance

To our partners in the statutory services and voluntary sector: guaranteed readiness and response whenever you need us

To governments: the commitment to provide medical and humanitarian care, in areas of armed conflict or disaster, with our traditional impartiality and neutrality

To the International Red Cross and Red Crescent Movement: to show, through our actions, our total belief in our fundamental principles of humanity, impartiality, neutrality, independence, voluntary service, unity and universality.

SUMMARY OF KEY POINTS

The strategic management process

- The essential components of strategic management are concerned with clarifying the organization's vision and mission, establishing overall objectives and strategies for achieving them, and setting up systems to manage performance.
- Strategic management provides the intellectual connection between service users, campaigns and funders.
- The process of developing strategy helps to weld together the coalition of interests that is needed for organizations to thrive.

Choosing where to start

- Before promoting any initiatives to strengthen strategic management, organizations should determine which of the following management topics will deliver the greatest improvement in effectiveness:
  - — governance arrangements
  - — management processes
  - — management structures
  - — organization learning and development.
- If strategic management is the priority, choices need to be made about which aspect to focus on.

The concepts of vision, mission and values

- Vision is a description of a desirable future situation for the organization's users and for the world at large.
- Mission is concerned with what the organization exists for.
- Values describe the underlying beliefs that the organization holds and that inform its policies and decisions.

Creating and refreshing visions and missions

- Organizations can increase the strength of feeling about their vision and mission by involving stakeholders in a debate about why the organization exists and what, overall, it aims to achieve.
- Once the visions and missions have been created, continuous effort is required to keep the sense of mission alive in the organization.
- Vision and mission statements document the outcomes of a process to refresh the organization's purpose. The process of preparing them should involve as many people as possible.

6 Establishing Overall Objectives and Strategies

6.1 THE NEED FOR OBJECTIVES AND STRATEGIES

Most organizations need a structured process for periodically revisiting their longer-term objectives and strategies. They need board members, managers and staff to gain an understanding of the recent history of the organization and its desired future development.

The process of strategic planning is a powerful tool for uniting the board, the senior management team and the staff behind a shared conception of future plans and priorities. It can re-ignite the mission and motivate staff to focus their contribution more sharply on new priorities. It enables senior management to concentrate resources on achieving agreed outcomes, rather than dissipating them over many activities. This chapter is about the process of developing objectives and strategies for the whole organization. The process will often involve working on the mission as well as the establishment of new objectives.

Strategic planning has had a very chequered history. It migrated to the third sector in the 1980s and, more often than not, promised more than it could deliver. Massive effort was put into preparing plans, involving endless meetings and lengthy documents. With a huge sigh of relief plans were approved by the board, and within a year or two the plan either would have been forgotten or would be so out of date as to render it irrelevant. People rightly grew cynical about the whole idea.

However, people working in an organization do require a clear understanding of its objectives and strategies. Third-sector organizations in particular have fuzzy boundaries and countless opportunities to drift away from their primary purpose. They are working in an increasingly turbulent environment and need to revisit their purposes and priorities more frequently than in the past.

Strategic planning therefore needs to establish direction, priorities and perhaps specific targets, but it should not attempt to tie them all down in detail. The process needs to give a framework within which people can develop detailed plans for individual services. It needs to establish priorities and broad timescales. It needs to be developed in less time than that given to the preparation of corporate plans in the past; it needs a shorter time horizon, and it needs to be reviewed more frequently.

A major review of strategy used to be on the agenda every five years. Now major reviews often take place every three years, and sometimes every second year. Organizations working in more rapidly changing environments need more regular reviews than those in more stable environments.

In today's turbulent times, planning should be viewed as a process of learning and discovery. It should help people to understand how their part of the organization fits into the overall picture. From this new perspective, planning aims to build coalitions of people who can work together to achieve common objectives.

This chapter describes:

- the hierarchy of objectives
- how to clarify strategic objectives
- where strategy comes from
- the concepts of strategic reviews, positions and choices
- the strategic planning process
- common strategic dilemmas.

Planning strategy for individual services is covered in section 7.2, below.

6.2   THE HIERARCHY OF OBJECTIVES

> ALICE: Which way should I go?
> CAT: That depends on where you're going.
> ALICE: I don't know where I'm going!
> CAT: Then it doesn't matter which way you go!
>
> Lewis Carroll, *Through the Looking Glass*, 1872

Objectives are statements of the aims of the organization. They can be both qualitative and quantifiable. They help to focus different parts of the organization on achieving the mission. They concentrate people's attention and guide their actions.

Organizations need objectives at every level of operation, from the board to individual service providers. The notion of a hierarchy of objectives is therefore a useful way of organizing long-term strategic objectives, more specific medium-term objectives and very precise short-term objectives.

A hierarchy of objectives can also be related to the layers of an organization. At the top there are precise but broad objectives. Lower down, departments have more focused objectives, and below that individual services have very specific objectives.

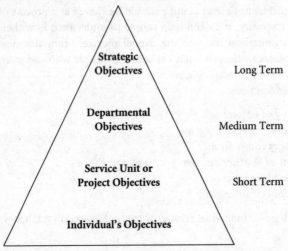

Typically there is a need for a limited number, perhaps between four and seven, carefully chosen objectives for the whole organization, and a similar number for each department, service unit and individual manager.

Strategic objectives

Strategic objectives focus the organization on achieving those things that are most critical to its success. They should be couched in words that focus and guide people's actions. They should avoid the common trap of being well-meant statements of good intentions that could be applied to many different organizations.

NATIONAL ASTHMA CAMPAIGN STRATEGIC OBJECTIVES

The National Asthma Campaign is a highly successful organization which resulted from the merger of a medical research charity with an organization of people with asthma. Its strategic objectives are to:

1. develop membership, volunteer activity and support at all levels throughout the United Kingdom
2. promote and fund research that is driven by the needs of people with asthma
3. make the services we provide to all the charity's users responsive, appropriate, and capable of helping diminish the impact of asthma on those who live with it
4. work as a partner with government and relevant authorities, at national and local levels, in developing public services for people with asthma
5. consolidate the National Asthma Campaign's position and influence as a campaigning health charity
6. maintain and develop best planning and management practices.

Having to put strategic objectives into a few words should provide sufficient discipline to force an organization to identify the most critical issues, but at the same time allow for the diversity that is an essential ingredient of most third-sector organizations.

Even so, an element of conflict between objectives is unavoidable. Most arts organizations want to present challenging works but also want large audiences. Development agencies want to maximize their income with dramatic appeals during emergencies, but they do not want to devalue the pride of hard-working people who are struggling to survive in difficult circumstances.

Although strategic objectives have a long time horizon, they should not be seen as being entirely fixed. Circumstances do change. Some objectives are achieved while others become a greater priority. Strategic objectives are therefore a tool that focuses people on specific goals that the organization as a whole wants to achieve at any particular time.

Departmental objectives

Departmental objectives tend to be more specific, they are easier to quantify and have a wide range of time horizons. Clearly they need to fit within the strategic objectives.

Ideally, departmental objectives should be SMART – Specific, Measurable, Actionable, Realistic and Timetabled. This mnemonic is a useful quality check on proposed objectives.

OBJECTIVES OF THE EDUCATION DIVISION

The Royal National Institute for the Blind agreed a five-year corporate strategy (in line with the vision and mission described earlier) with four over-arching priorities:

- to challenge blindness by raising awareness and tackling discrimination
- to extend services to more blind and partially sighted people
- to increase the priority given to older blind and partially sighted people
- to improve the quality of service to users and supporters.

The Education Division subsequently reviewed its objectives so that its priorities could be adjusted to meet the new corporate objectives. It established its aims under five headings:

- early identification and assessment
- information and support to parents
- education services
- staff development
- learning resources.

Within each heading it established between one and three specific aims – for example, to ensure that all visually impaired infants are identified at the earliest possible stage, that their needs are effectively assessed and that the services and support they and their families need are provided.

Then, within each of these broad aims, it agreed a series of more specific objectives for the Division as a whole, for example:

- to develop a database of all visually impaired children and their families
- to develop an effective way of delivering materials to parents, including those from ethnic minorities.

HOUSING 21

Housing 21 is a national housing association which manages 14,000 homes for older people, mainly in sheltered courts. It developed a national corporate plan for the period to year 2000. Its six corporate objectives were:

1. to be an effective not-for-profit housing and care business
2. to provide measurable and accountable services and to be responsive to the views of tenants, leaseholders and service users
3. to offer tenants a home for life
4. to provide a range of care and support services to older people which promote independence and choice
5. to increase the range and provision of suitable accommodation for older people
6. to be well known as a specialist provider of social housing, care and support services for older people.

Each of its regions also prepared its own objectives and strategies. The south-west regional strategy aimed to achieve twelve objectives, each of which contributed to the national priorities. Examples of its objectives are:

- to improve tenant and customer involvement in evaluating our delivery of services
- to increase by 5 per cent the housing stock in management by new development, agency arrangements, mergers and acquisitions

- to re-model 10 per cent of 'courts' to meet the changing needs of current and future tenants
- to develop care services that complement our role as a housing provider.

Cross-departmental objectives

An organization's objectives seldom fit all together into a neat hierarchy. Some objectives cut across two or more divisions. These are entirely legitimate, but they do present additional management challenges. They are easy to establish but more difficult to deliver, because greater co-operation across the management structure is required (see section 9.5: Strengthening cross-departmental working). As far as the establishment of objectives is concerned, the key is to ensure that there is a good fit between the departmental and the cross-departmental objectives, and that the departmental objectives in particular reflect a commitment to achieving the cross-departmental objectives.

Service delivery unit, project and campaign objectives

These are even more specific and will almost always be quantified. Service delivery units are the lowest level of the organization at which people and money can be managed to produce a desired result; they are defined more fully below, in section 7.1. They can have long-, medium- and shorter-term objectives – their own hierarchy within the overall scheme. They ought to be very SMART.

Internal objectives

Many organizations also find it useful to distinguish between external and internal objectives. External objectives relate very specifically to the organization's mission and the tasks it is trying to achieve. Internal objectives, on the other hand, are primarily concerned with building the capacity of the organization to achieve the external objectives. Internal objectives typically fall into five categories:

- **strengthening the governing board** – for example, implementing a new induction scheme, improving working relationships with staff
- **developing human resources** – for example, establishing a one-to-one supervision process, creating management-development programmes
- **investing in management information systems** – for example, improving financial management systems, developing performance indicators, investing in information technology
- **investing in plant and buildings** – for example, purchasing new equipment, renovating offices
- **expanding fund-raising** – for example, developing the public profile, marketing the cause and establishing the systems for raising money.

MENCAP'S OBJECTIVES

Mencap provides a wide range of services for people with learning disabilities. It has 550 small group homes for 2,750 residents, 700 leisure clubs (known as Gateway) and employment schemes that have placed 3,000 people in employment. Together, the national organization and the local societies employ 5,000 staff and 10,000 volunteers.

Their strategic plan established five objectives for the organization as a whole:

- to fight for the rights and dignity of people with a learning disability
- to campaign for top-quality statutory services
- to develop advice and information services
- to improve Mencap's direct services
- to create an efficient organization.

Each overall objective was supported by a series of more specific objectives. The objectives for creating an efficient organization were:

- to get communication right
- to develop the Mencap and Gateway partnership
- to strengthen the relationship between the national organization and the local societies
- to align Mencap's committee structure with its objectives
- to recruit and retain high-calibre personnel

> ● to secure the organization's financial position
> ● to increase voluntary income.
>
> Managers developed a summary strategy for achieving each objective, each of which was no more than one paragraph long.

The value of having clear objectives and of ensuring that everyone has a deep understanding of what they are and what they mean cannot be overstated. The fuzzy and ever-changing environment in which third-sector organizations exist means that managers need to be continuously asking themselves what they are trying to achieve, and communicating their answers to all the relevant stakeholders.

6.3 CLARIFYING STRATEGIC OBJECTIVES

Clarifying strategic objectives is a task that requires continuous attention. Managers need to ensure that:

● people affected are involved in agreeing them (usually the more wide-ranging the objective, the more people who need to be involved)
● they are as specific as possible, particularly in fields where it is easy to avoid being precise, such as arts organizations, development agencies and churches
● they are debated and developed in close consultation with the board, the staff and volunteers
● they are reviewed regularly.

Most organizations are pursuing a number of strategic objectives simultaneously, so there may be an element of contradiction between different objectives. Organizations are coalitions of people with different aspirations, so the strategic objectives need to reflect the widest range of interests without producing objectives that are so general they are of little practical use.

Setting strategic objectives

Strategic objectives are usually developed as part of the process of creating proposals for a strategic plan. A strategic review will have identified the key issues to address, and the proposals for addressing them will all need to begin with a statement of the strategic objective.

The process of establishing an objective is iterative, starting with an individual or a group and evolving as different people help to refine the thinking. Strategic objectives usually go through many drafts before the most effective way of casting and communicating the ideas is discovered.

STRATEGIC OBJECTIVES FOR RELATE – NATIONAL MARRIAGE GUIDANCE

After much discussion and debate, RELATE 2000, the organization's strategic plan, established six priority objectives for the agency; together these aimed to increase the number of clients the agency saw and the quality of the services they received.

1. Implement a standard **intake and assessment system** to enable quick, appropriate and effective responses to clients' needs.
2. Develop **career patterns** for paid and voluntary counsellors, other practitioners and managers, involving training, new work opportunities and clear contracts.
3. Create a network of **payments for service** at all levels for training, practising, supervising and managing, to allow each activity to respond to changes in demand.
4. Establish a **research and evaluation programme** to monitor the effectiveness of the services and to speak with authority on family and social policy issues.
5. Strengthen the **supervisory networks** to underpin quality and respond to varying needs.
6. Build an **integrated and participative approach** to management to ensure that the ambitious programme of change is well co-ordinated and sensitively implemented.

Each of these objectives was accompanied by a strategy and a time-table for implementation.

Checking the quality of strategic objectives

Clear strategic objectives help to focus everyone on the task. Check that:

1. They are realistic and not wildly ambitious. Most organizations have limited resources and limited management capacity, yet the scope of the problems they are attempting to address is huge. It is always tempting to adopt objectives that far exceed the organization's resources. Having realistic objectives and achieving them is always more motivating than failing to achieve unrealistic objectives.

2. They are as specific as possible. It is easy to produce any number of generalized statements of good intentions, but much more difficult to find the concepts and words that clearly fit with the mission and are seen as being practical by front-line staff.

3. They are not gratuitous. Strategic objectives are sometimes accepted because people are afraid to say 'no'. A number of people may have hobby-horses or views that are not shared by everyone else. It is always tempting to add additional objectives to the list. Managers should aim to gain agreement on the few objectives that are critical. Being disciplined will help focus people and avoid the accusation of being 'all things to all people'.

Getting strategic objectives right is ultimately a matter for board members' and managers' professional judgement. Unfocused objectives need clarification, ambitious ones need tempering, irrelevant ones need to be dropped. Effective managers spend time on strategic objectives and strive to keep them clear and appropriate.

THE FUND-RAISING DILEMMA

'Our objective is to increase fund-raising income by 10 per cent per annum above inflation,' said the Fund-raising Director of the development agency. 'To achieve this ambitious target, we need to highlight the desperate plight of poor people. Pictures of starving children will form the centrepiece of a new hard-hitting campaign to change complacent attitudes,' she continued. 'My aim is to bring in new money and give the field staff more resources for their work.'

'My objective is to change the public attitudes and policies in developed countries, because they are one of the causes of poverty,' the Director of Campaigns replied. 'People don't want us to portray them as poor and helpless. They are proud and honourable. Their problems are caused by exploitation by banks, local elites and middlemen. Hard-hitting campaigns might raise more money, but they will only increase the sense of dependency of poor people in the South on the rich people of the North. I think we should be tackling the root cause of poverty – not just addressing the symptoms.'

'But if I can't use the most effective fund-raising method, you'll have to accept less money for your campaign,' the Fund-raising Director retorted. 'I can't achieve the fund-raising target if you tie my hands behind my back.'

6.4 STRATEGY EVOLVES

Strategies are broad categories of action which indicate how human, financial and other resources will be deployed in order to achieve agreed objectives. They focus people on a small number of concepts that enable them to fit the activities of the organization into a context. They also provide a rationale that explains how resources will be allocated to different objectives or activities.

In today's demanding environment, managers need to have a clear concept of how their work fits in to the overall strategy of the organization. They need to anticipate relevant changes in the external environment and develop appropriate responses. They also have to demonstrate to funders precisely what will be achieved with their money.

Strategy is not static. It changes with time and is influenced by circumstances and people. Strategy evolves in three ways. First, it is an **incremental process.** It usually changes in a series of small steps. New ideas are tested. Experience is gained before major new strategies are agreed. Organizations reduce the risks inherent in any new idea by experimenting, learning from the results and modifying proposals as they are developed. Strategy should therefore not be seen as something that happens only when a strategic plan is produced.

The evolution of strategy is also a **political process.** Strategy results from a process of bargaining, negotiation and trade-off between people with competing interests in the organization. Powerful individuals and groups therefore have a strong influence over an organization's strategy. How they view an issue may be more relevant than the factual accuracy of their arguments. Strategy is therefore not only the result of dispassionate analysis – it is more often a reflection of the power and influence of different stakeholders.

Finally, strategy is the result of an **analytical process.** From this perspective, strategy emerges from a systematic and logical analysis of the organization's environment and its current activities. This leads to the establishment of new objectives and strategies which usually take the form of a strategic plan. Although planning is an essential element of managing third-sector organizations, the analytical approach to the evolution of strategy needs to be seen as only one of the three processes determining strategy.

POLITICS AND STRATEGY

The National Orchestra faced many competing demands when it began to think about future development:

- the musicians wanted good pay and opportunities to play new and challenging pieces of music
- the education department wanted more musicians to support their community music schemes in schools
- the fund-raisers wanted a popular programme of events to attract corporate sponsors
- the board wanted high-profile public events to increase the status of the orchestra
- the conductor wanted more rehearsal time to improve the quality of performances.

Endless attempts at strategic planning failed to solve the problem. These competing demands on money and musicians' time had to be resolved through negotiation and agreement.

Strategy is required at every level

Most organizations deliver more than one service. Some deliver many services to the same service user group (for example, the professional association that sets standards for the profession and also promotes members' services). Others deliver different services to different groups (for example, the disability organization that provides technical aids for young people and benefits advice for older people).

So, just as objectives are required at every level of an organization, strategies are also required at every level. In a smaller organization, strategy may operate at two levels: there will be an overall strategy for the organization as a whole and separate strategies for each service or each service user group. Large organizations that are divided into different operational divisions may require:

- an overall strategy
- divisional strategies
- service level strategies.

The overall strategy in both large and small organizations is concerned with the definition of the service user group (i.e. who is included and who is excluded), the range of services to be offered to these people, and the allocation of resources among different groups of people or different services. The divisional strategy is concerned with the strategy for a group of services, and the service level strategy is concerned with the objectives and performance of individual services.

6.5 STRATEGIC REVIEWS, POSITIONS AND CHOICES

The management of strategy can be divided into five basic elements (shown overleaf).

These are shown as a diamond to emphasize that developing strategy is not a linear process. Although there is a logical sequence to reviewing the organization, considering alternative ways forward and developing

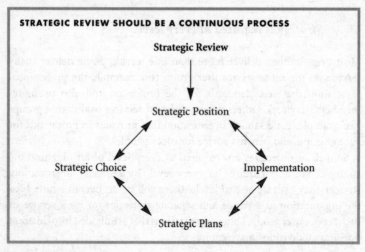

an implementation plan, most of the time all the processes are going on simultaneously, each continuously informing the others.

Strategic review

Reviewing strategy is a process of monitoring changes in the external environment and developments within the organization in order to gain a deeper understanding of the organization's strategic position. It may involve reviewing the mission, the objectives or the strategies the organization is pursuing, or any combination of all three.

The process involves collecting data about the way the world around the organization is changing and assessing the impact of these changes. Although organizations are often swamped with data, key strategic information is frequently not collected or is not available in an appropriate format to give clear insights into past achievements and key external trends.

The aim of reviewing strategy is to focus people on the strategically significant trends – those few things that are 'driving change'. From an improved understanding of the organization's strategic position, managers can identify the key strategic issues that need to be given attention.

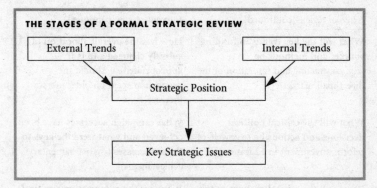

Formal strategic reviews are usually undertaken every few years at the beginning of a strategic planning process. These formal reviews help people to learn about the underlying trends influencing an organization's strategy. They often point to important data that the organization should collect systematically on a regular basis.

Questions which the review may need to answer include:

External review	*Internal review*
What are the key social and economic trends directly relevant to the organization and its objectives (e.g. benefit levels, social exclusion)?	**Who are the organization's users** (e.g. age, gender, minority representation)? **How will their needs change in the plan period** (e.g. services may need to change as users grow older)?
What are the key political trends that will affect the organization during the plan period (e.g. growth of higher education, European legislation)?	**What proportion of the total population of potential users is the organization reaching** (e.g. the percentage of each user group that the organization supports)?
What significant technological developments are likely during the plan period (e.g. for helping people with disabilities to communicate)?	**How much subsidy is the organization allocating to each service and user group** (e.g. the amount of unrestricted funds spent on residential homes or on young service users)?

External review (continued)	*Internal review* (continued)
What will the key trends in funding sources and methods be (e.g. contracting and saturation of the direct mail market)?	**How has the overall allocation of subsidy changed and is it appropriate** (e.g. should the proportion spent on older users increase)?
What will the critical political decisions and actions be (e.g. welfare reform, investment in education)?	**What campaign successes have been achieved and what were the keys to those successes** (e.g. parliamentary achievements)?
What will the critical changes in the demographics of service users and funders be, and how will their needs change (e.g. demand for different types of services or methods of delivery)?	**What are the organization's critical human, physical and financial resources, and how have they changed** (e.g. people's skills, funding sources)?
What cultural trends will the organization have to respond to (e.g. user-centred service delivery	**What are the organization's key intangible resources** (e.g. its key relationships, contacts, reputation)?
Who will the organization be competing with during the plan period (e.g. new competitors from the private and third sectors)?	

Reviews invariably generate a great deal of information. The key is to distil the data, focusing on the information that is most pertinent to the future development of the organization.

STRATEGIC REVIEW OF GUIDE DOGS FOR THE BLIND ASSOCIATION

Guide Dogs for the Blind Association provides dogs for 4,600 visually impaired people and assists a further 2,000 people each year through its rehabilitation service. It carried out a major strategic review in preparation for the development of a new corporate strategy. All services and activities were reviewed. This is the summary of the findings:

'There is plenty of good news . . .'

Service strengths
- GDBA has led the world in training dogs to help visually impaired people.
- It offers a unique service and has no competitors.
- The service is highly valued by guide dog owners.
- The number of guide dog owners has increased by 29 per cent in five years.
- Other services (such as holidays, hotels) are highly valued.

Organizational and financial strengths
- GDBA has a strong national infrastructure of centres and voluntary supporters.
- It has an investment fund of £144 million.
- It is a leading legacy fund-raiser.
- It is widely recognized by the general public.
- It has a skilled and dedicated staff.

'But there are symptoms of loss of strategic direction . . .'

Service strategy
- The client group for guide dog and rehabilitation services and their needs are not well defined.
- Service levels and quality vary widely across the country.
- Dog users per staff member (i.e. productivity) has fallen over the last five years.
- Other services are not complementary to the guide dog service.
- They require a growing subsidy from the organization.

Organization
- There is no clear financial framework to underpin efficiency, fund-raising and management of reserves.
- Income sources are vulnerable.
- The management culture is technical and individualistic rather than managerial and corporate.
- The organization is inward-looking and isolated from the visual-impairment sector, visually impaired people and the charitable sector.

This honest assessment led to the development of a new mission, strategy and plan for the organization.

Developing insights into strategic position

Strategic position sets the organization or the service in its environmental context. It draws together the information from the internal and external reviews to produce a summary of the situation. There are a number of techniques which can be used to enhance understanding of the strategic position of an organization or a service. These may sound rather elaborate, but in practice their greatest use is as thinking tools to help people look at the review from different perspectives.

Gap analysis is a method of focusing attention on service users' needs. It involves preparing an assessment of service users' needs and comparing these with services currently available. This can be done with a survey of users, by talking with other providers or by seeking views from knowledgeable people inside or outside the organization.

GAPS IN SERVICES FOR PEOPLE WITH AIDS

In the late 1980s provision of services for people with HIV and AIDS grew rapidly as central and local government provided funds for a wide range of entrepreneurial initiatives established by voluntary organizations.

It soon became unclear what the greatest unmet needs of people with HIV and AIDS were and which services required additional funding. Interviews with providers and funders led to the conclusions that:

- in London, the most pressing gaps for the 2,100 people with AIDS and 19,000 HIV-positive people were for:
  — residential care
  — home support
  — drop-in centres
  — transport to service providers
  — welfare rights and housing advice
- outside London, gaps in services for the 500 people with AIDS and 4,600 HIV-positive people varied within the seven cities where the largest numbers of people with AIDS lived. The only common gap was for terminal-care services.

The aim is to make judgements that help identify the most pressing unmet needs of service users and therefore point to areas where new services are required or where existing services need to be expanded.

Value for money analysis is a method of comparing the benefits of different services to service users with the cost and, more specifically, the subsidy which needs to be found from fund-raising or other sources. This involves calculating the subsidy required to provide each service and dividing it by the number of service users to give unit subsidy figures. These can then be compared with people's judgements about the importance of each service. This does not mean that services with higher subsidies are less valuable, but it does help to pinpoint the cost of expanding each service and the savings gained from reducing them.

COMPARING COSTS AND BENEFITS

An organization of people with disabilities carried out a review of the cost of services; it yielded the following figures:

	Income £'000	Expenditure £'000	Subsidy £'000	Users	Unit subsidy
Holiday service	15	55	40	200	£200
Help line	—	25	25	2,500	£10
Residential care	100	120	20	10	£2,000
Employment advice	50	60	10	400	£25
Equipment loan	10	25	15	500	£30

As a result of the review, the board agreed a strategy of:

- expanding employment advice because it was providing excellent value for money
- reducing the holiday service because similar holidays were available from other charities at a lower cost
- negotiating increased fees from local authorities to reduce the unit subsidy of the residential care home.

SWOT is a well-known mnemonic; it stands for the **S**trengths, **W**eaknesses, **O**pportunities and **T**hreats of an organization or of particular services. These are compared, the aim being to produce a one-page summary of the organization's strategic position. This is a valuable way of summarizing data obtained from a strategic review. It is often used as a group brain-storming technique; this is a useful tool to encourage people to think about the strategic issues facing the organization. However, when the material is generated in this way, it should be tested thoroughly against the evidence of a review, otherwise there is a real danger of producing a series of platitudes.

Identification of key strategic issues

Having gained an understanding of an organization's strategic position, the final stage of a review is to distil all the learning into a set of key issues that need to be addressed. These are the limited number of critical factors that it is thought will determine the long-term success of the organization. This is one of the most critical steps in the process; it provides the foundation upon which to build the strategic plan.

Strategic issues are generated by comparing the mission and the objectives with the information generated in the review about the achievements and performance of the organization. This can be done by individuals and by groups, and it is likely to be an iterative process in which first thoughts are developed and refined until consensus emerges around the really fundamental questions.

KEY ISSUES FOR MENCAP

Following a major review of its overall strategy, Mencap consulted its staff, board, local societies and other stakeholders on six key questions to determine the overall shape of its long-term strategy:

● Who are the people and groups that Mencap should be supporting?
● What services should Mencap be expanding?
● Should Mencap put more emphasis on campaigning and information and leave the development of new service areas to others?
● What should be the 'unique' role of Mencap?
● Should we become more active in the field of research?
● How do we build a closer relationship between the different sections of the organization?

In some circumstances, the resulting questions will raise big issues that will influence the future direction of the whole organization. In other circumstances, the overall direction will be secure and the issues will be about minor adjustments to current strategies.

Strategic choice

The process of strategic review identifies key issues; it may highlight any or all of the following: new needs among service users, new or better ways of meeting needs, or new threats (such as changing funding arrangements or competition from other suppliers). The priorities may initially seem daunting – too much to do and too few resources to do it. So, governing boards and managers need to make choices.

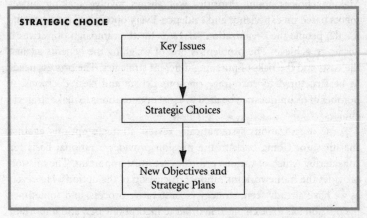

STRATEGIC CHOICE

Key Issues

↓

Strategic Choices

↓

New Objectives and Strategic Plans

There are a number of pitfalls to avoid. Some organizations, quite rightly, thrive on opportunism. The third sector is known for its ability to produce social innovations. New ideas and new funding sources drive the organization's strategy in a series of unplanned and incremental steps. In these organizations opportunism is a crucial ingredient of a successful strategy. Nevertheless, the organization that is driven exclusively by opportunism risks becoming a hostage to external funders; forced to pursue only those things for which it can raise money, it puts its future at the whim of its funders. In comparison, organizations that gain control over their strategy begin to determine their own future.

Some organizations compromise when it comes to strategic choice. In part this is necessary – their diverse constituencies are often held together by giving a little to all the contributors. But too much compromise is dangerous. Organizations that step incrementally from focusing on a few key objectives to a brief so wide that it ends up doing a little of everything risk not doing anything particularly well.

Finally, some organizations write the strategy in such general terms that everyone can agree to it. This avoids making difficult choices, but it greatly reduces the value of the strategic management process.

Concepts for making strategic choice more rigorous

Making choices about priorities will always involve making judgements based on experience and evidence. Every option will have benefits for the people the organization serves or for the campaign objectives it wishes to achieve. The problem is one of weighing the benefits against the costs and the risks of pursuing different strategies. The process needs to be structured to encourage rigorous debate and clear decisions. A number of techniques can be used to assist organizations to make strategic choices.

Some organizations systematically **review strategic options against the mission**. Going back to the mission provides a rational basis for considering which of various priorities are most important. The mission provides the framework for rational discussion of the options. However, as we have already seen, strategy is an iterative process, and sometimes the mission has to be changed in order to incorporate new and important objectives. So the method is far from foolproof!

Another approach is to **attach a weighting** to proposals that are competing for limited resources. Line managers putting forward a number of proposals are asked to rate them according to criteria such as:

- critical strategic importance
- important but not essential
- pursue when funds available.

This exercise can be carried out twice, once for projects requiring capital funding and once for projects requiring revenue funding. A similar approach involves identifying the different audiences that the organization is trying to influence and giving each a 'more stars the better' style weighting to the questions:

- What is our potential impact on this group?
- What is our current impact on this group?
- To what extent do the proposals increase our impact on the group?

Another frequently used method is **scheduling**. This is similar to weighting methods, in that those projects which have a higher priority are scheduled to take place before those with a lower priority. Scheduling is useful because it allows management to say that one project or initiative needs to happen before another. Furthermore, it confronts people with the fact that financial and managerial resources are limited and choices have to be made.

An important source of information for making choices is **the organization's recent experience** of things that worked and things that did not work. Learning from that experience can provide valuable insights which can be used to inform the strategic choices.

Finally, as the market for funding becomes more competitive, some business techniques are becoming more appropriate. Organizations can compare themselves with other organizations receiving funds from the same sources. They can ask what their **distinctiveness** will be in future compared with their competitors. They may be better placed to become a low-cost high-volume supplier of the service, or alternatively to become a niche provider, servicing a carefully targeted service user group. These considerations then influence which projects and initiatives to pursue.

Before choices are finally made, organizations can **test strategic choices**. One test is to consult relevant stakeholder groups and seek their reactions to the proposed choices. Another test is to analyse the sensitivity of particular projects to changing assumptions, looking for example at the implications of the loss of grant funding or the impact of new government regulations. Looking at the financial effects of a growing or declining demand for a service can test the economic sensitivity of proposals to different assumptions.

In practice, making strategic choices will always be a highly judgemental process. Techniques help to structure the problem, but ultimately they cannot replace experience and wisdom.

Once the strategic choices have been made, the strategic plan can be prepared.

6.6 DEVELOPING STRATEGIC PLANS

This section focuses on the process of planning. It establishes the circumstances that need to exist for an organization to develop its strategy in a formal way. It explains how to plan the planning process and how to improve existing processes, and finally it identifies common pitfalls.

COMMON OBJECTIONS TO PLANNING

'We need a strategic plan to guide our development over the next five years,' said the recently appointed chief executive.

'There's no point,' said the head of services. 'I've been here for ten years and the one thing I've learned is that you can't predict the future.'

'We can't predict everything,' the chief executive agreed, 'but many of the changes that will affect us, such as welfare reform and the creation of new partnerships, have been agreed. We need to anticipate how we will respond to them.'

'But even if we anticipate change, plans always depend on increasing funding,' the head of services replied. 'Planning is an academic exercise until we know where new funding will come from.'

'My experience is that we will only raise the money if we know what we want it for,' said the chief executive, recognizing that he was on to a good argument.

'Well, my experience is that we need to be flexible, able to adapt to new circumstances and not be constrained by the straitjacket of a plan,' the head of services said.

'That's true, but I don't see the plan as being fixed for ever. It is a route map and, if circumstances change, we can adjust our plan. Itwill enable us to see clearly the implications of making these changes,' the increasingly frustrated chief executive retorted.

'This argument illustrates the very point I want to make,' said the head of services, sensing victory. 'Planning will raise too many tensions that are better kept below the surface. If we can't agree on the need for a plan, we certainly won't agree on its contents.'

The need for planning has to be widely accepted for it to be a useful tool.

Preconditions for strategic planning

There is never an ideal time for strategic planning, and the major determinants of when to initiate a strategic planning process will be the time that has passed since the last plan was produced and the extent to which it has dated. However, there are a number of circumstances in which strategic planning will be less appropriate or will not work effectively as a management tool:

1. **Organizations need to have sufficient independence to select their own objectives and deploy resources to achieve them.** If the organizational unit is an integral part of a larger system (usually a public body), strategic planning may not be appropriate.
2. **Commitment of the chair and the chief executive.** A high level of commitment, particularly from the chief executive, is an essential ingredient of strategic planning. If the chief executive is not seen to be in command of the strategic planning process and is not dedicated to using the plan as a managerial tool, scepticism will creep in and planning will not be effective. In a similar vein, the chair needs to be involved and committed to demonstrate to the board that planning is for real, not just a paper exercise.
3. **The senior management team needs to be stable.** If two or more senior managers are in the process of leaving or if a major reorganization of the senior management team is imminent, strategic planning will be dominated by the inevitable politics of reorganization. It is not a moment for sitting back and dispassionately reviewing the organization and its prospects.

    Similarly, if new members have recently joined the team or if a team has just been established, the dynamics of a group in 'forming mode' (see section 12.3) may interfere with strategic planning.

4. **Lack of major crises.** If the organization is in crisis or if one is imminent, short-term pressures will predominate. The loss of a major source of funding, fundamental divisions over future directions, the resignation of a number of board members or the dismissal of a senior member of staff are all circumstances that militate against a participative approach to planning. There needs to be adequate stability in the organization and a willingness on the part of senior staff and the board to be dispassionate for planning to be effective.

In strategic planning, both the planning process and the substance of the plan are ultimately matters for the board and senior management, in consultation with the staff and sometimes with service users and other stakeholders. In operational planning, the board and senior management are responsible primarily for establishing the process, and individual departments and service managers are responsible for the content.

Planning in different types of organization

The substance of strategy clearly varies from one organization to another. It is nevertheless possible to make some generalizations about the overall substance of strategic plans. This helps to guide organizations to focus planning effort on those matters where planning is most likely to yield the greatest value added.

Two questions deserve consideration:

1. **How much strategic freedom does the organization have?**

   Some organizations have a great deal of strategic freedom. They have broad objectives, most of their income is not tied to any specific purpose (in the jargon, it is unrestricted) and they can choose not only what they do but how they do it.

   Other organizations have very little strategic freedom. They have limited objectives, most or all of their income is restricted to tightly prescribed projects, and there are few options for raising unrestricted income.

   Organizations with great freedom can be expansive in their strategic thinking. They can carry out wide-ranging environmental reviews, establish significantly different strategic objectives and reallocate resources to different or new activities. Their plans can therefore be wide-ranging. There is, however, a danger that they may become too broad and general and not focus on the specific objectives that the organization wishes to achieve in the next few years.

Organizations with little freedom have to focus sharply on strategic developments that are within their control. They may plan to increase their strategic freedom, but the core of their strategy is likely to be about developing existing services.

2. **How predictable is the organization's environment?**

Some organizations have a comparatively predictable environment. They know broadly how many users there are in their area of work and how their needs will change as they grow older; some housing organizations fall into this category. These organizations can plan for the longer term and they need to revise their plans less frequently.

Others have a much less predictable environment which may change significantly in a short space of time; campaigning organizations are a common example. These organizations need to plan to have the capacity to respond to different circumstances. Their plans will have shorter time horizons and should focus on building the institutional infrastructure so that the organization can act decisively when the next opportunity arises.

In practice, most organizations are not at either end of this spectrum, so they may need to focus parts of the organization in one way and parts in the other. The key point is to acknowledge that the fundamental nature of planning will vary, depending on the extent of their strategic freedom and the predictability of their environment.

Planning the planning process

The objective of strategic planning is to build a widely shared conception of the future of the organization and its managerial priorities – not to create a glossy document that sits on people's bookshelves. The key to effective strategic planning is therefore to focus on the process of preparing the plan as well as on the plan itself. Issues that managers should consider as they embark on a planning process include:

1. **Legitimizing the process throughout the organization.** People in significant positions in the organization need to be committed to planning. Their involvement in the decision to embark upon strategic planning and in the design of the strategic planning process is consequently an essential ingredient for success. Some people may have genuine concerns about the process and its implications for the organization and for their job. These need to be aired at the start and during subsequent stages of the process. Similarly, line managers and service unit managers need to be given an opportunity to raise their concerns and to be involved in the design of the process.

2. **Clarifying who will be involved at different stages.** Ideally, strategic planning should involve as many people as possible from the organization's different constituencies. However, there is a trade-off to be made. Consultation takes time and not everyone can be involved in all the stages of carrying out a strategic review, identifying key issues and making strategic choices. Therefore decisions have to be made on whom to involve at different stages of the process and how to involve them, in order to maximize their commitment to the plan. Once these decisions have been taken, everyone should be told how and when they will be expected to make their contributions.

3. **Integrating with other management procedures**. The strategic plan needs to fit with other procedures for agreeing budgets, submitting applications for grants and being prepared for performance reviews commissioned by funding bodies. Managers should anticipate having to make trade-offs because the timetable can never meet everyone's requirements. In practice, strategic planning, even in a small organization, is likely to take at least three or four months. In larger organizations and those where more extensive consultation is required, between six and nine months is more likely to be appropriate, and those planning for the first time should expect to have to add two or three months to allow time to learn how planning works and fits with other management processes. Successful integration implies that the timetables for planning, budget-setting and making funding applications all fit together.

4. **Challenging conventional wisdom.** Strategic planning is a process of challenging existing beliefs, checking whether assumptions still hold

and developing new perspectives. This may require the involvement of outsiders and of people who are close to the organization but not an integral part of it. Designing them into the process will help to ensure that there is an independent challenge to conventional wisdom.

5. **Communicating strategy.** Communication is an essential ingredient for effective implementation. In many organizations there are frequently stakeholder groups who can contribute more to the organization if they understand its strategic priorities. These can include funding bodies, members, major donors, service users, branches, local centres, local committees and any other group that has a relationship with the organization.

6. **Developing systems to monitor strategic performance.** Once the plan has been agreed, both the board and management need processes for gathering data and reporting on the overall performance of the organization. This element is frequently forgotten. Allow time to identify the measures that will be used to monitor performance and to agree ways to report on progress in implementing the strategy (see Chapter 8).

Preparing strategic plans

Preparing strategic plans needs to be thought about in terms of a 'social process' that involves different people at different stages. It usually starts with management designing a process and consulting on their initial ideas with staff and board members. It should result in a short document that describes the proposed process and is formally approved by the board as the basis for planning.

The document about planning the planning process should answer the following questions:

● Why is the organization embarking on planning?
● What is it intended the planning will achieve for the organization?
● What are the key stages of preparing the plan?
● Who will be involved at each stage?
● How will board members and staff be consulted at the end of each stage?

- When will decisions be taken?
- How will planning be integrated with other planning processes?
- What is the overall timetable?

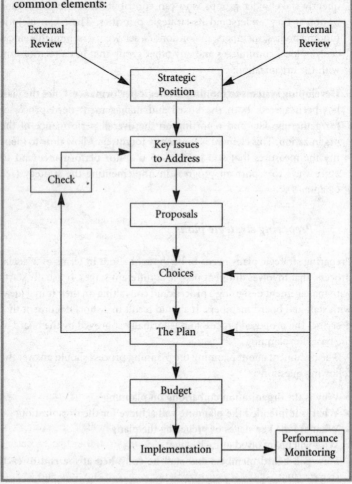

THE INTELLECTUAL PROCESS

A strategic planning process usually incorporates the following common elements:

Once the process is agreed, the review stage can begin. Organizations that have not engaged in planning for some time and organizations with a relatively new senior management team find the internal and external reviews time-consuming. This is unavoidable, not least because a great deal of learning is taking place while the review is being carried out. New data is discovered and much-needed data may not be available or will be available only in a very different form from that required.

Even when basic facts and figures have been collected, it takes time to interpret the data and develop new insights into the changing circumstances. Allow time to draw out conclusions before summarizing the strategic position of the organization and identifying the critical questions that the strategic plan will need to address.

The end of the review stage is often a convenient point at which to have a period of consultation. A review document can be circulated to a wide variety of stakeholders, and workshops can be held with key groups to explain the conclusions of the review in order to seek their input and to explain the next stages in the process.

Sometimes the review will point to a small number of critical strategic choices that the organization needs to make. One of the keys to successful planning is to confront these choices rather than agreeing strategies that are so generalized that they meet everyone's aspirations but avoid choosing between alternatives. These choices may need to be the subject of a consultation process, leading to decisions by the board on future directions and priorities. When consultation takes place, management needs to be very clear with everyone as to who is being consulted, when consultation ends, who is taking decisions, when they will be taken and how they will be announced.

Sometimes the review will lead to the establishment of a series of task groups to address specific issues that the plan needs to resolve. These can involve staff and board members working together, since this will increase ownership of the final plan.

Eventually the time comes to put the plan together. It may include contributions from task groups and from senior managers, and it may be put together by a senior manager. In the end, though, the content of the draft plan needs to have a significant input from the chief executive. He or she has the overview, understands the politics of the organization and needs, more than anyone, to own the plan. A temptation at this stage is to be excessively ambitious and to adopt priorities that far exceed the organization's resources and, more usually, its management capacity. This should be avoided by ruthless prioritization.

Draft plans benefit from widespread consultation with staff and the board and, sometimes, other stakeholders. Following a number of re-drafts (usually necessary to get the thinking really straight), a final plan can be put to the board for approval.

SCENARIO PLANNING

Scenario planning is a technique used in business to encourage managers to think the unthinkable. It is particularly valuable when significant changes in the external environment are anticipated and when managers have become set in their ways and need to be encouraged to be more imaginative.

One way to prepare scenarios is to put together a group of managers and ask them to prepare scenarios for the future based on fundamentally different assumptions. The assumptions could be significant increases or declines in unrestricted income, the possibility of a major technological breakthrough or the consequences of a new government policy.

Managers should work in an iterative way, brainstorming the possibilities, working out the consequences and then writing them up in a series of different scenarios. Generally three scenarios are developed: an optimistic one, a pessimistic one and a middle-of-the-road one.

These can then be used by other managers to test the consequences of the scenario on their area of work. The results can be fed into the strategic plan in the form of a sensitivity analysis that shows where the plan is most sensitive to changes in assumptions.

THE PLANNING PROCESS AT INTERMEDIATE TECHNOLOGY

Intermediate Technology is a multi-million-pound development agency which creates and implements low technologies for non-industrialized countries. It was asked, at relatively short notice, to prepare a new strategic plan for its main funding body. It adopted the following process:

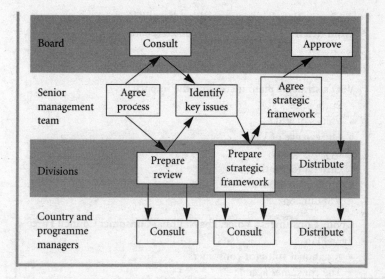

Content of plans

The content of plans needs to reflect the outcome of the planning process. Long, dreary documents incorporating everything discussed are less useful than short, accessible documents that:

● reflect the organization's values
● communicate the key messages
● provide the basis for reviewing progress.

In smaller organizations the document is usually called the strategic plan. In larger organizations, which have separate strategic or operational plans for each of their services, the document is sometimes called the 'strategic framework'. This sets the overall context within which detailed operational and service plans will fit.

When it comes to preparing the plan itself, the most useful documents:

● are **short** and to the point – say 10–20 pages
● **mix communication methods** such as text, diagrams, bullet-point lists and charts

- are **inspirational** – demonstrating what will be done
- **avoid detail** – that can be documented separately.

EXAMPLES OF THE CONTENTS OF STRATEGIC PLANS

VSO's strategic plan: increasing the impact
- Purpose of VSO
- Values of VSO
- The essence of VSO
- Key directions
- Criteria for work
- Implementation
- VSO in 2003

Giving Consumers a Voice: The National Consumer Council Three Year Plan
- A national voice for consumers
- The consumer agenda
- Priority 1: Public utilities
- Priority 2: Public services
- Priority 3: High Street goods and services
- Priority 4: Legal services
- Priority 5: Credit and debt
- Working for change
- Resourcing the plan

Countryside Commission Strategy
- The strategy at a glance
- Chairman's introduction
- The heart of the matter
- The challenge
- Our main aim
- Main areas of future work
- Our role

Requirements for top-quality plans

The best plans have the following characteristics:

They embody clear thinking and good judgement. The key to successful planning is the synthesis of data to focus people on critical trends that will have a significant impact on the organization. This allows people to engage in clear strategic thinking. Penetrating thought and good judgement are the prerequisites for a powerful strategy.

They are specific but adaptable. They should not be set in concrete and be so inflexible that they cannot be adapted if circumstances change. But they should also not be so generalized that they mean anything to anyone.

They focus on generating resources as much as on using them. Strategies for raising money from donors are usually prepared separately from strategic plans. The two need to be brought together.

They set a clear financial framework. This is likely to include financial assumptions and may also include a high-level financial forecast to indicate the likely level of resources available for delivering the strategy.

They contain an implementation timetable. Targets without a timetable are not real targets. Every plan ought to contain approximate dates by which key actions will have been put into place.

They need to have clear measures of performance. Good intentions are not enough. Plans need objectives with measures of performance attached to each. These should be a mixture of qualitative and quantitative measures.

The allocation of responsibilities is clear. When a strategic plan is completed, key individuals need to be clear as to what they have to achieve and the deadline by which they have to achieve it.

Strategic frameworks are likely to be a little less specific than strategic plans. Frameworks tend to establish overall directions and set the context for more detailed plans. Strategic plans, on the other hand, should be more specific, particularly in establishing timetables for implementation and measures of performance.

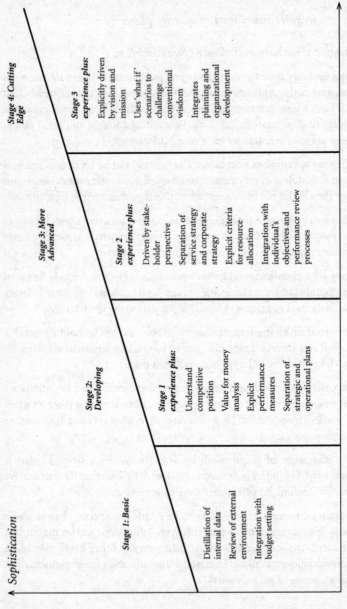

Sophistication →

Time →

Stage 1: Basic

Distillation of internal data

Review of external environment

Integration with budget setting

Stage 2: Developing

Stage 1 experience plus:

Understand competitive position

Value for money analysis

Explicit performance measures

Separation of strategic and operational plans

Stage 3: More Advanced

Stage 2 experience plus:

Driven by stakeholder perspective

Separation of service strategy and corporate strategy

Explicit criteria for resource allocation

Integration with individual's objectives and performance review processes

Stage 4: Cutting Edge

Stage 3 experience plus:

Explicitly driven by vision and mission

Uses 'what if' scenarios to challenge conventional wisdom

Integrates planning and organizational development

Finally, some organizations fall into the trap of assuming that planning will solve all the organization's problems. 'We can't agree that until the plan is completed' is a common sentiment, but it is usually an excuse for avoiding a decision. Plans are not a panacea; they are a structured means for conducting a rational debate and coming to an agreement about future priorities.

Each time a planning process is undertaken, the organization will learn how to create more effective plans. The first time is usually the most difficult. Subsequent processes should become more sophisticated, use a wider range of techniques and drive the organization up the planning learning curve.

To conclude, what does a typical organization do about strategic planning? A survey of over 100 voluntary organizations (ACENVO, 1996) showed that:

- 82 per cent had a plan
- the major reason for preparing it was the arrival of a new chief executive
- most plans were for 2–3 years
- users and supporters were rarely consulted or sent copies
- the average plan was fourteen pages long
- 40 per cent prepared a summary version
- the most used planning techniques were SWOT, gap analysis and cost–benefit analysis
- 64 per cent felt the plan had a strong influence on the organization's overall success.

6.7 COMMON STRATEGIC DILEMMAS

When organizations are skilled at strategic planning they often discover that there are some fundamental dilemmas to be considered. These are common to many organizations, and they usually emerge at the strategic choice stage.

Strategic choice is a key stage in developing future strategy. Making choices between alternative strategies is ultimately a matter of judgement, based on the values and beliefs of the board and the staff. There are no right and wrong choices. The appropriate choice for one organization with its set of skills and aspirations may be entirely inappropriate for another organization working in the same field but having different capabilities and motivations.

The strategic dilemmas which appear time and time again are set out here to illustrate some of the common issues that organizations have to address. When the strategy-making process has reached one of these dilemmas, managers know the time has come to make judgements.

1. A little help for many or a great deal of help for a few

Many organizations can focus their resources on making a substantial difference to a limited number of people or spreading them out and giving a little assistance to many people:

● Organizations for homeless people have to balance giving a few people an extensive service, including a roof over their head, psychiatric support, employment training and help in finding a job, with the provision of basic shelter for a large number of homeless people.

● Development agencies have to balance efforts to make a substantial difference by concentrating all their resources on a few communities with the desire to spread their resources across the many countries that desperately need their assistance.

● Disability organizations have to balance the need to offer substantial support to a few service users (perhaps people with the most profound disability) with the desire to give a little assistance to the many people with a mild disability.

2. Treat the symptoms or the cause

Most organizations can identify fundamental causes of the problem they seek to address, but it is usually beyond their resources to do much about it:

● Health and disability organizations have to decide how much money to spend alleviating the pain and suffering of people with the illness or disability and how much to put into research to discover the cause (and perhaps a cure) for it.

● Social service organizations have to balance meeting people's immediate needs with working on the more fundamental causes of the problems. RELATE, for example, gives people counselling but also provides an education service to help people establish healthy relationships in the first place. The Samaritans can befriend people with suicidal thoughts, but they could also commission research into why people commit suicide.

3. Provide services or campaign for change

Many service-giving organizations start to campaign for changes in government policy or funding when they realize that their contribution will always be small compared to the size of the problem. Similarly, some campaigning organizations start to provide services to demonstrate what needs to be done:

- Disability organizations have to find a balance between providing services and campaigning. They recognize that they can potentially achieve so much more by changing people's attitudes towards people with disabilities than they will ever achieve through direct service provision. Campaigns for the rights of people with disabilities have consistently demonstrated the value of achieving policy changes. But they also recognize that people need services now, not when the policy battle has been won.
- Development agencies have to balance their lobbying activities with their practical projects. They recognize that, for example, successfully campaigning for write-offs of non-industrialized-country debts will achieve much more than all the practical projects they fund – but it may take many years to achieve, and people need help now.
- Medical charities have to balance lobbying government to put more money into their field of research with using that money to fund their own research programme.

4. Focus or diversify services

Organizations can choose between concentrating on relatively few services and building their expertise in those tightly specified fields, or diversifying their expertise and delivering a wide range of services.

Many pressures encourage diversification. Funds may be offered for a new service; members or service users may call for new services to meet different needs, often as they grow older and have different needs; and staff may push for new services because they offer new challenges and career-development opportunities.

Despite these pressures there are powerful arguments for focusing on particular services. Economies of scale mean that services can be provided to more people at lower cost. Focusing leads to increased expertise in all aspects of the service.

- Colleges have to choose between systematically strengthening particular departments and programme areas or investing resources evenly across a number of fields.
- Campaigning organizations have to choose between spreading their efforts over a number of campaign fronts or focusing on the achievement of a few tightly specified objectives.
- Hospitals have to choose between putting new investment money in a limited number of specialities, gaining a reputation in these fields and, perhaps, being able to offer a lower-cost service to purchasers, or spreading the money over a wider range of specialities.

5. Hold virtuously to beliefs or be tempted by new resources

Many organizations face the dilemma of whether to hold righteously to their core beliefs or to compromise in order to gain new resources:

- Voluntary organizations have to choose between accepting funds from government initiatives or turning the money down because they are being seduced away from their core cause. In the 1980s many accepted money for employment and training projects that, in retrospect, consumed substantial management time and contributed little to help the organizations achieve their objectives.
- Organizations have to decide whether to accept sponsorship from the tobacco and alcohol industry. For environmental and health-care organizations this is a difficult decision.
- Fund-raising organizations know that pushing the emotive side of the cause (the starving baby, the child with disabilities) will raise more money. But it distorts the public's perception of the beneficiary group when people want a fair chance in life – not charity.

● Housing associations have to balance sticking to their core user group with bidding for money from the latest funding scheme, which may divert management time (and financial resources) away from their historic purpose.

KEY ISSUES FOR FAMILY SERVICE UNITS

Family Service Units is a national organization which helps disadvantaged families through a network of centres that provide a wide variety of family support services.

At the end of an extensive review of corporate strategy, set up to clarify the alternative ways forward for the organization as a whole, the FSU Planning Team summarized three strategic issues facing the organization as a whole:

1. **Focus on specified client group or general community needs**
   FSU's reputation and experience lies in providing intensive support to families facing severe difficulties. Yet an increasing number of Units are devoting resources to providing a variety of services to broader sections of their communities. FSU needs to decide whether it will be more effective if it concentrates on meeting the needs of a specific client group, or if it aims to respond to the differing needs of a wider range of clients.

2. **Aim for a consistent approach throughout the country or aim to promote diversity**
   Each Unit has developed its own priorities and practices. FSU as a whole offers an enormous diversity of services. The dilemma is how to establish a clear identity and focus for FSU while retaining local responsiveness. Too much diversity makes it difficult to identify what is distinctive about FSU and creates a confused message for potential funders. A too-rigid model of service provision would limit the Unit's ability to respond flexibly and effectively to local need.

3. **Develop national standards for performance or encourage Units to adopt their own**
   There is great variation in the quality and management of FSU services. Expectations about standards are determined by each

Unit. To promote a high level of performance, FSU could develop standards and performance measures which would be adopted by each Unit. Alternatively FSU could encourage local responses and accept different standards in different parts of the country.

Overcoming disagreements on strategy

Agreeing long-term strategy is not always plain sailing. Examples of problems of significant disagreements on strategy include:

- a theatre where opinion was deeply divided on whether to put on a programme of more challenging plays or to produce popular plays that would improve its financial security
- a social service organization with service users from all socio-economic groups, where there was much disagreement about the principle of charging for the service
- a social welfare organization in which funders and volunteers just could not agree about monitoring the effectiveness of volunteers' work.

These are just a few of the disagreements that can stop a strategy process in its tracks. Disagreements of this type often come down to different values and assumptions. Overcoming them may require:

- allocating time to enable representatives of the different viewpoints to explore the reasons for their different views and discover whether they can find common ground
- use of an independent third party to act as a facilitator in a review of alternative ways forward and the consequences of pursuing different strategies.

Sometimes agreement is not possible. If talking and the use of independent outsiders cannot resolve the differences, some people may need to leave, to allow the organization to un-stick itself and continue to function effectively.

More often, the disagreement results from misunderstandings and the allocation of insufficient time to talk through different assumptions and viewpoints. In these circumstances, time spent debating differences can be both motivating and rewarding; it can shed light on the 'messy' nature of these organizations and the fact that few issues have clear-cut solutions. It often leads to robust outcomes that provide firm foundations for the long-term development of the organization.

SUMMARY OF KEY POINTS

The need for objectives and strategies
- Strategic planning establishes direction, priorities and key targets. It helps people understand how their work fits into the organization's broader strategies.

The hierarchy of objectives
- Objectives exist in a hierarchy that is related to levels of the organization.
- Strategic objectives are few in number; departmental and service unit objectives are increasingly specific.
- Most organizations have external and internal objectives.
- Some organizations have cross-departmental objectives.

Clarifying strategic objectives
- Strategic objectives are usually established as part of the strategic planning process. They are required for each key issue that the organization wishes to address.
- Strategic objectives need to avoid being wildly ambitious, highly generalized and gratuitous.

Strategy evolves
- Strategies are broad categories of actions which indicate how human, financial and other resources will be deployed in order to achieve the agreed objectives.
- Strategy evolves in three ways: as an incremental process, as a political process and as an analytical process.
- Strategy is required at the corporate, divisional and service levels of an organization.

Strategic reviews, positions and choices
- Strategic reviews gather data on internal and external trends, summarize the organization's strategic position and identify the key issues which the strategic plan needs to address.
- Different techniques can be used to develop insights into strategic

position, to identify key issues and to make choices between alternative strategies.

Developing strategy

- Preconditions for planning include: commitment of the chair and chief executive, a stable senior management team and lack of major short-term crises.
- Planning the planning process is critical. Key considerations are:
  — legitimizing the process
  — clarifying who will be involved at different stages
  — integrating planning with other management procedures
  — challenging conventional wisdom
  — communicating the new strategy
  — developing systems to monitor strategic performance.
- Top-quality plans embody clear thinking, are specific but adaptable, show how funds will be raised and have a clear allocation of responsibilities, an implementation timetable and measures of performance.
- Planning is a 'social process' that typically happens in stages:
  — agree the planning process
  — carry out a strategic review
  — consult on key issues from the review
  — make strategic choices
  — draft the plan
  — consult on the plan
  — approve the plan.

Common strategic dilemmas

- Many organizations face fundamental dilemmas about strategy:
  — provide a little help to many people or more help to a few
  — treat the symptoms or the cause
  — provide services or campaign for change
  — focus or diversify services
  — hold virtuously to beliefs or be tempted by new resources.
- These are best resolved by allocating time to discuss and debate alternative ways forward.

Service Strategies and Operational Plans

Overall strategies are needed to give an organization a broad sense of direction and to build stakeholder commitment to the main thrust of its efforts. Within the umbrella of the overall strategy, organizations need strategies for each of the services they offer and operational plans that demonstrate how the strategy will be pursued in the coming year.

This chapter:

- explains how and when to separate services and campaigns into separate 'units' for planning and management
- demonstrates how service strategies should be developed for national and local services
- shows how operational plans are created.

7.1 DEFINING SERVICES AND CAMPAIGNS

Most organizations deliver a range of interconnected services, often to the same user group. A prerequisite for developing strategies for these services is the definition of exactly what constitutes a service. This enables management to put a boundary around the work and to identify clearly who is responsible for it.

Defining services requires careful thought. The very nature of services with social objectives is that the problems they attempt to address are multi-faceted:

- Organizations for homeless people may put a roof over people's heads, but they soon discover that the underlying problems many homeless people face may be medical, psychological, lack of skills or the need for a job.

● Disability organizations start providing services for people with disabilities, but they soon discover that the attitudes of able-bodied people are a greater obstacle to improving their lives.

Consequently the nature of the services offered tends to evolve. When a housing association uses existing staff to offer residents benefit advice or employment training and other 'foyer' services, they are initially inseparable from the housing service. But when they become a significant activity, perhaps with their own staff and top-up funding, they may need to be considered as a separate service. Similarly, when an orchestra's musicians do a few school workshops to drum up interest in a particular locality, they are inseparable from its main purpose. When the orchestra is selling its school education service to local authorities and using significant amounts of players' time, it eventually becomes a separate service.

The idea of distinct services is central to strategic management. Only when the services have been separated in people's minds can each develop a strategy to pursue specific objectives. Without this distinction it quickly becomes impossible to manage services efficiently, and everything becomes a tangle of activity without a clear logic to drive management and decision-taking. This is not to say that, once they have been clearly defined, they do not co-operate and co-ordinate with each other. Indeed, in today's environment, units are having to work more closely together than ever before. But it is essential to start by defining what a service is and who is responsible for it.

Defining services is a matter of judgement. Individual managers cannot manage more than a limited number of services, so excessive sub-division is not helpful. Conversely, failing to distinguish between different activities that may be expanding or declining at different rates – or, more importantly, that may be consuming different amounts of subsidy – can be dangerous.

It is therefore necessary to think about separate **service delivery units.** The concept is analogous to the idea of strategic business units in the private sector. Companies that produce a number of products for different customer groups in different parts of the world have strategic business units that cut across traditional, functional or geographical management structures to encourage managers to focus on customers and their needs. The concept builds on the idea of a project centre or cost centre, but it is concerned with management of the strategy and services of the unit as well as its income and expenditure.

Criteria for establishing service delivery units

An activity can be considered as a service delivery unit only if it:

- has a clearly defined service user group
- has specified objectives to be achieved for or with the service users
- can plan a strategy and deploy the resources needed to achieve the objectives
- can monitor achievements against plans
- has financial management information that sets out income and expenditure of the unit and the subsidy required to run the service
- has a manager who is responsible (either part-time or full-time) for planning, delivering and monitoring the service.

To create a service delivery unit, managers have to define the service offered, identify the staff who provide the service and quantify the income it attracts and the expenditure it incurs. This is not always straightforward because staff sometimes work on a number of services. It is then necessary for staff to estimate how they anticipate using their time and, ideally, to record how it is actually used. This needs to be introduced sensitively, because some people feel uncomfortable recording how they allocate their time. Time recording is being used in organizations where work can be divided into discrete projects.

Establishing service delivery units may require managers to divide funding that has been given for a variety of purposes and allocate appropriate amounts to each unit. It may also be necessary to adjust the accounts system to separate out the relevant costs for each service.

Similar issues arise with campaigns. An environmental organization, for example, may be campaigning for the protection of wildlife, but it needs to clarify whether its marine eco-systems campaign or its habitat protection initiative are separate activities, with their own budgets, managers and staff, or are all part of one strategic initiative.

Nevertheless, the concept of service delivery units is a powerful idea that helps to divide complex operations into manageable units. Each unit and each potential new unit becomes a building block in the development of the overall strategy.

7.2 DEVELOPING SERVICE STRATEGIES

Organizations need a planning architecture that defines how the overall strategy, the service plans and the operational plans fit together.

Theoretically, organizations could have strategic and operational plans at the corporate, departmental, regional and local levels: it would be a planner's paradise, but real work would grind to a halt. Choices have to be made. The current trend is away from complex networks of formal strategic and operational plans. The greatest value comes from having an overall strategy at the corporate level and succinct strategies and operational plans at the level of individual services which are tightly linked into the overall strategies. Strategies and plans may exist at other levels, but there is often little value to be gained from the bureaucratic process of documenting them at every level.

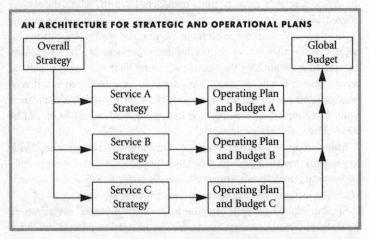

AN ARCHITECTURE FOR STRATEGIC AND OPERATIONAL PLANS

When the planning architecture is clear, each service delivery unit needs to prepare its own strategy, usually covering a one- to three-year period, which sets out objectives and how they will be achieved. Conceptually, the process for developing service strategy is very similar to the corporate strategy process. It involves two stages, beginning with a review and ending with the preparation of a plan. In the review stage, management gathers data about the external environment and the service itself to pinpoint key issues that the plan needs to address. Options can then be developed, choices made and a plan prepared.

However, service managers sometimes need help with their strategic thinking. Some may have been promoted from a service delivery role to their first management post. Well trained in their own specialism, they may be unfamiliar with the task of bringing together service delivery, human resource, financial and other concepts to create a strategy. Some may feel that senior management ought to take responsibility for service strategy. Others are driven by seemingly never-ending demands for their service and feel that they do not have time to stand back from the daily pressures of crises in the hostels, refugees queuing desperately for advice or the deadline of the opening of the night shelter. In all these circumstances, senior management is responsible for providing service managers with the level of support they require to produce a top-quality plan.

Preparing the first review of a service is particularly challenging because it requires definition of the service and the nature of the service user population, and the collection and analysis of data which may not have been drawn together before.

Process for preparing service strategies

Managers need to involve staff (and, depending on circumstances, board members and volunteers) in the preparation of service strategies. Their involvement will lead to greater commitment to implementing plans and a deeper understanding of how their services fit into the overall strategy.

A good approach would involve staff and board members in a discussion of how the review and planning are to be carried out, and a series of meetings to consider the review data, define the key issues that need to be addressed and prepare the plan. The service manager may need to procure additional resources to ensure staff have the extra time needed to help prepare the plan.

In larger organizations offering a number of services, senior management needs to develop and co-ordinate an organization-wide process for service strategic planning. This involves the practical work of timetabling when they should take place and how they fit with the corporate strategy and budget-setting processes.

Tidy logic suggests that service managers should prepare their strategies when the corporate strategy has been completed. In practice this is not always possible, because the total timetable for preparing corporate and service strategies and then preparing operational plans and budgets becomes too extended. Senior managers may also need to spread reviews out so that each can be given detailed attention. In addition, changing external circumstances may require reviews of service strategy at times that do not fit in neatly with the corporate planning timetable. An overall timetable is therefore required which results in each service considering its longer-term strategy about once every three years but does not require them to do their planning just after they have completed a budget cycle (because that is very demoralizing for staff).

Senior managers should expect to make a significant contribution to the content of service strategy. Senior managers are usually more experienced strategists; their job is to provide the insight and judgement that can help turn an adequate service strategy into an excellent one. This means being involved in helping managers to define the key issues and providing input into the shape of the emerging strategy.

Service reviews

Service reviews should provide answers to the following questions:

External Issues	Internal Issues
How are current and potential users' needs changing? Looking at changing expectations, and different ways of meeting them.	**Who are the current service users?** Segmented by such criteria as need, age, socio-economic group, and geography. In some cases the service users may be other organizations rather than individuals.
What are the trends in the numbers of people requiring the service? Reviewing demographics of the user group and the numbers requiring the service but not receiving it.	**How many benefit from the service?** Trends in the number of each type of user receiving the service.

Who are the competing suppliers and what distinguishes them? Identifying other organizations (including private- and public-sector bodies) that provide similar services, and understanding what is distinctive about your or their services.

What are the relevant legislative and political changes that will affect the service? For example, voluntarization of local authority services and European legislation.

What are the trends in funding for the service? Including income from sales, government, donations and membership.

What are the benefits to service users? Requiring an assessment of the quantitative and, equally important, the qualitative outcomes of services, where appropriate using service user 'satisfaction' surveys.

What skills are being used? Identifying the critical competencies the organization requires to deliver the service.

What have we learned? Focusing on what the organization has learned from the users and others about the services provided. Identifying what needs to change in order to improve services.

What staff skills and staff training are required to improve the service? Looking at different ways to develop people's skills.

How much does it cost? Pinpointing how much the service costs to provide, the overall subsidy required to finance the service and the income, expenditure and subsidy per user.

The data gathered needs to be distilled to pull out those items that are most critical to the future of the service and to identify information that needs collecting on an ongoing basis.

Campaigning organizations can consider a similar set of issues for each campaign. External considerations include:

- changing public perceptions on the issue
- changed circumstances that affect the objectives of the campaign or the strategy for achieving objectives
- forthcoming political decisions that provide campaigning opportunities

- changing policies of political parties
- new coalitions required to make an impact on the issue.

Internal considerations include:

- the specific objectives of the campaign
- achievements to date
- effectiveness in the use of people and money
- learning about why some campaign objectives and not others have been achieved.

Service strategies

The service strategy should be succinct, establishing objectives, articulating a strategy and setting out groups of actions needed to achieve the objectives. Typical contents might include:

- summary of the review
- description of the service
- summary of existing and potential service users
- objectives for the next three years
- the overall strategy
- specific targets
- timetable for implementation
- human resource requirements
- financial resource requirements
- sources of funding.

7.3 OPERATIONAL PLANS

The purpose of an operational plan is to link proposed activities with a budget. Most organizations put a huge amount of effort into establishing a budget. Some do not link the proposed expenditures with the activities planned for the next twelve months. The operational plan and the budget should therefore be a single short document that **integrates activity and money.**

In an ideal world, operational plans flow from strategic plans. Strategic plans give broad directions and the operational plans set out a programme of work for the next twelve months or two years. Operational plans should focus on what will be done and by when, and how much it will cost. They are a vehicle for managers to discuss and agree future priorities. They:

- provide a basis on which to delegate work and responsibilities
- describe desired outcomes and, where appropriate, specific targets
- establish the activities upon which the budget will be based
- create a tool for measuring progress.

Most organizations benefit from having a process that requires managers of all services to prepare short, succinct plans. Whether they are called campaign plans, operational plans or work programmes, they provide a structure to the work and are an important tool for communicating across organizational boundaries. They can apply equally to the service delivery parts of the organization and to the support services such as finance, personnel and information technology.

Operational planning process

Operational planning processes generally start with the board and senior management agreeing planning guidelines. These set the parameters for the process. They may set broad targets and budget boundaries (for example, no additional subsidy). In a small organization, the guidance may cover a single sheet of paper on which the board sets out its aspirations for the next twelve months. In a large organization, they will inevitably be more detailed because of the need for consistent budget data across services for the corporate budget-setting process.

Managers then work with their staff to prepare the plan, which, again, needs to be a succinct summary. The best plans are a few pages long, encapsulating critical thinking and proposed actions.

Draft operational plans and budgets **need to be reviewed and challenged** before being agreed by line managers. Once approved, the documents need to be brought together into an overall operating plan and budget for the organization as a whole. This should highlight key proposals for the year, the timetable of major events, and the budget. It should be approved by the board shortly before the start of the organization's financial year.

Content of operational plans

Operational plans need to highlight:

- the benefits that will result (i.e. what)
- the scale of the results (i.e. how much)
- the quality standards
- the cost of each type of help given
- the implementation timetable
- mechanisms for reviewing performance and outcomes.

In some cases, establishing outcomes is relatively straightforward. It is easy to describe how many homes are to be built or to set a target for the number of people who should pass an examination or receive a qualification. In many cases, it is more difficult. Outdoor education centres can plan how many people will attend their team-building courses, but it is more difficult to measure how they have benefited. Social service organizations can plan to offer a number of counselling sessions, but detailed follow-up is required to measure the benefits that arise from this service. Development agencies can aim to distribute a specific number of grants to projects, but it is much harder to specify the desired achievements of the projects.

In some cases, it is virtually impossible. Drug prevention schemes cannot measure the number of people who did not take drugs because of their preventative work. The Samaritans cannot measure whether the people who called subsequently committed suicide.

The final ingredient of an operational plan is a budget which establishes:

- income to be raised from supplying the service
- the cost of providing the service
- the surplus generated or subsidy required.

OPERATIONAL PLANNING AT LONDON LIGHTHOUSE

London Lighthouse exists to provide support and residential care to people with or affected by HIV and AIDS.

Each year it produces a corporate plan which integrates the plans of each of its departments. These are set in the context of three-year strategic directions. Each department has to state its achievements in the previous year, the overall priority for each of its services, the specific objectives it plans to achieve in the coming twelve months, the milestones it will use to monitor performance and the resources it will apply to deliver the plan.

For example, one priority of the Health Care Department was to introduce a named-nurse system as specified in the Patients' Charter. The specific objective was to review the present system and to determine ways of introducing the system. The milestones in achieving this priority were:

- consultation with nursing staff on alternative ways of introducing the system by April
- recommendations for a new nursing structure by May
- consultation with Personnel in June
- introduction of a new recruitment and selection system
- system fully operational by March.

Drawing plans, timetables and budgets together from eight departments ensured a high level of integration across the organization and good understanding of everyone else's priorities.

Common mistakes

The most common mistake is to allow the process to become too bureaucratic. A year or two after initial enthusiasm for the process, it is easy to fall into this trap. The process becomes so routinized that once a year everyone automatically cranks out a plan. People give it little thought and quickly come to regard the plan as work that, although needed to satisfy the system, is not a useful managerial tool. There is, to some extent, a degree of inevitability about this. All new processes have greatest leverage when they are first introduced, but this decays with time. This difficulty can be overcome by carrying out a brief review shortly after completion of the process to identify what went well, where problems were encountered and how it could be improved next time.

Senior management therefore needs to see its task as continuously revitalizing the process. Each year the guidance needs to be adjusted to meet new circumstances. Managers need to be pushed harder to identify real benefits to service users, to seek ways of streamlining their services, to improve quality and reach out to more people.

The second mistake is for senior management to require the plan well before the implementation dates. Long timescales are a particular problem in large organizations where the operational plan for each service may need to be approved by departmental management, then by the committees for each service, then by senior management, then by the finance committee, before being finally submitted as a global budget to the board. In the worst cases, the plan is being prepared a year or more before its start date. This type of bureaucratic process needs to be streamlined to fit the fast-changing world we live in. The scope needs to be agreed (for example, one page each describing benefits to users, actions, a timetable and a budget) so that the minimum number of steps needed to involve people in preparing and agreeing it can be established.

OPERATIONAL PLANNING IN SENSE

SENSE provides pre-school education, post-sixteen education and long-term support for people who are both deaf and blind. Services are delivered regionally, and their annual budget is £30 million. Every four years the organization reviews its overall strategy.

Their operational planning process works as follows:

21 October	Finance Committee to agree inflation and cost-of-living assumptions
26 October	Senior management team agrees guidelines and timetable for operating plan and budget preparation, together with assumptions on fee increases
3 December	Current year budget, expenditure to date and blank pro formas mailed to senior management

	team members. Directors review plans with service managers and consolidate them into departmental and regional plans and budget bids
9 December	Progress report to Governing Council
17 January	All completed operating plans and budgets to be with Director of Finance
18 February	Summarized national operating plan and budget mailed to senior management team
27–28 February	Residential meeting. All Directors present plans for scrutiny by colleagues. Revisions agreed for submission to Governing Council
22 March	Council agrees operating plan and budget
1 April	New financial year begins.

SUMMARY OF KEY POINTS

Definition of services and campaigns

- The notion of service delivery units helps to distinguish separate services.
- An activity can be considered a service delivery unit only if it has:
  — a defined user group
  — its own objectives and strategy
  — outputs that can be monitored
  — financial information to control income and expenditure
  — a manager to plan, deliver and monitor the service.

Service strategies

- Organizations need a planning architecture that defines how overall, service and operational plans fit together.
- Service plans describe the objectives, strategies and plans for each service the organization delivers. They are prepared in two stages: the review and the plan.
- The process for preparing service plans needs to be co-ordinated at the corporate level.

- Typical contents include:
  - — summary of the review
  - — description of the service
  - — summary of existing and potential service users
  - — objectives for the next three years
  - — the overall strategy
  - — specific targets
  - — timetable for implementation
  - — human resource requirements
  - — financial resource requirements
  - — sources of funding.

Operational plans

- Operational plans link proposed activities to budgets.
- The process starts with approval of guidelines by the board and ends with agreement of a budget for the year ahead.

8 Managing Strategic Performance

8.1 STAKEHOLDERS NEED MEASURABLE RESULTS

Performance management is the fourth essential component of strategic management. Third-sector organizations have put great effort into strategic planning over the last fifteen years, but they have found that the most difficult problems are associated with implementation of their plans. Many were disappointed when the organization's momentum kept moving in the same direction. The 'push' behind the plan existed, but there was nothing to 'pull' people in new directions.

Organizations therefore need a tool to focus people at all levels on the new priorities and to let them know how well they are performing against the plan targets. Establishing a performance-management system is one way of focusing people on implementation.

Performance management is particularly important in third-sector organizations because, unlike businesses, few have the benefit of strong market forces to provide an external check on performance. Since they also do not have the discipline of accountability to shareholders, self-imposed measures of performance are needed to ensure that the best intentions do result in effective services.

It is rather surprising that most third-sector organizations have well-developed systems for monitoring their financial performance, but remarkably under-developed systems for monitoring achievements for their users. One reason for this is that it is much more difficult to monitor achievements; unlike financial management, there is no common currency for monitoring performance. However, the expectations placed on third-sector organizations are growing, both from within and from external stakeholders.

Stakeholders want to know what is being achieved, whether quality is of the required standard and whether users are satisfied. Funders want to know what their money has achieved. As the third sector grows, funders have more options as to which organizations to fund. Organizations that can demonstrate the results they have achieved with the funds provided and, more ambitiously, that they offer best value for money will inevitably receive more resources than those that do not have the evidence to support their case.

Users are also taking a growing interest in how organizations are performing. Examples include people with disabilities who want to know more about the achievements of the organizations that assist and represent them, housing association tenants who want to know how their association is performing, and parents who want to know how their children's schools are performing.

People throughout the organization benefit from having a clear view of its overall performance so that they can see what it has achieved. Board members need to take particular interest in strategic performance and ensure that the organization is providing value for money. Senior managers need tools with which to manage the overall performance of their organization. Divisional directors need to know how the various parts of their division are performing, and service managers need to know how their part of the organization is performing, and keep staff focused on the critical issues.

Performance monitoring gives management the evidence they need to determine whether their decisions are leading to the desired results. It also provides a way of holding people more accountable for their work.

Four great benefits flow from strengthening performance-management processes. First, it **focuses people on results**. Although targets often have a slightly artificial feel about them, their existence encourages people to think more clearly about the relationships between the work they do and the results that are achieved.

Secondly, it forces people to be more **realistic about the objectives** they set. People who work in third-sector organizations are notorious for setting themselves particularly ambitious objectives – an understandable characteristic, given their commitment to their cause. The introduction of performance monitoring forces people to think much more rigorously about what can be achieved with given resources in a given timescale and consequently set plans that are more achievable.

Thirdly, the existence of a performance-management system helps **people to concentrate their attention on the agreed priorities** when the very nature of these organizations is that people are surrounded by other opportunities that may all fit within the mission but are not the most pressing matters.

Finally, organizations that have strengthened their performance management report that great benefit comes from **the process of establishing the system**, as well as the resulting performance reports. Time spent thinking about performance at each level in the organization helps to clarify priorities and deepen understanding of how resources should be deployed to achieve the desired outcomes.

This chapter sets out:

- the concepts behind performance management
- a typology of performance indicators
- methods for strengthening performance-management processes
- how to use benchmarking to improve performance
- quality-management techniques for improving performance
- how to ensure financial information systems support performance management.

8.2 CONCEPTS BEHIND PERFORMANCE MANAGEMENT

There are two key concepts that underpin the idea of managing strategic performance. They are:

- the performance-management cycle
- the system of accountability.

Requiring managers to think about measurable results helps to move people beyond the good intentions of planning and into the realities of implementation. Performance management closes the loop that begins with strategic planning and ends with a better understanding of how effectiveness can be improved. Performance management is therefore the system that helps people at each level understand how they are doing and how they should subsequently adjust their plans.

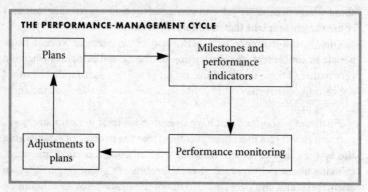

THE PERFORMANCE-MANAGEMENT CYCLE

Plans → Milestones and performance indicators

Adjustments to plans ← Performance monitoring

Secondly, performance management provides a basis for holding people accountable for their work in a more structured and systematic way. Accountability needs to exist at each level in an organization. Trustees should be holding the chief executive accountable for the overall performance of the organization, senior management should be holding their managers accountable, and they in turn should be holding individuals accountable for performance. All need to be in a constructive dialogue that focuses on results and priorities for future action.

When considering strengthening performance monitoring, it is useful to distinguish between strategic and operational monitoring because they require different approaches and have different timescales. Strategic performance is concerned with information about the overall and longer-term performance of the organization and its main services. It addresses questions about:

- what, overall, the organization, division or service has achieved
- whether agreed developments have been introduced on schedule
- what funders and users think of the services
- whether they are providing value for money.

It is undertaken annually (less frequently if the organization or service is running well and there are no significant changes in the external environment). One way of thinking about performance monitoring is to see it as 'regularizing' the strategic reviews which were probably carried out both when the organization prepared a strategic plan for the first time and when individual services prepared their first strategic plans.

STRATEGIC PERFORMANCE OF RNIB

RNIB's strategic plan had four over-arching aims, supported by twelve specific objectives for services and fifteen for resourcing the organization. Here is a sample of the objectives, the targets and achievements halfway through implementation of the plan.

Aim	Target	Achievement at halfway point
Raise awareness and tackle discrimination		
Raise awareness of RNIB and its services	Increase total awareness among the public from 74% to 85%	84%
Reduce discrimination	One significant campaign success for each age group every three years	Young people: 1 Working age: 3 Elderly: 1 All ages: 5
Extend services		
Increase the number of people reached by direct services	Young: +67% Working age: +50% Elderly: +110% All:	+38% +22% +74% +70%

This illustrates a good mix of quantitative and qualitative measures. It also demonstrates that some achievements may not have been anticipated (e.g. the initiatives to reach all blind people).

Operational performance is concerned with measuring ongoing achievements for beneficiaries. Just as strategic-performance information is valuable at both the organization-wide level and for its main services, so operational performance is needed at both levels. It provides information on:

● trends in numbers of people assisted

- trends in types of assistance given
- trends in the use of the organization's resources.

It should be part of a system that produces information regularly and in reasonably standard formats.

The greatest value of performance monitoring is that it forces people to think about the ways in which their work is linked to benefits for end users. In the maelstrom of daily activities it is easy to get so caught up in the means by which work is done that the end purpose is forgotten.

8.3 PEFORMANCE INDICATORS

Performance indicators are an important concept for performance management. Organizations need measures to determine the extent to which they are achieving their objectives. Some of these measures will be descriptive and qualitative; others will be statistical and quantitative in nature. Together they are known as performance indicators.

Indicators can be used to inform people how well a service, a division or an organization as a whole is performing. They help board members and managers stand back from the detail of day-to-day operations and see whether their efforts are achieving the desired results.

Indicators of service users' views are particularly important because user information tells managers how users rate the services they offer, what they appreciate and where they think improvements can be made. User information can be compared across services by asking people for their overall opinions of different services.

There are compelling reasons for having a range of performance indicators:

- **They focus people and resources on the achievement of objectives** – rather than allowing effort to be dissipated on many activities.
- **They provide information on how efficiently services are being delivered** – so managers know where to focus their attention.
- **They give managers feedback on users' views** – so managers know what to improve.
- **They identify trends and allow comparisons with other similar**

services – so managers know how they compare with internal and external benchmarks.

However, performance indicators can be the subject of much controversy, with protagonists arguing that, without indicators, no one knows how well the organization is doing, and those opposed arguing that the complexity of third-sector organizations means that indicators are of little practical use. The most common objections are that:

● **It is difficult to measure the quality of services** – and quality is often as important as quantity. A simple measure will seldom reflect people's complex needs.

● **It is difficult to link cause and effect** – because the relationship between actions and results is not clear-cut. For example, campaigns that result in policy changes are usually the result of actions taken by many different organizations.

● **Monitoring overemphasizes the quantifiable** – because it encourages people to put more emphasis on measurable results, leading staff to focus on achieving specific targets rather than an improvement of the service as a whole.

● **It is hard to obtain reliable data** – for example, information that is dependent on people reporting on their behaviour (such as drug misuse). There can also be issues of confidentiality (where service users do not wish to be followed up) and of accuracy (where people who are dependent on a service do not wish to be critical for fear of losing it).

● **Indicators seldom shed light on the overall performance of an organization** – they usually relate to individual services that are different in nature, so achievements cannot be aggregated to give an overview of performance.

● **It is an unnecessary expense** – particularly when resources are scarce and people believe that funds should be focused on improving or expanding the service rather than measuring it.

● **What gets measured gets manipulated** – a well-known adage pointing out that all measurement systems can be distorted by their users.

Over the last few years managers have been taking much greater interest in performance indicators and striving to find ways of overcoming the difficulties and objections. Learning is at an early stage of development, but more and more examples of successful applications are emerging.

Performance indicators for services and overall strategy

Indicators to measure the performance of services and overall strategy can be categorized into:

- **input indicators**, which measure the resources the organization uses
- **process indicators**, which measure the activities the organization undertakes
- **output indicators**, which measure the work the organization does
- **outcome indicators**, which measure the consequences of the organization's work.

SOME EXAMPLES OF PERFORMANCE INDICATORS

Input indicators	income, staff time, volunteer numbers and time contributed, gifts in kind
Process indicators	response times, backlogs and arrears, clear-up rates, seat and bed occupancy, length of waiting lists
Output indicators	people housed, inquiries answered, courses delivered, counselling sessions held, number of performances
Outcome indicators	people who secured employment, people who stopped using drugs, people successfully housed, qualifications gained

---

Some organizations draw a distinction between **outcomes** (the results of the work for the individuals concerned) and **impacts** (the ultimate achievements for the wider community).

Indicators can be combined together to create measures of **efficiency**. Efficiency measures how well the resources were used and is usually expressed in terms of the cost of achieving one unit of the desired output, for example cost per inquiry or cost per course participant. Efficiency can also be measured in terms of time to achieve the desired output, for example time to place volunteers or time to house homeless people.

Indicators can also be combined to create measures of **effectiveness.** Effectiveness measures achievements from the available resources and is usually expressed in terms of the cost of achieving one unit of the desired outcome. Examples include the cost per successful placement or the cost per qualification gained. Effectiveness can also be measured in terms of time taken to achieve the desired outcome, for example staff hours per person successfully rehabilitated.

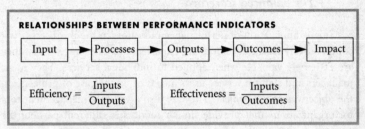

RELATIONSHIPS BETWEEN PERFORMANCE INDICATORS

Input → Processes → Outputs → Outcomes → Impact

$$\text{Efficiency} = \frac{\text{Inputs}}{\text{Outputs}}$$

$$\text{Effectiveness} = \frac{\text{Inputs}}{\text{Outcomes}}$$

User satisfaction indicators

User satisfaction indicators can be qualitative and quantitative. Both are important in getting an overall picture of user satisfaction. Qualitative information comes from asking users open questions about a service, then looking at the patterns in the responses to determine how users view the service. Quantitative information comes from asking users to rate each aspect of a service, usually on a scale of 1 to 5. This numbering is important because it allows managers to aggregate the scores and find out which aspects of the service deserve attention. It also allows organizations to follow trends over time to determine whether users are becoming less or more satisfied.

Performance indicators for projects and special initiatives

Projects and special initiatives may require different types of indicators, since progress rather than ultimate achievements may be more important to management. Progress is best measured using **milestones**. Plans and projects can be divided into stages, and timetables can be attached to the achievement of each stage. This is sometimes called a milestone plan. It sets out what will be achieved and by when, and it can be used by managers as one way of holding people accountable for their work. Milestones are particularly useful for 'one-off' pieces of work, where other performance indicators are just not appropriate.

The balanced scorecard

Systematic application of performance indicators in the third sector is a comparatively recent development. Experience to date suggests that they are extremely valuable when applied to individual services. They focus managers and staff on service users' needs or, in the case of projects, on the objectives of the project. They are also a valuable management tool for organizations that provide similar services in different parts of the country, as they can be added up to give a national overview.

They are more problematic when organizations that provide a wide range of different services wish to develop an overview of their performance. In many cases the indicators cannot easily be added together to give an overview. One alternative is to focus on the performance of the major services as a proxy for monitoring the achievements of the organization as a whole.

Another alternative that is gaining popularity in the private sector is to identify a basket of measures and report on these on a regular basis and in a standard format. These reports can be used to make judgements about the achievement of the organization's overall objectives. This is known as the **balanced scorecard**. It is a range of indicators that gives an overview of performance on all the dimensions that are critical to an organization's future success. Indicators have to be chosen to suit each organization; they could include service-output indicators, user feedback, investment in organization learning, financial results and other data that will tell people about the overall performance of the organization.

Despite the challenges, organizations are increasingly moving towards gathering data that helps to monitor performance. They are collecting quantifiable data on the results of services and qualitative and quantitative information from users.

8.4 STRENGTHENING PERFORMANCE-MANAGEMENT SYSTEMS

Strengthening performance-management systems is the final stage in creating a strategically managed organization. It is also the most challenging and is dependent on other stages having been successfully introduced. Organizations that embark on developing their performance-management systems therefore need to be sure that:

● directors and managers are clear about the overall strategy of the organization and the objectives of individual services
● there is a well-established planning process
● there is strong commitment to further developing the organization's strategic management process.

All organizations have some form of performance management. Existing systems may include:

● the annual report
● reports to board meetings
● reviews of strategy
● verbal reports at AGMs
● reports to funders.

Strengthening this system is a significant task. Every organization has to tailor the system both to the types of services it provides and to its own management and governance structures.

At present, many organizations do not have systems that capture and distil high-level information about overall performance. Often the information required is located in various parts of the organization and is held in a mixture of manual and electronic systems and sometimes at different geographical locations. Sometimes it exists as raw data but has not been summarized and presented in ways that help people to make judgements about performance against targets. Sometimes effort has been put into gathering the information together, but processes that enable the board and senior management to review overall performance regularly and systematically have not been established.

Experience from the private sector suggests that it takes many years to create a culture in which performance management is an integral part of every manager's work. Given that third-sector organizations are often more diverse and that measuring performance is less straightforward, managers should anticipate that they will have to put significant effort into this final stage of establishing their strategic management process.

DEVELOPING PERFORMANCE-MANAGEMENT SYSTEMS AT NSPCC

The National Society for the Prevention of Cruelty to Children runs 150 child-protection teams and projects. Its primary aim is to prevent child abuse and to help families at risk.

For many years the organization had collected information on the numbers of children treated, assessments carried out and abuses prevented. Management wanted to take this further and probe into the organization's efficiency and effectiveness. They began by asking board members to define what information they needed in order to do their job. Their requirements were comparatively straightforward, but meeting them was a nightmare:

- similar activities were defined in different ways
- activity data was collected on a number of different systems
- costs were counted in different ways in different parts of the country
- there was considerable scepticism from staff about the value of collecting this information.

Before any useful data could be gathered, the Finance Division had to restructure the accounts so that all management information was derived from the general ledger. Senior management had to redefine activities from 137 down to 35 clearly specified services, and new software had to be installed to take data from a variety of different sources and produce managerially useful information. Costs had to be defined and categorized in consistent ways, and discipline over submitting data had to be greatly improved.

Two years into the initiative, it was widely recognized that, while progress had been made, it was going to take more effort and time both to get full ownership of the system and to produce the data that the board required in a consistent, timely and regular way.

Practicalities of strengthening performance-management processes

The first step is to decide whether to work on strengthening the strategic or the operational performance-management process. If the monitoring of operations is not well developed, then that is likely to be the place to start. The next step is to decide whether to start with a pilot. As performance management is a comparatively new development, there is much learning to be done. Pilots are therefore a good way of getting started.

Establishing or strengthening strategic or operational performance-management processes should be treated as a project. It needs to have clear objectives, a timetable, a team of people from each department affected by the proposals and a project champion who has clear responsibility for seeing it through to completion. The champion and the project team need the authority of the chief executive and the senior management team to ensure that the actions required in each division will be carried through.

In medium- and larger-sized organizations the team will probably have to meet between four and six times over a three- to six-month period to agree:

- the data that needs to be captured to inform people about the extent to which objectives have been achieved
- the format in which data will be reported
- how often to review performance
- who will be responsible for preparation of performance information
- how the results and any associated commentary will be communicated to the board, the staff and other stakeholders
- how feedback from the board and senior management will be reported back down the line.

PERFORMANCE INDICATORS AT THE ROYAL NATIONAL INSTITUTE FOR THE BLIND

RNIB (income £65 million) provides over sixty separate services for visually impaired people. It has developed a corporate performance monitoring system which aims to draw together for each service:
- the number of people assisted by each service

- the outcomes of services (where this information can be captured)
- the cost of providing the service
- the subsidy RNIB invests in the service
- qualitative and some quantitative data on service quality.

This information is circulated regularly to senior management and the governing board with a commentary on the significant trends.

The services also collect performance data for use at the operational level.

The stages of a project to strengthen performance management could be as follows:

1. Check the prerequisites are in place:
   - that there are clear objectives and strategies for the areas of work to be monitored and well-established planning processes
   - that people are clear whether it is strategic or operational performance monitoring that requires strengthening.

2. Establish a project team:
   - involve a cross-section of people at different levels and people from parts of the organization that will be affected by the proposals.

3. Build commitment to the value of managing performance:
   - discuss the purpose and need with staff and allow people an opportunity to raise their concerns
   - plan how the process of strengthening performance monitoring will be undertaken with staff and trustees
   - set boundaries on the scope of the project to ensure that it is not too ambitious
   - agree that proposals will be piloted.

4. Decide what data to capture:
   - this is likely to require a 'trial and error' approach to match what ideally might be needed with the information that is realistic to collect.

5. Ask line managers to propose targets:
   - focus initially on a very limited number of measures (no more than 3–5 per service)

- ask for a mixture of quantitative and qualitative measures
- keep them simple.

6. Set up a reporting process:
   - agree report formats
   - keep it to the minimum necessary to avoid over-bureaucratizing the process. Ideally, the report should be a 'scorecard' that can be distributed in the same way as budget performance is reported to staff and directors
   - agree frequency of reporting to different groups.

An important test of the use of strategic performance management is to ask whether the report led to any actions.

PERFORMANCE MONITORING AT BROADCASTING SUPPORT SERVICES

BSS provides follow-up services to the public on behalf of broadcasters, to advance education, promote health and relieve poverty. It identified lack of a performance-monitoring system as a key reason for difficulty in implementing a strategic plan. Consequently, when a new plan was established, management went to great lengths to involve as many people as possible to ensure ownership of the corporate priorities.

The plan has seven strategic objectives which guide all activities in the organization. These objectives are hung on the wall of every office to ensure that people do not lose sight of them! The main report to regular board meetings is organized under seven headings, corresponding to the seven objectives. Each section of the organization reports quarterly on its achievements, broadly following the seven objectives. The Senior Management Team reviews progress against the plan objectives quarterly.

According to BSS, 'the key to the success of our system is that we have kept it short and simple. Our first attempt was too complicated. Now it's simplified it keeps staff and the board acutely aware of the corporate priorities. It has been a major contributor to our successful development over the last few years.'

Performance management will become increasingly important in the coming years. Organizations that have worked on making improvements in this area say:

- it is an enabling tool
- it disciplines people to be more realistic about objectives
- it provides vital feedback from users on a regular basis
- it gives people a framework for looking at achievements more systematically
- it drives people to think about implementation when they've got stuck in a planning mode.

8.5 BENCHMARKING CATALYSES PERFORMANCE IMPROVEMENTS

Benchmarking is a systematic process for improving performance by making detailed comparisons between organizations and using the information to catalyse improvements. It has been defined as 'the search for best practices that lead to superior performance'.

It is widely used in the private and public sectors and is growing in popularity in the third sector. It is a valuable tool for developing an understanding of how an organization performs in comparison with others and why its performance is different.

It is undoubtedly an effective catalyst for change, and some see it as a means of operationalizing the idea of continuous commitment to learning.

However, it is not a panacea. While it supports a process of incremental change, it is not a source of innovation. It helps management to understand how their existing processes and services compare with other organizations, but it is unlikely to be the source of a major breakthrough.

Benchmarking has great potential in the third sector because:

- the sector has a culture that values co-operation as a way of achieving the best results for service users
- there is a strong tradition of developing best practices – an important outcome of benchmarking exercises
- it can be a highly participative process.

Benchmarking is not just about **comparing statistical data** on performance. Indeed there is much evidence that excessive effort applied to gathering ever more detailed numbers can be counter-productive. It is also about **identifying good practices** that are qualitative in nature. Most important of all, it aims to understand **why** performance differs and **what** needs to change for an organization or service to achieve or exceed the benchmark.

There are three types of benchmarking:

● **service benchmarking** – which is used to compare the performance of each service an organization offers
● **process benchmarking** – which is used to compare the processes, work practices and management procedures an organization uses
● **strategic benchmarking** – which is used to compare organization structures and strategies.

These categories are useful for thinking about which type of benchmarking would have the greatest impact on an organization's performance, but they may have to be applied in combination. For example, benchmarking a service might require managers to compare the processes used to deliver the service or even differences in the service strategies being pursued by different organizations.

Benchmarking is usually carried out by making comparisons between organizations. However, in larger organizations comparisons can be made between different parts of the organization. In some areas self-assessment benchmarking schemes have been established that enable organizations or services to assess themselves against a previously defined set of benchmarks.

Sometimes benchmarking is undertaken by one organization taking the initiative to gather data to compare its performance with other organizations. More often, people form a benchmarking club, in which all the members of the club compare performance with each other. Club members can both share the information and work with one another to **identify the underlying reasons** for the differences in performance. They can even support one another in developing ways to improve their performance in areas that are below the benchmark.

Before embarking on a benchmarking exercise it is important to make a realistic judgement about the time and effort that will be put into it. A survey of benchmarking in over a hundred businesses found that the average project lasted twenty-three weeks and involved thirty person-weeks in total.

A benchmarking exercise typically has six stages:

1. **Determine what to benchmark**. The first step is to determine where performance is thought to be low and to decide whether the service, the process or the strategy should be benchmarked.
2. **Form a benchmarking team**. Using a team ensures that many people feel ownership of the project. Decisions need to be taken about leadership of the team and whether to involve service users, board members and other stakeholders.
3. **Identify benchmarking partners**. Decisions are required about whether to gather data independently or to form a benchmarking club. Either way, one of the most difficult areas of agreement is which organizations to compare performance against. The options include:

● organizations in the same sector and field of work (e.g. another housing organization providing a similar service)
● organizations in the same sector but in a different field (e.g. charities in different fields of work)
● organizations in different sectors that provide similar services (e.g. comparing third-sector suppliers with organizations in the public and private sectors).

It is worth putting considerable effort into this stage, as the experience of the other organizations will be a major determinant of the overall success of the exercise.

4. **Collect and analyse benchmarking information**. Decisions need to be taken about what information to collect, how to collect it and how it will be drawn together. Issues of confidentiality may arise at this point. Where people have concerns, a third party can be used to collect and analyse the data. It can then be reported back in a format that allows each organization to compare their performance with the other contributors, but without identifying them individually.

It is tempting at this stage to attempt to collect a wide range of information to ensure that all participants are confident that nothing important will be missed. However, experience suggests that there is a grave danger of being over-ambitious and unrealistic about the time it takes to analyse and report on findings.

There is also a trade-off to be made between collecting a lot of poor-quality information and a little really good information. Since the credibility of the benchmarking process is entirely dependent on the data gathered, it is usually better to err on the side of caution and, if necessary, collect further information when the value of the initial information has been proven.

5. **Identify the underlying reasons for differences in performance**. This stage is critical for moving beyond interesting information to gaining insights into why performance differs among organizations. A process of discussion and investigation within and between the participating organizations is needed to explore how things are done differently and to identify what might be changed to improve performance.

6. **Take action on the findings**. This final stage requires organizations to take decisions on changes and to establish groups to implement agreed actions. This will ensure that the results of all the effort are turned into improved performance.

BENCHMARKING COMMUNITY DRUGS AGENCIES

A project was undertaken to compare the performance of eighteen community drugs agencies, funded by the Department of Health. Information on what to benchmark was gathered through a series of interviews and workshops with leaders of the agencies. A questionnaire was prepared and tested on a sample of agencies.

Topics covered included overall management of the agencies, governance, service delivery methods and performance of each of the services offered, such as needle exchange, counselling, drop-in and therapy. The project identified good practices in governance and management and developed a set of performance benchmarks which agencies could compare against their own performance. The report made a series of recommendations on ways in which community drugs agencies could increase their effectiveness.

The range of topics that third-sector organizations can benchmark is wide and includes:

- service delivery and quality
- user involvement and satisfaction
- membership services
- trading operations
- volunteer management

- personnel practices
- training
- contracting practices
- financial management.

Benchmarking does take time and investment of effort. It requires strong support from senior management and it works best if there is a project champion. When these are provided, it is particularly good at convincing people of the need for change, identifying creative ways to improve existing services and helping people to establish more ambitious object- ives.

It should be stressed that benchmarking is always the start of a process. It is an unthreatening way of introducing people to change, enabling people to share best-in-the-class performance, and to go on to establish ambitious aims and action plans to achieve or exceed current best practice.

In an increasingly competitive environment, third-sector organizations are under growing pressure to demonstrate that they deliver value for money. Until recently this has required management to address the 'big picture' issues of strategic planning, structures and governance. Now that the agenda is moving on, organizations have to focus on fine-tuning their services and management processes. Benchmarking is a powerful tool that helps organizations to work systematically on maximizing both their effectiveness and their efficiency.

8.6 CONTINUOUS IMPROVEMENT THROUGH QUALITY MANAGEMENT

Quality management is widely seen as having an important role to play in increasing the effectiveness of third-sector organizations. Although organizations have always striven for quality in their work, many now wish to take a more formal and rigorous approach to improving quality. Some have acquired formal accreditation for their quality-management regime and some seek external assessment to compare their standards with their achievements.

Quality management is concerned with improving all aspects of an organization's work; it is not just concerned with the quality of its services. It should lead to improvements in people, processes and performance.

Everyone aspires to achieve quality in their work, so it is reasonable to ask why quality systems are needed or whether they are just another management fad. Quality-management systems are required because directors and managers need to be able to answer the question, 'How well are we doing?' They need to be able to give answers to users, purchasers, funders and other stakeholders. And when an organization is not working to the highest standards, they must have the evidence needed to convince people of the need for change.

To do all this requires the establishment of standards and then monitoring performance against those standards. The organization is then in a position to make improvements in those areas that do not meet the agreed standards. Although it sounds simple in theory, the practice is not quite so straightforward.

The field of quality management is at an early stage of development in the third sector and most of the work to date has drawn on experience from the private sector. Much of this is based on quality systems that help people think through the issues of quality and use tested techniques to improve quality. Three systems (Investors in People, Social Audit and Codes of Practice) and one overall framework (the Excellence Model) are particularly relevant to the third sector.

However, systems are only as good as the people who operate them, and the key to quality is building people's commitment to quality and an organization culture that encourages people to strive to make continuous improvements.

QUALITY PRINCIPLES

The National Council for Voluntary Organizations Quality Standards Task Group established six principles that define a quality voluntary organization. An organization committed to quality:

- strives for continuous improvements in all it does
- uses recognized standards as a means to continuous improvement and not as an end
- agrees requirements with stakeholders and endeavours to meet or exceed these first (and every) time

- promotes equality of opportunity through its internal and external conduct
- is accountable to stakeholders
- adds value to its end users and beneficiaries.

This section describes the quality systems that are most appropriate to third-sector organizations and how to apply them.

Investors in People

Investors in People aims to improve organizations' performance by linking objectives to investments in people's skills and abilities. The system focuses on performance in:

- business planning
- communication
- induction
- setting objectives
- management effectiveness
- training and development procedures
- evaluation
- performance review.

Investors in People is based on four principles:

1. **commitment:** to invest in people to achieve organization goals
2. **planning:** how skills of individuals and teams are to be developed to achieve these goals
3. **action:** to develop and use necessary skills in a well-defined and continuing programme directly linked with organization objectives
4. **evaluation:** measuring progress towards goals, added value and future needs.

Organizations applying for Investors in People status have to collect evidence to show whether they meet the required standards. Investors in People status is achieved in stages in a process that can take one to two years. This involves reviewing how the organization compares with the standards, preparing and implementing an action plan to bring the organization up to the standards, assessment by an external assessor and continuous improvement in preparation for re-assessment three years later.

Social Audit

Social Audit is a process that helps organizations to account for, report on and improve their social performance and ethical behaviour. It is based on the idea that organizations should have their achievements audited just as their accounts are audited. Organizations are expected to record information about their performance (social book-keeping), prepare social accounts and have them independently audited.

It is based on six principles. A social audit should be:

1. **multi-perspective** – reflecting the views of all stakeholders
2. **comparative** – comparing performance over time and with other organizations
3. **comprehensive** – embracing all aspects of an organization's social and environmental performance
4. **regular** – usually completed annually
5. **verifiable** – by people who have no interest in the results
6. **disclosed** – made available to all stakeholders.

The external verifiers should ensure that the **process** has been carried out fairly and that the **results** are a fair representation of the organization's performance.

Codes of Practice

The aim of this initiative is to help organizations develop codes of practice so that they can demonstrate their accountability and effectiveness. Aimed at voluntary organizations, it proposes that codes of practice be developed under eight headings:

- effectiveness
- accountability
- standards
- user involvement
- governance

- voluntary action
- equality and fairness
- staff management.

This approach is not exclusive. It could be combined with other approaches to quality, since it focuses on the development of standards that organizations should aspire to achieve.

The Excellence Model

The Excellence Model is a self-assessment framework which recognizes that there are many approaches to improving quality. The model has nine elements, each of which can be assessed to determine the organization's progress towards achieving excellence. The nine elements are divided into two categories: **enablers**, that are concerned with how the organization is managed, and **results**, that are concerned with what the organization achieves.

Each element is measured using a set of criteria. For example, the definition of **processes** is:

'the management of all value-adding activities within the organization. How the organization identifies, manages, reviews and improves its processes.'

The criteria for this element are:

- how processes key to the success of the organization are identified
- how processes are systematically managed
- how processes are reviewed and targets set for improvement
- how processes are improved using innovation and creativity
- how processes are changed and the benefits evaluated.

The elements are weighted to determine the overall performance of the organization (e.g. leadership accounts for 10 per cent, processes 14 per cent, results 15 per cent). In total, the enablers account for 50 per cent of performance and results account for 50 per cent.

The Excellence Model has recently been selected by the NCVO Quality Standards Task Force as the preferred model for voluntary organizations, and they are now tailoring it to suit this sector.

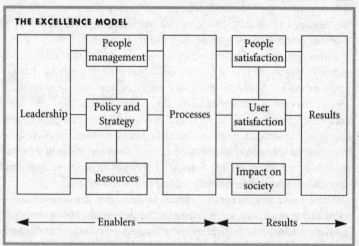

THE EXCELLENCE MODEL

These quality systems are tools that help organizations to take a structured approach to developing the quality of their work. They provide an intellectual framework which managers can use to launch a quality initiative. They also allow organizations to demonstrate to their stakeholders that they take quality seriously.

Managers need to decide which system best suits their organization's circumstances. Some third-sector organizations have sought recognition by Investors in People and report that the process enabled people at all levels of the organization to work on improving quality. Some are experimenting with Social Audit and others are applying the Excellence Model.

8.7 ENSURING FINANCIAL INFORMATION SUPPORTS MANAGEMENT

The final section of this chapter looks at financial information. It is included here because financial information is so critical to managers who wish to improve performance.

Financial management systems are one means by which organizations give people responsibility and hold them accountable for their actions. Organizations that develop a culture of delegating responsibility can encourage people to feel accountable by providing timely information in the required formats. Good financial management information is an essential corollary to delegation of authority.

Third-sector organizations often do not compare well with either the public or private sectors in the sophistication of their financial management processes. Many business and public-sector managers expect to receive relevant, accurate and up-to-date figures within a few days of the end of each month. These are set out in ways that highlight the performance information managers need to control their organizations. In third-sector organizations, financial information is sometimes not presented in ways that assist management to understand the performance of individual services and campaigns or of the organization as a whole.

Three financial concepts are central to managing the performance of third-sector organizations. All three are fundamentally about presenting information in ways that trustees and managers need in order to discharge their responsibilities effectively.

This section explains:

● why management accounting should be treated as a service that meets needs defined by its users, i.e. other managers
● why managers should price services using total costs but be held accountable only for the variable costs that they control
● why trustees should focus on how unrestricted income (i.e. income that is not attached to particular projects or services) is allocated to each service.

Management accounting is a service

The essential elements of a good financial management process are straightforward. Organizations need a budget, a system that records income and expenditure and provides up-to-date accounts relevant to each level of the organization. Service managers need information about the income and expenditure that they control and the subsidy they require. Departmental managers need summaries of the services for which they are responsible. Senior management and the board require an overview of income and expenditure, a balance sheet and a cash-flow forecast.

That is the ideal, but it takes hard work to achieve it. A series of common problems ensures that many managers may not have the information they require in an appropriate format. These include:

- management accounts that arrive late – sometimes 30–60 days after the month end, when seven days is quite achievable
- accounts that are inaccurate – as a result of misallocation to budget holder accounts, late payments or early receipts
- overhead costs that are not separated out of service managers' accounts, so they cannot distinguish between the costs they control and those that they do not (for which they should not be held accountable)
- expenditure not subtracted from income, so managers cannot see at a glance whether their service is generating a contribution to overheads or requiring a subsidy
- costs that are incurred continuously but charged infrequently (e.g. heating), and that are not accrued, so accounts look good until a bumper invoice hits the system
- budgets that are not varied month by month to take account of cyclical demand or skewed expenditure patterns
- accounts that are produced in a standard format that suits the accounts department computer system but not the needs of service managers
- information needs of different users, such as board members, senior management and service managers, that are not differentiated to help them focus on their responsibilities.

Even when the information is available, some managers are unable to use it properly because they have not had the training or received clear explanations of how to interpret the information.

To overcome these problems, the finance department needs to see financial management as a service that has to meet the different needs of its different users. These users include the board, directors and managers, each of whom needs financial information for different purposes. In return, service managers need to ensure that their financial submissions are accurate and made exactly on time. In particular, service managers who come from non-financial backgrounds need to acknowledge that financial management is a central part of their job.

The job of the management accounts service is to work with each user group to agree what their needs are and how they can be met. Appropriate formats, frequency of reporting and levels of detail should be established so users get what they need (consistent with the cost of producing the information, of course). Training and support should be provided to help people understand how figures are derived and how to analyse reports.

FINANCIAL MANAGEMENT INFORMATION AT SENSE

SENSE provides a dozen different services for children and young adults who are both deaf and blind. Income of £30 million p.a. comes from statutory sources, foundations, companies and donors. It is structured into geographical divisions.

The board and the senior management team receive: an overall financial statement showing income, expenditure, surplus (and deficit) figures for each main service for:
● last month
● the year to date.

All figures show:
● budget
● actual
● variance
alongside each other for easy comparison. These are set beside the annual budget with notes explaining unexpected differences.

Regional and departmental directors receive: income and expenditure statements broken down into cost centres, with budget, actual and variance figures for easy comparison.

Service managers receive: cost-centre reports broken down into single budget codes with budget, actual and variance figures.

On request, any manager can receive a nominal account listing of all transactions on a single budget code. Managers at regional centres can access this directly from their own terminals.

Hold service managers accountable for financial contribution

Financial contribution is a fundamental principle of management accounting that is particularly applicable to service delivery organizations funded by statutory authorities and service users. The principle is used widely in commercial organizations, but less often in third-sector bodies. As contract funding grows, it has become increasingly useful.

The principle is that managers should be held accountable only for the income and expenditure that they are responsible for controlling. They should not be held accountable for costs that may be attributable to their service but which they cannot control in practice (for example, a proportion of the cost of the headquarters).

In summary, a service manager's account should have the following lines:

	£
Income from providing the service (grants, sales)	a
Direct costs of the service (costs incurred exclusively in providing the service)	b
Contribution to overheads (or subsidy required to finance the service)	a−b
Overhead costs (i.e. proportion of fixed overheads charged to the service)	c
Surplus or deficit from the service	a−b−c

Service managers are responsible for managing the contribution line. They usually have control over the income, which can be increased by raising prices (for example, to purchasing authorities) or by seeking additional grant funding. They also control expenditure, and they should be in a position to reduce expenditure if income falls or increase it if demand for the service and income rise. They should not, however, be held accountable for the bottom line (surplus or deficit), because they do not take the decisions that affect overhead costs.

Service managers need to know what the bottom line is, because this information will influence the setting of prices. Furthermore, they should be informed of the overhead costs that are being allocated to their service so that they can make judgements about whether overhead expenditure is providing value for money.

Once accounts have been set out on a contribution basis, the contribution budget of each service can then be built up into a contribution account for the organization as a whole.

The contribution approach neatly illustrates one of the perverse aspects of managing third-sector organizations. In business, when a service is

CONTRIBUTION BUDGET FOR CARE HOMES

Care Homes manages a number of homes and also has a care-in-the-community scheme. The homes are mainly funded by fees from local authorities but, in order to provide a high quality of service, Care Homes provides a subsidy from its unrestricted income.

Most of the headquarters' income is unrestricted money, raised from direct mail. It also receives a grant for a research project. Headquarters' human relations costs include finance since it is more cost-effective to provide these corporately. However, where these costs relate to homes or the care-in-the-community project, they are recharged.

£'000	Homes	Care in the community	Head-quarters	Total
INCOME				
Grants	30	50	50	130
Fees	950	140	0	1090
Donations	20	20	320	360
TOTAL	1000	210	370	1580
EXPENDITURE				
Staff	800	150	180	1130
Materials	250	50	90	390
TOTAL	1050	200	270	1520
CONTRIBUTION[1]	(50)	10	100	60
REALLOCATED OVERHEAD COSTS	30	10	(40)[2]	
SURPLUS/DEFICIT OF THE SERVICE	(80)	0	190	

[1] Service managers are responsible for managing income and expenditure to meet this target
[2] Costs recharged to Homes and Care in the Community for pricing purposes.

successful, growth in the number of customers leads to a larger financial contribution. The line a–b (above) grows and, provided overheads do not grow, the business makes a larger profit.

Some third-sector organizations have inverse economic equations. When direct costs are more than service income, every increase in the number of users leads to a larger deficit. So the more successful the service is at meeting users' needs, the greater the financial loss. As any experienced manager knows, this is a fact of life in the third sector. The advantage of the contribution approach is that it makes the economic equation of the organization entirely explicit. When each service has its own economic equation, it becomes much easier for the board and senior management to understand the financial consequences of decisions to expand or contract different services.

Focus trustees on unrestricted income

Most third-sector organizations receive money from a mixture of sources, with some restricted to particular projects and some (known as unrestricted funds) available to be spent as trustees determine. Typically, donations and profits from trading are unrestricted and grants are restricted. In recent times the proportion that is restricted has been increasing as funders have wanted to link their money with the achievement of specific objectives. Money that is unrestricted is particularly important because trustees can use it as they wish. Indeed, unrestricted income is a measure of the degree of independence the organization has to determine its own future.

The budgets and accounts that trustees and senior managers use to set overall priorities and monitor performance should clearly identify the sources of unrestricted income and how they have been applied. When information is presented in this way, management and board members can make judgements about whether funds at their disposal are being used effectively. Without this information there is a danger that valuable unrestricted income will be spent subsidizing services that trustees did not wish to subsidize.

USE OF UNRESTRICTED INCOME AT CARE HOMES

The following simple example takes data from the Care Homes management accounts in the previous box to clarify how unrestricted income was applied.

Unrestricted income

Surplus of grants and donations after headquarters' costs	100
Surplus from care-in-the-community service	10
TOTAL	110

Allocation of unrestricted income

Subsidy to homes service	50
Available for investment as trustees determine	60
TOTAL	110

Characteristics of an effective financial management process

Getting useful information to each level of management requires continuous effort. Every new development and every change in management structure has implications for the financial information system. The aim should be to keep the system bang up to date with developments in the organization.

Once the process has been agreed, it needs to provide information which is:

- relevant only to that service
- accurate
- appropriately formatted to highlight the key numbers for managing performance
- timely.

Complex multi-national businesses can produce accurate financial management reports within hours of the week- or month-end. While it is sometimes difficult to persuade board members to invest in financial systems and the associated IT, third-sector organizations should aspire to achieve similar performance standards in their finance functions.

SUMMARY OF KEY POINTS

Stakeholders need measurable results

- Monitoring strategic performance produces information on achievements.
- The benefits of a system are that it focuses people on results, makes people more realistic about objectives and keeps attention on agreed priorities.
- The greatest benefits often come from the process of establishing the system rather than the resulting performance reports.

Concepts behind performance management

- Performance management makes explicit connections between planning and implementation.
- Performance management creates a system of accountability.

Performance indicators

- Indicators can be either descriptive or statistical.
- They focus managers on objectives, show how well services are being delivered, give managers feedback on users' views and allow comparisons with other services.
- Developing really useful performance indicators requires commitment and persistence. It can be difficult to measure quality, link cause and effect, emphasize qualitative measures, obtain reliable data, summarize organization-wide performance and minimize the cost of the system.
- Indicators can be combined to give valuable measures of effectiveness and efficiency.

Strengthening performance management

- Performance-management systems have to be tailored to the types of services provided and to the organization's governance and management structure.
- Improvements should be treated as a change of management project, with objectives, a timescale, a project team and a champion.
- The processes of strengthening operational performance management should be separated from strategic performance management.

Benchmarking catalyses performance improvements
- Benchmarking aims to show why performance differs between organizations and what needs to change to exceed the benchmark.
- A benchmarking exercise typically has six stages:
  — determine what to benchmark
  — form a benchmarking team
  — identify benchmarking partners
  — collect and analyse benchmarking information
  — identify the reasons for underlying differences in performance
  — take action on the findings.

Continuous improvement through quality management
- Quality management is concerned with managing all aspects of an organization's work that should lead to improvements in people, processes and performance.
- Quality systems appropriate to the sector include:
  — Investors in People
  — Social Audit
  — Codes of Practice
  — the Excellence Model.
- Managers need to decide which quality system best suits their circumstances.

Making financial processes work for management
- Management accounting is a service that should meet the specific needs of different users of management information.
- Managers should be held accountable for the financial contribution of their service, not for costs that they do not control.
- Trustees should focus on how unrestricted funds are applied.

9 Creating Flexible Management Structures

9.1 CHANGE BY CONTINUOUS ADJUSTMENT

Structures are central to our understanding of organizations. When people describe their organization, they talk about it being structured into five departments, or having nine regions. Structures define the way the parts of the organization should fit together.

However, it is well known that the structure itself is seldom a fundamental determinant of an organization's performance. It is all too easy to blame the structure for all sorts of management problems, to invest great effort in designing and implementing a new structure, and to cause much personal angst during the transition. Months later, the original difficulties reappear because underlying problems have not been resolved.

Nevertheless, organizations do grow, new ventures are established, new posts are added and spans of control become elongated. Within a relatively short period, what looked like a rational structure quickly becomes ambiguous to people inside and outside the organization. In these circumstances, structural change is required.

In the past, structures were seen as relatively fixed and were changed infrequently, usually in one last grand effort to get them right. This view is no longer appropriate. The environment around organizations is changing much more rapidly. New sources of funding, new methods of delivering services and the need for greater efficiency all mean that organizations need to be highly flexible. The aim, therefore, is not to design the ideal structure, but to inculcate into the organization the assumption that continuous adjustments to the structure are an essential part of effective management. Those organizations that are flexible will be better able to adjust to the more uncertain and more demanding environment than those with more rigid arrangements.

This approach enables management to move beyond the traditional approach of reorganizing to catch up with changing circumstances. It encourages managers to anticipate future needs and organize around them. Growth, changing priorities and new funding methods may all require new structures. Management's task is to anticipate and adjust the structure in preparation for these new demands.

This chapter explains:

- the need to overcome obstacles to change
- options for management structures
- common dilemmas in organization design
- how to implement changes to the structure
- how to make inter-departmental groups effective.

Overcome conservatism

It is an ironic truth that many organizations committed to change and development are often conservative when it comes to changing themselves. Sometimes people who have been with an organization for a long time find it difficult to see new ways of structuring it. In other situations, people who are highly committed to the cause find it hard to put time and effort into restructuring when other pressing service and campaign matters require their attention. Similarly, professionals with expertise in fields such as health care, education and social work can be opposed to change because they fear it could threaten their professional independence.

The aspiring organization designer therefore faces an uphill task. Evidence of organizations with arrangements that have long passed their 'use-by' date is widespread:

- Small organizations committed to consensus-style management, with everyone having a say in everything, grow beyond the point where this is possible.
- Medium-sized organizations continue to operate with one person attempting to co-ordinate everything, when a senior management team is required to manage cross-departmental boundaries.
- The hierarchical structures of some long-established organizations

make decision-taking tortuously slow, even when urgent action is required.

Some organizations are easier to change than others. The pressures for change are strongest in organizations funded by the sale of their services. Here, market forces work to demonstrate a clear linkage between the need to change and the organization's survival. The pressures are weakest in donor-funded organizations where money may continue to flow in long after the organization has lost its cutting edge. Campaigning organizations, churches and development agencies therefore need to put extra effort into changing their organization if they are to maintain efficient structures for changing circumstances.

Choice of design ultimately boils down to one person's judgement against another's. Typically the protagonists for change will argue in terms of increasing efficiency and improving the organization's attractiveness to donors, and those in favour of the *status quo* will argue that the proposed changes breach important values held by the organization, such as a commitment to consensus decision-making, and they will plead for 'a period of consolidation'. Usually there is more than a grain of truth in both positions and, before long, urgently required change gets stuck in a quagmire of competing arguments. A strong-willed board, a new chief executive or the use of a consultant may be the only way to bring about change.

9.2 OPTIONS FOR STRUCTURING MANAGEMENT

The term 'management structure' refers to the way in which paid management and staff are organized into units that are held accountable to senior management and ultimately to the chief executive. At the most fundamental level, management divides into services (or campaigns) and support infrastructure (i.e. finance, fund-raising, human relations, etc.). Both of these can then be subdivided, depending on the size of the organization.

A useful way to think about the overall structure of an organization is to consider the theoretical alternatives.

THEORETICAL STRUCTURES

The theoretical alternatives for dividing an organization into divisions, departments or units are:

Structure	Examples	Advantages	Disadvantages
By function	Services Finance Fund-raising Human resource Public relations	Reflects different functional skills required to manage the organization	Risks senior management team's work being dominated by internal rather than service issues
By service users	Young people Adults Elderly	Focuses the organization on the particular needs of each client group 'Market oriented' in business language	Less suitable when service delivery is dependent on a limited pool of professional skills
By services	Education service Housing service Accident & Emergency Benefit rights service	Focuses on professional skills needed to deliver the service Recognizes different nature of services	Cumbersome for service users who need to access different services
By funder	Contract services Charitable services Sales-funded services Membership services	Focuses the organization on its funders Separates out different logic that applies to charitably funded services	Risks fragmentation of service delivery
By geography	Countries Regions	Puts decision-making close to ground Allows for regional differences	Danger of over-stretching professional skills

In practice, most organizations recognize that the structure needs to be a mixture of each type. They find that they need one or two functional departments (such as finance and fund-raising) and structure the other departments by type of service user or by service.

ALTERNATIVE STRUCTURES FOR VOLUNTARY SERVICE OVERSEAS

VSO has 1,600 volunteers working on overseas assignments in 50 different countries. In a typical year 75,000 people inquire about volunteering, 8,000 apply, 2,000 are interviewed, 1,200 are selected and 900 are placed. VSO gives training to volunteers before they leave and support while they are abroad. It also uses volunteers after they have returned and provides public education on its work. During a review, the organization considered four different structural alternatives, simplified here for clarity:

By region	*By service*
Africa	Services for poorest countries
Asia	Services for more developed countries
Latin America	Reconstruction programme
Eastern Europe	Cultural and sports programme
Fund-raising	Fund-raising
Central Services	Central Services

By volunteers' profession	*By function*
Education	Overseas
Health	Recruitment and Education
Business development	Fund-raising
Natural resources	Communications
Central Services	New services
	Finance and Administration

Following discussions among senior management team members and consultation with staff, the Director and the Board decided to retain and adjust their functional structure. They wanted to increase accountability for achieving departure targets, give special attention to the development of new services and maintain a creative tension between education and fund-raising.

The issues to consider when designing the structure include:

- the size of the senior management team
- the strategic importance of different functions
- current managers' skills and experience.

Size of the senior management team

The first issue to determine when structuring an organization is how many people should report directly to the chief executive. The main considerations are:

- **the rate of change in the external environment**: more rapid change requires faster responses by the organization and calls for a smaller senior management team that can meet at short notice and take quick decisions
- **the complexity of the organization:** more complex organizations require smaller senior management teams so that members can spend more time together co-ordinating activities and coping with the complexity
- **the stability of the senior management team:** when a group of managers have been in a post for a few years and they understand each other's assumptions, styles and skills, teams can be larger
- **past experience of the senior management team:** when the experiences of members of the team are very divergent (for example, from private, public and the third sectors), large senior management teams are difficult because members are making judgements based on different assumptions
- **the chief executive's span of control:** a larger management team means that the chief executive will take more decisions in sub-groups rather than with the team as a whole. A smaller team, however, can lead to more levels of management, with the attendant increase in bureaucracy and communication problems.

Although the size of the senior management team depends on circumstances, many chief executives find that teams of between five and seven people (including the chief executive) are optimal.

In making decisions about size, a choice has to be made between the desire to maximize the opportunities for team members to participate in decision-taking (which requires a smaller team), the need to bring specialist knowledge to the team's deliberations (requiring a larger membership), and the need to involve different stakeholder groups (also pushing up the size of the team).

The strategic importance of different functions

The size of a department has to be taken into account in designing a structure. A department that accounts for a large percentage of the organization's staff and activity usually has better claim to be represented at the top than a small department. Similarly, a department that is going to play a greater role in the future (e.g. communications) may have a better claim than one which is likely to play a smaller role in the future (e.g. legal services).

Ease of combining functions is another factor to take into account. Regional managers, for example, can often be combined together under one person more easily than a range of unrelated functions.

EVERYONE WANTS A SEAT AT THE TOP TABLE

Every department can make a compelling case for having a seat on the senior management team:

- Regional Managers argue, 'We deliver the services – without us the senior management team moves into an ivory tower, utterly removed from practical service management issues.'
- The Fund-raising Department makes the case that, 'We need to be in a position to give donors a strategic view of the organization and to represent their views to the senior management team.'
- The Communication Division reasons, 'Unless we are on the team, we will not have an overview, so we won't get our public image right and consequently won't be able to raise the money or win the campaigns.'
- The Research Department suggests, 'We hold the keys to long-term success. If we're not on the team, investment may be wasted.'

- The Personnel Department pleads, 'People are our main asset; human-resource management must have an overview and be represented.'
- The New Initiatives Team believes, 'We represent the future services that will be critical in the long term – we cannot be demoted to a second-tier position.'

And so on. The only department that seldom has to argue its corner is Finance.

Tough choices have to be made to create a workable team.

More than one team at the top

One option which a number of organizations have found helps resolve some of the design problems is to have different teams for different functions. While there will always be overlaps, it is possible to separate out some of the top team's functions. A larger team can meet less frequently to maintain an overview of all activities, and smaller teams can meet more frequently to progress matters on behalf of their colleagues.

SENIOR MANAGEMENT STRUCTURE OF UNITED RESPONSE

United Response has grown rapidly over the past ten years and now has an annual income of £27 million, with 1,800 staff. It provides a wide range of small-scale community-based support services for people with either a learning disability or a mental health problem. These include 24-hour residential care in ordinary housing, support for people within their own home, a portfolio of day services, including employment and training, mental health resource centres, supported housing, advocacy for individuals and adult family placement services.

Until recently, senior management structure was as follows:

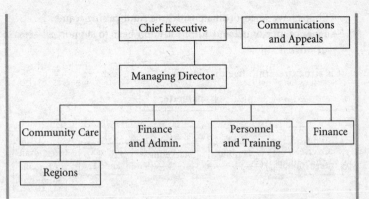

This group was divided into three teams: a **national management team** which consisted of all these managers, and met three or more times a year; a **strategic planning team**, which included the four headquarters-based directors but not the regional directors (it met monthly and was responsible for the strategic management of the organization, and it was chaired by the chief executive); an **operational management team**, which consisted of the regional directors (it was chaired by the managing director, and met monthly).

Further growth led the organization to re-structure and appoint three Regional Directors to join a streamlined senior management team.

OXFAM GB

Oxfam GB funds health, social development, agriculture, education, production, humanitarian and emerging programmes in seventy countries. It raises over £90 million through a network of over 850 shops, fund-raising appeals, direct-marketing activity and institutional fund-raising.

It is a hugely complex operation, employing over 1,000 staff in Great Britain and 1,800 internationally. There are many interdependencies within the organization:

— Fund-raising has to work closely with campaigning
— Trading imports products from overseas operations

— Shops have to co-ordinate with area fund-raising teams
— Finance, personnel and administration have to support all areas of work.

It is structured into five divisions:

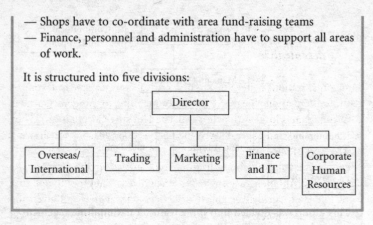

Current managers' skills and experience

The final determinant of management structure will always be the current managers. Their skills and their development needs cannot be separated from the structural issues. Holding on to talented people, giving them growth opportunities and widening people's experience are all important matters. The aspiring structure designer needs to remember that the people are the organization and that the primary purpose of the structure is to create arrangements that enable people to work together effectively to achieve the organization's objectives. Structures that are perfect on paper are of no use if they do not capitalize on the available people.

Judgements by the chief executive and board members about individuals and their potential are therefore often the most crucial element of an effective design.

9.3   **DESIGN DILEMMAS**

Organization design is an art, not a science. There are no right and wrong answers – just more effective and less effective arrangements. There are two common dilemmas:

Some want to centralize – others want to decentralize

Some organizations believe this to be a critical issue. People in favour of centralization argue the need for accountability to funders (such as government and local authorities and The Housing Corporation). They see lack of skill and experience in the field as good reasons for drawing more responsibility into the centre.

People in favour of decentralization argue just as forcibly that local or departmental differences have to be recognized. They point out that front-line staff can deliver effective services only if they are given the power and resources to do the job relatively unhindered by central control. They see the centre as a bottleneck which hinders progress and development.

The argument about centralizing or decentralizing is generally misplaced; the key is to determine which critical matters need to be managed by the centre and which can be delegated to the field. This is what business calls the **loose-tight organization**. A few matters need to be tightly controlled from the centre (e.g. resource allocation and overall strategy), and many things can be delegated to front-line managers and be subject only to loose control.

Some organizations fall into the trap of not decentralizing activities as they grow; as a result, the centre becomes a bottleneck. Despite the ever-increasing efforts that senior managers devote to the organization, the workload grows inexorably. So, someone needs to determine what tasks can be decentralized. It is seldom whole areas of work; more often it comes down to decentralizing certain aspects of each area of work. The management accounts computer needs to be centralized, but data input and report generation can be localized. Service standards need to be agreed centrally, but application is a local responsibility. The overall budget is a central responsibility but – despite the temptation to meddle – the detail should be delegated to front-line managers.

At the same time, the centre of some organizations fails to control those issues that are the critical determinants of success. The centre should have a tight grip on the overall allocation of resources to different objectives or services; it should be very clear about what specifically is being achieved for each group of service users, and it should know what it costs to achieve the benefit. Sometimes the centre may not gather information in ways that allow it to control these critical variables.

Commissioning a review to determine which management issues should be centralized and which decentralized will sometimes shed more light on management problems than restructuring exercises. A review provides the basis for managers to have a systematic discussion about the allocation of work and consequently to delegate more responsibilities and release the log-jam that can occur at the top of the organization.

A common problem occurs in organizations that have capable middle and front-line managers who are not, however, given clearly specified boundaries to their work. In these circumstances it is tempting for senior managers to involve themselves in the detail of the services to the detriment of their primary task of setting objectives and boundaries and delegating practical responsibilities to their unit managers.

The deputy director dilemma

Overstretched chief executives sometimes yearn for an efficient deputy: 'Someone to deal with all the detail that comes across my desk.' The pressures are very real: delivering services, campaigning for new laws, raising the money and reporting to multiple stakeholders all make the chief executive a busy person. Sadly, in many circumstances the seemingly simple solution of a deputy does not work as intended.

There is much confusion about deputies, because people use the same word to mean different things. The **four types of deputy** are:

1. The person who already has a line-management responsibility but who 'deputizes' for the chief executive when he or she is away. This is a common and sensible arrangement, which gets difficult only when the chief executive does not give the deputy adequate authority, when the deputy has a different agenda from the chief executive's or when managers prefer being managed by the deputy.
2. The person who accepts responsibility for a group of services (for example, finance, personnel, administration, information systems) to reduce the chief executive's workload and span of control. This is one way of overcoming the problem of the overloaded chief executive. One consequence of this arrangement is either that people have to accept three 'tiers' of managers on the senior management team or people

who are excluded will feel demoted and frustrated. Neither alternative is entirely satisfactory unless there is a great deal of trust and goodwill among all team members.

3. The 'floating' deputy director who has no line responsibilities but is used as a fixer and is given specific time-limited tasks to reduce the burden on the chief executive. Successful operation of this arrangement depends on close working relationships between the deputy and other members of the team. The deputy needs to work very closely with departmental heads to avoid them feeling she or he is interfering in their responsibilities. The potential for trust to break down is high!

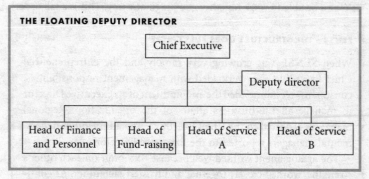

THE FLOATING DEPUTY DIRECTOR

Chief Executive

Deputy director

Head of Finance and Personnel

Head of Fund-raising

Head of Service A

Head of Service B

4. The deputy who line-manages the staff and allows the chief executive to focus on external relations and overall strategy. This works only when there is total trust between the chief executive and the deputy and when senior managers do not bypass the deputy to get decisions from the chief executive. It can be successful when the two individuals have been working together for some time and the arrangement evolves. It works best when people are totally clear about the different roles of the two posts. This might mean the chief executive taking responsibility for external affairs, campaign work and new initiatives, while the deputy takes responsibility for the efficient management of current operations.

Organizations considering the appointment of a deputy should take this decision with extreme care. The idea of appointing a deputy director is sometimes an excuse for not addressing a more deep-seated problem in the organization. It may be that the chief executive is not delegating effectively or is failing to appoint more capable senior staff or is not getting the senior management team to share responsibility for the organization as a whole. It can also result from a waning in the interest of chief executives or their unwillingness to do parts of the job they do not enjoy. In any of these circumstances, tackling the root cause of the problem can be more productive than appointing someone to a post that is often a very difficult role to fulfil satisfactorily.

In circumstances when it is appropriate to have a deputy, the position is heavily dependent on the relationship between the director and the deputy. Ideally, they should know each other well, be loyal and open with each other, have complementary skills, get job satisfaction from different tasks and be able to work together in a pragmatic way. This is a tall order!

SENSE – THE STRUCTURE GOES FULL CIRCLE

When SENSE was growing very rapidly and the entrepreneurial Chief Executive was overloaded with management responsibilities, consultants recommended the appointment of an Executive Director to manage all the business affairs of the organization. Regional managers reported to the Chief Executive, and all the other departmental managers reported to the Executive Director.

The arrangement worked well because they built on each other's strengths, worked closely together and trusted each other. As confidence grew, the Executive Director was promoted to become Managing Director with full responsibility for managing the Senior Management Team.

When, eight years later, he became Chief Executive of another charity, SENSE promoted one of its regional managers to take on the additional responsibility of co-ordinating all the regions, and business managers once again reported to the Chief Executive.

9.4 IMPLEMENTING CHANGES TO THE STRUCTURE

Making major changes to the management structure is a sensitive and time-consuming task. Getting agreement to the process, developing alternatives, consulting the board and staff, and dealing with the human implications all consume effort and energy. It is a major decision which should not be taken lightly. Furthermore, as has already been stressed, the cause of ill-defined management problems may not be the structure at all. It is always worth checking whether other, less tangible issues (such as an unclear strategy or poor management processes) are the real problems that need addressing.

The relative importance of strategy and structure is a significant consideration. In most circumstances, organizations should avoid changing the structure and the strategy simultaneously. A major review of strategy requires that managers work closely together in a dispassionate way to consider alternative futures for the organization. This cannot happen effectively if some managers are worried about the effect of a reorganization on their work and, more critically, whether they will have a job in the new structure.

Senior management has to decide which to tackle first. In some cases, a new strategy or an organization development programme may be needed before decisions can be taken about the structure. In others, the structural problems may be so pressing that management has to accept the current strategy and wait until the new senior management team is established before working on the strategy. Although logic suggests structure should follow strategy, sometimes it is necessary to get the right people in place in order to develop a top-quality strategy.

Alternatives to changing the management structure include:

- improving management processes
- making better use of existing processes
- changing the meetings structure
- creating cross-departmental working groups
- changing one or two key people
- appointing an 'interim manager'.

The option of appointing 'interim managers' is becoming more popular in the third sector. Interim management is well established in the private sector, where there is a reservoir of experienced people willing to fulfil these roles. People are appointed for a limited period of time to carry out an agreed role or set of specific tasks. They may work full-time or part-time for the organization and they may or may not be members of existing management teams. They are paid higher salaries to compensate for the short-term nature of the contract.

This is a valuable option for chief executives because it can be used to fill a position at relatively short notice. It can also buy time when a chief executive wants to avoid making a permanent appointment. It also allows very specific and sometimes short-term skill gaps to be filled. A longer-term arrangement, which may require different skills, can be made at a later date.

Since major structural adjustments are disruptive, managers should try to avoid 'big bang' changes. If the chief executive and the board have a view of the structure needed to deliver the strategy, they can use opportunities of growth, departures, retirements and promotions to make a series of alterations that eventually create the desired structure.

When the structure lags far behind the organization's needs, major change becomes unavoidable. In these circumstances, chief executives should be prepared for the issues that frequently arise. First, the interests of each individual involved in the change (for example, for promotion, for a new role or for more status) are virtually never the same as the interests of the organization as a whole (for example, for a more stream-lined structure or a smaller senior management team).

Secondly, there is the expectation in some organizations that there will be democratic consultation over every aspect of the changes. In most cases, consultation leads to better decisions and greater commitment to implementation. But consultation about future structures has to be handled with precision and sensitivity because some structures may not include all existing posts.

It is virtually impossible for anyone involved in the process entirely to separate purely structural issues from issues about people. This becomes particularly important when some people are perceived to be under-performing. In these circumstances, widespread consultation with the people who report to them may be inappropriate. So, before any changes can be made, the chief executive may have to deal with the underlying problem of one or more individual's performance.

Stages of a major reorganization

The work of making major changes to the organization structure can be divided into five stages. Some stages can be combined in organizations that are smaller or have a less consultative tradition or when the reorganization involves few people. In practice, minor reorganizations also follow these stages, but they may take place in the chief executive's head rather than as a wider process. The stages are set out separately here, to clarify the logic behind structural change.

STAGE ONE: AGREE THE PROCESS

The chief executive should seek agreement with the board that a major reorganization is necessary. Since reorganizations are a sensitive issue, this is likely to require preliminary discussion with the senior management team and, sometimes, an announcement to other staff that the issue of structure is to be put on the agenda. The chief executive should agree with the board:

- the major reasons for considering a restructuring
- the scope of the exercise (involving all departments or just a few; involving senior management or more junior levels as well)
- the way the review will be carried out and when staff and board members will be consulted (i.e. the process)
- how final decisions will be taken (for example, by the board, based on a recommendation from the chief executive)
- the timetable for consultation and decisions.

This preparatory stage is vitally important. The aim is to ensure that everyone involved is clear from the start why changes are necessary and how they will be consulted. It will also help to clarify that, while there will be consultation, a final decision will be taken by the chief executive and the board. In many circumstances, a chief executive will want to retain the right to propose a preferred structure to the board. But the board may also want an input into this sensitive decision because it affects the overall balance of power and the importance attached to different activities. Ultimately the best decisions are those in which the board and the chief executive together agree their preferred structure. When agreement is not possible, it is nearly always inappropriate for the board to impose a structure on the chief executive; this allows her or him to blame the board if things go wrong.

STAGE TWO: INSTIGATE A REVIEW

A review needs to be carried out to pinpoint specific problems with the organization design. This is sometimes carried out by an independent person. It may involve looking at management processes as well, since it is difficult to separate the two issues. This review may conclude with a shortlist of key issues that the reorganization needs to resolve. The review is a vehicle for gaining agreement among staff and board on the exact nature of the structural problems. It should also be used to establish clear objectives for changing the structure. In straightforward circumstances, stages one and two can be combined.

STAGE THREE: DEVELOP OPTIONS

Options need to be created and the advantages and disadvantages of each set out. At this point, options should be about principles (for example, to structure around services, regions or functions). Detailed organization charts are generally inappropriate because they encourage people throughout the organization to consider their own position rather than the principles.

STAGE FOUR: PREPARE A DETAILED STRUCTURE

The preferred option needs to be worked up into a detailed structure, fitting individuals into the structure, so that management can identify:

- posts that will remain unchanged
- posts that disappear
- posts that change partially
- entirely new posts.

At this stage, individuals who will be affected need to be spoken to by their line managers and told about the implications if the reorganization proceeds as planned. An implementation timetable should be attached to the proposals.

STAGE FIVE: TAKE DECISIONS

The chief executive needs to take decisions, in consultation with the board and the senior management team. Individuals affected need to be informed personally about the implications for their jobs before general announcements are made.

Appropriate consultation is an important element of a successful reorganization – and a legal requirement in some circumstances. There will always be people who gain and those who feel they have lost out in the changes; however, if the chief executive has been demonstrably fair in the process, there is less cause for complaint. Consultation with staff and trade unions can be undertaken between any of the five stages. However, since some stages may have been combined together, it would be common to have either one or two rounds of consultation, often after the review stage and after the options have been prepared.

Common mistakes made during reorganizations include:

- springing surprises on people
- reorganizing too many levels in the organization at the same time
- using restructuring primarily to solve other problems (such as an underperforming member of staff)
- being heavily influenced by lobbying from powerful individuals or groups.

So, when preparing for a reorganization:

- ensure people understand that there are no ideal solutions – compromise is always necessary
- recognize that the skills of people currently in the organization will be a significant determinant of the appropriate structure
- ensure the board supports the proposals
- consult openly with the staff and their trade union or staff association
- set a tight timescale, let everyone know when decisions will be made, and stick to the timetable
- be willing to see changes through – this is not a time for vacillation.

Criteria for change

The absence of profit as a primary objective means that there is no simple logic to help managers drive through necessary changes. Consequently, adjustments to the structure have to be evaluated against other criteria. The value of criteria is that they help to focus people's minds on what the change is designed to achieve. They provide a framework for making difficult decisions. The debate moves from abstract ideas about structures to a discussion about change and the desired outcomes. Management can evaluate alternatives against agreed criteria. Use the following list to choose which criteria are most suitable for the circumstances. Will the changes:

- enable services to be significantly improved, for example by integrating the delivery of fragmented activities?
- strengthen the organization's fund-raising capability, for example by separating out types of fund-raising that require different skills?
- enable the organization to deliver its strategy, for example by grouping services together in a different configuration?
- create teams with greater potential for high performance, for example by streamlining senior management?
- reduce divisions between service delivery or campaign departments and support functions such as communications, fund-raising, finance and personnel?
- strengthen co-ordination across the organization's boundaries, for example by having integrated units at a lower level in the structure?
- incur costs that are small in relation to the anticipated benefits?

Even with criteria, there is no way round the reality that organization design is a matter of opinion and judgement, and that ultimately the board and the chief executive are responsible for making judgements about the overall structure. Chief executives can listen to advice from many people, but in the end a key part of their job is to create a structure and a team that enable them to do their job.

9.5 STRENGTHENING CROSS-DEPARTMENTAL WORKING

An organization of more than a few people needs a structure which gives individuals areas of responsibility and enables management and ultimately the board to hold people accountable. However, any management structure creates barriers which can become obstacles to effective working. Departments find themselves competing against each other for resources, people become protective of their departmental interests and managers' egos become attached to the success of their department.

There are many ways to encourage cross-departmental working and to discourage departmentalism. Managers can be encouraged to promote people across, rather than within, departments. People can shadow colleagues in other departments as part of their professional development. In some circumstances, people can swap jobs for a limited period of time to broaden their experience.

However, one of the most powerful ways of breaking down barriers is to create cross-departmental groups. These require people from different departments to work together on specific tasks with well-defined objectives. In all but the smallest organizations, these groups are needed to deliver effective services and to ensure that the organization itself is working in the most efficient way possible. Increasingly, many organizations are finding that some of their most exciting initiatives arise from the opportunities of working across departmental boundaries.

Cross-departmental groups can be temporary or more permanent. Temporary groups may be called a task group or a project. They have a specific task to carry out in an agreed timescale and should be dissolved when it is completed. They do, however, have a tendency to develop a life of their own. Groups sometimes recommend that further research is required or that they need to continue to monitor outcomes. Rigorous challenge is required to check why nobody felt strong enough to say, 'We've done our work, it was enjoyable; now other things are more important.'

Permanent groups are valuable when integration across departments is required on a continuous basis. The membership of the group may change from time to time, but its purpose remains comparatively constant.

Examples include groups that integrate service divisions with fund-raising divisions and groups that integrate IT users across the organization.

Cross-departmental groups provide an excellent opportunity for involving people from different levels of the organization in management. They will bring new and different perspectives to the issue and, by forging personal links across departmental boundaries, will strengthen the ability of the organization to resolve issues at the front line, rather than passing them up one line of the hierarchy and down the next before they can be resolved. Involving people from different levels is also an ideal opportunity to give them a professional development opportunity that may demonstrate their potential for future promotion.

Effective cross-departmental working depends on:

- ensuring the group has the resources and authority to achieve the objective
- integrating cross-departmental planning with line-management plans
- managing the group as a team.

Establishing cross-departmental groups

Establishing cross-departmental groups with the potential to succeed requires that:

- **the brief is clear.** It should specify the objective and also the scope of the task. It is easy for a group to drift into many issues that are not central to the task, so specifying the boundaries helps to keep the group focused.
- **the group has a leader with the authority and internal credibility to carry out the task.** The leader must command the authority needed to complete the task either through his or her position in the organization or through personal persuasiveness and the support of senior management. The leader's brief should clarify whom the group reports to, what they must make judgements about and when to refer items for advice or decisions.
- **the group has the resources to carry out the task.** In practice this means giving the group a budget so that it does not have to prise resources from other departmental budgets. A budget also signifies that the group is important and that its task is being properly resourced.

- **team members have the time required for the task**. The most common reason for groups not working is that members have not estimated the time the task will require nor taken this into account when planning the rest of their work. A good discipline is to require members to make the estimate and agree the time allocation with both the team leader and their line manager.

Integrating plans

Cross-departmental groups need to have a plan that establishes objectives, desired outcomes, performance indicators and milestones to monitor progress.

For permanent groups, plans should be integrated into the organization's planning cycle. In some cases, groups may need to circulate outlines of their plans to line-management departments to ensure that their requirements are incorporated into departmental and service delivery unit plans. In other cases, cross-divisional group leaders may wish to review line-management plans before they finalize the cross-divisional plan. In both cases time may have to be included in the organization's planning cycle to mesh together the line and the cross-division group plans.

The resulting plans should be subject to the same rigorous scrutiny that line-management plans receive and be approved in a similar manner. This will usually involve the senior management team. Their approval will help to give the group the authority to command the time and resources required to carry on with or complete the task.

Managing cross-departmental groups

The essential requirements for a well-managed cross-departmental group are that:

- **leaders report in to the management structure.** The line of accountability of the leader should be known in all the departments contributing to the group.
- **groups should ideally be of between three and eight people.** With

more than eight, co-ordination becomes increasingly complex and time-consuming.

● **members work to the leader on cross-departmental tasks.** Members of the group should be accountable to the group leader for their cross-departmental tasks. They can delegate work to other members of their line department, but they remain accountable to the group leader for delivery.

● **group leaders are responsible for maintaining communication with line management.** This work should be delegated to group members, each of whom should take responsibility for reporting progress and problems back into their own departments, and sometimes to other cross-departmental groups as well.

CROSS-DIVISIONAL PROJECT TEAMS AT CHRISTIAN AID

Christian Aid is the agency of the British and Irish churches that provides more than £40 million to support relief and development work in sixty countries. It had a matrix structure based on regions of the world (Africa, Asia, Latin America and UK/Ireland) with cross-cutting functions for education, communication, fund-raising and finance. Although this worked for ten years, it was eventually replaced by a conventional structure, supported by a series of cross-divisional project teams. A high level of cross-departmental working is essential to the success of Christian Aid, so, to ensure that project teams were successful, the Senior Management Team agreed the following guidelines for project teams:

Definition
A cross-divisional project is a major piece of work that can be implemented only by two or more divisions or teams working together. Cross-divisional projects have to be approved by Directorate. The current cross-divisional projects are:

● Christian Aid Week
● Change the Rules Campaign
● computer systems
● major emergencies
● fund-raising.

Project planning

- **All projects must have a plan** that establishes the goals, specific objectives, actions and performance indicators of the project. The timespan for achieving each of these must be clearly stated. Project plans must also have responsibilities allocated to teams or individuals, a financial budget and a time budget. The time budget should include unallocated time to take account of the unexpected.
- **Project plans should be prepared as part of the annual planning cycle**, except in the case of emergencies. Projects may have timescales of more than one year but they will still have a new plan each year.
- **Planning formats for projects should be the same as those for teams.**
- **Project managers must be responsible for agreeing time estimates** with each team leader and staff member who is responsible for implementing part of the plan.
- **Project plans must be approved by the Directorate** before implementation can begin.

Integration into the annual planning process

- **The objectives of cross-divisional projects should be sent to all teams** at the same time as the paper on 'really important priorities'.
- **Embryonic cross-divisional project plans should be circulated** to all teams before they start to prepare their annual plans.
- **Directorate should take responsibility for providing robust challenge** to project plans and for ensuring that each is realistic and achievable.
- **The planning process must allow time for team leaders to mesh team plans** with project plans before Directorate approves the annual plan.

Project management

- **All projects must have a project manager** who has overall responsibility for achieving the goals and objectives. Project managers should be responsible specifically for planning, managing and evaluating their project. They should take decisions, consulting where necessary, chase progress and directly manage the work of people who contribute to the project. Project managers will usually be Associate Directors.

- **Line accountability of project managers** to the Director or an Associate Director should be clear to all staff. Team leaders and staff should have an up-to-date list of project managers and their accountability.
- **Project managers should be responsible for holding group members accountable** for carrying out agreed tasks within agreed timescales and budgets.

Cross-departmental groups are an essential part of an organization's structure. However, if too many are established, they can become an obstacle to effective working. People find themselves in a never-ending round of meetings and have no time to meet the commitments they have made to all the groups to which they belong.

Responsibility for making good judgements about the numbers and tasks of groups lies with senior management; if the organization is overloaded with groups, senior management needs to take decisions about priorities. Actions may be required to:

- abolish groups that are not critical at this point in time
- reduce the scope of their work so their tasks are achievable
- reduce the size of groups so they take less staff time in total
- set tighter timescales so tasks are completed and groups disbanded
- improve working practices so groups are more effective
- establish time budgets to ensure that more realistic judgements are made about the tasks that can be achieved within the available time.

SUMMARY OF KEY POINTS

Change by continuous adjustment

- Management needs to inculcate into the organization the assumption that continuous adjustments to the structure are essential in today's turbulent world.

- Third-sector organizations need to overcome their innate conservatism and develop structures that anticipate future needs.

Options for structuring management

- Organizations can be structured by function, service users, services, funders and geography. Usually they are a mix of two types.
- The key issues to consider are:
  — the size of the senior management team
  — the strategic importance of different functions
  — current managers' skills and experience.

Design dilemmas

- Arguments about centralizing or decentralizing need to focus on creating a loose-tight organization, with some matters closely controlled by the centre and others firmly delegated to the field.
- Appointing a deputy director is seldom straightforward. Chief executives need to review whether the problems they face could be solved in other ways. In the rare circumstances that one is required, they then need to select someone whom they can trust.

Implementing changes to the structure

- Chief executives need to decide whether they can achieve the desired structure using opportunities created by retirements, departures and promotions or in one 'big bang'.
- The process for major structure change needs to involve a review, options and a proposal. Consultation is an essential element of the process.
- Establishing criteria helps to evaluate proposed changes in a systematic way.

Strengthening cross-departmental working

- Cross-departmental groups can be temporary or permanent.
- They require clear briefs, a strong leader and the authority to carry out the task.
- Members need to be clear that they have the time to make a contribution to the group before agreeing to join.

- Group plans need to be fully integrated with line-management plans.
- Group leaders are responsible for communicating progress and problems to the rest of the organization.
- Senior management must make judgements about the number and scope of groups and take care not to overload the organization with too many tasks.

10   **Managing Change**

10.1   **MANAGING CHANGE IS AN ESSENTIAL SKILL**

Third-sector organizations have had to respond to an increasingly turbulent and competitive external environment in recent years. Rising expectations of users, funders, staff and the public have all contributed to the need for more frequent, more rapid and better-managed change:

- Users expect to be more closely involved in organizations providing services than they were in the past.
- Staff and volunteers expect to get learning opportunities as part of their compensation for working with the organization.
- Funders expect to give fewer handouts for loosely defined purposes and more contracts with tightly specified performance requirements.
- The public expects good governance, low overhead costs and high standards of probity.
- Developments in technology are having an increasingly significant impact.
- Partnerships and coalitions with other organizations are presenting new ways of working.

Taken together, these mean that organizations face a significant 'change management' agenda, and all the evidence suggests that these pressures are all likely to grow in coming years.

In addition, some organizations, including some household names that were once at the cutting edge, have fallen well behind the times in terms of their overall strategy, service quality and management practices. They face the additional challenge of catching up with current best practices and at the same time responding to more rapid changes imposed from outside.

Change management draws together a group of ideas that help managers to understand what type of change they are embarking on and how to make appropriate changes happen. Change management is an approach to management that underpins many of the activities described in other parts of this book (such as strategic planning, changing structures and developing management processes). The approaches to change set out in this chapter can therefore be applied in all those circumstances.

The principles of change management can also be used to underpin the successful implementation of a wider range of tools and techniques for making an organization more effective. Examples include people development programmes (such as Investors in People or the introduction of management competencies), quality standards initiatives (such as the Excellence Model), customer care projects, cost-reduction programmes or process redesign projects.

Change management has to be led by a 'change leader'; this is the person responsible for managing the change initiative. Change leaders have to drive change with enthusiasm and commitment in order to maximize the probability of success.

This chapter sets out the principles and practices of effective change management. It starts with a short section on the theory of organization culture, because understanding organization culture is an essential pre-requisite to a successful change programme. Insights into culture help managers to identify which levers of change will have the greatest impact, to understand which communication methods will be most effective and to ensure that changes are fully embedded into culture.

The chapter then describes:

- the fundamental concepts of change management
- some characteristics of change processes
- the eight critical stages of a major change initiative
- the essential skills of successful change leaders.

10.2   INTRODUCTION TO ORGANIZATION CULTURE

Culture has been described in many ways, including:

● the way we do things around here
● the way we think about things around here
● the commonly held and relatively stable beliefs, attitudes and values that exist within an organization.

Three levels of organization culture

Culture is best understood by considering the three different levels at which it is expressed. At the most superficial level, there are the **visible representations** of an organization's culture – its buildings, the routine procedures of meetings, the management structure and the language that people use. Visit a well-established housing association with its offices in the business park, and one cannot help but notice the smart photographs of its properties on the wall, the tidy reception area and the sense of calm organization. Contrast this with a campaigning organization with its offices in a dilapidated property in a rundown area of town, newspapers piled high waiting to be clipped, desks cramped close together, walls piled to the ceiling with T-shirts, pamphlets and posters, and the sense of pressure and urgency. Two extreme cases, perhaps, but they illustrate the different physical manifestations of culture.

At the second level of culture, there are common patterns of **group behaviour**. This level is about how people act and react in various circumstances. Organizations work in subtly different ways: decision-making processes are different, respect for different groups varies, and the processes that are important and those that are disregarded are different. Examples of group behaviour include:

● how the organization treats users
● how trustees behave towards staff
● how the senior management team behave towards staff
● how staff treat each other.

Once behaviour patterns have been established, they strongly influence people who join the organization. New managers and trustees watch how people conduct themselves and adjust their own behaviour accordingly. As a result, the way the organization works becomes embedded in their unconscious behaviour patterns.

At the third and most fundamental level, there are the **underlying beliefs** held by the staff, trustees and members of the organization. These are assumptions that are taken for granted. They are the unconscious values that inform people's behaviour. For example:

- social welfare providers may have underlying beliefs about respecting service users
- managers may have underlying beliefs about the costs and effectiveness of services provided
- campaigners may have underlying beliefs about social policy.

The underlying beliefs of the different groups of people and different departments will vary within an organization, but there are also common values that exist across the whole organization. These values are virtually invisible, which is why it is so difficult to change them. Their power in determining how an organization works should not, however, be underestimated.

Embedding changes into an organization's culture requires action at all three levels. The easiest level is the visible representational one – but this also has the least long-term effect. The most difficult level to change is that containing the underlying beliefs. When these are altered, change becomes part of the unconsciously accepted culture of the organization.

Characteristics of culture

The concept of culture can be understood more thoroughly by considering some of its characteristics:

1. **It is learned.** It results both from people's experiences before they joined the organization and from the influences of the organization itself.
2. **It is determined by the organization's history.** It is defined by decisions people have taken in the past, particularly those taken by significant individuals such as the founder.
3. **It is partly subconscious.** Over time, assumptions develop and become

implicit influences on people's behaviour. These beliefs and assumptions affect the way people think about things.

4. **It is heterogeneous**. Different parts of an organization have different cultures. A commonly observed difference is that between staff in the headquarters of an organization, who may be concerned with public profile, fund-raising, lobbying and the inevitable politics of large organizations, and people in the local branches, who may be more concerned with service delivery and valuing volunteers.

A BRIEF GUIDE TO DIAGNOSING CULTURE

People who understand their organization's culture are in a strong position to manage change more effectively. The understanding gives managers insights into what to do to maximize the impact of their efforts. It points to the 'levers' to pull at different moments in time in order to have the greatest effect.

Understanding can come partly from conscious observation of the patterns of behaviour in an organization. Reflecting on changes that were successful and identifying the elements of the approach that contributed most to achieving the change can shed light on the culture.

Culture can also be brought to the surface more systematically by working in groups to develop a description of the culture. An outsider who can bring an independent eye to the organization and act as a facilitator in making the cultural diagnosis is usually necessary.

The stages of a cultural diagnosis include:

- establishing a group to make the diagnosis
- agreeing an understanding of the concept of culture and the language that is used to describe it
- brainstorming, to build a picture of the visible representations of culture and distilling them to identify the most pertinent ones
- building an understanding of group behaviour by reviewing how things happen and asking in particular why people do things in the ways they do, without being judgemental
- reviewing behaviour to tease out some of the underlying beliefs

- exploring how these beliefs help or hinder the management of the organization
- preparing a summary of the group's diagnosis of the culture.

Further information on cultural diagnosis can be found in *Organizational Culture and Leadership*, E. Schein, 1992.

10.3 CHANGE MANAGEMENT CONCEPTS

This section:

- defines change management
- describes different types of change
- explains the art of combining leading and listening.

The nature of change management

The ideas that underpin change management are vitally important to managers who wish to introduce significant change into their organization. Organizations are littered with examples of changes that did not produce the desired results. Indeed, much of the cynicism that managers encounter when they wish to make changes results from the failure of previous initiatives to have a significant impact. Introducing change is a subtle and sensitive process and a misjudgement in any of the stages of change can easily result in good proposals being consigned to the pile of failed management initiatives.

Change management is **the skill of catalysing significant improvements in the performance of organizations**. It is a set of skills that managers need to apply in order to achieve the greatest results for their efforts.

Change management **involves people from many parts** of the organization. The actions usually cut across departments and may involve users, branches and board members.

Change management is a **combination of substance and process**. It is about developing a clear view of the improvements that are needed and integrating this with a sequence of activities for achieving the change. It combines the head (the vision and the analysis) with the heart (the people and their emotions).

At a more fundamental level, change management is about **'re-framing' a situation** so that people see their circumstances in a different way. It is about creating a new mental model or 'paradigm' that enables people to think and act in ways that will help the organization achieve its objectives more effectively.

There is **no one approach** that can be applied to all change situations. While this chapter aims to help managers to plan and implement major changes by setting down some principles and a general approach, there is no avoiding the harsh reality that good judgements at each stage of a change process are critical to success. It is impossible to predict how the change process will evolve – something will always go awry in a complex set of changes.

Flexibility is therefore critical. Plans have to be prepared, communication methods agreed and timetables established. But, particularly in large-scale change, effective managers are always ready to make adjustments and sometimes to take a different approach in order to achieve the desired objective.

Types of organizational change

Three types of organizational change have been defined (by L. Ackerman):

- **developmental change** – concerned with the improvement of current activities or ways of working (for example, by doing more or doing it better)
- **transitional change** – concerned with replacing current activities or ways of working with new ones (for example, introducing new services or systems)
- **transformational change** – concerned with changing beliefs and awareness about what is possible, requiring a leap of faith (for example, redefining the mission or adapting an entirely new strategy).

Transitional change may also involve an element of developmental change, and transformational change may involve both the other types.

Two particular types of transitional change that are common in the third sector are project management and programme management. The term 'project management' is often used to describe the planning and implementation of specific pieces of work with well-defined boundaries. Programme management is concerned with the management of a number of projects simultaneously. The principles of change management can be applied to both project and programme management. However, the stages of change are likely to be much more compressed, and some will be done more informally. Nevertheless, the ideas that underpin transitional and transformational change provide a rigorous basis for managing projects and programmes.

The key point for aspiring change leaders is to determine the type of change they are embarking upon, since the complexity and resource requirements grow exponentially from developmental to transformational change. This chapter focuses on transitional and transformational change.

TRANSITIONAL CHANGE AT VOLUNTARY SERVICE OVERSEAS

Redesigning the recruitment process

VSO aims to send over 900 people per annum on two-year overseas assignments. They are selected from 75,000 applications in a complex process that has to:

● recruit people with a wide range of skills and abilities
● prepare applicants for selection boards
● select people as potential volunteers
● post people to appropriate overseas assignments
● train people for the post
● prepare them for departure.

The Recruitment Division wanted to increase the number of volunteers working overseas, reduce the time from initial inquiry to departure, and reduce the unit costs of the Division. It used the principles of change management to diagnose the problem and develop new ways of working.

A Steering Group, led by the Division Director and representing all parts of the Division, was established to oversee the whole process. It established eleven Task Groups to investigate every aspect of the problem. Their reports were drawn together by the consultants assisting the Director into an overall diagnosis of the situation. There was widespread consultation on this to ensure that it was owned by key people in VSO and the Recruitment Division.

The Steering Group established specific objectives and targets which the new process needed to achieve. A new process was designed and piloted for eighteen months and evaluated against agreed success criteria. After detailed consensus-building work between the Steering Group and the other staff, more radical changes were made. The new structures and systems were then implemented throughout the Division. Although some issues remained (particularly around workloads in the new structure), most staff believed that the new process provided a better way of working.

Combining leading and listening

Change management has two historical roots. One root was a 'top down' approach to change, inspired by a vision, pushed by senior management and driven energetically through the organization with plans, briefings and an element of razzmatazz. This approach tended to be strong on analysis and aimed to achieve a predetermined objective. The other root was a 'bottom up' approach in which leaders facilitated change, managers helped their staff to use skills and experience that were already embedded in the organization, and the development of people was seen as the key to successful change. In this approach, sometimes called 'organization development', change happened in incremental steps.

Modern views of change management stress the need to adopt both approaches simultaneously. The most effective change happens when there is a combination of:

Leading	Listening
● a clear view of the future	● a desire to build on the best of the past
● strong leadership	● strong commitment to listen to the concerns of people at all levels of the organization

- a focus on action .... ● time for reflection

- investment in training .... ● commitment to learning

- a plan with targets and .... ● freedom to act within broad
  timetables   guidelines

This combination is particularly important because trustees, managers and volunteers place a very high value on the meaning of their work to them personally. People are closely attached to their work because one of their fundamental motivations is to improve an aspect of the world in which they live. Since change management is about altering an aspect of people's work, it can threaten to take away some of the value of that work to those people. It may therefore be perceived as the organization placing less value on that person, department, region or branch.

These concerns are expressed in many different ways. Sometimes they are expressed in terms of the implications for service users of the proposed changes. Sometimes the objections are practical and sometimes they are philosophical. They are seldom expressed in terms of people's anxieties about how the organization is perceived to be placing a lower value on some people's work. In these circumstances it is difficult to untangle people's concerns about the value of their work from legitimate views that they are expressing about the proposed changes.

If these concerns are not listened to, or if their underlying meaning is not understood, there is a danger that change will be opposed. Such opposition may be voiced through the organization's formal decision-making processes, but it may also arise through the powerful networks of informal communications that determine how any change initiative is viewed in the organization. Successful change managers go out of their way to meet concerns head-on and to understand what people have to gain and to lose from the proposals.

People's concerns have to be treated as genuine. Managers have to try to bring to the surface the underlying meaning of the proposed changes for the people affected and find an accommodating way forward before the opposition becomes an insurmountable obstacle to the overall change process. Railroading proposals through may be possible, but there is often a large price to pay in terms of people's reduced motivation and willingness to co-operate with the new arrangements.

Broadly speaking, people affected by a change initiative can be divided into those who are committed to change, those who are uncommitted and see it neither as an opportunity nor as a threat, and those who are likely to oppose change. The key group to win over is that of the uncommitted, who may well be the silent majority. They need to be motivated by the proposed changes, and their concerns about the consequences need to be given particular attention.

Maintaining coalitions

One of the distinguishing features of third-sector organizations is that every one is a coalition of different interests, held together by shared objectives and interests. There is no financial imperative to tie these organizations together.

Major change puts the coalition at risk. Any significant part of the coalition (volunteers, branch members, board members in particular) that does not support the change or feels that their views have not been listened to can threaten to leave. In many circumstances this can have very damaging consequences on the organization's ability to deliver its services and campaigns.

A key requirement of a change process is that it should keep all the stakeholders on board at every stage. This means that massive effort has to be put into communication at every stage, critics have to be listened to and decisions have to wait until it is quite clear that the change will receive the support of the majority.

In circumstances where there are fundamental disagreements, the consequences of taking actions that alienate a group need to be carefully weighed before taking decisions. This is particularly important in organizations with a high public profile, as any stakeholder group can threaten to go to the press with their views and cause significant damage to the organization's fund-raising prospects.

10.4 **CHARACTERISTICS OF CHANGE PROCESSES**

Large-scale change processes have three common characteristics:

● complexity and clarity vary with time
● confidence and support vary during the process
● change is demanding on leaders.

Complexity and clarity vary with time

Change leaders and their teams should anticipate that the complexity of a change initiative will vary with time. At the start of the assignment the issues often look remarkably straightforward. However, gathering data and building the case for change produces masses of detail, and soon the problem can look overwhelmingly complicated. Then, as the information is analysed, perhaps assisted by the preparation of a summary review, the big picture usually starts to come clear again. The key issues that have to be addressed become more obvious, and consensus about the next steps emerges.

When planning starts in earnest, matters may once again look exceedingly complex, and the discomfort of being overwhelmed with detail returns. However, preparation of the plan itself should clarify and simplify the actions that are required to make a success of the initiative.

Finally, when implementation begins, the team may yet again feel swamped in detail, but, as issues are resolved and new mind-sets are established, clarity should once again return.

Confidence and support vary during change processes

People's feelings and attitudes towards change will vary during the process. Their support for it and their confidence about coping with change will fluctuate as the project proceeds.

Typically, at the start of a change process some people will enthusiastically support the need for change; some will feel the way things worked in the past has always been successful, so changes are not required; yet

THE COMPLEXITY OF A CHANGE MANAGEMENT INITIATIVE VARIES WITH TIME

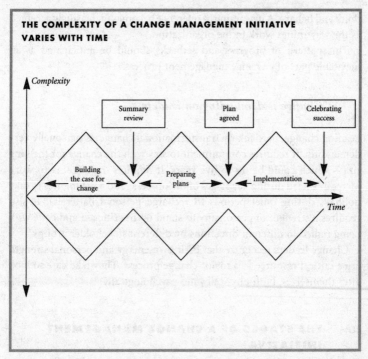

others will feel anxious about the implications of the initiative and concerned for their jobs. Once the initiative is underway, more people will come to understand the need to change, and support will begin to grow.

However, there are often one or more false dawns. People see glimpses of a new future but feel overwhelmed by the scale of change required to achieve the new vision. Frustration levels rise and some begin to be sceptical as to whether the desired changes will ever be achieved. Some may feel that they do not have the skills or the energy to make the necessary changes.

As time passes, the need for change becomes more apparent and people start to see how the change can have positive impact on their work and offer them new opportunities. They start to let go of the history of the situation and acknowledge that new approaches are needed. Small steps forward increase their confidence in implementing change. People start to internalize the progress, and they incorporate changes in the way they think and behave. A new frame of reference becomes increasingly accepted as the way things work in the organization.

This pattern of progress and setbacks should be anticipated as an inevitable part of a change management process.

Change is demanding on leaders

Leading change, particularly transformational change, is personally very demanding. It requires commitment to stay with the change for the long run – which could be up to five years. It requires the stamina to work incredibly hard during key stages of the process (and a willingness to take holidays during quiet periods to recharge personal batteries). It also requires a strength of personality to stand up to criticism and cope with being pulled in different directions by different stakeholder groups.

Change leaders recognize that their own energy and personal strength are a critical resource in a major change process. They take care to look after themselves, both physically and psychologically.

10.5 **THE STAGES OF A CHANGE MANAGEMENT INITIATIVE**

The success of transitional and transformational change is highly dependent on following a series of stages, and not falling into the trap of beginning a new stage prematurely. This section sets out eight essential stages that need to be followed in order to implement change successfully. It draws on the experience of third-sector organizations and the thinking of a number of people who have written about change, including Professor John Kotter of Harvard Business School.

Reduced to the core, these stages are:

1. to **clarify the scope and scale** of the proposed change initiative
2. to **establish a change team** with the power and expertise needed to ensure the change will succeed
3. to **prepare a diagnosis of the problem** so people can understand why change is needed
4. to **build strong commitment** to the need for the change and listen to people's concerns

5. to **develop a motivating vision** for what the change will achieve
6. to **plan and communicate** extensively about the proposed change
7. to **implement by empowering** people to take the required actions
8. to **incorporate change** into the culture of the organization.

The key to successfully managing change is to start the stages in order and not be tempted to jump on to a new stage before the preceding stage is substantially completed. The change leader and members of the change team need to be thinking ahead about subsequent stages, and indeed these thoughts may influence their approach to a current stage. However, ensuing stages should not be rolled out more widely into the organization until people have understood and internalized previous stages.

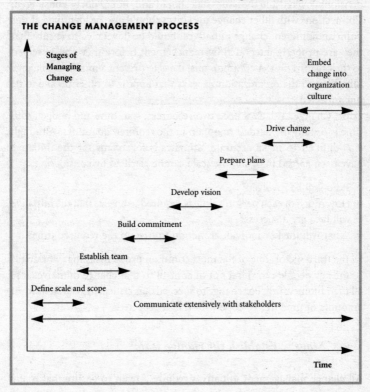

THE CHANGE MANAGEMENT PROCESS

Stages of Managing Change

Embed change into organization culture

Drive change

Prepare plans

Develop vision

Build commitment

Establish team

Define scale and scope

Communicate extensively with stakeholders

Time

Stage 1. Clarify the scope and scale of the proposed initiative

Before deciding to proceed with a change initiative, critical judgements need to be made about its scope (what its boundaries will be) and its scale (how significant it will be).

Scope: It is all too easy for a change initiative to stray into many different areas that seem to be connected to the issue, leading to loss of the sharp focus required for success. Clear boundaries need to be established around levels of the organization to which the initiative applies, the departments or divisions covered and the issues that should and should not be considered. Connections with other change initiatives should also be identified at this point and different change initiatives should be dovetailed to ensure that they are properly integrated by management before they are presented to the organization. A common mistake is to present a number of change initiatives to the organization in ways that appear to other people to be unconnected.

Scale: Change initiatives need two resources, staff time and budget; staff time is usually the hardest to obtain in the required quantities. Although it is difficult to make accurate estimates before plans for the initiative have been agreed in detail, the scale can be clarified by considering:

● Who will be involved?
● How much of each person's time is required to ensure that the initiative will be a great success?
● What will the key individuals *not* do to free up the required time?

In the third sector, one of the most common problems is that workloads of the key people can spiral out of control so that change initiatives lose all their momentum. For change to succeed, it is critical to keep significant amounts of time free to cope with the unexpected.

Stage 2. Establish the change team

All change management initiatives require a team to ensure that many perspectives can be considered, to give the initiative champions in different parts of the organization, to improve the quality of decision-making and to take effective action.

The team needs a leader who cares about the issue and has the skills and authority to deliver a successful result.

Four types of team can be considered:

- a **line management team** – consisting of the managers responsible for the areas where the change is happening
- a **cross-cutting team** – consisting of managers from the different parts of the organization that will be affected by the initiative
- a **representative team** – consisting of carefully selected representatives from those levels and parts of the organization that have a stake in the initiative (including trustees, front-line staff, regions, branches and volunteers). This is sometimes called a 'diagonal' or 'slice' team
- a **mixed team** – consisting of a combination of the above.

The critical tests are whether the team has sufficient:

- **expertise to do the job.** The specialist and managerial skills required to review the problems and implement solutions should all be represented
- **power to drive through the changes**. People with the power to make the change happen and those with the power to block it should all be represented. This may include board members, staff association officials, branch members, user representatives and individuals who are significant opinion-formers who may not hold any formal positions of power
- **connections to listen to the views of everyone affected**. The tentacles of the team should reach out to all parts of the organization that will be affected by the changes.

When change is transitional, the chief executive should create the team. This confers immediate authority on the initiative – though, as time passes, the team will have to earn their authority from their work and their actions. When it is transformational, the chief executive will almost certainly be the team leader.

The team leader should estimate the time that will be required from each team member from the start so that everyone realizes the level of commitment that is likely to be required. The team leader will then need to agree people's availability with their managers. Being explicit about the time required and reducing team members' other commitments ensures that they can allocate sufficient time to make a success of the initiative.

Loyalty to the whole of the organization is a critical ingredient of a successful change team. If team members are more committed to their department or their region or to a section of the organization than they are to the organization as a whole, the change process will be more difficult. Team members should be willing to put the team's work ahead of these allegiances in order to ensure the success of the initiative. Applying other good practices in team working, as described in section 12.3, will help to ensure that the change team works effectively.

The team is the core of people who champion the initiative. Their influence will need to spread out across the organization as the initiative gains momentum. In particular, they will need to listen to, involve and influence the key stakeholders as the change process gets underway. These key stakeholders will in turn have to do the same with an ever-widening group of people.

Stage 3. Prepare a diagnosis of the problem

The first task of the change team is to develop a diagnosis of the situation. This may involve an analysis of the issues that led to the creation of the team and the development of a shared understanding of the underlying causes of the problem.

Start by thinking through how the diagnosis should be prepared. Topics to consider include:

● the issues to be investigated
● the division of the issues into manageable chunks of work
● responsibilities of individuals and teams preparing parts of the diagnosis
● the method of bringing elements of the diagnosis into an overview
● the timescale for the work
● the process for agreeing the diagnosis.

For a comparatively minor change initiative, members of the change team may do all the work. In larger initiatives, sub-groups may be needed to do specific jobs and feed their work into the change team. Involving people across the organization in gathering data helps to build commitment to the change process. Setting up task groups to gather information on specific issues, each of which could be led by a member of the change team, is one way of gaining support. External and internal sources of information will be needed to review the current situation, identify the key issues and summarize the reasons why change is required.

External information ensures that the case for change is based on the perceptions of people who see the organization from outside. These external views and comparisons are valuable, even when the change initiative is mainly about internal matters, because they bring new perspectives which can catalyse change.

User information is particularly valuable because it helps to challenge any complacency that may have developed about the quality of the services provided. With appropriate support, and guarantees about confidentiality, information can be gathered from virtually everyone who receives services from third-sector organizations. People with learning difficulties contributed to Mencap's strategic review; people attending counselling with RELATE provided feedback at specified times after the counselling was completed; and drug misusers gave feedback on the use of illegal substances.

Other sources of information include funders, members, visitors, other organizations in the same field, suppliers, prominent people who know the organization, past employees, trustees, patrons and people from the media, and others (such as elected representatives who know the organization).

Internal information is equally important in building the case for change. Gathering people's views – as well as facts and figures – has the added advantage of involving people in the initiative and listening to their opinions. People need to be given time to raise their concerns about the issue and to explain previous decisions that led to the current situation. This ensures that people feel fully involved in the change process.

Remember to ask what works well and do not allow the change initiative to become an opportunity for people to do nothing more than air their grievances. People forget that, for much of the time, many things are working well, and a natural desire to highlight problems may lead them to give undue emphasis to the difficulties.

When pulling new information together, task groups and the change leader should go to great lengths to **be respectful of the past**. Acknowledging the commitment people have given to improving the organization in the past ensures that their previous work is appreciated and is not unintentionally devalued.

Change leaders also **build on achievements**, rather than criticizing what people did previously. Each person who feels that his or her previous hard work is not being appreciated is potentially someone who will not give wholehearted support to the change process. A good test is to check that all reports and presentations give as great a weight to strengths, capabilities and achievements as they do to weaknesses, problems and criticisms.

The diagnosis stage usually involves the preparation of a summary document that clarifies the many issues raised. It is the first point at which people should be clear about why change is needed and how the process will proceed. The stage can end by confirming the original thoughts on the nature and extent of the problem. Alternatively, it can end by redefining the problem. In either case, the diagnosis will clarify the issues and provide the evidence needed to convince people of the need for change. The stage can also end by concluding that no change is necessary or that the costs and upheaval of change outweigh the anticipated benefits.

Whichever way it ends, decisions will be required from the sponsor of the change about how to proceed.

Stage 4. Build commitment to change

Change initiatives are most successful when a critical mass of the people involved has a deep understanding of the need for the changes and the benefits that will be gained. The best way to achieve this understanding is to build a **robust case for change**.

Change is easiest when there really is external pressure for change: a financial crisis, loss of public confidence, demonstrably poor performance or a succession of missed opportunities. However, well-managed organizations anticipate change. They see new opportunities or issues on the horizon and introduce change in anticipation of their arrival. Such changes require stronger and even more robust cases to be made.

The case for change needs to **take account of both the facts and the emotions** of the situation. Change therefore requires hard information on the situation which can be analysed and summarized for presentation

GUIDE DOGS FOR THE BLIND ASSOCIATION

GDBA provides guide dogs and mobility services for over 2,000 visually impaired people in the UK. At the start of a transformational change process, an analysis of internal stakeholder views was prepared in order to identify contributions people could make and obstacles that they might present:

Group	Major concerns	Key contribution	Obstacles they might present	Actions to win their support
Trustees	Financial viability	Setting new direction and targets	Division of view on future	Staged approach to key decisions
Senior managers	Personal futures	Communication with stakeholders	Opposition to proposed changes	Focus on benefits to clients
Staff	Jobs and professional integrity	Champions for change	Lack of response to required changes	Massive consultation and communication at every stage
Branches	PR image of the organization	Continuing support for GDBA	Declining support for GDBA	Keep branch chairs well informed
Guide dog owners	Security of guide dog service for life	Understand situation facing GDBA	Public opposition to proposals	Keep them well informed
Other visual impairment organizations	Effect on them of new GDBA strategy	Form new partnership with GDBA	Lack of co-operation	Consult at each stage of change

The analysis identified where the change team needed to concentrate its effort and pinpointed the need to increase the effort put into communication with stakeholders.

to key stakeholders. It should diagnose the problem and pinpoint what needs to change, without making proposals for the actual changes required. The case for change also requires a deep understanding of people's concerns about the current state of affairs and their future aspirations, both for the organization and for themselves. By taking these on board, the change team will earn the support and respect of the people who may be most affected by the change process.

One way of ensuring that all the appropriate groups are considered is to list key stakeholder groups and, for each, to identify:

- their major concerns
- the key contribution they need to make
- the obstacles they might present
- the actions required to win their support.

The summary case for change should be limited to the arguments for change. Although proposals may be beginning to emerge, do not be tempted to put them forward at this stage; that would be premature and would risk generating opposition about proposals before the reasons for change had been accepted.

Stage 5. Develop and communicate the change vision

Change initiatives need a vision that describes the desired improvements. The vision should not be confused with the organization's overall vision as described in Chapter 5. The change vision should state as succinctly as possible the ultimate objectives of the initiative. It should describe **desired objectives and outcomes** and, where possible, these should be quantified.

The vision should be **motivating**. It should inspire people to support the project by connecting its aim with the overall mission of the organization. People should be able to see how the initiative will help the organization to achieve its overall objectives more effectively.

A clear and powerful vision provides a solid foundation for a change initiative. It should help to identify both appropriate and inappropriate actions of the people who will be involved in the initiative. This also enables task groups and other people to work with a degree of autonomy, and it should result in easier decision-making. It is therefore worth taking time to get the vision right.

The acid test of clarity is whether team members can describe the purpose and vision of the change initiative to people inside and outside the organization in a few sentences.

When it is reasonably well developed, the change team can sound out key stakeholders both to get them to 'buy in' to the vision and the change process and further to improve the vision itself.

VSO RECRUITMENT DIVISION VISION

The change process in VSO's Recruitment Division (described in an earlier box) was driven by its vision to:

- increase the number of volunteers working overseas
- increase the satisfaction of overseas organizations that employ volunteers
- increase the average length of stay of volunteers
- fill a higher percentage of vacancies
- fill vacancies more quickly
- become more responsive to volunteers' requirements
- give staff more responsibility and hold them more accountable.

Each of these objectives was accompanied by a quantitative target for the Division to achieve from its redesigned recruitment process – for example, reducing the early return rate to less than 15 per cent, filling 80 per cent of placement opportunities within three months of the agreed start date, and ensuring that 80 per cent of volunteers depart within three months of their availability.

The case for change and the vision should be communicated to stakeholders in the change initiative and more widely through the organization. A wide variety of means should be used to ensure that people get the messages by different methods and at different times. Workshops and briefing sessions are likely to be more powerful than written communications, which tend to get swamped in the morass of internal communications circulating in any organization. Events also have the advantage of allowing two-way communication, so people can raise their concerns and alert the change team to potential obstacles to change.

When planning communications, remember also that the change team will have spent many hours building the case for change and developing the vision, so allow other people the time to consider, discuss and understand the purpose of the initiative, its scope and the problems that it is designed to overcome. This may involve holding a number of workshops with different groups of people and tailoring presentations to meet the needs of different stakeholder groups. The effort required here should not be underestimated. It is a critical investment in the long-term success of the initiative.

Effective change leaders do not expect to get things right first time, so both the case for change and the vision should go out as drafts to enable people to improve and buy into them before they are finalized.

Stage 6. Plan the changes

It is tempting to start a change initiative by thinking about solutions and preparing detailed proposals for change. This is a mistake. Unless the preceding stages have been completed, proposals are likely to land on unfertile ground. However, once the preparatory steps have been concluded, a plan is an essential element of any change initiative.

The plan needs to address both the substance of the change and the process for implementing it. The substance may include:

- **models** – of different ways of working in the future
- **options** – setting out alternative solutions to the issues
- **proposals** – describing what the changes will be.

The process part of the plan needs to address:

- **practical issues**: what will happen, in what order
- **people and group issues**: who will do things, who needs to be consulted, and how activities will be co-ordinated
- **timetable issues**: deadlines, milestones and fitting in with existing decision-making processes.

A critical judgement at this point is the **division of the work into manageable pieces** that can be completed within available resources and the available time. This provides another opportunity to involve people through task groups. The change team should identify each of the tasks that need to be undertaken and estimate the number of days required to complete the task and the time it will take to complete the change. When this has been done, tough decisions may have to be made either to cut out some activities or to increase the resources available to the team. It is extraordinarily easy to underestimate time and resources, and a misjudgement at this stage can lead to unduly ambitious commitments that cannot be met at later stages.

This is the stage when pilots of possible ways forward may be appropriate. This allows managers to discover whether proposals will really work. Practical experience helps to improve the proposed solutions and, most critically, it helps to build commitment to the proposals. Pilots may delay organization-wide implementation, but they ensure that when change is rolled out it is rooted in practical experience and has champions who have real credibility.

There is nothing more disillusioning for managers than being asked to support initiatives that appear to conflict with other programmes in the organization. The plan therefore needs to consider other initiatives and activities running concurrently in the organization. It should identify them and their timetables, to ensure there are no conflicts. This avoids inconsistency later in the process and demonstrates to everyone that the initiative has taken account of other activities and will integrate its work with them.

This stage often ends with the documentation of a plan and formal decisions to proceed on the proposals set out in the plan. It is the second point in the process when everyone should be clear about what will happen, why it will happen, and when it will happen.

TRANSFORMATIONAL CHANGE AT GUIDE DOGS FOR THE BLIND

The Board of GDBA began a process of transformational change by appointing a new chief executive, who was briefed to address some fundamental issues faced by the organization. It also reviewed its own ways of working and decided that, for the period of major change, all Board committees would be suspended and that the Board would meet monthly instead.

With the help of consultants, the chief executive embarked on a change process that had the following steps:

1. A plan for the first few stages was prepared, consulted upon and agreed.
2. A Steering Group of representatives of all stakeholder groups was established.
3. A review of the strategic position of the organization, the key

issues it faced and broad options for the future, involving contributions from Task Groups, was prepared.

4. A major consultation exercise, involving the chief executive attending workshops in all regions of the country, was carried out.

5. The review was published and stakeholders were asked to respond.

6. The board took two major decisions on the overall direction of the organization and agreed six principles as the basis for preparing an implementation plan.

7. The plan was prepared, as was the subject of further workshops throughout the country.

8. The plan and the implementation document were published.

9. Ten Task Groups, involving staff and board members, were established to drive implementation. Some were due to last a matter of weeks – to ensure some 'quick wins'. Others had tasks that were likely to take one to two years.

10. The board agreed a programme of decision-taking, timed to coincide with completion of the work of each Task Group, and to re-launch the organization after eight months' work had been completed.

Communications strategy was central to the whole process. The chief executive wrote a letter to all staff every few weeks to report on progress. After key board meetings there was a cascade briefing, to inform staff of decisions. Regional meetings were held for guide dog owners and branch representatives. Video reports by the chief executive were sent to each region, because people preferred to hear news in this way, and 'hot news' from the Steering Group was circulated 48 hours after each meeting.

Stage 7. Implementing change

When all the previous stages have been meticulously followed, implementation can begin. A key role for the change leader, supported by the team, is to keep track of progress. This means anticipating deadlines and chasing people before it is too late to take remedial action.

The leader and the team also need to keep their ears close to the ground as work progresses, to enable them to identify issues as they arise and deal with them before they become an impediment to the change pro-gramme. The change team should meet regularly to review progress and take remedial action when problems begin to emerge.

PRIORITIZE QUICK WINS

Change initiatives need to demonstrate results in order to maintain enthusiasm and momentum. If people work for months without seeing significant results, the whole project begins to lose credibility. People become available for meetings less often, will put in less effort and will focus on other matters.

So 'quick wins' are a critical element in a change initiative. Unfortu-nately, they do not necessarily come easily; they have to be vigorously sought after and pushed up the change team's agenda.

Examples of quick wins include:

- a successful pilot for a new way of working
- a new service up and running
- a marked improvement in quality in one area
- a new performance report that captures information of the type required to work in new ways
- an old or disliked process or set of forms being scrapped.

Any initiative should aim to achieve a quick win within six months of the start; a smaller initiative should expect a quick win sooner than that. Once achieved, a quick win provides an ideal opportunity to communicate the success to all stakeholders and give the initiative new momentum.

PILOT EXTENSIVELY

The consequences of change are inevitably difficult to predict; it therefore makes sense to pilot anything that can be tested on a small scale before rolling out the proposals more widely. Opportunities for piloting might include:

- piloting a new service in one area
- testing a new process with a group of people who are keen to pursue the idea

- trialling user-involvement initiatives in one part of the organization
- reorganizing one part of a department to see if the new arrangements produce the desired results.

The disadvantage of piloting is that it may delay final implementation. However, the advantages are huge. Unanticipated problems can be identified and corrected at low cost and with less effort. Proposals can be further developed and refined with the benefit of practical experience. If the pilots begin to show signs of success, commitment to the proposed changes will grow in other parts of the organization as people not involved in the pilot come to see the positive results.

SUPPORTING IMPLEMENTATION

Change leaders can take a number of actions to support implementation:

- **Offer training**. People may need training, the opportunity to shadow someone who has done something similar before, or additional support to implement the change proposals. A mini skills audit to determine whether individuals or groups of people have training needs may shed light on the requirement for training.
- **Adjust people's personal objectives and performance review targets.** Increasingly individuals have annual objectives. These may not include points related to the change initiative or, worse still, they may contain expectations that are in conflict with the new priorities. A review of personal objectives will help to assimilate change at all levels of the organization.
- **Appoint new staff**. Appointing new staff who bring new assumptions and ways of working is one of the quickest and most effective ways of making change happen. Making one or two key appointments can significantly increase the speed of change and implant new beliefs into the organization culture.
- **Encourage consistency**. Changes inevitably lead to inconsistencies with existing activities and processes. Change leaders need to ask people to identify inconsistencies at the earliest opportunity and then attend to them before they become irritations.
- **Hold celebrations**. Change is always hard, so every opportunity should be taken to record progress with activities and events that mark progress.

● **Promote people who implement the initiative**. In the long term, promotions for people who embody the new behaviour and methods of working will do more to ensure long-term success of the change initiative than many other measures.

When implementation runs into problems, it is often because either a misjudgement was made at an earlier stage about the scale or scope of the initiative, a stage was carried out only superficially or one was completely missed out. In these circumstances, it may be necessary to go back a stage rather than pressing on against the odds.

IMPROVING SERVICES AT THE PRINCE'S TRUST – ACTION

The Prince's Trust – Action is the part of the Trust that provides direct services to young people, including courses, study support, grants, awards, special projects to address issues facing young people and contact opportunities with peers in Europe. It operates through some sixty voluntary local committees that historically had operated with a high degree of autonomy. This led to wide variations both in the services provided in different parts of the country and in the evaluation of those services.

A review had led to the appointment of fourteen full-time Network Development Officers to support local committees and a Network Development Committee to co-ordinate activities across the country. This resulted initially in a lack of clarity concerning the responsibilities of voluntary committee chairs, the paid NDOs, the Committee and the staff at national headquarters.

A two-day conference called to review the situation led to a change management project that lasted for nine months. It was a particularly challenging assignment because it involved head office staff, field staff, volunteers and a sub-committee of the governing board.

The project had a **vision** 'to improve the consistency and quality of PT–A's services to young people and to continue the development of appropriate management structures and processes of the Network'.

It had a **Steering Group** of six people: the Executive Director of PT–A, the Director for Network Development and the Chair of the Network Development Committee, and the Chairs of three **Task Groups**. Together they had the power to drive the change process.

It met four times to co-ordinate the process and plan next steps. The **Task Groups** had briefs to:

1. clarify responsibilities of the main parts of PT–A
2. develop a new structure model for local committees, based on best current practice
3. establish minimum standards for local committees.

Each Task Group had a Chair, a timetable of three meetings to do its work and the support of a consultant to prepare the reports and co-ordinate thoughts across the Groups.

A second conference reviewed and improved the reports, which were then drawn together into an overall document for approval by the PT–A Board.

Implementation followed swiftly, as the proposals commanded widespread support. A vital process of change had been legitimized, and implementation to clarify responsibilities and develop new structures moved forward swiftly.

Stage 8. Incorporate changes into the organization's Culture

Ideally, change leaders want their initiatives to be long-lasting. Changes are irreversible only when they become fully embedded in the organization's culture.

Changing culture is undoubtedly the hardest part of change management; it takes the greatest time and requires the most consistent effort. Experience suggests that culture change happens as a consequence of actions and the results of change programmes, rather than as a consequence of attempts to change the culture directly.

Change leaders should recognize that the timescales over which culture change happens are long – usually measured in years rather than months. However, effective change leaders do speed up the process of change by judicious application of the most appropriate actions at the most appropriate times.

Ways of embedding changes into the different levels of an organization's culture include:

- changing visible representations of culture:
  — develop a new performance report
  — introduce a new corporate image
  — rename the organization
  — reorganize office space
  — move to new offices.

- changing behavioural norms:
  — create new management processes
  — reorganize the meeting's structure
  — develop new meeting agendas
  — improve or create new internal communication mechanisms
  — establish user groups to strengthen 'customer' orientation
  — hold joint board/management meetings to create a new strategy
  — celebrate specific achievements with a memorable event.

- changing underlying beliefs:
  — recruit people who hold the new beliefs
  — promote people who show commitment to the new ways of working
  — demonstrate how new practices are improving results.

Change management and changing people

The staged approach to change can become significantly more complicated when the need to change key posts or people is itself part of the change programme. Frequently the arrival of a new chief executive in an under-performing organization presages the beginning of transformational change. In some circumstances, the board will have appointed someone with a mandate to bring about substantial change. In other situations, ambitious chief executives will see their appointment as an opportunity to make a significant difference by bringing new ideas and methods to organizations that are looking for strong leadership. Similarly, the arrival of new senior managers with a brief to transform a department can be the trigger for a major change process.

Large increases in income and significant changes in legislation can also lead to transformational change. They imply the need for new services, new appointments, new structures, new roles and new ways of working. This is likely to add up to transitional or transformational change.

In any of these circumstances major change often implies changes in people's jobs. Some people may be required to take on additional responsibilities, some may have to make significant changes to their roles (and apply for newly created posts), and some may not be required by the organization at all. This greatly complicates change because the team that a change leader has at the start of the process may not be the same group that will be implementing the agreed changes.

It means that change leaders sometimes have to make decisions about people, often when they do not have much evidence as to their performance or their potential. Change leaders have three options. They can **change the team before initiating the change process**. This is appropriate when leaders judge that the organization does not have the management capacity to bring about major change and that there is time to establish a new team before change becomes unavoidable. This may be appropriate when funding is secure and the board is comfortable that change can await the establishment of a new team. It minimizes the potential for people changes and a change programme interfering with each other.

When the pressure for immediate change is stronger, change leaders may have to **change the team during the change process**. This significantly complicates change, because success requires openness, transparency and extensive communication. However, the process of changing people – and, in particular, moving people out of the organization – requires discreet discussions, private negotiations and confidentiality. It may therefore not be possible for the change leader to be completely open with colleagues about the future of some members of the team. It is a particularly demanding time for change leaders as there are many aspects of major change and of people change that just cannot be delegated.

While the process of changing people is underway, those who will be part of the new team will have to trust the change leader. Once changes have been agreed, remaining members should be given reassurance concerning their own future at the earliest opportunity. People who are not directly affected, but who may be worried when the people changes are announced, should also be told that their position is not at risk.

The third alternative is to **adjust the team after the change process**. This is appropriate when it would have been difficult to predict the required changes at the start and when the change process itself has shed light on people's capacity to contribute in the new circumstances. However, if this route is chosen, the change-management process may have to be revisited once the new appointments have been made, so as to help new people understand the rationale behind the changes and the actions required to implement the agreed changes fully.

Ups and downs of change

Presenting major change as a sequence of eight stages makes the process appear as a sequence of events that always move forward. In practice, organizations going through significant change tend to take two steps forward, followed by one step back. At first there may be enthusiasm. This can be followed by denial of the need for change or a sense of being overwhelmed by the scale of the problem. When the need is re-established, people may want to rush ahead, only to be frustrated by the pace of change. When proposals are agreed, people may find it difficult to let go of the past and start behaving in new ways. There may be false starts, followed by great successes.

The critical point for the change leader is to anticipate that there will be ups and downs in the process and that it is difficult to predict when a down will come and what will cause it. Experienced change leaders are not disheartened. They know there will be setbacks, but they also have the confidence and commitment to adjust the process and ensure that they do not lose sight of the overall objective.

STREAMLINING SYSTEMS AT THE WORLDWIDE FUND FOR NATURE

WWF UK spends £13 million per year on some 200 projects that seek to slow down and eventually reverse the destruction of species and habitats throughout the world. The Programme Division has five main departments (International, UK and Europe, Scotland, Policy, Education). Each has managers responsible for project management.

As part of the transition from being a grant-giver to being an organization that has a strategically managed programme, a major project was established to streamline the whole process of agreeing programme goals, integrating fund-raising and programme activities, taking decisions on grants and monitoring performance against the agreed goals.

A Steering Group of twelve people from all parts of the organization involved in the decision-making process was established to undertake the work in three stages: diagnosis, solutions and implementation.

In the first stage, ten Task Groups were established to document existing procedures and prepare a concise diagnosis of the critical problems. This took four months and the results were drawn together by the consultants into an overview. The diagnosis identified the need for:

● multi-year budgets to take account of multi-year projects
● a multi-year Operating Plan and Budget for the Programmes Division
● evaluation of the whole of the 'programme' against the corporate objectives
● integration of two budget allocation processes.

The proposal stage involved eight different Task Groups. They took five months to develop solutions, which were drawn together into an overall package of proposals covering:

● the production of an organization-wide timetable to integrate all planning and budgeting activity
● the use of total costs in financial planning rather than separate internal and external budgets
● the introduction of multi-year budgeting
● a pilot scheme for budgeting staff time
● a process for evaluating programme achievements.

The most difficult problems encountered were:

● finding time to develop new proposals when the existing time-consuming processes were still in place
● maintaining communication about the initiative in a large and complex organization when many people have to spend significant amounts of time away from the office and overseas
● working in a culture which valued individual actions, due to its historical grant-giving role, when a more strategic approach required much higher levels of team work.

One year after the changes were agreed, the organization had an organization-wide timetable, was using total costs, had multi-year budgeting and had successfully piloted time budgeting.

10.6 SKILLS OF THE CHANGE MANAGEMENT LEADER

Managing change is an art. In addition to the skills described so far, change leaders need to:

- **be very clear about the key issues and flexible about the detail**. Leaders need to keep the process sharply focused on the critical changes that are required and to ensure that timely decisions are taken on the big issues. They also need to give the change team and other stakeholders plenty of freedom to make their own contributions in imaginative ways

- **understand people's frustrations**. When people feel that their concerns are being listened to, they are more likely to support change initiatives. Leaders listen particularly to people who are resisting change and understand what fears underlie their opposition. Addressing such fears allows people to contribute constructively to a change programme

- **manage the sponsor**. Change leaders are ultimately accountable to another manager, the chief executive or the board. Their continued support for the change will help to give the initiative priority and send important signals to the other stakeholders about how it is regarded. Take steps to build the sponsors' support, to involve them as work proceeds, and ensure that they champion the initiative

- **expect to be criticized.** It is not possible to keep everyone happy all the time, so anticipate criticism. The key skill is to separate out the vocal minority who do not endanger the overall process from a quiet majority who may not be fully supportive and who could at a late stage endanger the initiative

- **allow time for reflection**. In the maelstrom of activity in busy organizations, it is easy to forget that learning comes in part from reflecting on progress and problems. This helps change leaders to keep their eye on the big picture and ensure that their efforts are directed towards the critical issues and not the minutiae.

The task of the change leader was succinctly summarized in a recent book which said, 'effective leadership of change involves bringing together apparently contradictory qualities. Successful leaders shape the future *and* they adapt to the world as it is. They are clear about what they want to change *and* they are responsive to others' views and concerns. They are passionate about the direction in which they want the organization to go *and* they understand and value the current reality of the organization, why it has been successful and what its people are good at. They lead *and* they learn' (*Leaning into the Future*, Binney and Williams, 1995).

Common obstacles to overcome

Unfortunately, change management is best learned by practice and not by reading books on the subject! And all change initiatives encounter obstacles somewhere in the process. Perhaps the most common one is a lack of time to devote to change initiatives. Hard choices have to be made about priorities and the endemic problem of being realistic about what can be achieved. If managers want change to be successfully implemented, they have to ensure that people have the necessary time. The alternative is a change process that loses momentum and credibility.

Sometimes this may mean convincing board members and funders to adopt realistic priorities for the organization. Sometimes it will be a matter of persuading colleagues. All the evidence suggests that the changes which are the most successful and have greatest impact are those in which all the stakeholders are persuaded from the start to invest the necessary time and effort.

The following guide is designed to help change leaders to overcome common problems that they are likely to encounter:

The problem	Possible solutions
No one has sufficient time to commit to the initiative	• Review resources and time budgets. They may need to be increased and agreed with the appropriate managers • Go back a stage and build more commitment to the initiative
There is lots of action, but nothing fundamental changes	• Ensure the diagnosis is correct. Effort may be focused on the wrong issues or on the symptoms, rather than on the fundamental causes

The problem	Possible solutions
Inability to make real and significant progress	• Ensure key stakeholders are behind the initiative • Ensure the leader has a strong team with the authority to drive the change process • Check the scope has not been defined too widely for change to be achievable
Change appears to be blocked by key people	• Review whether these people are fully committed to the change. If not, it may be necessary to arrange for them to leave in order to secure the best interest of the organization as a whole
Insecurity among staff and managers	• Identify the root causes of the insecurity. Some concerns may be assuaged, others should be acknowledged as real
People are not changing their habits	• Identify what needs to change and then go back a stage in the process
Too many initiatives are crowding each other out	• Establish priorities. One success is better than two failures
A gap between the people driving the change and people who feel they are being driven	• Create opportunities to listen harder and to respond to people's concerns • Increase two-way communication significantly

SUMMARY OF KEY POINTS

Managing change is an essential skill

- As stakeholders' expectations of organizations rise, change management becomes an essential skill for managers at all levels.
- Organizations that have fallen behind the times face a particularly tough change management agenda.
- The principles of change management can be applied to a wide range of management processes.

Introduction to organization culture

- Culture is the way we do and think about things.
- Culture has three levels: visible representations, group behaviour and underlying beliefs.
- Culture is learned, historically determined, partly subconscious, and heterogeneous.

Change management concepts

- Change management is the skill of catalysing significant improvements; it is a combination of substance and process that enables people to see why an issue has arisen and consequently to act in a different way.
- The three types of change are developmental, transitional and transformational.
- Change leaders need to listen closely to people who oppose change to understand the underlying meaning of their concerns and to meet objections head on.

Characteristics of change processes

- Well-managed change processes have periods of confusion and complexity, followed by periods of clarity and simplicity.
- Change leaders expect setbacks but maintain the momentum of the initiative.
- Change is demanding on leaders.

The stages of a change management initiative

- The eight essential stages of change management are to:
  — clarify the scope and scale of the proposed initiative
  — establish the change team
  — prepare a diagnosis of the problem

— build commitment to change

— develop a motivating vision

— plan and communicate extensively about the changes

— implement change by empowering people

— incorporate change into the organization culture.

● Implementing change can involve training, adjusting personal objectives, encouraging consistency, holding celebrations and promoting change implementers.

● 'Quick wins' are an essential element of a change process.

Skills of the change management leader

● Change leaders need to be clear about the key issues and flexible about the detail, understand people's frustrations, manage the sponsor, expect to be criticized and allow time for reflection.

● Change processes inevitably encounter obstacles, often because the leader has missed one or more of the essential stages of a change process.

11   Leading, Directing and Managing

11.1   MANAGEMENT JOBS ARE DIFFERENT

Everyone recognizes that managers' jobs differ by function; the Director
of Finance clearly has a very different job from that of the Director
of Services. Equally important, however, is an understanding of how
managers' jobs differ by level. It is easy to assume that senior managers
have greater responsibility than junior managers, but that the tasks of
managing are essentially the same. In practice, nothing could be further
from the truth. The roles of chief executives, divisional directors (a level
which exists in larger organizations) and managers are fundamentally
different.

Chief executives have particular responsibility for leadership of their
organization, for managing the crucial relationship between the board
and the staff, and for ensuring that the mission and strategy are clear.

Divisional directors are people who manage a group of services and
report to the chief executive. Examples include Director of Operations
and Director of Human Resources. They have two different roles. As
members of the senior management team, they have to share responsibility
with the chief executive for the overall management of the enterprise.
Within their divisions, they have to be able to build their own team,
support and coach their managers, set strategy and hold accountable the
managers who report to them.

Managers' jobs are different again. They are responsible for managing
people to provide direct services, campaigns or internal services (such as
finance and personnel). They have a 'small business' within the enterprise
and have to develop strategy and deliver services and campaigns that

achieve agreed objectives within an agreed budget. In a small organization they report to the chief executive, and in larger organizations they report to divisional directors.

Chief executives, divisional directors and managers all have to deploy the skills of managing their boss, getting teams to perform, delegating work and encouraging learning. But each has to deploy an additional range of skills:

- chief executives have to provide leadership
- divisional directors have to direct
- managers have to manage.

The skills that need to be deployed at each level are additional. Managers of services have to be able to use the broad range of skills needed to manage a service. Divisional directors need to apply all these management skills, and in addition they must be able to use the special skills required to manage managers (known as directing). Chief executives have to have mastered the art of directing, and they also have to know how to employ the wider range of skills required to lead an organization.

This chapter describes these different skills and how people acquire them.

11.2 SPECIAL CHARACTERISTICS OF THE CHIEF EXECUTIVE'S JOB

The role of chief executive in third-sector organizations has changed dramatically over the last thirty years. The post used to be called General Secretary or Clerk to the Council, and the role was seen as being the administrative servant of the board. The post-holder was given comparatively little strategic authority and the board could take a hands-on role because most organizations were small.

During the 1970s, the title 'Director' started to creep on to organizations' letterheads, reflecting a change in the duties that the board expected the office-holder to discharge. In the 1980s the language and the role changed again. Organizations began to seek 'chief executives'. They wanted people with substantial management experience who could take charge of these increasingly large and complex organizations.

It is now widely accepted that having a talented chief executive is a critical ingredient of a successful organization. Chief executives are expected to be figurehead, politician and manager all rolled up in one person. The job is undoubtedly demanding; understanding why this is so requires some insight into why it is so different from all other posts.

It is less structured. Being responsible for everything means the chief executive can become involved in anything. This lack of boundaries differentiates the job from all other posts. As ex-ICI boss John Harvey-Jones says, 'It is only when you become aware of the range, scope and incredible responsibility of the job that you realize that there is an almost limitless opportunity to be ineffective unless you are totally clear about how you are going to set about it.'

It is highly exposed. The chief executive has nowhere to hide. He or she is expected to speak in public, to make press statements, to report to the board, to make presentations at gatherings of staff, and to approve publicly available documents. Chief executives are on stage every day of their working lives.

It requires the widest range of abilities. Chief executives need to master an extraordinary range of skills. They need to understand the fundamentals of finance, marketing, service and human-resource management; they are expected to deploy strong inter-personal skills and at the same time master the policy issues of their field; they need consummate political skills to make things happen; they need to be tough when hard decisions have to be made and tender when compassion and sensitivity are required.

It involves the widest range of constituencies. Chief executives have to operate with many different groups, including funders, service users and umbrella organizations, as well as staff and board members. They have to adjust their style and approach to suit groups that often have different interests and different motives for contributing to the organization.

It is a lonely position. The chief executive often has no one inside the organization to seek advice from on any sensitive issue, because the very act of raising it can cause unnecessary anxiety, particularly if it is an idea that is not subsequently pursued.

It depends on maintaining a reservoir of goodwill. Chief executives need the trust and active support of their board and their staff. They have to maintain the confidence of both groups in order to do the job.

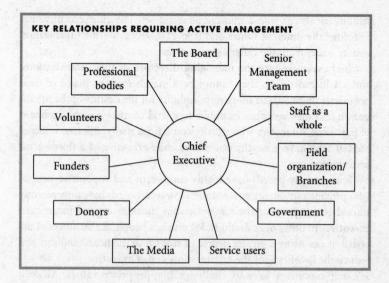

KEY RELATIONSHIPS REQUIRING ACTIVE MANAGEMENT

- The Board
- Senior Management Team
- Professional bodies
- Staff as a whole
- Volunteers
- Chief Executive
- Field organization/ Branches
- Funders
- Government
- Donors
- The Media
- Service users

It is the critical link between the board and the staff. The chief executive has to operate effectively both as head of the senior management team and as the servant of the board. These two groups frequently have different working styles and priorities. The chief executive has to work with both and manage the information flows between the two.

It requires a longer-term perspective and short-term actions. Chief executives have to think months or years ahead, and simultaneously solve current problems that have not been resolved elsewhere in the organization.

Five further aspects of the role are common in managing third-sector organizations.

It is not well understood. The special characteristics of the chief executive's job are often not well understood by the board, the staff and other people outside the organization. This results in conflicting expectations that will pull the chief executive in different directions until these people become clear about the role.

Chief executives have to **bridge many fundamentally different value systems.** Third-sector organizations all have a skill base such as medicine, education, social welfare, and so on. Each skill base has associated with it a set of values that are predominant in that field. These values are seldom consistent with a managerial mind-set. The chief executive has to bridge the different values and help each group see the organization and its issues from the other's perspective.

Chief executives are the **managing directors** of their organizations, and yet in most cases they cannot be a member of the board of their organization. They bear more responsibility for the destiny of the organization and they are often its public face, and yet they report to a board of part-time volunteers who usually come from many different walks of life but who have generally not been a chief executive of a third-sector organization.

Clearly, many boards have highly competent and supportive people, who provide top-quality governance. However, boards have only recently started to ensure that their membership includes one or more chief executives of other organizations. When such people are members of the board, it can bring a greater degree of realism to the board and can also reduce the loneliness of the organization's chief executive.

Chief executives have to **challenge inappropriate values.** Modern management textbooks (including this one) stress the importance of the organization's culture and values. But values can also be a source of difficulty for the chief executive when they permeate all aspects of an organization's work in ways that are inappropriate. Take, for example, the training organization whose commitment to training its own staff grows out of proportion to their need to perform their jobs; the trade union that is frightened to challenge the union that its own staff belong to; the human-rights organization that uses the language of human rights to argue for equality of status for all staff; or the social-services agency that cannot bring itself to sack members of staff who are consistently not performing to the required standard. In these circumstances, it falls to the chief executive to challenge the inappropriate application of values and beliefs.

Finally, third-sector chief executives have to **deploy a combination of entrepreneurial and political skills**. They need the entrepreneurial abilities of taking risks and seizing opportunities that are usually associated with the private sector. They also need the ability to unite diverse political constituencies behind activities that everyone is willing to support – a skill that is more often associated with public-sector management.

11.3 STRUCTURING THE CHIEF EXECUTIVE'S WORK

Because the chief executive's job entails endless variety, it is all the more important to structure the work. Without structure there is always the risk that chief executives will become the servants of their in-trays – dealing with what appears to be most urgent rather than with those things that are most important (and which usually do not appear in the in-tray).

One way to structure the chief executive's work is to think in terms of his or her responsibilities for the three Ps:

- the **purpose** of the organization
- the **processes** of managing it
- the **people** who work closely with the chief executive.

The purpose

Chief executives have a wide range of responsibilities relating to the purpose. Their first responsibility is to ensure that all parts of the organization are **focusing on achieving the purpose**. This is easier said than done. It is tempting for chief executives to allow the process of getting things done to become more important than the task itself. For some, managing by consensus is assumed to be the best way of working; it unites different constituencies behind a common purpose. But achievement of the task sometimes needs to take precedence over the process of gaining consensus. The balance is a delicate one. Chief executives who take too many initiatives to strengthen the purpose without seeking consensus will ultimately encounter opposition. On the other hand, chief executives who miss opportunities, or who slow the pace of change because they are always striving to gain consensus, risk losing momentum and being branded as weak and indecisive.

Chief executives need to concentrate on the **quality of the organization's services.** Ultimately, the organization is about providing services to an agreed user group (or campaigns on agreed issues), to a specified standard and within agreed cost and time parameters. The chief executive needs to know whether this is happening, what the organization is doing to improve the quality of its services and what has been learned about the most effective ways of improving them.

Chief executives also need to ensure that all the **internal functions are providing high value-added services** to the rest of the organization. These include finance, marketing, personnel, information technology, property maintenance, and so on. It is remarkably easy for them to become engrossed in their own concerns and gradually slip away from the objective of meeting the needs of the organization's service providers. The absence of market mechanisms to keep them on their toes means that chief executives have to ensure that they are meeting their internal users' needs.

Chief executives are also responsible for ensuring that the organization has a **viable economic equation.** In the past, some chief executives believed their financial role was to ensure a balanced budget; as long as income was approximately the same as expenditure, chief executives had met their financial responsibilities. This, however, is insufficient, even in times of low inflation. Ambitious chief executives should ensure that the organization makes a surplus to pay for future investments, innovation, experiments and working capital, and to give them managerial flexibility.

In many third-sector organizations, fund-raising plays a role in balancing the economic equation. Although most have professional staff running fund-raising, chief executives need to play **three critical roles in fund-raising**. They have to:

1. ensure that the organization has an ambitious, realistic and achievable fund-raising strategy. This is a challenging task. Fund-raising is among the most difficult and subtle activities in third-sector management. It is surrounded by opportunities to make errors of judgement. Chief executives have to challenge fund-raising plans, ensure that they are robust, provide imagination when they are dreary, and give special support to the person who is responsible for their delivery.
2. give personal attention to key fund-raising initiatives. Ultimately, large donors and grant-makers expect chief executives to be personally involved in fund-raising. They need to be assured that their grant or donation is being given special attention, and the best way to signify that is by the presence of the chief executive.
3. ensure that each type of fund-raising investment is producing a return appropriate for that source of funds.

Finally, chief executives have to **encourage innovation**. They have to ensure that the organization is continually moving forward and finding ways to campaign and deliver services that meet new circumstances. It means searching for new ideas, sometimes from other countries, sometimes from local branches and sometimes from organizations in other fields. It means putting staff time and money into new ideas and acknowledging that, while many will fail, a few will become the engine for the organization's future development.

The processes

More than anyone else in the organization, chief executives are responsible for managing the processes that are required to make things happen. Chief executives are responsible for ensuring that the necessary processes for good management are established and continuously developed to meet changing circumstances. They also have a day-to-day responsibility for guiding the processes used to take individual decisions. They have to define:

- the precise nature of each decision
- when the decision should be taken
- who needs to be involved
- the period of time over which the decision should be taken.

Chief executives also have to decide **how to structure the big decisions**, so as to make it easy to proceed. Structuring decisions in ways that fit with staff and board perceptions makes decisions easier. For example, a decision concerned with improving the quality of a service could be cast as a decision about:

- the need for improved performance-monitoring to pinpoint problem areas
- the need for a new service plan
- a pilot improvement programme to demonstrate a new approach to quality management
- an opportunity to raise new funds from a donor who wants the service to be successful
- firing the manager responsible.

More than anyone else, the chief executive has to decide which way to approach the problem in order to achieve the desired results.

Judgements about **whom to involve** in a decision are the next consideration. Consultation is an essential ingredient of the chief executive's job. The problems most organizations have to deal with are highly complex. Expertise and knowledge often reside with many different people whose contribution will often lead to better decisions. Furthermore, their commitment to implementing decisions will be greater if they feel they have been consulted.

Consultation is also essential to hold together the coalition of stakeholders who constitute a third-sector organization. If funders, board, managers and employees have been consulted, they are more likely to back the decisions the organization makes, even if the decision is not the one they wanted.

However, consultation slows decision-making. When there is too much consultation, people become frustrated at the lack of progress and may feel that the chief executive is abdicating his or her responsibility for taking decisions. So chief executives have to be making a continuous stream of judgements about whom to involve in different types of decisions and when to involve them. They have to **pace decisions**. An attempt to rush key decisions through too quickly can lead to a build-up of opposition. But leaving issues to fester unresolved begins to immobilize organizations. Chief executives have to make frequent judgements about how fast to push people on critically important issues.

Chief executives have to **take decisions**. Although the major decisions are likely to have been widely discussed and are formally taken by the board, chief executives have to make up their own minds at an early stage and drive decisions through the organization. They have to listen to their colleagues and take advice, but often this will be contradictory. So chief executives have to decide when to listen to advice and when to note it but proceed in order to achieve a desired objective.

Chief executives also have to take critically important decisions about **the amount of work** an organization should commit itself to achieving. It is always tempting to make more commitments than the organization can meet. Indeed, a common mistake chief executives make is to take too many management initiatives without taking full account of the limitations on people's time to implement the desired changes. Consequently they are either not done to the required standard or they are so delayed that they lose their impact.

The **timing of initiatives** often rests in the hands of chief executives.

It is tempting to concentrate on the substance of a decision and forget that the timing is equally important. Pushing for an urgently needed change (for example, the restructuring of a team) when no one favours the idea might lead to no change at all. A half-anticipated departure, however, might create circumstances in which the same change is agreed without resistance or difficulty.

Finally, chief executives are responsible for ensuring good **communications** within the organization. People need information in order to do their jobs effectively and to set their work in the wider context of the organization. Chief executives have to work to ensure that:

- clear and concise information about why particular decisions have been taken is communicated to managers and staff
- information reaches everyone who needs to know (including part-time employees, people working away from the head office and people on leave)
- the organization is not overloaded with news and facts, but is failing to communicate the essential information.

Chief executives need to make effective use of a wide range of methods of communication, including:

- regular team briefings
- chief executive's newsletters
- managers' meetings and staff conferences
- internal news-sheets
- user group meetings
- e-mail and intranets
- telephone conferences
- videos.

The people

Building relationships with a wide range of people is a critical part of the chief executive's job. Chief executives have to work particularly closely with board members and the senior management team. They need to form relationships with, and maintain the confidence of the majority of, the individuals in both groups.

Chief executives need to **build strong senior management teams**. This is an essential prerequisite for making a success of the chief executive's job. It requires the chief executive to create good working relationships with each member of the team and with the team as a whole. These are the people who make the organization work and, without capable directors working as a team, organizations quickly become unmanageable.

Chief executives have to secure and maintain the confidence of the senior management team. If there are more departures than anticipated or if vacancies are unfilled for too long, chief executives will quickly lose the confidence of their remaining team members and find that their job is at risk.

Chief executives have to decide on the desirable structure for their senior management team and on the timing of any changes that need to be made. These are sensitive issues, where support from the chair and the board will often help a chief executive come to the right judgement.

Chief executives have to hold members of their team **accountable.** They have to agree objectives with each member of the team and review their performance at regular intervals.

Chief executives are also responsible for the professional development of members of their team. They can be encouraged to network with similar organizations or to pursue an interest in a field which personally intrigues them. They can be encouraged to take on additional responsibilities or to take time out of work to study. Sometimes chief executives may need to be particularly aware of people's personal circumstances and of stresses in their lives. At other times they may need to give members of their team extra support on an assignment. Chief executives cannot work miracles, but they can hold on to good people if they do all they can to look after the individual professional development needs of team members.

A particular problem chief executives face is in their relationship with the individual who is responsible for the function that is also the **chief executive's own area of professional expertise.** An example that is known to cause problems is in the relationship with the Director of Services when the chief executive's background was service management.

Sometimes chief executives are tempted to take the limelight and intervene a great deal in an area because it is their area of expertise. They feel that they can make a particularly strong contribution here. This can cause problems for the director or manager of that area, who may feel constrained and lacking freedom that is given to the other directors or managers. Conversely, chief executives may realize that this is a sensitive issue and over-compensate by not becoming sufficiently involved in that area. In this circumstance, directors or managers may feel that they are receiving insufficient attention compared to their colleagues. Either way, it is an issue worth bringing to the surface so that both parties come to a mutually satisfactory relationship.

AVOIDING BAD HABITS

Working with many chief executives has given me an opportunity to observe some habits that need to be avoided. They include:

- failing to take decisions
- talking too much in meetings
- allowing team members to talk too much
- blaming the board
- failing to hold people to account for their responsibilities
- always seeing people's weaknesses rather than their strengths
- not delivering on tasks they committed themselves to
- not delegating explicitly
- criticizing team members behind their backs
- revealing by their attitude, behaviour and non-verbal communication whom they like and whom they dislike.

Everyone makes mistakes. Successful chief executives strive to learn from their errors and to find their own formula for working effectively as a leader.

Chief executives also have to form a **close working relationship with their board**. They have to understand their needs and their concerns, and maintain their confidence at all times. This is not straightforward, since chief executives sometimes have to carry a recalcitrant board along with their proposed changes. Pushing change too far or too fast carries the risk that members of the board will begin to lose confidence in the chief executive. As soon as more than half the members have concerns (often about very different matters), the chief executive's job is at risk.

To overcome this danger, chief executives should **form an effective working relationship with the chair**. This means putting time aside to meet alone with the chair to share concerns, plan board meetings and build and maintain trust in each other. This is not always easy, as these two people are chosen for different reasons, at different times, and seldom because people think they will work well together. Nevertheless, the consequences of a poor working relationship can be very significant for the organization. The absence of good co-ordination between the chair and the chief executive can lead to misunderstandings and growing mistrust between the board and the staff. So, even though the two people in these positions may sometimes not be the best of friends, each needs to be able to respect the other and to find the time and motivation to work together as a partnership (see section 4.4 for details).

11.4 CHIEF EXECUTIVES PROVIDE LEADERSHIP

Management is concerned with the efficient administration of the organization. It is about the establishment of processes that make the organization work, the creation of structures that link people together in an organized way, the development of plans, the control of budgets and the costing of services. Chief executives have to master all these and more.

But truly effective chief executives have to rise beyond management and provide leadership. Leadership is required to clarify the mission, to motivate people, to seek new opportunities, to give organizations a sense of purpose and to focus people on the task.

The boundary between management and leadership is not crystal clear. It is not that management is all boring administration and leadership is the enjoyable activity; they sit on a continuum. But the distinction is important because organizations need an appropriate combination of management and leadership for their circumstances. Those that are over-led and under-managed may be exciting places to work, but they may not have the practical capacity to deliver the work. Those that are under-led but over-managed may be capable of doing the work, but they are eventually overtaken by the imaginative organization with the flair and creativity to take entirely new approaches to achieving their mission and inspiring their people.

Organizations need leadership at the top. Since most chairs are volunteers and have limited time to give to the organization, chief executives have to lead both the board and the staff. This does not mean usurping the proper role of the board to control the organization. Indeed, chief executives' leadership role is a great deal easier when organizations have

LEADERSHIP AND MANAGEMENT

Although a little stereotyped, the following helps to make the distinction between leadership and management

The Leadership Task
Create a long-term vision
Set broad purpose and direction
Create a better future
Focus on the product
Inspire people to do more
Teach by example and praise
Create more effective systems
Focus on effectiveness
Look to the future

The Management Task
Plan to meet current objectives
Make best use of resources
Manage today's problems
Focus on making processes work well
Ensure people work to contract
Seek improvements through training
Establish standard procedures
Focus on efficiency
Look at the present

Adapted from *LEAD!*, Richard Lynch, Jossey-Bass, 1993

skilled and supportive chairs. But it is widely accepted that the most effective organizations almost always have chief executives who provide both the board and the staff with leadership.

Effective chief executives understand the difference between being a manager and being a leader. They strive to delegate managerial tasks so as to create the time to discharge their leadership responsibilities. They manage their time in such a way that they can turn their attention away from the daily deluge of seemingly urgent activities and on to the task of providing leadership.

They recognize that learning about leadership is a lifelong process. It takes time and practice to learn what it means and how to behave as a leader. One way to start working on the development of leadership skills is to review current behaviour against an inventory of leadershipskills.

The following checklist is based on ten points suggested by Richard Lynch:

1. **Recognize people's efforts**. Effective leaders praise the work of their managers, the staff, the board and local branches. As monetary rewards are less significant in the third sector, personal recognition is all the more critical. Recognition is best when it is:

- given frequently
- varied
- honest
- about the person, not just the work
- appropriate for the achievement
- consistent
- timely – given as soon after the event as possible
- individualized to suit the recipient's needs.

2. **Develop a power base.** The chief executive's power depends primarily on maintaining the confidence of the board, the staff and, in some cases, the broader membership as well. That implies both serving them well and, more importantly, gaining and maintaining their confidence. This requires chief executives to demonstrate that they are in command of the organization's affairs. Chief executives need to persuade the organization to face up to and resolve difficult issues; and they also have to stop the board or staff making decisions that would be difficult to defend. They also strengthen their power base by anticipating divisions of opinion between themselves, their boards and their staff. Each is a potential weakness that others can exploit if the chief executive is not in command of the resolution process.

3. **Use authority effectively**. Chief executives – and in particular those employed by caring organizations – find it difficult to combine caring values with the need to be tough and decisive when circumstances demand a decision that will not please colleagues. The temptation is to give relationships a higher priority when in practice the long-term interest of the organization should be paramount. Authority used effectively increases people's respect for the leader.

THE LESSONS OF EXPERIENCE

Douglas McGregor acted as teacher and consultant to many organizations. After being President of Antioch College in the United States, he had the honesty to admit that he had made some wrong assumptions about leadership:

'It took the direct experience of becoming a line executive, and meeting personally the problems involved, to teach me what no amount of observation of other people could have taught.

'I believed, for example, that a leader could operate successfully as a kind of adviser to his organization. I thought I could avoid being a boss. Unconsciously, I suspect, I hoped to duck the unpleasant necessity of making difficult decisions, of taking the responsibility for one course of action among many uncertain alternatives, of making mistakes and taking the consequences. I thought that maybe I could operate so that everyone would like me – that good human relations would eliminate all discord and disagreement.

'I could not have been more wrong. It took a couple of years, but I finally began to realize that a leader cannot avoid the exercise of authority any more than he can avoid responsibility for what happens to his organization. In fact, it is a major function of the top executive to take on his own shoulders the responsibility for resolving the uncertainties that are always involved in important decisions. Moreover, since no important decision ever pleases everyone in the organization, he must also absorb the displeasure, and sometimes severe hostility, of those who would have taken a different course.

'A colleague recently summed up what my experience has taught me in these words: A good leader must be tough enough to win a fight, but not tough enough to kick a man when he is down. This notion is not in the least inconsistent with humane, democratic leadership. Good human relations develop out of strength, not weakness.'

Essays of Douglas McGregor, MIT Press, 1966

4. **Use the power of the position**. People in positions of power, particularly those recently appointed, often shun the trappings of power. They stress that they are the same as everyone else and forgo the privileges relevant to the post. This is an understandable reaction, particularly in organizations with a history of equality and consensus decision-making. It can nevertheless be short-sighted because, like it or not, the status attached to the post is one source of the chief executive's influence. Effective chief executives ensure that they retain an appropriate status for the post in the prevailing circumstances. They have an office that

is appropriate for the job. They ensure that they have appropriate administrative support. They sit at the head of the table at meetings.

5. **Build a reputation**. Managers respect chief executives who have a reputation in their field of endeavour. Chief executives who have the expertise to make press comments or give speeches strengthen their position within their organizations. They gain a reputation by networking with co-ordinating groups and by building a profile in their field through writing or hosting seminars.

6. **Develop skills and abilities**. Leaders constantly strive to increase their expertise, both as managers and as people who understand the detail of their field of endeavour. When managers know that they can extend their abilities by working with their leader, their respect for the leader grows.

7. **Clarify personal objectives**. Leaders have a burning desire to achieve specific objectives. They are clear about what they want the organization to accomplish and how they are going to help the organization to realize it. When this is coupled with a passionate belief in what the organization can do, it rubs off on everyone else.

8. **Communicate with stakeholders**. Leaders listen to others and the language they use. They put great emphasis on communicating a vision of the future in language that people can understand. They take every opportunity to communicate in person and in writing with as many constituencies as possible.

9. **Develop a positive self-image**. Effective leaders are confident of their abilities. They strive to increase confidence in themselves and in others. They are optimistic. They get into a virtuous circle in which their success feeds their self-image, which in turn leads to further success.

10. **Combine vision with attention to detail**. Leaders judge when to focus on the big picture and when detail has to be given attention. Focusing exclusively on either is a recipe for problems.

This is a challenging set of attributes, and few chief executives will exhibit them all. It illustrates the point that chief executives have their own learning requirements and that these are just as important as the needs of other managers.

Chief executives' learning

Chief executives have to put time and effort into considering their own learning programme and taking the actions required to ensure that they are developing the range and depth of their skills. Some will be fortunate enough to have a chair or a board member who can assist with this task. Others may have to rely on close colleagues or a consultant to provide an external perspective on their development.

The first step is to acknowledge that personal development is an essential part of a chief executive's maturation and that, despite the very heavy pressures on people's time, it deserves attention and effort. Then, chief executives need to identify their development needs. These can come from:

● discussions with the chair
● feedback from managers as part of a 360° performance review
● discussions with a mentor
● conversations with other chief executives.

The next step is to decide how the identified needs can be met. Options include:

● joining an Action Learning Set (perhaps run by a professional association or a business school)
● attending appropriate training courses
● appointing a mentor specifically to attend to their learning needs.

Finally, the loop can be closed with a review of progress and the establishment of new learning objectives.

Responsibility for attending to learning needs is an ongoing requirement that should be given continuous attention by chief executives who wish to deploy the many skills that are expected of the role.

GOOD HABITS

Watching the chief executive of one of Britain's largest third-sector organizations, I noticed that:
● he went out of his way to praise staff for their achievements (both face to face and through personal notes)

- he demonstrated that he had listened to consultation by returning people's comments with his own views annotated in the margin
- he held a conference of all 120 senior managers once or twice a year to share the overall strategy and communicate his view of priorities
- he retained the authority of the position of chief executive by taking decisions when people could not agree
- he worked hard to retain the confidence of his board by keeping them well informed, anticipating difficult decisions and planning how they should be taken, often over a period of many months.

These are habits of chief executives who lead their organizations.

WHAT FOLLOWERS EXPECT FROM THEIR LEADERS

One of the characteristics of leadership is the ability to persuade others to follow. Research at Santa Clara University attempted to identify leadership characteristics that followers admire. It came up with some surprising results. It did not find that followers wanted chief executives to be the best strategic planners, the fastest decision-takers or to have the best 'people' skills. Following the survey of 2,615 managers, the researchers found the following four characteristics were most admired:

Characteristic	% of managers selecting this
Honesty	83
Competence	67
Forward-looking	62
Inspiring	58

This suggests that followers are not looking for someone with godlike characteristics. Rather they want their leaders to be good at the basics:

Honesty: keeping agreements, telling the truth, and behaving in a trustworthy way

Competence: having a good track record, being able to challenge, enable and encourage (but not necessarily having expertise in the core skill areas of the organization)

Forward-looking attitude: having a sense of direction, the ability to select a desirable destination for the organization

Capacity to inspire: being able to communicate a vision and to give people a greater sense of worth.

The Leadership Challenge: Kouzes and Posner, Jossey-Bass, 1987

11.5 **DIVISIONAL DIRECTORS DIRECT**

Divisional directors are people who report to the chief executive and have managers reporting to them. This level of management exists in larger organizations where services are grouped together under a divisional director. People working at this level are called divisional directors to emphasize the distinction between managers (who are responsible for managing individual services) and divisional directors (whose main task is managing managers). The term 'director' is not being used to imply any legal responsibility that may be attached to being a director of, say, an organization which is also a limited liability company.

Directors have two equally important roles. They are responsible for **managing their own department**. They have to craft into a team the people who report to them. They need to establish clear objectives for the team, agree operating plans and work programmes for the department, procure the resources needed to deliver the plan and hold their managers accountable.

They also share responsibility with the chief executive for the **overall management of the organization**. They have to support the chief executive in managing the overall strategy, shaping policies and plans and giving advice on major operational decisions. This second set of responsibilities requires directors to deploy a very different set of skills, which will be described in this section.

Directors of effective organizations may spend between a third and a half of their time on their responsibilities as directors. To do this, they have to delegate many of their managerial responsibilities, which necessitates building a strong team of managers. The nature of the delegation is different from that described earlier. When people are first appointed to a management post, they have to learn to delegate work in order to create time to manage. When people are appointed as directors, they have to learn how to delegate management in order to create time to direct.

Skills of effective directors

People generally need to have had substantial management experience before accepting a director-level post. They need to have a functional expertise (for example, service delivery, finance or fund-raising) and to have experience in using those skills. They should also have had management experience – perhaps running a unit of an organization, a geographical territory or an internal service. This will have given them experience of building a team, delegating work and getting performance from people. These skills will be invaluable when it comes to managing managers and coaching them to perform their tasks.

Once appointed as a director, a new range of skills has to be developed. First, directors have to learn to see problems from an **organization-wide perspective.** Each director has to step into the shoes of the chief executive and contribute constructively to the overall management of the organization. This may mean shaping the development of the organization's policies, helping to establish organization-wide priorities or improving processes such as strategic planning, management information, budget-setting and performance review. It may involve chairing a task group or representing the organization in the media. Whatever the activity, directors need a clear overview of the organization and its work.

Secondly, directors have to learn to **think at a strategic level.** It requires the ability to stand back from practical details and take a longer-term and more conceptual view of the organization and its environment. This necessitates allocating significant time to reflecting, talking to other people about strategic issues and building the capacity to contribute constructively to the strategic thinking of the senior management team. This is not easy for managers who are used to being action-orientated, resolving today's crises and taking tomorrow when it comes.

To see the current situation in its correct context, directors need to learn about the organization's past. They need to develop a deep understanding of the organization's present situation and accurately anticipate key elements of the future. This requires an ability to stand back from the detail and summarize the current circumstances into a clear overview. It means talking to people to gain the 'helicopter' view of the organization. Directors need to make a contribution to the senior management team that moves beyond providing details of their area of work. When they are equipped with this high-level context, directors can discharge their responsibilities for the strategic development of the organization.

Thirdly, directors have to be much more aware of the changing **social, political and technical environment** around their organization. Changes in social policy, government policy and party policy are important issues for directors. Such developments require adroit changes to the way the organization thinks about its work. Directors therefore need to read widely and network extensively to keep their finger on these important external trends.

Fourthly, directors need to learn how to **hold managers accountable for their work.** In part, this is achieved by requiring their managers to prepare strategic and operational plans for each service managed by the division. A key role of a divisional director is to support managers in the preparation of their plans, to scrutinize them closely before they are approved and to use them in a regular and systematic way to hold managers accountable for their performance. Divisional directors are discharging their responsibilities most effectively when they keep their eye on the overall performance of each service and avoid the trap of being pulled into the detail.

Finally, directors have to **judge when to intervene** in a situation and when to stand back. Although managerial experience will help here, it is more complex for directors. They have to judge both when to intervene in managers' work and when to delve one level deeper to have a hands-on involvement in front-line service delivery. Effective directors can use their experience to make a substantial difference at both levels, but they have the time to get involved only in those few decisions where they can make a significant contribution. Examples of circumstances in which directors are likely to have a hands-on involvement include capital investments, exploiting wholly new sources of funds or responding to significant changes in government policy. It is a mistake to intervene too often. 'He never lets me do my job,' is a common complaint and one that is often justified. Moreover, effective directors just do not have the time to become involved in the detail of all the services in their division.

Learning directorship skills

Ensuring that directors learn directorship skills is a responsibility that is shared by directors and their chief executives. Chief executives help, usually through one-to-one meetings, to identify development needs, to guide directors on changing their priorities, and on actions to develop the required skills. As well as helping directors, this also sets an example to directors (and to other managers) who need to pay attention to the development needs of the people who report to them.

Directors also have to take personal responsibility for their own development. The chief executive may be able to help, but the mark of a good director is that he or she is someone who knows their own strengths and weaknesses and who takes action to develop the skills that require attention.

There are a variety of ways of encouraging learning:

- **Use a mentor**. Directors can use someone outside the line-management structure as a sounding board or mentor. A trustee with directorship experience, a director of another organization or a consultant can all be used to review experiences and make learning a more systematic process.
- **Use your own team**. The people who report to you are an important source of learning. By regularly asking for feedback, directors gain important data on their performance and how to improve it.
- **Review learning alone**. Directors can keep a personal record of learning points and routinely update it to build a body of experience and personal learning. They can also read and reflect to consolidate experiences and help to ensure that what is learned is applied in subsequent situations.

CREATING AN ACTION PLAN FOR PERSONAL DEVELOPMENT

Start by thinking back over an issue, a meeting or a decision. Consider what happened and select a part of it that was significant to you:

- Write a detailed account of what happened during that period of activity. Don't at this stage put any effort into deciding what you learned – just concentrate on describing what actually happened.
- Then list the conclusions you have reached as a result of the

experience. These are, in effect, your learning points. Don't limit the number and don't worry about the practicality or quality of the points.

- Finally, decide which learning points you want to implement in the future, and work out an action plan which covers:
  — what you are going to do
  — when you are going to do it.
- Spell out your action plan as precisely as possible so that you are clear what you have to do and that it is realistic.

A. Mumford *et al.*, *Director's Development Guidebook*, Institute of Directors, 1990

In some organizations directors are located in different parts of the country (and sometimes in different parts of the world). For these people to work as directors and to be effective members of a senior management team, special attention has to be paid to communication and working together. Extra time has to be given to meetings, because team communication has to be squashed into fewer occasions. Telephone conferencing is a particularly good way of keeping all team members in touch with one another between meetings.

In summary, the work of being a director is very different from that of being a manager. It requires a new layer of skills that can be learned and developed. The task of a director is to understand the differences and to use every means available to acquire the necessary skills. The rewards are potentially high. The divisional director who has mastered the skills and is making a substantial contribution to the overall management of the organization is well prepared to start applying for chief executive positions.

THE EFFECTIVE DIVISIONAL DIRECTOR

Watching the divisional director of a national organization providing a wide range of services for people with a common disability, I noticed:

- she had reduced the number of managers reporting directly to her to give her time to discharge her director's duties
- she built her managers into a strong team and encouraged them to solve each other's problems

- she took the team out of the office three times a year to plan and monitor progress
- these actions gave her time to think about senior management team meetings, enabling her to have something useful to contribute to each item
- she worked hard to build a network of contacts outside the organization and used them for advice on organization-wide issues
- she volunteered to help on strategic problems in senior management team meetings
- she kept abreast of major developments in the disability field so that she could see her organization in perspective.

These are the actions of an effective divisional director.

11.6 MANAGERS MUST MANAGE

In many third-sector organizations, management was, until recently, not a valued skill. A legacy of this belief is that some managers are expected to learn the skills they need by some mysterious process of osmosis. There is an assumption that management is all common sense – something an intelligent person has the innate skills to do. To make matters worse, managers are often managed by people who themselves have been promoted because of their specialist skills and in consequence have had little management training. Some chief executives and divisional directors have, unfortunately, not developed the skills of coaching newly appointed managers.

Faced both with a poor understanding of what being a manager means in practice and with a culture that tends not to value management, some managers fall into the trap of doing rather than managing. It often appears easier to do a task than to manage someone else to do it, particularly when you were promoted because you were good at doing that task. Managers feel comfortable when they are busy, and they know that they can usually do the work more quickly than their successors and probably to a better quality. But doing the work is not the job of a manager.

The essential skills of a front-line manager are:

- setting objectives
- building teams

- developing individuals
- taking decisions
- monitoring performance
- resolving problems.

The problem for managers is, however, that seemingly straightforward tasks are often much more complex in practice. This section explains some of the special characteristics that affect managers in third-sector organizations and suggests ways of becoming a more effective manager in these circumstances. Some of these points are relevant to chief executives and divisional directors as well as to front-line managers. They are grouped together here because they impact most directly on the work of front-line managers.

The task of managing people in this sector has to be seen in the context of the types of people who work in it. The third sector attracts employees with different motives, particularly when compared to the private sector (P. Murvis, writing in *Non-profit Management and Leadership*, autumn 1992). This research has shown that they tend to have stronger ideals; they attach greater value to job satisfaction; pay is less important; and job content is seen to be part of the compensation package. People who work in the third sector have been shown to be more caring in spirit, to be more trusting of others and less cynical in their attitude.

The same research showed that people working in the third sector tend to have higher educational qualifications than people in equivalent jobs in the private and public sectors. They also have greater difficulty balancing their work lives and their private lives. This is hardly surprising: when people live for a cause, the distinction between work and home becomes very blurred.

Special challenges for managers

The first challenge managers have to face is that most third-sector organizations have extraordinarily high ambitions. They all want to have a significant impact. Objectives such as saving endangered species, discovering a treatment for an incurable disease or alleviating poverty are ambitious and lack clear boundaries. For front-line managers this means that there is always more they could do. Effective managers consequently have to learn to be realistic about what can be achieved and **ruthless in setting priorities**.

This means that an annual work plan is an essential management tool. It should set out what will be done by whom, and it should leave space every month to deal with unforeseen problems. It also requires managers to check frequently in their own mind what their objectives are, and whether some of their current workload can be avoided because it is not a top priority.

The second challenge is to **carve out an appropriate role** for the circumstances. The space in which managers have to work is often squeezed by various pressures. There is pressure from board committees, which expand their roles from their proper governance duties into the day-to-day problems of management. These interventions into management are often well intended, and sometimes even needed. But a board or committee that slips incrementally over the boundary of governance and into routine management reduces managers' authority and the scope of the managerial task.

Similarly, managers can face constraints from their boss not giving them sufficient freedom to get on with their job. The hands-on boss who wants to be involved in all the detail can be a significant impediment to a front-line manager.

Yet another pressure comes from professional groups (such as doctors, social workers and teachers) and articulate individuals, who quite rightly guard against managerial incursions into what they perceive to be their professional domain. The boundaries here are invariably grey. However, faced with a powerful board, an interventionist chief executive and strong professional interests, weak managers can find it increasingly difficult to define the contribution they can make. They need to be totally clear about what they are doing and why they are doing it in order to have the freedom to discharge their managerial duties.

The third challenge is to overcome the common belief that organizations should be managed by consensus. People quite rightly expect to be involved in decision-making, but this expectation can shift subtly from the realistic desire to be consulted on some decisions to the unrealistic demand that all decisions should be taken by consensus. Managers have to **earn their authority** by distinguishing between situations requiring consensus and circumstances in which they should take responsibility, make a decision and be held accountable. Managers consequently need to keep issues which are heading for decisions under constant review and decide when to prolong discussion in order to achieve consensus and when to take command and make decisions.

The fourth challenge is that, in some organizations, the very notion of management sits uncomfortably alongside strongly held values about empowering disadvantaged people. From this perspective, users have rights to define their needs and the way services should be provided. Many no longer want to be given charity; they want to determine what the organization should be doing for them and not allow management to take decisions, sometimes in a paternalistic and demeaning way. Managers of these organizations have to combine a strong commitment to **representing users' views** with an ability to make things happen when decisions need to be implemented.

MANAGERS' TASKS ARE EXTRAORDINARILY VARIED

Third-sector managers are expected to perform an extraordinarily wide range of tasks. Leonard Cheshire has 140 homes and services in the UK and a further 200 homes in fifty countries around the world. Each home or service has a manager who has to deploy a wide range of skills. A survey identified the following skills which a home manager needs:

- strategic planning
- marketing to purchasing authorities
- negotiating fees
- agreeing contracts
- building staff teams
- involving residents/clients in decision-taking
- preparing and monitoring accounts
- budgeting
- training staff
- disciplinary skills
- managing meetings
- dealing with the media
- delegation
- day-to-day management of a home
- purchasing of equipment and services.

The fifth challenge is to overcome unnecessarily strong pressure to keep administrative overheads to a minimum. While cost control is entirely appropriate, it can lead managers to penny-pinch in circumstances when spending on overheads could lead to significant improvements in effectiveness. Managers are responsible for avoiding wastage of resources, but they also have to **argue for sufficient resources** to do their work efficiently.

The sixth challenge is to ensure that managers receive the necessary **induction, one-to-ones and personal development**. When senior managers are overloaded (or unable to establish their priorities), supporting their staff can be the activity that is squeezed out. This problem is particularly common in geographically spread organizations, where staff are at separate locations. Because of physical separation these are often the very people who ought to get extra support. When managers are not receiving assistance, they have to push for the support they need to do the job effectively.

Finally, managers face particular challenges when it comes to **changing people's roles**. People believe in their jobs; they have often worked tirelessly for the cause, so managers' suggestions for change are sometimes most unwelcome. An extreme example is the difficulty of moving people out of the organization altogether when their performance falls below expectations, when redundancies have to be made and when people have to be dismissed. Caring organizations are expected to care for their staff – so managers have to be particularly sensitive when they need to adjust the structure or change the membership of their team.

In summary, while the skills front-line managers have to learn and use are those common to most managerial situations, the people the sector attracts and the nature of third-sector organizations combine together to create demanding circumstances which can be overcome by better training, greater line-management support and hard-won experience.

SUMMARY OF KEY POINTS

Management jobs are different

- Chief executives have to provide leadership.
- Divisional directors have to direct.
- Managers have to manage.

Special characteristics of the chief executive's job

- The chief executive's job is different from all other posts.
- It is less structured, highly exposed and lonely. It requires the widest range of abilities, involves the widest range of constituencies and depends on maintaining a reservoir of goodwill.

Structuring the chief executive's work

- Chief executives can avoid becoming servants of their in-trays by focusing on the three 'P's:
  - — the purpose of the organization
  - — the processes of managing it
  - — the people who work closely with them.

Chief executives provide leadership

- Management is concerned with efficient administration, making processes work, creating structures, developing plans and controlling budgets.
- Leadership is concerned with clarifying the mission, motivating people and giving the organization a sense of purpose.
- Chief executives can systematically develop their leadership skills by recognizing people's efforts, developing a power base, using authority effectively, using the power of the position and building a personal reputation.
- They also need to develop their skills and abilities, clarify their own objectives, communicate with their followers, develop a positive self-image and combine vision with attention to detail.

Divisional directors direct

- Divisional directors have to manage their own department and contribute to the overall management of the organization.
- To become effective, divisional directors have to learn to take an organization-wide perspective, think at a strategic level, follow trends in the external environment, hold managers accountable

for their work and judge when to intervene and when to leave matters alone.

- Divisional directors can strengthen their directorship skills by using a mentor, learning from their team and reflecting on their experiences.

Managers must manage

- The essential skills for front-line managers are setting objectives, building teams, developing individuals, taking decisions, monitoring performance and resolving problems.
- The special challenges of managing third-sector organizations mean that managers have to carve out an appropriate role, be ruthless in setting priorities, earn their authority, represent users' views, argue for sufficient resources and push for personal support.

12   **Managing People**

12.1   **DEVELOPING PEOPLE IS AN ART**

The ability of third-sector organizations to achieve their objectives depends almost entirely on the skills of their people. Those organizations that have the strongest base of skilled and experienced people are in the best position to raise the largest sums of money and deliver the best-quality services and campaigns. The capacity of their staff and volunteers is determined by the quality of the people who are recruited and by the organizations' investment in developing their expertise.

Investing time and effort in developing the capabilities of managers at all levels of the organization brings great benefits both to the individuals and to the organization. It presents people with new challenges to the way they work and consequently makes work more interesting and stimulating. The new skills and abilities they gain make them more rounded and capable individuals. Organizations that strive to develop the capabilities of their staff attract more talented people, who grow personally and perform to higher standards. Organizations that neglect this crucial area have higher staff turnover and a less motivated workforce and they achieve less with the resources at their disposal.

The potential for increasing the effectiveness of third-sector organizations by developing people's skills is huge. Many managers could improve their delegation skills and give their staff greater responsibility within clearer boundaries. They could also learn more from the people to whom they delegate.

Improving team leadership skills can also yield great benefits. Teams are very sensitive to both good and poor leadership. When they are working at their most effective they are a powerful means of making things happen. Teams are also a great source of opportunities for managers to learn about themselves, each other and ways of increasing the productivity of the team itself. When they are mismanaged, they are a great obstacle to organizational effectiveness.

There are many ways of encouraging personal development. Coaching, mentoring and shadowing help people to improve their performance. Regular one-to-ones for managers hold them to account, provide support and create opportunities for coaching. Annual reviews present an opportunity for a more thorough appraisal of performance; they also create a situation where managers can learn about their performance from the person they are supervising.

This chapter sets out how to increase the capacity of organizations to be really effective. It describes how to:

● manage your boss
● get better performance from teams
● delegate work and empower people
● supervise, develop and coach people.

12.2 MANAGING YOUR BOSS

Managing your boss (an idea propounded by John Gabarro and John Kotter in *Harvard Business Review*) is a foundation-stone of being a good manager. It is possible to be excellent at all the other aspects of management, but fail because people forget to manage this crucial relationship.

Everyone has a boss, from the chief executive who reports to the chair, to front-line staff who report to their supervisors. Some people have two bosses; regional and branch managers often report to a line manager as well as to the chair of the regional or branch committee; departmental managers sometimes report to both a manager and a committee chair. These people have the additional challenge of managing two sets of relationships simultaneously.

Managers and staff can do their jobs more effectively if they have a strong and constructive relationship with their boss. Each is dependent on the other: bosses need help, guidance and advice from their managers in order to do their jobs. They need to feel confident that they can depend on their managers. Similarly, managers and staff depend on their bosses for guidance and support. Managers and staff need to understand how their work fits in to the wider context; they need information from their boss and, most of all, they need their boss to help procure the resources required to achieve their objectives.

Poor relationships are often put down to personality conflicts. 'I don't get on with the boss,' is a common sentiment. However, this description sometimes conceals simple misunderstandings about the mutual dependencies in the relationship. Managing a boss is not about political manoeuvring to seek advantage. It is a process of working with him or her to obtain the best results for the organization and using every opportunity to learn from each other.

The first step in managing bosses is to understand their context. This means having a sense of their priorities, their aspirations and the issues that are being addressed at a higher level. It means tapping into their information systems, networking with other managers and asking questions when the broader context is not clear. It requires managers and staff to recognize that their bosses are not there to do everything but to ensure that everything gets done.

The second step is to understand her or his strengths and weaknesses. Successful people avoid making the assumption that their boss is omniscient. They recognize that all bosses are different: some are full of creative ideas but need guidance to come to decisions; some are decisive but need to have all the options developed for consideration. Some are good at networking outside the organization but need to be briefed on developments within the organization. People who understand their bosses actively exploit their strengths and support them in their weaker areas. This is particularly important when their boss is the chief executive.

The third step is to understand his or her preferred working methods. This requires watching their behaviour and gaining insights into the way they work. Some people prefer to learn about things on paper; others prefer an oral report. Some like solitary time to think; others prefer to work things out together. Some are lateral thinkers, others are better at making quick judgements. People can get better value from their bosses if they understand their working styles.

TWO MANAGERS AT CITY HOUSING ASSOCIATION

Jane, the chief executive of City Housing, was formal and well organized. She paid attention to detail and liked to have written reports, and formal meetings with set agendas.

Nick, a flamboyant and creative manager, preferred a more informal and intuitive style. He had great difficulty with the chief executive. Their meetings were always fraught with problems as the chief executive tried to piece together the information she felt she should have had before the meeting. Nick often felt that Jane was meddling in the detail when what he wanted was guidance and support.

Juliet, another manager, worked hard to manage her relationship with the chief executive. She asked what information Jane would like to have before they met. She noticed that the chief executive was most effective when she had time to think about issues before a meeting. Although it took time to prepare the paperwork, her department grew and flourished because it was able to exploit both her own and her chief executive's talents.

Managers and staff can conceive of their boss as a resource which needs to be used effectively. A boss's time is always limited, so it needs to be used judiciously. Wasting time involving the boss in detailed issues which people ought to resolve on their own is a common mistake; briefing the boss on the issue and the action taken is far more helpful. Similarly, judging when an issue needs the boss's attention, preparing thoughts about the problem and knowing what to ask helps make effective use of the boss's time.

All relationships have frustrations. Successful people learn how to handle them. Those who rebel against their boss and who undermine him or her are not creating the conditions for succeeding in their own job. Similarly, people who bottle up all their frustrations and do not share their concerns with their boss are storing up problems for the future. Effective managers and staff work hard to address their frustrations with their boss in constructive ways.

They also seek opportunities to learn from their relationship with their boss. There is a potentially rich resource to mine here, provided both parties are willing to strive to learn. Managers and staff can take the initiative by praising their boss when she or he has done things well or has changed their behaviour to improve the relationship. They can offer to support their boss when he or she needs assistance. They should raise anxieties openly and make positive proposals about ways of working together more effectively.

In summary, people who wish to learn should:

● understand the broader context in which their boss is working
● discover their boss's preferred working style
● use their boss to help with tasks they are good at
● expect their boss to provide them with support and one-to-ones
● see the relationship as an opportunity for each to learn from the other
● look elsewhere for the support their boss is unable to provide.

12.3   **GETTING PERFORMANCE FROM TEAMS**

In addition to creating relationships upwards, managers also have to create relationships with the people who work for them. More than anything, managers need to create and lead a team of people who are dedicated to achieving agreed objectives.

Ultimately, managers' success depends on getting high performance from teams. Their job is to build strong teams, release the potential that is within team members and ensure that the achievements of the team as a whole are much greater than the sum of its parts. Teams are important not only in the line-management structure, but also as an essential integrating mechanism across the departmental structure.

This section describes:

● the characteristics of effective teams
● creating teams
● changing team membership
● developing teams
● leading teams
● adopting different styles for different tasks.

The art of encouraging teams to learn from their experience is described in Chapter 13.

Characteristics of effective teams

Organizations have different types of team including:

● **management teams** – consisting of managers and their boss (e.g. the Senior Management Team)
● **staff teams** – consisting of staff and their manager (e.g. the Help-line Team)
● **project teams** – consisting of a cross-section of managers and their staff (e.g. the Lottery Project Team).

Many of the attributes of effective teams are common to all three types. The important differences are that:

● Management and staff teams have a longer life, so it is worth investing more effort into ensuring that they work well
● Management and project teams need to pay close attention to good preparation and paperwork to maximize their effectiveness
● Project teams have deadlines, so they need to become effective quickly, achieve their objective and dissolve themselves.

When teaching about teams, Ashridge Management College, a research and management school, summarizes the characteristics of highly effective teams as groups that are:

● persistent in pursuit of their goals
● inventive in overcoming obstacles
● committed to quality in all aspects of teamwork
● inspired by a vision
● action-orientated
● committed to the success of the organization as a whole
● able to distinguish the important from the urgent
● willing to take risks and be innovative and creative
● always looking for ways to do things better.

This, no doubt, reflects many team leaders' intentions. However, two special characteristics of third-sector organizations have to be overcome in order to attain this ideal. First, there is the fact that the sector attracts an extraordinarily wide range of characters to its organizations, many of whom are intelligent, charismatic, opinionated, but sometimes obstinate when it comes to being a team player.

Secondly, managers have to understand that their role is different from that of other members of the team. The democratic values of some organizations and the deeply held desire to represent users' views can spill over into team behaviour. Sometimes managers start from an assumption that their primary duty is to represent the views of their staff or service users. They put their loyalty to their staff or service users ahead of their role as a member of a more senior team in which they have to make trade-offs between the interests of different parts of the organization. They feel more accountable to the people they represent than to the senior team. They find it hard to accept collective responsibility for management decisions and to support those decisions when they have to report back to their own team.

Managers therefore need to understand the techniques they can use to create teams that perform well. This section briefly introduces some of the behaviours and actions managers can apply.

LIFE CYCLE OF A TEAM

Groups mature and develop. Like individuals and organizations, they have a fairly clearly defined growth cycle. This has been categorized as having four successive stages:

1. **Forming**. The group is not yet a group but a set of individuals. This stage is categorized by talk about the purpose of the group, the definition and the title of the group, its composition, leadership pattern and life span. At this stage, each individual tends to want to establish his or her personal identity within the group and make an individual impression.

2. **Storming.** Most groups go through a conflict stage when the preliminary (and often false) consensus on purposes, leadership and other roles, and norms of work and behaviour, is challenged and re-established. At this stage a lot of personal agendas are revealed and a certain amount of interpersonal hostility is generated. If handled successfully, this period of storming leads to a new and more realistic setting of objectives, procedures and norms. This stage is particularly important for testing the norms of trust in the group.

3. **Norming.** The group needs to establish norms and practices: when and how it should work, how it should take decisions, and what type of behaviour, level of work and what degree of openness, trust and confidence is appropriate. At this stage there will be a lot of tentative experimentation by individuals to test the temperature of the group and to measure the appropriate level of commitment.

4. **Performing.** Only when the three previous stages have been successfully completed will the group be at full maturity and be able to be fully and sensibly productive.

From *Understanding Organizations*, Charles Handy, 1994

Some theorists have added two further stages: **re-forming**, to account for changes in the group's membership, and **mourning**, the necessary process of properly marking the end of a group's life.

Creating the team

The first issue to consider is the **size of the team**. Teams that are too small may not contain all the skills required or generate enough variety of thought. Teams that are too large are cumbersome and frustrating for members.

Larger teams are appropriate when:

- some of the posts are similar (for example, managers of similar centres or regions) because they will have common problems
- members are experienced team players who require less support, one-to-ones or coaching
- a wide range of skills is essential to the team's effectiveness (for example, resolving very complex problems).

Smaller teams are appropriate when:

- there is high interdependence between members (for example, an assessment and rehabilitation centre where tight co-ordination is required); they need time to work closely together
- the team works in a rapidly changing environment (for example, a campaign team); people will need lots of short meetings.

Any rule has exceptions, but for many situations a team of between four and seven people is a common compromise.

REORGANIZATION OF A MANAGEMENT TEAM

A British development agency recognized the need for radical change in its management. Senior management team meetings were lengthy and often inconclusive, personal relationships were poor, meeting discipline was deteriorating.

'It's because we can't agree whether our primary objective should be in emergency aid, long-term development, empowerment of local people or institutional change,' said one group. 'If only we could agree upon our fundamental purpose, our problems would be solved.'

'The problem is: we aren't sticking to our strategy,' argued another group. 'We spent a year agreeing a strategic plan, but we never use it to guide our decisions.'

'We can't work together as a team,' argued a third group. 'We need training in team development and facilitation to help us discover ways of working together.'

In practice, none was right. The central problem was that the team of nine people was too large and too heterogeneous to work together. Too many big personalities, each in charge of a large division, just could not work together.

Reorganized, the team became a group of five people. The creation of a smaller team, three of whose members were recruited from outside the organization, was enough to break the mould and establish new ways of working together.

The next issue to consider is the **characteristics of team members**. For teams to perform to the highest standard, people have to work closely together, support each other and balance team needs with their own. A balance has to be found between having people with similar backgrounds and experience who work together well but who see issues only from one perspective, and having a more heterogeneous team drawing on people with different skills. The need for homogeneous teams increases as the tasks they have to undertake become more complex. Heterogeneous teams are more productive when dealing with more straightforward tasks, but they can expect to experience more conflict.

Then there is the issue of **sensitivity and trust**. Groups of people who get along well, who trust each other and are sensitive to each other's needs, are more productive than those where members are suspicious of one another. Sensitivity and trust should grow as the team works together and as members gain deeper insights into their colleagues' strengths and weaknesses.

The fourth aspect of creating an effective team is allowing **time for people to get to know each other** both professionally and personally. Teams are more effective when people understand each other's personal backgrounds and personalities. They work more efficiently when members have a deep understanding of each other's strengths and weaknesses. This can take many months and often years to assimilate fully. Time for team 'away-days', social events and – particularly in the forming stage – lots of team meetings all help to provide the foundations for a high-performance team.

Changing team membership

Sometimes managers need to change the size, structure or membership of a team in order to improve its performance. Teams can be restructured but, as Chapter 9 demonstrated, this does not always have the desired results. Another option for changing team membership is to make judicious use of opportunities created by people leaving or retiring. A departure gives managers the space to reconsider everyone's responsibilities and either reduce or enlarge the team.

Another, more subtle option is to **change the definition of the team**. Team membership can be adjusted by redefining the scope and purpose of the team and incorporating or excluding people to increase its effectiveness. For example, if a team is too small and the organization has talented people who are not on the team, it can be expanded for certain types of meeting. A quarterly review of strategy, for example, or a series of planning meetings provide an ideal opportunity to enlarge the team. If the team is too large, it may be necessary to reduce the frequency of meetings and create a smaller group to co-ordinate activities between meetings.

Creating a team with an appropriate size and composition is an essential prerequisite for getting performance from a team. However, there is a trap to avoid. Some managers mistakenly assume that getting the right group of people is their single most important task. They continually adjust the structure and the membership of the team – not recognizing that **each adjustment is a disruption** to team dynamics. Developing appropriate team behaviour and coaching members so as to help them become better team players can have more effect than adjusting its membership. Each time team membership is adjusted, its behaviour takes a step back in the 'forming, storming model' (see the box, above), a consequence that is sometimes overlooked. In short, oversize or undersize teams with good team behaviour can be more productive than a team with appropriate size and composition and no accepted ways of working.

ADJUSTMENTS TO TEAMS CAUSE DISRUPTION

'We trained hard . . . but it seemed that every time we were beginning to form up in teams we would be reorganized. I was to learn later in life that we tend to meet any new situation by reorganizing, and a wonderful method it can be for creating the illusion of progress while producing confusion, inefficiency and demoralization.'
Petronius Arbiter (AD 65)

Developing the team

Teams need objectives. Everyone on the team needs to be totally clear about what the team is trying to achieve. The team needs both to have words that define the objectives and to be clear about the context in which they have to be achieved. The objectives need to be understood from many different perspectives and from the different viewpoints that each team member brings.

Ideally, all team members need to be directly involved in agreeing the objectives. Everyone also needs to believe in them. It is easy to support the words, but the high-performance team needs people who are motivated to achieve the objectives and demonstrate by their behaviour in and outside the team that they believe in the objectives. This can be achieved only by working on the objectives, taking time away from the office to explore the options and develop the thinking. Objectives can then be tested on other groups (up, down, across and outside the organization) to make them more robust.

Teams plan together. Successful teams spend time planning their work. Sometimes individual members of sub-groups will prepare plans for achieving a particular objective and bring them to team meetings. In other situations, planning the work will be done in team meetings. If the team has been created to undertake a specific project, it may well identify the factors that are critical to the project's success (see Eastlink Housing box, below). Whatever the circumstances, effective teams are clear about how the objectives will be achieved.

Teams need coaching. Managers are responsible for setting the standards for team behaviour. As well as guiding the team in its work, managers encourage members to contribute constructively. They praise good team behaviour, they criticize loose or poor contributions and they help people to improve their work.

Teams need good administration. Preparation for meetings and communication outside meetings are essential elements of effective teams. The major topics for meetings need to be planned so that papers can be commissioned, reviewed by the manager and distributed in advance. Timing of meetings, appropriate venues and circulation of action notes may all be details, but they are crucial elements of an effective team.

IDENTIFYING CRITICAL SUCCESS FACTORS

Project teams enhance their effectiveness by identifying the factors that are critical to their success. These are the limited number of action areas that are both necessary and sufficient to achieve the objective.

Working to identify the actions, boiling them down to a manageable list and checking that they are both necessary and sufficient provides team members with a deeper understanding of the objective and how it will be achieved. Descriptions of critical success factors usually begin with the words, 'We must . . .' or 'We need to . . .'

Eastlink Housing Association put together a cross-departmental team to manage a major conversion project. They established the following objectives and critical success factors:

Objective:
to convert three old people's homes into local centres for frail elderly people over the next three years.

Critical success factors:
- We must raise a total of £3.6 million from statutory and charitable sources to complete the project.
- We must create an in-house development team of three people, dedicated to this project alone for at least two years.
- We must find superior-quality accommodation for existing tenants and give them a minimum of six months' warning of the move.
- We must recruit people with expertise in managing centres for frail elderly people to start work four months before each centre opens.
- We need to create new management committees for each centre, incorporating the seven specialist skills identified as critical to their success.

Leading teams

Finally, the most effective teams are those that have strong leadership which is sensitive to team members' needs and not dominant or authoritarian. Team leadership is an art. It requires the adroit use of different skills in different circumstances. The critical elements of effective team leadership can be summarized as follows:

Start modestly. Managers should set realistic objectives at the beginning, build the team's confidence in itself and then increase expectations. If leaders are too ambitious, they risk losing credibility when the objectives are not achieved.

Promote the mission. Teams are motivated by missions. They need to feel that their work is vitally important and be able to set it in the broader context of the organization's overall objectives. Managers should emphasize the value of the work being done and remind people that bureaucracy and management are necessary activities only to achieve the broader mission.

Encourage openness. Teams under-perform when individuals have private agendas or when one group is making different assumptions from those of another. Managers need to tease out private issues and ensure that their own agenda is open and explicit.

Support each other. Members of high-performance teams take particular care to support each other. They build on each other's arguments in meetings, show concern for each other's welfare and assist each other in their work. Managers set the tone by being seen to support team members.

Face up to differences. Managers with strong teams encourage differences of opinion. They expect members to make their differences clear, but to be willing to compromise when decisions are required. They also expect team members to support decisions, once they have been made.

Review performance regularly. Managers set aside time for the team to review its own performance. They identify behaviour that worked well and review situations where improvements could be made. They encourage critical discussion of the team's performance and expect the team to agree actions to improve team performance. They remind the team of agreed actions when behaviour slips below expectations.

Encourage systematic decision-taking. Teams make better decisions if they are systematic about gathering information, diagnosing problems, seeking opinions and evaluating options before taking decisions. Effective leaders encourage a rigorous approach to decision-taking.

Make the team visible. Managers promote their teams both inside and outside the organization. They communicate up, down and across the organization, ensuring that their team's work engages with the rest of the organization.

Encourage action. Managers encourage action. They clarify what needs to be done and ensure that agreed actions are followed through.

Celebrate success. Managers make sure that successes are celebrated. They mark achievements with praise, publicity and parties.

Different styles for different tasks

Leading an effective team also requires the selection of an appropriate style of working for the task at hand. When the team needs to crack through the routine work of communicating with each other, co-ordinating activities and making regular decisions that do not raise wider issues, it is appropriate that there should be tight chairing, short interventions and timetabled agendas. Where there are disagreements on minor matters, the team leader can impose a decision on the group.

However, where there is a great deal of uncertainty around the issues being addressed and the decisions will have widespread repercussions, an entirely different mode is required. All the skills and all the experience of team members are required to consider the issue. Chairing needs to be more flexible, ownership of the way the discussion is going may move around the team, and timetables need to be less fixed (see also section 13.5 about 'discussions' and 'dialogues').

The dividing line between different styles is clearly not absolute. Indeed, some issues which may have seemed clear-cut may turn out to raise much wider concerns, and some seemingly open issues may be more clear-cut than anticipated. An experienced team adapts and adjusts its approach according to the circumstances. The more mature a team becomes, the more it will find it can work with sharper differences in style and increase its effectiveness.

STAGES OF THE DEVELOPMENT OF A TEAM

Charac- teristic	Undeveloped team	Experimenting team	Consolidating team	Mature team
Atmos- phere, feelings and conflict	Tense, individual self-interest; feelings not dealt with; conflicts seen as inappro- priate	Dynamic; expressions of mutual interest; feelings begin to be opened up; groups inward-looking	Confident, open approach; resolves interpersonal issues	High commit- ment to the task and each other; individuals' needs for recognition low; confrontation handled easily

Characteristic	Undeveloped team	Experimenting team	Consolidating team	Mature team
Talking and listening	Very little listening; points of view queuing up	More listening and thinking, less talking in unconnected ways	Listening very good, constructive use of ideas, good balance of agreeing, disagreeing and behaviours	Easy but careful listening; lots of building and extracting benefits of ideas; summaries stated regularly
Working method	Stick to the established method; scared of changes; little time spent considering how to operate	Increasing dissatisfaction with procedures initially established; increased concern with internal processes	Further examination of methods; willingness to change; better understanding of method through discussion	Conscious observation of group process; discussion of its effectiveness; flexible use of procedures and time-keeping; readiness to change
Time management	Ignored; 'speaking clock' tends to operate	Realization of need to plan and manage time; tentative steps	More realistic time-allocation to the various stages of working	More flexible use of time-allocation and readiness to change to facilitate the task
Understanding the task	Leader's view is often different from the rest; others tend to be confused	Understanding increases through discussion and questioning, but little willingness to vary it	Better understood through questioning, leading to a group version of the task	Continual monitoring of the task; modification depending on progress and feedback
Decisions	Mostly taken by the leader	Decisions still taken mostly by the leader or by voting	Shared responsibility for decisions; group tries for consensus	Taken by the group by consensus, but leader's role in reasoned arbitration is recognized

Charac-teristic	Undeveloped team	Experimenting team	Consolidating team	Mature team
Using each other's abilities	Individuals keep to narrow roles; low recognition resources available	Increased readiness to deal with quiet members	Clear understanding of strengths and weaknesses; moves to use resources outside the group	As for consolidating team, but stronger
Personal weaknesses	Covered up; mistakes used to judge people, not to identify learning opportunities	Increased readiness to look at people's preferences and at tasks they feel unhappy with	Now well understood and taken account of in a positive and acceptable way	As for consolidating team
Resilience to the outside	Defensive to outside 'threats'; proposals increase bureaucracy	Increasingly insular and competitive	External demands and conflict handled constructively	Team copes constructively with problems

12.4 DELEGATING WORK AND EMPOWERING PEOPLE

Delegation is the art of sharing work among the team, giving people the freedom to make decisions, but retaining responsibility for achievement of the task. Empowerment is a broader concept; it is concerned with giving people more latitude around how tasks are completed and holding them accountable only for the results. It implies less detailed monitoring and an expectation that the delegatee will request assistance when required.

There are many forces that work against delegation in third-sector organizations. Managers are often highly motivated by the nature of the work they are doing; they believe in the cause they are working for, put in long hours and enjoy the detail. It is very tempting not to delegate enough in these circumstances.

Then there is the fact that staff feel overloaded. They too are committed to the cause and often believe that they could not work harder. So, before work can be delegated, managers have to find ways to help their staff review priorities and stop doing some things that they believed were important in order to create the time to do the new work managers wish to delegate to them. The issue is usually not lack of willingness but the ability to set priorities that are consistent with the manager's view of their relative importance.

A frequent obstacle to delegation is the pressure of time. The work needs to be done quickly, so the easiest solution is for managers to do it themselves. It takes time to brief someone, explain what is required and help them to adjust their priorities, so it often appears easier just to do the task. This, however, is a recipe for overload. Effective delegators anticipate the need for the work and decide how it can be done before they become trapped into doing it themselves.

Another obstacle to delegating is the fear that the individual will not be able to do the task. Sometimes this may be entirely justified and the task should not be delegated to that person. But sometimes managers have to take small risks in order to give the person who is delegated the task an opportunity for learning. They can assist in these circumstances by being particularly clear about the objective of the task, its scope and its time-frame, and explicitly checking that the person concerned understands the task.

Successful managers delegate as much as they possibly can. They delegate in stages as people's skill and experience grow; they monitor the individual's performance; and they maintain the level of control needed to ensure a successful outcome. They start by delegating low-risk tasks and, as the person's experience grows, higher-risk tasks are delegated.

To delegate effectively, managers have to trust their staff and be confident that they can do the delegated tasks. Simultaneously, they must reduce the amount of direct control they have over the way the individual does the task. Once the boundaries have been agreed, managers should hand over control. The less control they retain, the more the individual will feel responsible for completing the work to the required standard.

However, delegation is not simply a matter of handing over tasks to another person. It is the skill of giving someone additional responsibilities that are within his or her abilities and providing appropriate advice and support as that person takes greater responsibility for the task. The amount and nature of work that can be delegated depends on the person's experience, the confidence of the manager and the risk attached to the task.

The manager and the person doing the work need to agree the objectives that are to be achieved – ideally by the person who will do the work proposing the objectives and the manager amending and agreeing to them. The manager is then in a position to 'manage by objectives' – an old adage that is still very pertinent today.

Learning the art of delegating

Becoming an effective delegator requires a new attitude of mind. Good managers instinctively think ahead and ask themselves how to achieve each task for which they are responsible. Anticipation is the critical ingredient. Managers have to allow time to brief people to whom tasks are delegated and for those people to fit the work into their already busy schedules. They have to allocate time to review progress, to give advice and to support the delegatee.

Managers also need to clarify why they are delegating tasks. They can delegate:

● **to make better use of time**. Managers are paid to manage, not to do the work. They have to create time to discharge their many managerial responsibilities, and this invariably means delegating as much work as their staff can handle.

● **to give staff development opportunities**. All staff need to develop their skills and abilities. Giving staff responsibility for additional tasks is an ideal method of enabling and encouraging professional development. It provides new challenges within carefully selected boundaries.

● **to use people's skills**. Staff have strengths in areas where the managers may have weaknesses. Managers delegate to maximize the use of staff members' skills.

DELEGATING WORK IN A TRADE UNION

'I know I need to delegate more,' the union official told the management consultant. 'I've read all the books on it and even attended a course. It's just not that straightforward.'

'You need to sit down with each member of your team and agree what can be delegated. I'll help by providing an independent perspective,' said the consultant, spotting an opportunity to sell his time.

'That isn't the problem,' said the union official. 'My difficulty is that all the committee members expect me to deal personally with every problem. Committee chairs in particular feel their status is not being recognized if I delegate their problems to my staff. Chairs feel they can do the job they have been elected to do only if they deal with me.'

'Well,' said the consultant, 'we'll have to think about how to persuade them to allow you to delegate.'

Delegation is seldom straightforward.

Some activities cannot be delegated. **People-management responsibilities**, such as one-to-ones, performance reviews, chairing team meetings, discipline, praise and resolution of disputes, are responsibilities that managers should retain in all but the most unusual circumstances. **Policymaking** cannot be delegated. The work of preparing papers, doing research and making proposals can be delegated, but decisions on matters that have widespread repercussions cannot be delegated. **Crisis management** usually requires judgements to be made from a broader perspective; these situations can seldom be delegated. Matters involving **confidential information,** such as sensitive personnel information, cannot be delegated. Finally, the **rituals** of celebrating successes, rewarding long service and representing the organization or department at major occasions should not be delegated. Position and status both add significantly to the value of rituals.

Improving delegation skills

Good practice in delegation involves:

● creating a well-informed team of people who understand the broader context into which their work fits. When tasks are delegated, people will understand why the work needs to be done

● giving people appropriate information about the task. Hard information about what needs to be achieved is as important as soft data about the people and problems that might be encountered

● being clear about the objective but allowing the individual to take the initiative in how it is achieved

● being clear about available resources, the milestones that will mark progress, the timescale for achieving the result and the arrangements for reporting on progress

● being honest about the task and what it will involve

● leaving no confusion about accountability for the work

● giving credit for a job well done, and taking responsibility if it does not go well

● using mistakes as learning opportunities and not as reasons for allocating blame.

Delegating is a skill that is learned with practice. It is an essential ability that managers need to grasp. Too often managers fail to delegate and so overload themselves, or they delegate without providing the support and guidance that are needed to produce the required outcomes. Managers need to practise delegation so that it becomes an instinctive way of working.

Empowering people

Empowering people is a process of giving **greater ownership** of a task or a set of responsibilities to an individual or a group. It is about going one step further than delegation, being very clear about the 'ends' that people are expected to achieve, but allowing them greater freedom in managing the 'means' of achieving the desired end. In an empowered organization, people are held accountable for their achievements and not for the methods used to accomplish them. Empowering people allows them to take charge of their situation within clearly agreed boundaries and to take more decisions. Empowering people requires that the fundamentals of good management are securely in place. It is appropriate in organizations that already have very clear objectives, strong teams, well-established management processes and good personal relationships.

Initiatives to increase empowerment also require managers to have reached a comparatively experienced stage of their personal development. They should be sufficiently mature to be able to share their anxieties with other people, willing to learn from failures, and able to challenge people confidently, to stand back from detail and to command people's respect.

In its most developed form, the manager is not a 'member' of the empowered group. He or she builds the environment in which the group can do its job, coaches people when support is required and monitors the results.

The most critical judgement that managers have to make is the **extent of empowerment** that is appropriate. On the one hand, managers who hold on to too much power frustrate their staff and do not allow them to perform at the highest level. Staff end up wasting time, working out how to 'get round' the system. On the other hand, managers who expect people to work to very wide briefs when they are not ready to have so much scope run into great difficulties. Activities start to feel less well controlled and people begin to express anxieties about the abilities of their managers. This is a particular problem when it is inherently difficult to set clear and limited objectives for work, such as in campaigning. At its worst, this leads to an element of organizational anarchy in which everyone is running his or her own initiatives with insufficient co-ordination to allow a coherent strategy for the department or the organization as a whole to be constructed.

Similarly, attempting to give people power over huge issues with long timescales is just as inappropriate as giving people power over trivial matters. A useful catchphrase is to think about giving people '**freedom within a framework**', in which the manager is responsible for defining and agreeing realistic conditions within which the empowered person can work.

Empowerment is likely to be appropriate in organizations that are well established and which, over the years, have developed controls and procedures that are now an obstacle to effective entrepreneurial working.

However, care needs to be taken to avoid raising inexperienced managers' expectations that they will suddenly have more power over the organization and will be participating in all the major decisions. They need to be aware that increased empowerment also means increased responsibility, both for their own work and for their interventions into broader management issues.

Increasing empowerment is a long-term process, requiring changes in trustees', managers' and employees' behaviour. A **two-year time-frame** might be appropriate in many circumstances. Empowerment should therefore be treated as a change management project, with stages including a diagnosis of the problem, building commitment to the need for new ways of working and the preparation of plans and actions to bring about the required changes.

Empowerment generally requires greater change from managers than from the people they manage. Managers have to put more effort into clarifying objectives and boundaries, coaching staff, giving them links to other people and resources, and encouraging two-way feedback.

Actions to empower people

Managers can take many actions to empower people. Choices will depend on circumstances and on people's views on what will have the greatest impact. The stages of increasing empowerment might include:

- **involving people in planning** so that they share the ownership of objectives in addition to the means of achieving them. A deep understanding of the purpose and boundaries around the work of an individual or a group is a prerequisite for devolving power
- **communicating extensively with staff** to keep them well informed about the changing context in which they are working and how their work affects the organization's overall effectiveness. Such communication should be a two-way dialogue that also encourages people to submit new ideas. The best of these can then be fed back in subsequent communications to maintain the dialogue
- **removing institutional barriers** that prevent people making changes in their own area of responsibility. Managers should have freedom to make changes that they know are necessary and feasible. Where such changes cross departmental boundaries, set up a 'bureaucracy-busting'

task force to find imaginative ways of overcoming obstacles. Examples include forms that gather data that has been collected elsewhere, statistics that hardly anyone uses, onerous authorization procedures and requirements to consult committees on matters of tiny detail

- **asking staff to keep you appraised** to ensure that you get feedback on your performance
- **increase people's spending limits** to indicate confidence in their ability to make good decisions
- **reducing the formal reporting requirements placed on staff** to an absolute minimum and requiring reports on results not activities
- **encouraging people to come with solutions** rather than presenting problems.

Empowering people to take greater responsibility significantly increases an organization's capability. It releases senior people to put more effort into their critical role of integrating changes in the external environment with the current work of the organization. However, it cannot be done in short timescales. It is achieved over months and years, and results from incremental behaviour changes that become embedded in the organization's culture.

SUMMARY OF KEY POINTS

Developing people is an art
- Investing time and effort in developing the capabilities of managers at all levels of the organization brings great benefits both to the individuals and to the organization.
- Individuals have to take responsibility for their own learning and development.
- Organizations should deploy the full range of methods for encouraging learning to maximize the potential of their people.

Managing your boss
- Managers need to manage their relationships with their bosses.
- They need to understand his or her context, strengths and weaknesses and preferred working methods.
- Managers should use their boss's strengths and look elsewhere for the support that they are unable to provide.

Getting performance from teams

- The size of the team needs to be related to the task.
- Team membership can be adjusted by including additional people for certain topics or creating sub-groups to address specific issues.
- Successful teams need clear objectives, to plan together, coaching from the leader and good administration.
- Teams offer great learning opportunities that should be exploited to maximize organization learning.

Delegating work and empowering people

- There are many forces that work against delegation.
- Delegation is the art of giving people responsibilities that are within their abilities.
- People management, policy-making, crisis management, matters involving confidential information and organization rituals should not be delegated.
- Empowerment is a process of giving people greater responsibilities within clearly defined boundaries.

13 Creating a Learning Organization

13.1 ENCOURAGING LEARNING THROUGHOUT THE ORGANIZATION

A learning organization has been defined as 'an organization which facilitates the learning of all its members and continuously transforms itself' (Bob Garratt) ... 'an organization which harnesses the full brainpower, knowledge and experience available to it, in order to evolve continually for the benefit of all its stakeholders' (Mayo and Lank). The central idea behind the learning organization is that a high priority is given to learning at all levels of the organization. This means encouraging:

- **individual learning**, through induction, coaching, one-to-ones, performance review, shadowing and mentoring
- **team learning**, through understanding different team roles, reflecting systematically on the ways teams function and discovering more effective methods of working
- **organization-wide learning**, through establishing processes that enable learning to take place and a culture that promotes and is seen to value learning.

Organizations that encourage learning expect people and teams to take responsibility for their own learning and development. They expect people to take every opportunity to enhance their abilities. They encourage people to acknowledge mistakes openly and see them as learning opportunities. They establish systems that require people to see every situation as a learning opportunity and to put that learning into practice. In this way they enhance the abilities of their people and therefore the capability of the organization itself. When people are learning from each other, the organization has its own 'brain' and consequently much increased capacity to change and develop.

Learning is under-valued in third-sector organizations. Surrounded by demands to deliver more services, campaign for change, respond to media opportunities, and resolve the endless stream of short-term crises, the need to invest in learning can be neglected. Yet the benefits are potentially enormous. Increasing the efficiency of the way people work together and of the way work is done yields benefits that far exceed the time and effort put into learning. For example, in many third-sector organizations huge amounts of time are spent with people working together in meetings. Learning to work more effectively and, for example, saving one hour in an eight-person meeting creates a whole day of time for other activities.

Organizations need to work on the assumption that, if their people are not developing as fast as the changes in their environment, they are losing their capacity to be effective. Organizations have to adapt to changing circumstances, and that depends on people's ability and willingness to learn and then to change their work practices and habits. People have to be prepared to change as a result of their learning so that organizations can keep up with changes in their external environment.

The single most critical action in creating a learning organization is that the chief executive and the directors set an example through their own actions. This means that they are properly inducted, supervised and appraised. They coach, mentor and shadow other people, and they go out of their way to learn from other organizations. They acknowledge that learning is a dialogue in which people are learning from each other in a structured way. They are seen to be using the good practices that they wish other people to adopt.

Learning is a practical process and it take time and effort to acquire the necessary skills. In already over-stretched organizations, this can appear an impossible challenge. However, organizations that are too busy to improve themselves will not develop and their abilities will remain fixed at their current level.

This chapter explains how organizations promote learning by:

● developing individuals
● prioritizing one-to-ones and performance review
● encouraging coaching, mentoring and shadowing

- encouraging teams to learn
- ensuring organization-wide learning.

Successful implementation of all of these is dependent on organizations having a culture that encourages, values and gives real priority to everyone's learning. The learning culture is created, not by trying directly to change the culture, but by senior management setting an example by taking the actions that encourage people to learn and rewarding those who adopt the new beliefs and values.

13.2 **DEVELOPING INDIVIDUALS**

Developing individuals is concerned with extending their skills and experiences:

- to enable them to be more effective in achieving the organization's goals
- to give them opportunities for personal growth.

Managers can play a significant role in helping individuals to develop. Their enthusiasm, their willingness to think about others' needs, their discipline in holding regular one-to-one sessions, and their ability to give individuals work that provides development experiences and to help their staff learn from them are all important ingredients. However, the extent to which individuals develop depends ultimately on their motivation and willingness to learn. Their attitudes are, in the end, the crucial determinant of their development.

RECOGNIZING DEVELOPMENT NEEDS

By observation, working together and discussion, you will have a sense of someone's strengths and weaknesses; you will also come to know the areas of work that they enjoy, those that they find less satisfying, and their longer-term aspirations. You will also know about the demands and possibilities of the work. In addition, you may have information or ideas about the emerging priorities for the organization as a whole, and about the prospects and requirements that these may involve. These aspects are represented in the diagram.

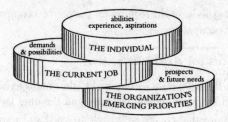

Ideally the three 'discs' would stack neatly on top of each other, meaning that the work being done fitted perfectly with the individual's aspirations and abilities and with the organization's priorities. Unfortunately, the reality is more complex; the fit is rarely 100 per cent and the 'discs' keep shifting in relation to each other. For example, the work being done may lag behind the latest priorities; or the individual may have to do work that she or he does not feel capable of, nor want to do. Moreover, one 'disc' can cause another to shift with it (as happens when an individual shifts the job to suit her or his abilities, or when an organization changes its plans in the light of the possibilities revealed by a job). Alternatively, a 'disc' can shift in the opposite direction to the others in reaction to developments (for example, when individuals try to set up a new project to ensure greater opportunities for themselves). So the 'discs' keep moving and your aim can only be to maintain *a reasonable alignment* between them by adjusting the job, by developing the individual, or occasionally by seeking to adjust the organization's priorities (to take advantage, for example, of under-used skills).

From *Managing Voluntary and Non-profit Enterprises*, Book 6, *Choosing and Developing Staff and Volunteers*, Open University Business School

It is sometimes assumed that individual development will somehow happen automatically and that it requires little more than casual inquiries about the progress of their work. Nothing could be further from the truth. In practice, promoting learning is a challenging task and organizations need to set up systems both to ensure individuals are taking the required actions and to monitor their implementation.

Building a **clear view of an individual's current skills** is the starting place. This can be done by reviewing the person's abilities against a 'ladder' of the skills he or she requires for that job or a competency profile for his or her occupation.

COMPETENCIES FOR MANAGING PEOPLE

Identifying the competencies required to do a managerial job helps to pinpoint the skills individuals have and the ones they need to develop.

The Management Charter Initiative is an independent organization set up by employers and backed by government. Its mission is to shape and promote competence-based management development, for the benefit of both organizations and individuals.

MCI is responsible for researching, developing and promoting the national Management Standards. It has identified seventeen competency areas for managing people. They include the ability to:

- manage yourself and develop your own resources
- enhance your own performance
- create, develop and enhance productive working relationships
- contribute to the selection of personnel
- select personnel for activities
- contribute to the development of teams and individuals
- develop teams and individuals to enhance performance
- develop management teams
- lead the work of teams and individuals to achieve their objectives
- manage the performance of teams and individuals
- delegate work to others
- deal with poor performance in your team
- redeploy personnel and make redundancies.

Each of these is supported by the elements of the competency that managers should be able to apply. For example, the elements of the competency, 'develop teams and individuals to enhance performance', are the abilities to:

- identify the development needs of teams and individuals
- plan the development of teams and individuals
- develop teams to improve performance
- support individual learning and development
- assess the development of teams and individuals

> • improve the development of teams and individuals.
>
> This approach provides the basis for managers and their staff to identify where people's skills are strong and where there are gaps, and hence to agree the skills requiring development.

Managers and their subordinates then need to agree the **next skills or capabilities to be acquired**. The objectives should be highly tailored to the individual's present work situation, the demands that are currently being placed on him or her and the expectations that both the manager and the subordinate have for his or her future development.

Managers can then play a significant role in helping people to learn. Personal development experiences come from many sources, including:

- the nature of the work that people are doing
- the teams that people are working with
- the one-to-ones and performance reviews that people receive
- the training that people receive
- the books people read!

Finally, they need to **monitor progress** in using the skills and abilities so that both are aware of improvements. They need to have arrangements to review individuals' development on a regular basis so that the whole approach is embedded in their way of working together.

Managers should recognize that individuals learn in different ways. Alan Mumford has identified four different learning styles:

Activists learn from new experiences and problems and prefer to be involved with other people. They like methods such as role-playing and they dislike solitary work and being asked to review their experiences.

Reflectors like to collect data, to analyse and review. They dislike being thrown into things without thought, being rushed or placed under time pressure.

Theorists learn from models and concepts. They want to question assumptions and logic and be intellectually stretched. They tend to discount methods emphasizing emotions and feelings.

Pragmatists want links between the subject-matter and their work. They like techniques that provide immediate opportunities for application.

They dislike learning concerned with environments quite different from their own.

Managers who want to know more about how their staff learn could suggest that they complete a 'learning styles' questionnaire to identify people's preferences (see Further Reading, below).

The idea of the learning cycle (known as Kolb's learning cycle) is a useful reminder of the necessary steps for effective learning. It suggests that four steps are essential for learning: hands-on experience, reflection, abstract conceptualization and active experimentation (see the box, below). More often than not, busy managers take actions, observe what happens and then take further actions or move on to new projects. This does not allow time to reflect, to learn from successes and failures or to develop models or 'rules of thumb' that can be applied in similar situations in the future and, finally, to communicate that learning to the rest of the organization.

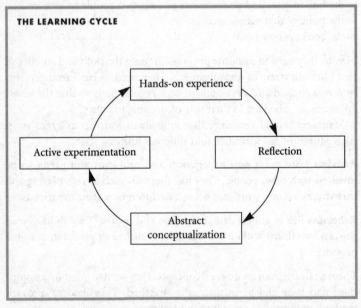

THE LEARNING CYCLE

Hands-on experience

Reflection

Abstract conceptualization

Active experimentation

Building a commitment to learning and to continuous personal development begins when potential recruits receive their first communication from the organization – even when they are sent a recruitment pack. This can stress the organization's commitment to learning, set out the skills that the potential recruit will be expected to deploy and point to possible development paths within the job or within the organization.

The induction process needs to ensure that new staff have a learning experience which:

● teaches them how the organization works
● communicates the organization's values
● clarifies their role in achieving the organization's mission
● explains the support and resources that are available to help them achieve their objectives.

The process can stress the importance the organization attaches to learning by comparing the incumbent's skills with the person specification for the job. The skills that the individual lacks provide the basis for agreeing some initial learning goals.

The importance of using every situation as an opportunity for learning can be instilled at the beginning of new recruits' careers by asking them about their experience of the induction process and what they think could be done to improve it.

13.3 PROMOTING LEARNING THROUGH ONE-TO-ONES AND PERFORMANCE REVIEW

This section is about the formal and regular arrangements organizations should have for managing people and their work on a continuous basis (one-to-ones) and, more thoroughly, at the end of each year (performance review).

One-to-ones

The term 'one-to-ones' is increasingly used to describe regular meetings between managers and each of their staff. These used to be called supervision meetings, but that word has a top-down connotation that was inappropriate in organizations that are promoting learning and enabling. The term 'supervision' also has a more formal meaning in social work and counselling that is different from one-to-ones.

One-to-ones provide the discipline of thinking about individuals' performance and their development needs on a routine basis. In some organizations, the daily pressures of work conspire against finding time for one-to-one sessions. The latest crisis always seems more important than the one-to-one session which inevitably has a longer-term pay-back. Discipline in holding the meetings and commitment to preparing for them are needed to ensure development takes place.

One-to-ones follow on directly from delegation. When managers delegate work to individuals, they have a corresponding duty to review progress, help people overcome problems and give constructive feedback.

An individual's objectives and the support the organization has agreed to give that person set the context for one-to-ones. It should be linked to annual performance reviews, during which objectives will have been agreed. One-to-ones need to revisit these objectives, monitor progress in achieving them, identify obstacles and agree new actions. One-to-ones are a structured opportunity to review progress and problems which should:

- review performance against objectives
- ensure that delegated work is done to the agreed standard and within the agreed timescale
- check that people have received the resources required to achieve their objectives
- enable staff to clarify how their work fits in to the broader context
- enable staff to learn from their work experiences and develop their skills
- provide a channel for two-way feedback on any other work-related issues (including problems outside work that may affect people's performance)
- allow managers and their staff an opportunity to remind each other that they are a valued part of the organization and that their work is appreciated.

The frequency of one-to-ones depends on both the work that has been delegated and the experience of the person being supervised. When the work is challenging, one-to-ones need to be more frequent and more supportive. Similarly, when the person being supervised is highly experienced and has been in the job for many years, one-to-ones can be less frequent and more consultative in nature. Frequency is likely to vary from weekly (for a new, inexperienced person or someone working in a challenging environment) to quarterly (for an experienced person in a stable environment). For many people, monthly or every other month will be appropriate.

ACTIVITIES IN EFFECTIVE ONE-TO-ONES

Task-related activities

Shaping	structuring the task
Target-setting	setting or agreeing specific goals and deadlines
Explaining	selling policies and plans
Delegating	devolving tasks and responsibilities
Guiding	giving advice, information, being a role-model
Limiting	setting boundaries, reining people in
Negotiating	matching individual ideas with organizational policy
Resourcing	arranging back-up, funds, etc.

People-related activities

Coaching	helping people to learn the work
Encouraging	being a sounding board, boosting morale
Facilitating	getting introductions and putting people in touch
Counselling	giving assistance in exploring approaches to situations/dealing with anxieties
Representing	speaking on behalf of individuals
Evaluating	making judgements about achievements/potential

From *Managing Voluntary and Non-profit Enterprise,* Book 6, *Choosing and Developing Staff and Volunteers,* Open University Business School

---

One-to-one sessions can cover many issues. Most are either concerned with the work people are doing or the development of the people themselves. It is important, therefore, for managers to ascertain from the people being supervised what they wish to achieve from one-to-ones. Explicit clarification of the expectations of both parties can lead to much more productive sessions.

Organizations need a system that encourages all staff to meet one-to-one with their line manager at an agreed frequency. Establishing a one-to-one system should involve all the participants, to ensure their active support and commitment to the one-to-one process; this will also help to incorporate it into everyone's work routines. Ideally, it should become part of the accepted culture that everyone expects a one-to-one at an agreed frequency. A series of workshops to tailor a one-to-one process to the organization's circumstances is a good way to build commitment. This should be followed by management decisions on the frequency of one-to-ones and training requirements to support implementation.

Setting an example from the top is crucial. Chairs are responsible for ensuring that chief executives have one-to-ones, either by doing them themselves or, in exceptional circumstances, by appointing another board member to perform this function. Managers who report to the chief executive should have one-to-one meetings with the chief executive before the process cascades down the organization. Support for people who are anxious about one-to-ones helps to build confidence and commitment to the process. This can take the form of training and opportunities to review progress with senior management.

It takes a concentrated effort to establish one-to-ones, but they bring huge benefits in focusing people on the organization's priorities and ensuring that they have the resources and support they require.

Performance reviews

Performance reviews are regular in-depth reviews of past performance and future expectations of an individual; they used to be called appraisals, another term that has connotations that are inappropriate in organizations committed to learning. Normally carried out annually, they are sometimes done more frequently for a new member of staff or for people whose performance would benefit from more frequent review.

Performance reviews compare an individual's performance with previously agreed objectives. These individual objectives need to tie directly into the objectives of the individual's organizational unit. Performance reviews need to be carried out in a scrupulously professional way. The assessment of an individual's performance must be objective. Areas for improvement should be presented honestly, and the whole process should aim to be a motivating experience.

Performance reviews are a powerful means of assisting individual and organization learning. By requiring people to stand back and review both their performance and their learning over the previous year, they encourage reflection and help to consolidate experiences at a higher level. They should also establish objectives and priorities for the next twelve months, usually proposed by the individual and agreed by the manager.

Preparation is critical for a successful performance review. Both parties should agree the broad topics that the performance review will cover before data-gathering commences. In larger organizations, there may be corporately agreed headings or a performance review form to complete. Data for a performance review should be collected by both parties.

A performance review should:

- review achievements, using both quantitative and qualitative criteria
- reflect on learning and personal development over the past period
- identify the individual's competencies in relation to the skills required to do the job (these might be National Vocational Qualifications skills set out in a job description, or a set of management competencies)
- identify next steps in the individual's development
- consider any changes in the way the manager works which might assist the development of the person whose performance is being reviewed
- lead to agreement on a package of actions (coaching, shadowing, training, reading) to meet the individual's needs
- consider the next career steps.

Establishing and refreshing performance review processes

Establishing or reinvigorating an organization's performance review process is a substantial task that requires significant time. The practical activities are similar to those needed to set up a one-to-one process. A programme of discussions among managers concerning the design or development of the process will help to build commitment and an understanding of the need for change. The scheme should be designed or developed, possibly using specialist external expertise, and subject to widespread consultation to strengthen commitment and support for the initiative.

Once an overall scheme is agreed, tailor-made training designed to suit the specific circumstances of the organization is essential in order to give people the necessary skills. Everyone should be offered training before being required to carry out a performance review.

The performance review process should roll out, starting with senior management and gradually expanding until it covers all employees. Top management commitment is essential and needs to be demonstrated by the chief executive having a review before reviewing members of the senior management team.

Once established, periodic actions are required to avoid the process becoming a bureaucratic necessity that does not add value to the organization. Changing the questions on performance review forms, requiring people to link performance reviews explicitly to strategic and operational plans, and listing the types of support the organization can provide and introducing 360° reviews are all examples of ways to give the process renewed life.

Introducing 360° performance reviews

A 360° performance review is a wider and deeper review. It gathers information from a range of people who work with the person being reviewed, to provide the fullest possible picture of his or her performance. Sometimes called a multi-input review, these use information from the person's boss, his or her peers and subordinates and, where appropriate, relevant board members and service users.

This data can be gathered by an independent person or, in organizations with appropriate experience, by the person being reviewed and the person conducting the review. Ideally it should include written feedback from people who work with the person being reviewed so that the person doing the review can draw out common themes.

These reviews can be both informative and motivating. They give people a more rounded view of their performance, and as a result the approach is becoming increasingly popular. It is particularly suitable for senior managers, whereby new insights can be gained from seeking the views of all the stakeholders with whom the individual interacts.

LEARNING FROM A 360° PERFORMANCE REVIEW

A charity chief executive wanted to take stock of her own development. Acknowledging one of the organization's values was 'to respect and value each other and those for whom we work', she commissioned a 360° review of her own performance.

The consultant she engaged interviewed seven people who knew her work well, including staff, clients and board members. The interviews were anonymous. The consultant reported back to the chief executive that she was seen to be:

● an excellent ambassadorial leader
● persuasive and intellectually consistent
● able to take tough decisions and confront difficult issues
● insistent on quality
● calm and focused
● an accomplished communicator
● an empowering manager for some
● good at giving and receiving feedback.

She was advised to focus her development on:

● her speed of decision-making
● appealing to emotion as well as intellect
● taking more risks
● providing more overt direction and consulting less.

On receiving this feedback, she was surprised to discover some of her strengths, which had not been apparent to her before. She planned a development programme based on the suggestions.

Fifteen months later, at her regular performance review, her chair told her that he had seen great developments in her skills and performance. She ascribed much of this to the motivation and focus she had gained from learning the combined views of those who knew her work best, through the 360° review.

Specialist expertise may be required to help set up a 360° performance review process, because the procedure of opening up a person's perform-ance for more widespread review can be destructive if not handled well, and conversely very motivating and empowering if done in a highly professional way.

Performance review and pay

The issue of linking performance review to pay is a much-debated topic. Those in favour of agreeing salaries shortly after a performance review argue that rewards should be seen to be linked directly to performance. Those in favour of separation of these two processes argue that people will be honest in their performance review only if they know that it will not have an immediate effect on their annual pay award.

Organizations that do not have well-established performance review processes and a deeply ingrained culture of learning may find that they need to separate the two processes. This can be done by having a six-month gap between the annual round of performance reviews and the annual pay award. This approach provides maximum encouragement for learning and minimizes 'game playing'.

Organizations that have a more developed management culture may find their staff and managers are more confident and recognize that there is little advantage to be had from 'talking up' their performance and a lot to be gained from an honest and thorough performance review. In these circumstances, agreement on salaries can take place shortly after completion of performance reviews.

Dealing with poor performance

Sometimes, despite managers' best efforts, individual performance does not meet the required standard, and action is required to move the person from her or his position. This is often not straightforward because, in many situations, a significant element of judgement is required in coming to this conclusion.

Moving people on can be difficult because:

● people continue to believe in the organization's cause, and sometimes it is the most committed people whose jobs have developed beyond their abilities

● people who have not developed the skills needed to manage their unit of the organization may be renowned leaders in their professional field

● it is a particularly sensitive issue in organizations whose missions are often about helping less able people.

Nevertheless, organizations exist to pursue a mission and not to give people employment, so poor performance always requires attention. Indeed, not attending to a performance problem sends signals to other people about the organization's expectations of people that are likely to be even more damaging to it.

Organizations should have a **redundancy policy** that sets out the terms people will be offered if their post is no longer required. It should be agreed by the board and referred to in employees' terms and conditions. Organizations should also have a **disciplinary procedure** that sets out the process for disciplinary action. When neither of these approaches is possible, there is no alternative but to **negotiate a job change or a departure** with the individual and agree terms and a financial package that is appropriate for the circumstances. Legal advice should be sought in these circumstances.

The process of agreeing a job change or departure should generally be well prepared over a period of time. The person should have been told where his or her performance is falling below the required standard and have had an opportunity to make improvements. If the problem is likely to lead to a dismissal, then the legally required procedures for verbal and written warnings should be followed.

When a decision is taken to ask someone to change jobs or leave, great care should be taken over the process to ensure that it is seen to be as fair as possible in what are inevitably difficult circumstances. Communication with other people in the organization needs to be given as much thought as communication with the person concerned. A badly handled departure can have a damaging and long-lasting impact on an organization's staff and its reputation. Handled professionally, a much-needed departure can enhance a manager's reputation for firm action in what everyone recognizes is a difficult situation.

13.4 ENCOURAGING COACHING, MENTORING AND SHADOWING

Coaching, mentoring and shadowing are all powerful and comparatively inexpensive ways of encouraging learning and they are all becoming increasingly popular.

Coaching

Coaching has risen up the management development agenda in recent years because it is perceived to be a highly effective and inexpensive way of advancing people's abilities. The aim of coaching is to assist people to learn through the medium of their current work. It uses people's recent experiences to draw out learning points around things that went well and things that did not go so well.

Coaching is about helping people to learn, rather than telling them what they should learn. It is about asking perceptive questions and guiding people towards learning points. It addresses the question, 'What can I do to help you do your work?'

Coaching should be an integral part of a manager's daily work, as well as an activity that takes place at one-to-one and performance review sessions. It requires managers to be more diligent about praising work that is well done and bolder about raising questions concerning work that did not go so well. It is effective when the coach and the person being coached have high respect for each other.

It can involve:

- offering an opportunity for the person being coached to shadow someone else
- providing additional support before an important meeting, presentation or the start of a new initiative
- using rehearsals as a way of exposing things that have not been fully thought through
- advising on relevant literature on a subject
- challenging people before they attend a training event to specify their learning objectives, and reviewing their achievements after the event
- guiding people to similar work that someone else did previously

● taking opportunities to give people tasks that will take their skills one step forward.

In a learning organization, coaching should be an integral part of the culture. Managers should be coached and should feel responsible for giving coaching.

Promoting learning through mentoring

Mentoring is the activity of one person providing individual support to another, to help that person to learn. The mentor is usually a more senior or experienced person who is not the individual's line manager. The mentor may be from the same organization or from another organization. A mentor's roles include:

● improving an individual's performance
● acting as a sounding board and an adviser
● sharing knowledge and experience
● encouraging individuals to reflect on their decisions and actions
● supporting an individual's career development.

Mentoring within and across organizations has grown rapidly in recent years because it is seen as a very effective way of helping people to learn in an unthreatening environment.

Mentoring relationships can be short term (to help a manager with a particular problem) or longer term (to help with skill and career development). The relationship typically has a series of stages:

● initiation – when agreement is reached on the nature of the relationship and practical ways of working together
● direction-setting – when the individual's needs are agreed and objectives are established
● working together – when they share each other's expertise, review progress and develop their relationship
● moving on – when the relationship is drawn to a close.

Mentoring is particularly valuable when managers do not have anyone they can turn to for advice. Reasons for this might include:

● the problem is their relationship with their manager or chair

- the individual does not wish to discuss an issue within the organization before testing it out on a third party
- a view that no one within the organization could provide the required support
- the individual wishes to discuss career development in private because public discussion might lead to a loss of authority in the organization
- the individual needs to adjust his or her relationships with former peers following a promotion.

Mentors need to agree and adhere to strict rules of confidentiality on both professional and personal matters. They should not mentor more than one person in the same organization at the same time.

Mentoring can be enhanced if it is combined with shadowing. When mentoring is done on its own, the mentor often does not see the person 'in action', so the only source of information is the individual himself or herself. When it is combined with shadowing, the mentor gains additional insights into the individual's ways of working that can point to further avenues for enhancing performance.

One danger is that mentoring can also be seen as a criticism of the managers of the people being mentored; managers may feel that they should be providing the support people require. Mentoring can also result in managers feeling threatened when people bring back different assumptions and ideas that may conflict with those their managers wish to promote.

Despite these anxieties, mentoring is another method of promoting learning and development that is already bringing great benefits to people working in the third sector.

THE ACENVO MENTORING SCHEME

The Association of Chief Executives of National Voluntary Organizations established a successful mentoring scheme to link new chief executives to those with experience and to support chief executives of smaller organizations that had no training budget.

Although members were asked to volunteer for the task and their names were published, private arrangements between members were also encouraged. The Association's Chief Executive also offered to be a matchmaker if required. A 'Guide to Mentoring' was published in the members' handbook.

People were advised to ensure that the personal chemistry was right before establishing a formal relationship. ACENVO suggested that people should envisage that the relationship would last for a year and then be reviewed. They were advised to meet every six to eight weeks.

The advice stressed that, in a mentoring relationship, both parties have opportunities to learn. Mentors were advised to be supportive and not judgemental. Individuals being mentored were advised to tell their trustees, go to meetings with a clear agenda and give them a high priority, despite the many other demands on their time.

Promoting learning through shadowing

Shadowing is a valuable way of giving people learning opportunities. It costs almost nothing and is comparatively easy to organize, but it does require proper preparation if it is to yield the greatest benefits. This takes time for both the shadow and the person being shadowed. However, learning does accrue to both parties. Shadowing can be done within organizations, between organizations in the sector or with people in the public and private sectors.

People who are shadows should specify their learning objectives before deciding whom to shadow. They should be briefed by the person they are shadowing on the situation they will be following before and during the shadowing activity. They should reflect on what they have learned with the person whom they are shadowing. Writing up their learning from the shadowing helps to relate the experience to their work situation.

Shadowing can involve following a manager over a period of days or following a sequence of activities that take place over a number of weeks. Examples of shadowing activities include following:

- a series of strategic planning meetings
- a board or senior management team meeting
- a chief executive or divisional director for a period of days
- a consultant working on a relevant assignment
- a manager in a similar job in another sector
- a task group working on a relevant project.

13.5 ENCOURAGING TEAMS TO LEARN

Teams have the potential to generate significant learning for individuals and for the group as a whole. They offer this potential because people see each other working together and inevitably they reflect on each other's behaviour. Some of these reflections will contain important insights, if they can be teased out in unthreatening ways.

To learn from the team, members need to be aware of how the team is working at three different levels. Members are usually conscious of how the team is working with the **task**. Comments such as 'We're making good progress' or 'We took a lot of decisions' relate to the task. Team members also need to be conscious of the **processes** of its work, the ways it is tackling its job. Comments such as 'She chaired the meeting well' or 'He brought the best out of her' are indicative of process. Lastly, teams need to be aware of team members' **emotions**. They need to be conscious of how people are feeling about the task, the processes and each other. Comments such as 'I really appreciated his constructive comments on my paper' or 'She was clearly feeling angry about that' relate to the emotions of the team.

Teams need to create opportunities to learn. Rich learning opportunities arise when teams are working in what Peter Senge calls a dialoguing mode. He draws the distinction between **discussions** and **dialogues**. When a team is having a discussion, different views are presented and defended, and the team searches for a solution to a particular problem. This is appropriate at times when a decision is required. A dialogue, on the other hand, is a 'free and creative discussion' of more complex and subtle issues, in which individuals listen closely to one another.

According to Senge, three conditions are necessary for a team to learn from a dialogue:

● Participants must be willing to expose their assumptions to the team and to have them examined by team members. Questions about what assumptions people are making and why they are making them are encouraged. Team members search for answers in an honest way, and members do not feel threatened by having their assumptions challenged.
● All team members must regard one another as colleagues and be willing to work on a level field. The benefits of open dialogue must be greater

than the privileges that individuals enjoy as a result of their positions.
● One or more members of the team have to 'facilitate' the dialogue and take responsibility for 'holding the context' and not allow the conversation to drift.

When a team is in dialogue mode, individuals gain insights that they are unlikely to have found on their own or when the team was in discussion mode. The team is likely to get a better understanding of the circumstances outside the team. More importantly, it should get nearer to the truth about what is going on inside the team – and that is really powerful learning.

Organizations that promote learning encourage teams to dialogue and to maximize the learning that they can generate from themselves.

Another method of learning from the team is to **review and reflect** how it is working. This can happen in many different ways. A good starting-point is to spend a few minutes (at the end of each meeting, say) reviewing how the meeting went. A comment from each member of the team can tease out thoughts on:

● What did we do well?
● What did we not do so well?
● What could we do better next time?

These questions can refer to all three levels of team working described above. Reminding people at the beginning of the next meeting what was agreed at the end of the previous meeting is a good way of embedding the required improvements into team behaviour.

Similar reviews can be carried out at the middle and at the end of a series of meetings related to a specific task. A more thorough review can be scheduled to take place less frequently. This might start with similar questions, but go on to consider deeper questions such as:

● What different types of contributions do different team members make?
● What changes are required in the way the team works?
● What changes would I like to see in the ways other team members work in the team?
● What changes would I like to make in the way I contribute to the team?

A thorough review might be combined with the use of one or two of the tests that help people to understand different personalities and the different roles that people play in teams. Myers Briggs is a well-developed test that helps to identify different personality traits, and the Belbin test helps to identify the different roles that people tend to play in the team. They also help to give a profile of the whole team that can point to gaps in skills or behaviours that need to be filled.

USEFUL PEOPLE TO HAVE IN TEAMS

Type	Positive qualities	Allowable weaknesses
Company Worker	Organizing ability, practical common sense, hard-working, self-discipline.	Lack of flexibility, unresponsiveness to unproven ideas.
Chairman	A capacity for treating and welcoming all potential contributors on their merits and without prejudice. A strong sense of objectives.	No more than ordinary in terms of intellect or creative ability.
Shaper	Drive and a readiness to challenge inertia, ineffectiveness, complacency or self-deception.	Proneness to provocation, irritation and impatience.
Plant	Genius, imagination, intellect, knowledge.	Up in the clouds, inclined to disregard practical details or protocol.
Resource Investigator	A capacity for contacting people and exploring anything new. An ability to respond to challenge.	Liable to lose interest once the initial fascination has passed.
Monitor-Evaluator	Judgement, discretion, hard-headedness.	Lacks inspiration or the ability to motivate others.
Team Worker	An ability to respond to people and to situations, and to promote team spirit.	Indecisiveness at moments of crisis.
Completer-Finisher	A capacity for follow-through. Perfectionism.	A tendency to worry about small things. A reluctance to 'let go'.

From: *Management Teams*, R. M. Belbin

All these actions help teams to become highly sensitive to their own performance and consequently make organization learning an integral part of their working. They help teams to understand their strengths and weaknesses and to use the team as a pool of skill and experience that is available to assist all members of the team.

When these relatively simple disciplines are adopted and used by the senior management team, it sends powerful messages to the rest of the organization about the type of learning culture that ought to permeate through the whole organization.

13.6 ENSURING ORGANIZATION-WIDE LEARNING

Organization-wide learning happens when learning is seen to take place at every level and in every corner of the organization. While easily said, it takes years to create a culture in which people see learning opportunities in everything they do.

There are three elements to creating a learning organization. It requires:

- **senior management to champion learning**. People at the top must be seen to be taking every opportunity themselves to learn, to encourage learning throughout the organization and to invest time and resources in learning. Without evidence of commitment to learning, it will be seen as well-intentioned but not real.
- **masses of communication and education**. People have to understand for themselves why learning is important, and they can be helped and supported by extensive communication up and down the organization that stresses its importance. This will include face-to-face, paper and electronic methods.
- **effective support systems**. People have to be supported by a range of systems, including training, facilitation, one-to-ones and team-building sessions.

Many of the management techniques described earlier in this book can also make a huge contribution to learning. Strategic planning is a tool for helping people to learn about their organization and its external environment. Performance management is a critical element in creating a learning organization because it establishes a systematic approach to reviewing achievements and feeding back learning into future plans. Management competencies are a means for people to learn how their skills compare with those of others. Investors in People helps people to identify their learning needs. Benchmarking allows people to understand why their organization's performance is better or worse than that of others.

Learning can also come from outside the organization. Managers can be encouraged to obtain insights from other organizations. This is a rich source of learning, both about different ways of working and about the strengths of one's own organization. To tap into this learning, managers should be encouraged to attend conferences and workshops, both within the sector and in the public and private sectors. Managers should also become involved in the professional groups that provide development for people in their particular profession.

Organization-wide learning therefore needs to be seen not as an initiative on its own but as a way of working that permeates all the activities and processes that an organization undertakes. This will demonstrate to people that the organization is deeply committed to learning and that it values people who learn.

These actions produce reciprocal commitments from individuals to the organization. They motivate people to learn and they encourage the openness and information-sharing that are essential to the learning organization.

SUMMARY OF KEY POINTS

Encouraging learning throughout the organization

- Organizations enhance their performance by encouraging individual, team and organization-wide learning.
- A structured approach to learning is often under-valued in third-sector organizations.
- Senior management has to set an example by being seen to prioritize learning.
- A learning organization requires people to take responsibility for their own learning. The organization provides support and encouragement to ensure learning opportunities are maximized.

Developing individuals
- Managers play a significant role in helping individuals to develop.
- Managers should have a clear view of individuals' current skills and the next skills they need to develop.
- Personal development experiences come from many sources.
- The induction process is an opportunity to stress an organization's commitment to learning.

Promoting learning through one-to-ones and performance review
- One-to-ones should:
  - review performance
  - ensure delegated work is done
  - check the required resources were provided
  - enable people to learn from their work
  - remind people that they are valued.
- Organizations need systems to ensure that one-to-ones produce real learning opportunities for staff.
- Performance reviews should:
  - review achievements
  - reflect on learning and personal development
  - identify current and required competencies
  - agree actions to meet the individual's learning needs.
- 360° performance reviews help senior managers in well-developed organizations to get a more rounded view of their performance.
- Organizations should have a redundancy policy, a disciplinary procedure and, when all else fails, should negotiate a job change or a departure to deal with irretrievably poor performance.

Encouraging coaching, mentoring and shadowing
- Coaches help people to learn from their work.
- Mentors can improve people's performance, act as a sounding board, share knowledge and experience and support career development.
- Shadowing enables people to learn from other people's work.

Encouraging teams to learn
- Team members need to be conscious of the task, the processes and the emotions.

- Teams should distinguish between discussions and dialogues.
- Teams need to review and reflect.

Ensuring organization-wide learning
- The essential ingredients of organization-wide learning include championing learning, masses of communication and effective support systems.
- Managers should encourage people to learn from other organizations.

14 Managing Different Types of Organization

14.1 ORGANIZATION LIFE CYCLES

The third sector consists of an extraordinarily wide range of organizations. So far this book has concentrated on approaches to management that are common to many organizations. This chapter looks at the management of organizations at different stages of their development and at the management of different types of organization

The management of organizations at different stages of development is best understood by considering the notion of their life cycle. This idea was first introduced in Chapter 3 in relation to boards, but it can also be used to help understand the development of the whole organization.

The central proposition behind the life cycle is the idea that organizations develop in stages. It was put forward over twenty years ago in a *Harvard Business Review* article entitled 'Evolution and Revolution in Organizations'. It argued that periods of steady evolutionary growth and development are followed by periods of revolutionary development when everything seems to be changing at the same time. This behaviour pattern is very common in third-sector organizations.

The idea of a life cycle does not imply that all organizations will necessarily move through a predetermined set of stages. That patently could not be true because organizations' futures are ultimately determined by governing boards and management taking decisions based on their judgements at a particular point in time. However, when one looks at many organizations and summarizes their behaviour, a surprisingly large number have a similar evolutionary pattern.

The value of this life cycle idea is that it helps boards and managers to

ORGANIZATION LIFE CYCLE

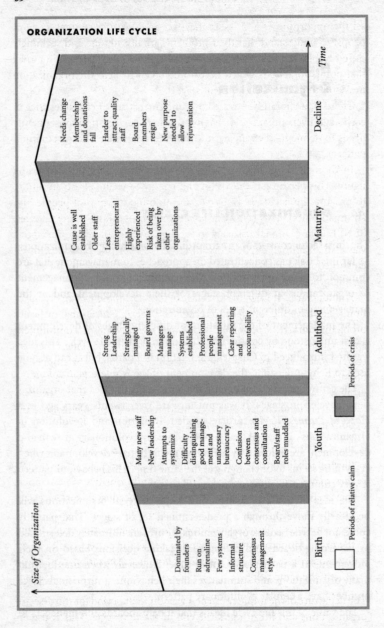

Size of Organization

Time

Birth
- Dominated by founders
- Run on adrenaline
- Few systems
- Informal structure
- Consensus management style

Youth
- Many new staff
- New leadership
- Attempts to systemize
- Difficulty distinguishing good management and unnecessary bureaucracy
- Confusion between consensus and consultation
- Board/staff roles muddled

Adulthood
- Strong Leadership
- Strategically managed
- Board governs
- Managers manage
- Systems established
- Professional people management
- Clear reporting and accountability

Maturity
- Cause is well established
- Older staff
- Less entrepreneurial
- Highly experienced
- Risk of being taken over by other organizations

Decline
- Needs change
- Membership and donations fall
- Harder to attract quality staff
- Board members resign
- New purpose needed to allow rejuvenation

☐ Periods of relative calm

▨ Periods of crisis

set the opportunities and issues they face in a broader context. It helps people to understand that their problems are not unique and seemingly unresolvable. It enables people to explain behaviour in terms of a model that points to actions which need to be taken to help the organization move on to its next development stage.

There is, it should be stressed, no one correct set of characteristics in each stage. Every organization has its own characteristics and consequently needs to define its own life cycle. There are nevertheless some common patterns.

In the first stage, organizations are often dominated by a founding figure. This person has the vision and energy to create an organization, to procure the necessary resources and to build a group of people into an organization. This stage can last from a few years to many decades. SENSE (The National Association for the Deaf and Blind), for example, was a small mutual-support organization for over thirty years before it embarked in the mid-1980s on a period of explosive growth that took it through the next two stages in less than ten years.

Founders are critical in the first stage of the development of an organization. They have the foresight to recognize a social, educational or health problem or an artistic opportunity, and they have the energy, commitment and charisma to create an organization to address the issue. They are entrepreneurial in approach and are usually unwilling to be stopped by obstacles. Without these people, organizations would never get off the ground.

However, founders are also a common source of problems once the organization has become established:

- they can find it difficult to let go of the reins
- they often fail to train and coach their successors
- they may be unable to adjust to the style and priorities of newcomers
- they may see the growth of systems and procedures as unnecessary bureaucracy
- they sometimes plot to overthrow new management in order to put the organization back on to what they see as the correct track
- they sometimes leave and establish another organization working in exactly the same field.

The departure of the founder can be a very difficult period for third-sector organizations and it can mark the end of the first stage. This is usually followed by a period of upheaval and a move into the second stage. New management brings different approaches and new ideas, and the organization moves forward. There is, however, still much to be learned in the second stage. Sometimes there is a clash of values between an 'old guard', who see flexibility and opportunism as the very reason for the organization's success, and the 'new guard', who see the need for improved planning, more formal decision-making processes, better information systems and more structured management. Sometimes the roles of the board and the staff remain ill-defined for a period of years. Until these problems are resolved, organizations stay in the youthful phase.

Eventually organizations grow into adulthood, perhaps following a change of leadership. In their idealized form, adult organizations separate governance and management, have a clear purpose and strategy, have effective management information and decision-making systems and develop people to achieve their greatest potential. In practice, not all organizations attain this potential. Changes in board membership, staff and the external environment mean that it is a never-ending struggle to keep the organization in top management form. Some organizations may slip back into the youthful stage and have to work on their management to return to the adult stage.

Others move on to maturity. Once the cause is well established, it becomes more difficult to remain 'fired up' about the issues. These organizations probably have good connections with funders and policy-makers, but they may not have the most motivated branches or attract the most ambitious staff and board members. They frequently become less entrepreneurial and risk being overtaken by other organizations.

Finally, as needs change, funding, members and donations may start to fall. Unless organizations in this predicament can find a new purpose, they will start to decline. Surprisingly, third-sector organizations seldom die. Some become smaller and less effective and slide into ever-increasing mediocrity; others eventually merge with a larger or newer body that injects new life into the organization.

The value of the life cycle is that it helps to explain the behaviour of organizations when a number of problems surface simultaneously. This can be a time of great trauma when different management issues all become entangled with one another. It is frequently a time when management consultants are brought in to help unbundle the problems and create an agenda of actions to move the organization on to its next stage of development.

The notion of life cycles is applicable to most organizations at different stages of their development. Further unpacking the management of different types of organizations requires an explanation of different ways of classifying them.

14.2 CLASSIFYING ORGANIZATIONS

Third-sector organizations are normally classified according to the activities they undertake: schools provide education, hospitals heal sick people, trade unions represent labour, disability organizations represent people with special needs, and campaigning organizations argue for policy change. The International Classification of Non-profit Organizations (see the box, below) is a good example. However, classifications that are more useful for managers sub-divide organizations according to characteristics that cut across these traditional groupings. These classifications help to explain the types of strategic developments that are workable and those that lead to major problems.

CLASSIFICATION BY ACTIVITY

The International Classification of Non-profit Organizations groups organizations by activity:

Group 1: Culture and Recreation
Sports, arts, museums, zoos, recreation, social clubs

Group 2: Education and Research
School and higher education, vocational training
Medical research, science and technology, policy studies

Group 3: Health
Hospitals, rehabilitation, nursing homes, mental health
Public health, health education

Group 4: Social Services
Child welfare, youth services, services for families, elderly and disabled people

---

Emergency relief, income support, material assistance

Group 5: Environment
Conservation of natural resources, pollution control
Animal protection and welfare, wildlife and countryside preservation

Group 6: Development and Housing
Economic, social and community development
Housing
Employment and training

Group 7: Law, Advocacy and Politics
Advocacy organizations, minority groups, civic associations
Legal services, crime prevention, rehabilitation of offenders, victim support
Political parties

Group 8: Philanthropic intermediaries and voluntarism promotion
Grant-making trusts, fund-raising organizations
Intermediary organizations

Group 9: International Activities
Exchange programmes, development assistance, disaster relief
Human rights and peace organizations

Group 10: Religion
Religious organizations

Group 11: Business, professional associations and unions
Employers' organizations, trade unions, professional associations

Group 12: Not elsewhere classified

'A Comparative Study of the Non-profit Sector', L. Salamon and H. Anheier, in *Researching the Voluntary Sector*, Charities Aid Foundation, 1993

This approach is the same as academic analyses of the private sector, in which organizations are divided into categories such as manufacturing and service businesses, capital intensive and non-capital intensive, vertically integrated and horizontally diversified. Such categorizations are valuable because they shed light on common behavioural patterns which cut across industries. The same process will lead us to a better understanding of their behaviour.

Third-sector organizations can be categorized in many different ways; for example, by size, by geographical scope (international, national, regional or local), by their institutional structure (linear or federal) or by historical stage of development. These are interesting and significant but, for managerial purposes, three types of classification are particularly useful. These are classification by:

● the **broad purpose** of the organization
● the **main source of funds**
● the **composition of the board**.

This section describes these classifications and how different types of organization fit into each of the classifications. It then looks at the implications for managing the different types of organization.

Classification by purpose

The first way of putting some coherence on this diverse sector is to classify organizations according to their primary purpose. This is a development of a typology that was put forward by Charles Handy in *Understanding Voluntary Organizations*. In this classification, the primary purpose of third-sector organizations is one of the following:

● to **provide services**; examples include housing associations, colleges, schools, arts organizations and many voluntary organizations
● to **provide mutual support**; examples include trade unions, professional associations, employers' organizations and self-help groups
● to **campaign for change**; examples include campaigning organizations such as Greenpeace, Liberty and Amnesty International.

This simple division into three main purposes is complicated by the fact that some organizations fall into two and some into three categories. For example, some that began life as mutual support organizations (say, for parents of children with a disability) start providing services. The services are successful, so they grow and develop. Before long, the organization is a multi-million-pound service provider. However, it will probably have retained its mutual-support role, so consequently it falls

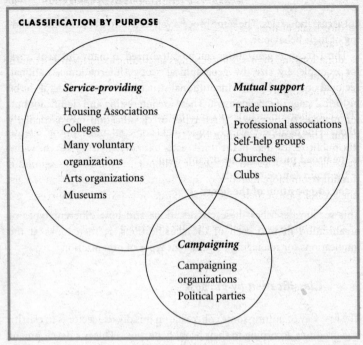

CLASSIFICATION BY PURPOSE

Service-providing

Housing Associations
Colleges
Many voluntary
organizations
Arts organizations
Museums

Mutual support

Trade unions
Professional associations
Self-help groups
Churches
Clubs

Campaigning

Campaigning
organizations
Political parties

into both categories and has the management issues of both types of organization.

Similarly, trade unions began as pure mutual-support or solidarity organizations representing the needs of their members. Today, many sell a range of services (such as insurance) to members and non-members alike, and also campaign for change. (As a slight aside, it is worth noting that the relative size of each group is not known. Service-providing organizations dominate the third sector, by comparison with which mutual-support organizations are small in number and size, and campaigning organizations represent a very small proportion of the sector, though they have a very high profile compared to their size.)

Classification by source of funds

A second way of putting some order on the third sector is to classify organizations by source of funds. Organizations are funded from four different sources:

- direct sale of their services
- grants
- donations and fund-raising activities (including investment and trading income)
- membership fees.

This classification includes organizations at the core of the third sector and those at the periphery (which, some might argue, sit more appropriately in the public sector than in the third sector). It nevertheless gives the widest possible perspective on the sector. Although some receive significant funding from more than one of these sources, most organizations receive the greater part of their income from one or two of these sources.

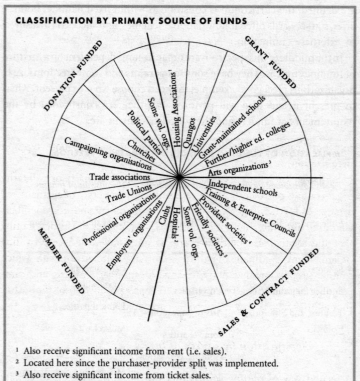

CLASSIFICATION BY PRIMARY SOURCE OF FUNDS

[1] Also receive significant income from rent (i.e. sales).
[2] Located here since the purchaser-provider split was implemented.
[3] Also receive significant income from ticket sales.
[4] Examples include BUPA, Private Patients Plan and Western Provident Society.
[5] After February 1993 no new Friendly Societies could be registered.

The primary source of funding has a significant impact on organizations' strategic freedom. Organizations funded by donations sit at one end of a spectrum. They have great freedom to determine what they will do and how they will do it. Their boards are comparatively unconstrained in how they choose to achieve their objectives. Development agencies, for example, have enormous freedom to determine the activities they will pursue, the parts of the world they work in and the mechanisms they employ for achieving change.

Organizations funded by contracts and, to a lesser extent, those funded by grants are more tightly constrained. Geographical coverage, type of service, qualifications and accreditation may all be fixed. Schools and further education colleges exist at this end of the spectrum. Their users are defined, the curriculum is constrained within fixed national boundaries, staff rewards often follow national schemes, and success is measured by external examination.

In the middle of this spectrum are organizations dependent on a mixture of funding sources. They have some constraints and some freedoms. Arts organizations are a good example; they can choose what to present, when to present it and who will perform, but they are constrained by the requirements of funders and their local catchment area.

IMPLICATION OF FUNDING SOURCES ON STRATEGIC FREEDOM

Tightly constrained funding	Mixture of funding sources	Unconstrained funding
Little strategic freedom	Some strategic freedom	Great strategic freedom
Schools	Hospitals	Campaigning organizations
Further Education colleges	Universities	Political parties
Training and Enterprise Councils	Arts organizations	Most charities
	Some charities	Foundations
	Housing associations	Membership organizations
	Churches	
	Trade unions	

Classification by composition of the board

The third way of classifying organizations is by the motives of the people who are appointed to its board. Organizations attract different types of people to join their boards. These people bring different skills and experiences. Although people do not necessarily fall exclusively into one category or another, three main types can be identified. They are:

● **experts,** who bring knowledge, experience and (usually) specific professional skills to a board
● **users,** who joined the organization to benefit from its work or services and who will usually have been elected to the board by the membership
● **concerned individuals,** who believe in a cause and wish to make their contribution by their voluntary effort as a board member.

Each group of people has different expectations of the role of the board and the way it should work.

Experts bring a series of assumptions derived from their work and professional experience. Users bring different assumptions to the board. They have a direct personal interest in the organization. The services help them as well as other members, sometimes making it difficult to separate the best interests of the organization from personal preferences and prejudices. Users may bring expertise from a profession as well, but their fundamental motivation for joining the board is different from that of the pure expert. Concerned individuals have another set of motives. They are distinguished by the fact that they feel so passionately about an issue they are willing to give significant amounts of their time to the organization. They believe in the cause and are willing to work tirelessly to pursue social or political objectives.

Each of these three groups works in different ways. Even when a board consists of one type, there will be differences of opinion within the group. However, these generally take much less time to resolve than the differences that arise from mixing experts, users and concerned individuals on boards.

In summary, the majority of provider organizations can be categorized on three dimensions:

- by purpose:
  - to provide services
  - to give mutual support
  - to campaign for change
- by source of funds:
  - sales and contracts
  - grant funding
  - donations
  - members
- by composition of the board:
  - experts
  - users
  - concerned individuals.

14.3 PUTTING THE CLASSIFICATIONS TOGETHER

The purpose of dissecting the third sector into a series of classifications is, first, to reflect the extraordinarily diverse nature of the organizations and, secondly, to identify combinations of types that work well and those that are more problematic in managerial terms.

The three classifications described earlier can be used to identify combinations that work particularly well and combinations that present greater managerial challenges. The combinations with a straightforward fit are:

Purpose	Main sources of funding	Composition of the board
Service	Sales, contracts and grants	Experts
Mutual support	Members	Users
Campaign	Members and donations	Concerned individuals

Although the boundaries between these types are not clear-cut, the central logic that drives each of these combinations is straightforward. These organizations are easier and less stressful to manage. Less time is spent resolving conflict and less experienced managers and board members are required.

However, in some circumstances it is entirely appropriate to mix types of organizations. When an organization has matured and has the management capacity to cope with running two logics simultaneously, the benefits can be considerable. Problems usually arise when organizations drift across the boundary from one category into another.

A common example is the mutual-support organization that believes it should help people outside its membership and starts to offer services. At first sight, this is an obvious and sensible decision. The consequences are nevertheless significant. A pure mutual-support organization has a straightforward logic: members pay fees and the organization provides members with services. When it moves into service provision for non-members, it needs a different logic, concerned with defining user needs, marketing services and seeking funds to pay for them. Furthermore, members' needs are no longer the organization's sole priority. The situation becomes more complicated when, as sometimes happens, the service activities become much larger than the original mutual-support activities. An organization with an institutional structure suitable for offering mutual support can become a multi-million-pound service provider which may need very different structures and management processes.

Another example comes from the service-providing organization that starts campaigning. Campaigning has yet another logic, concerned with defining policy objectives and devising strategies to achieve them. Campaigning needs new sources of funds (e.g. from donors) and new structures to manage the work (e.g. policy committees, press officers, lobbying skills).

Additional management challenges arise when organizations have funding sources that do not fit with their primary purpose. Combinations that cause problems include:

Purpose	Primary funding source	Potential problems
Service	Donors	Service dependent on continuing support from donors
Mutual support	Grants	Grants are often time-limited, which leads to instability in the organization
Campaign	Grants	Funders can (often unintentionally) have disproportionate influence on campaign priorities

The basic message is that an expansion from one purpose to two is a major strategic decision with wide-ranging consequences; it may require new funding sources, a different management logic and different skills on the board. It is a decision that should be taken with great care.

Having given this overview, the next three sections take the classification by purpose and look at the management of each type in turn.

14.4 MANAGING SERVICE-PROVIDING ORGANIZATIONS

Service-providing organizations dominate the third sector. Examples from the core of the sector include many voluntary organizations, arts organizations and housing associations. Examples at the periphery of the sector include schools, colleges, hospitals and universities.

These organizations were often founded by an individual or a group of social entrepreneurs. Examples from many years ago include the founding fathers of Oxford University and St Bartholomew's Hospital. Examples from the voluntary sector where the founder's name became enshrined in their organization's name include Dr Barnardo, Leonard Cheshire and Sue Ryder.

Service-providing organizations exist for service users. This contrasts with mutual-support organizations that consist of people who themselves benefit from their organization. The key characteristic of service-providing organizations is that they provide a range of services to specific groups of service users who are not necessarily members of the organization. This section therefore describes propositions that are particular to service-providing organizations.

Strategic questions

The first strategic question that many service-providing organizations need to answer is: **why are they providing the service?** This is not as straightforward a question as it may appear at first sight. It could be any one, or a combination, of the following:

- meeting users' needs
- demonstrating the value of the service

- testing a new approach
- providing experience to support campaign work
- making a surplus to invest in other services
- meeting volunteers' needs.

Answers to this question shed light on the primary objective of the organization's services. If, for example, the purpose is to test a new approach (e.g. to experiment with the French 'Foyer' approach to helping single homeless people in the UK), then the primary objective might be to monitor how it works. Alternatively, if the purpose is to support campaign work, the organization will have to gear itself up to fit the service into its campaign strategy and manage the service, not just for the benefits the service provides, but to demonstrate the results that were achieved.

This leads to the second strategic question: **how will the organization be financed in the long run?** Third-sector organizations are tremendously innovative when it comes to putting together a range of different sources of funds to finance a service. However, there are some organizations that do not monitor the extent to which their services are being funded by grants or contracts, subsidized by donors, or paid for by service users. In some cases, services which should be fully funded by the state are being unintentionally subsidized by donors. Managers of service-giving organizations need to be clear about who is funding the service, whether it should be funded in this way and whether the funding is sustainable in the longer term.

The third question is **whether the organization wishes to provide the service itself in the long term.** In the past, many organizations established services to demonstrate to the state how a particular objective could be achieved. Other organizations have established services with the intention of hiving them off as separate organizations. The National Council for Voluntary Organizations has been particularly successful at that, founding Age Concern, the Charities Aid Foundation, Citizens' Advice Bureaux and many other, less well-known organizations.

The fourth question is **whether the service should be provided by one organization alone** or as a partnership between different organizations. Partnerships between third-sector organizations themselves and with businesses are increasingly common. RNIB publishes its electronic newspaper in conjunction with the *Guardian*, housing associations undertake joint ventures financed partly by city institutions, and Oxfam imports products from small businesses in non-industrialized countries to sell via its mail-order catalogue.

Meeting users' needs

Having established the primary purpose of the service, the central logic that needs to pervade these organizations is that of understanding users' needs and providing services to meet them. This sounds simple in theory; however, there are many dimensions to user needs. They include the exact nature of the service, its quality, the way it is delivered, where it is provided, the times it is available, and so on.

In the private sector, these different aspects of the service are bundled together and a price is attached to delivery of the service. When the business is not meeting that bundle of needs, sales fall and everyone knows that action must be taken to pinpoint the problem and make improvements. Many third-sector organizations do not have such a sensitive feedback mechanism, because users seldom pay the full cost of the service. As a result, there are only muted signals about service quality. In some organizations there is virtually no connection between funder and user. Consequently other issues (such as the needs of staff, board politics and policy debates) can creep incrementally up the agenda. There is an ever-present danger that meeting the needs of service users will not be given the attention it requires.

The logic of managing service-providing organizations is therefore dependent on **developing and maintaining a deep understanding of user needs**. This may require research, data-gathering from user groups, focus-group discussions, feedback forms and so on to replace the market mechanism and ensure that managers develop a clear view of user needs. Much has been written about marketing for service-giving organizations (see Further Reading, below), so the concepts are not repeated here.

Having understood user requirements, the whole service delivery system needs **to focus sharply on meeting users' needs**. Objectives should focus on user needs and clarify what the organization aims to do to meet those needs. The strategy should focus on how the organization will meet those needs. The performance-monitoring system should gather information on the extent to which users are satisfied with the service.

The people-management process, including induction, supervision and performance review, should incorporate sections on meeting user needs. Finally, the system for monitoring overall performance of the organization should provide information on the number of users assisted, the extent of the assistance and its quality.

The effect of not having a direct market mechanism to keep service-giving organizations on their toes cannot be overestimated. Third-sector service providers have to compensate for this by taking every opportunity to ensure that all parts of the organization are geared up to seek out, listen to and respond to users' needs.

Demand management

In many service-providing organizations, demand for the service far exceeds the funds available to pay for it. Economic theory tells us that, as prices for a service fall, demand increases. In many of these organizations prices are zero – so demand could potentially be infinite.

Organizations therefore have to adopt techniques to manage demand that depend on factors other than money. Some organizations allow waiting-lists to grow. As they get longer, more and more people will seek the service elsewhere or solve their problem in some other way. Educational organizations have entry qualifications to manage demand. Housing associations measure the extent of people's housing need so that only people with the greatest need are eligible. Some organizations consciously avoid marketing or promoting their service, to avoid being swamped by demand.

Using various mechanisms to control demand is an important task for many service-giving organizations. It may require a balance of:

● qualifying criteria (e.g. degree of disability)
● means testing (e.g. income, savings)
● price (e.g. rents, ticket prices, user charges).

There is often an element of conflict between the need to market services (to ensure that their availability is known to those most in need) and the need to manage demand (to avoid being swamped by people wanting the service). Managers may feel that they are being pulled in two directions simultaneously. It is sometimes necessary to do both in order to concentrate resources on people with the greatest need. Marketing initiatives may need to be focused on particular groups, such as ethnic minorities, to ensure that they have access to the service; simultaneously, opening hours may need to be restricted as a way of controlling availability of the service.

Responding to the contract economy

One of the most significant changes in the management of many service-providing organizations has been the recent switch from grant to contract funding. For many years, the proportion of funding these organizations received from central and local government has been growing steadily. But the money came mainly in the form of grants, giving organizations considerable freedom as to how the money was actually spent.

The gradual change to funding by contract has had many implications. It meant:

- some organizations that had previously co-operated now find themselves competing with each other
- historically stable sources of funds can no longer be relied upon
- entrepreneurial newcomers are taking work from well-established organizations
- funding has increased, but it has been focused on the services that funders are obliged by law to provide and not on the education, advocacy and research that third-sector organizations have always seen as important
- the traditional focus on quality of service has been replaced by value-for-money considerations.

The change has two important implications for management. First, it requires organiz.   ns to revisit their fundamental purpose in order to determine whether to participate in the contract economy in the first place. Organizations that have been highly dependent on grants to fund their services may have little choice. Those that are funded by donations or the sale of services to users have greater choice in the matter. The decision is not as straightforward as it may appear at first sight, particularly for organizations that have not previously received significant government funding. The new money may appear attractive but:

● having to compete for contracts can be a restraint on organizations that mount campaigns against the policies or actions of government. These organizations worry that their campaign activity may tip decisions on contracts towards their competitors

● many organizations that were established as independent bodies, aiming to bring about change, unintentionally become surrogate suppliers of government services.

Having determined that seeking contracts is within the spirit and mission of the organization, management has to develop a new range of skills, some of which are described elsewhere in this book. They include:

● **understanding potential purchasers**: managers have to identify the (often limited) number of purchasers of services. They have to understand the purchasers' organization, their personnel and their decision-making processes, and ensure that potential buyers know of the supplier's ability to deliver the services

● **costing services**: managers need to know how to build up the costs of a service to ensure that their decisions on pricing contracts are based on the full cost of providing the service

● **tendering for contracts**: managers need to learn the art of submitting tenders, making pitch presentations, setting competitive prices and convincing purchasers to buy the service

● **negotiating**: before and after contract tenders are won, there is often a period of negotiation. Managers need to learn how to negotiate to ensure that the organization concludes a fair deal with its purchaser

● **financial management**: the financial management systems of most organizations are not designed to capture information by contract. Income and expenditure accounts by contract are essential to enable managers responsible for contracts to manage expenditure within contract income, and for the organization to ensure that it is not unintentionally subsidizing contract work

● **performance monitoring**: contracts usually require organizations to monitor services more closely than they had to previously under grant-funding regimes. Suppliers need to be able to inform purchasers how many people were assisted, what level of assistance was provided, what outcomes were achieved, and so on. Most organizations have to sharpen up their monitoring procedures in order to capture and evaluate this information

- **manage purchaser–provider relationships:** special skills are required to manage these relationships. They are concerned with keeping purchasers informed of progress and finding open and constructive ways of working together. These skills need development, particularly in organizations that are used to donor income and consequently are less experienced in reporting to funders.

To summarize, governors and managers of third-sector service-delivery organizations have to ask some fundamental strategic questions about why they are providing the service; they have to orientate all their organization's systems around meeting users' needs; they often have to market the service and manage demand simultaneously; and they need to develop new skills in order to survive in the contract economy.

14.5 MANAGING MUTUAL-SUPPORT ORGANIZATIONS

Mutual-support organizations include trade unions, professional associations, employers' organizations, trade associations and many voluntary organizations established and run by members.

The fundamental difference between service-providing and mutual-support organizations is that members both benefit from and control the management of mutual-support organizations. The special nature of the management of these organizations emanates from this critically important relationship.

Values and management are inseparable

Mutual-support organizations are distinguished more than anything else by the values and beliefs of their members. These organizations usually consist of people who are dedicated to the cause that the organization stands for: committed trade unionists, enthusiastic members of their profession, or dedicated members of a voluntary organization and hardworking members of trade associations.

In the case of voluntary organizations, many board members may have had a significant life-experience that motivated them to join the organization. Common examples include the birth of a child with disabilities, the death of a relative as a result of a terminal illness or an accident. Whatever the motive, members of these organizations have something in common. Consequently, the **culture is deeply influenced by members' experience** and the cause they champion.

The impact starts at the top with the board. It is elected by the members to represent their interests and views. Board members are therefore particularly aware of their constituency. They are not only thinking about the best interests of the organization, its staff and its lobbying actions; they also have to keep their minds clearly fixed on members' views concerning the decisions and actions they take.

The values and beliefs of members have another – less obvious but nevertheless significant – impact on the way their organization works. The very **nature of the cause spills over into management.** Take, for example, mutual-support organizations where there is hope for special training for children with disabilities. In these circumstances, members' ambitions and enthusiasm for the cause lead to positive attitudes towards achieving the goals. At the other end of the spectrum, organizations for people with terminal diseases can have a very different atmosphere. Unless values are fully acknowledged, as happens successfully in many hospices, anger, despair and resentment can spill over into the management of the organization. Members can become angry with staff, and sometimes with each other as well. Debates and decisions become highly politicized and increasingly divorced from the facts.

The point is that values are central in mutual-support organizations, both explicitly and implicitly. Management's task is to make things happen within the framework of the organization's values. Management may sometimes have to challenge the values (for example, to persuade members of the need to modernize their approach to the organization's work), but they will achieve significant change only if they bring the members with them.

Tensions between members and staff

Mutual-support organizations are created when people come together around a common cause. In the beginning and sometimes for many years, they have no staff. Members do the work until it becomes too much for volunteers and the organization appoints its first member of staff. This is often followed by a period of tension. Some members may begrudge paying staff to do work they used to do voluntarily. They continue to involve themselves in the detail of the organization, only to find that staff resent them interfering in what they believe to be their work. Time has to be set aside to clarify roles and to understand each other's perspectives to overcome these problems.

Even when this is done, **tension between members and staff is seldom far below the surface**. There are good reasons why this should be the case, and it is worth acknowledging them explicitly. Members believe, quite rightly, that they own the organization. They set it up, they pay their membership fees, and they control the governing board. However, their involvement is very much part time and, as the organization grows, they just cannot keep on top of the detail of the organization's work. They have to delegate to staff, who inevitably begin to feel that they are responsible for the future of the organization.

This problem becomes more acute when the organization has hired good-quality staff and has paid less attention to the quality of the organization's governance. Staff come to feel that they know what is best for the organization. These tensions should not be allowed to fester, because they demotivate members and staff alike. The respective roles of the staff and of the board and its committees need to be discussed, clarified and documented.

There is a further complication that affects management. **Tensions are common among members themselves**. Some may have high ambitions for the organization, some may vigorously argue a particular policy position, and some may have different ideas about the future direction of the organization. These differences need to be acknowledged. They are all part of the push-and-pull of a group of diverse people who share one common cause. They need to be talked through, because people often have many common views and a few differences of opinion. In difficult cases, independent third parties may help to resolve the problem. Where differences cannot be resolved, and they are incapacitating the organization, one side or the other should leave. The organization needs to go one way or the other, not remain in suspended animation, unable to proceed in any direction.

Employees may include people who are also members of the organization. Indeed, many organizations go out of their way to recruit people who have had or are having direct experience of the needs and services the organization provides; it means that user needs are built into day-to-day management. This, however, is not without its difficulties. **Employees who are personally affected can cause problems.** They do not always have a broad perspective on members' needs. They may hold strong views which can bring them into conflict with staff who are not personally affected by the problem. It requires adroit management and skilled supervision to have a user on the staff and not let the organization become dominated by her or his viewpoint.

Organizations for people with terminal diseases provide a particularly difficult example of this issue. Members with the disease inevitably hold very strong views about priorities and staff feel they have to be responsive to those views. It is difficult to challenge people when they have all the authority that is provided by their circumstances. However, it has to be done when they hold a minority viewpoint; management has to be seen to be sensitive and yet simultaneously move the organization forward for the benefit of the majority.

The special case of intermediary organizations

One particular type of membership organization is the intermediary body. This is an organization whose members are other organizations. It exists in most fields to provide an umbrella which enables a number of organizations to work together and speak with a common voice. The National Housing Federation, the National Council for Voluntary Organizations, the Long-Term Medical Conditions Alliance, the Confederation of British Industry and the Trades Union Congress are typical examples.

These organizations present a special set of issues. Many of the people who sit on their boards do so as part of their job rather than as an entirely voluntary activity. Their commitment is consequently very different from that of voluntary board members. Although their primary loyalty should be to the intermediary organization board, there is a danger that they will defer to the interests of the organization they represent. This makes the job of the chief executives of these organizations significantly more difficult. They have to be consummate politicians as well as effective managers. They have to be able to judge which issue or proposals will command the support of the majority of member organizations and which will not.

Like other membership bodies, these organizations become more complex to manage when they start to offer services to members. The core
skills required to manage effective services are very different from those
required to represent members. Indeed, the mind-set of the service
providing part of the organization is very different from that of the
representative machinery. The service provider has a business mentality
and is concerned with the market for the service, its quality and its cost.
Representation, on the other hand, is concerned with preparing policy,
lobbying and the mechanics of political processes.

The issue becomes particularly acute when the service-providing part
of the organization finds itself in competition with its members for funds.
This is surprisingly common, and it happens because it is often difficult
for intermediary organizations to raise sufficient funds from their
members for their representation work, so they start to offer services in
order to finance the representation work.

The consequences of their action can be deeply damaging to a representative organization. Members start to lose their commitment to their
umbrella body, speak less highly of it and begin to represent their views
individually rather than through their representative organization.
Further, the special purpose of the intermediary organization is diluted.
There is a real danger that the unique opportunity which the organization
has to represent its members' views will become secondary to service
provision and that the organization will become just another provider.

Organizations in this situation may need to review their fundamental
purpose, determine whether representation work can become economic-
ally viable and, if necessary, float off those services that are competing
with members for funds.

14.6 MANAGING CAMPAIGNING ORGANIZATIONS

Campaigning organizations are only a tiny proportion of the third sector
but they have a disproportionately large impact, despite their small
number and comparatively small size. Pure campaigning organizations
include Greenpeace, Amnesty International and organizations fighting
for minority rights, women's rights and against poverty and prejudice.
However, many service-giving and membership organizations also run
campaigns, so parts of this section are relevant to them too.

Campaigning organizations are particularly difficult to manage. They are often staffed by idealistic and highly articulate people. Many will have had little experience of managing people, working in a team or being a manager when they find themselves with significant management responsibilities.

The first ingredient of successful campaigning is **leadership**. Successful campaigns depend on individuals who believe passionately in the cause and can argue the case for change, both within the organization and externally to the press and media. Campaigning organizations need people who present a cogent case and who can simultaneously champion the cause and sound eminently reasonable.

Campaigning also depends on people with **creative skills** to mount campaigns that capture public imagination. It needs the skills that are found in advertising and public relations agencies. These people have to have the ability to think in images and to create new ways of communicating complex messages to the public. Only when the messages are clear can the organization build a strong constituency of people who support the cause both politically and financially.

This activity also depends on having the **political acumen** to identify campaigns that can be fought and won. Campaigning organizations need managers who can make judgements about changes that are achievable and who can then galvanize people into action around that change. Campaigns with unrealistic goals soon lose steam. Greenpeace has short-term objectives and it calls them 'small wins' – the essential steps in the political process that lead to desired long-term changes.

These organizations also require **management**. Fired up by the day-to-day tensions of running campaigns, people often put insufficient energy into looking after the organization itself. Organizations do not run on idealism alone; responsibilities need to be divided and individuals made accountable. Teams need to work both in and across the line-management structure; people need to be managed. Campaign managers need to work within budgets and have the information they need to control costs; fund-raisers need to be able to compare the cost effectiveness of different fund-raising methods. In short, tight management practices are needed to enable people to do the all-important campaigning work.

Boards of campaigning organizations play an important role in getting the right balance between campaign flair and sound management. Although board members will also be passionately dedicated to the cause, they need to be able to stand back from the details of individual campaigns and play a more strategic role. The board's role in securing effective management of the organization is equally important. Board members need to insist that staff put sufficient attention into looking after the organization itself, otherwise working for the organization can become so frustrating that even the motivation of the cause itself is insufficient to retain good campaigners. Since they are the critical resource, the board needs to ensure that time and money are invested in good administrative systems.

Strategic planning in campaigning organizations has to separate out the strategies of each campaign from building the capacity of the institution as a whole. Campaign strategy is concerned with the objectives of the campaign, the strategies that are chosen to achieve the objectives, and the resulting action plans. These are often given close attention; but equally important are the strategies for building a donor base, supporting local groups and creating an organization that can respond quickly and effectively to campaign opportunities.

A major strategic issue for campaigning organizations is the choice of campaign priorities. There are always more issues requiring attention than resources available. Difficult choices have to be made by the board about competing claims for staff time and money. The pressures against setting priorities are often overwhelmingly strong. Board members have their personal – often strongly held – views. Campaign managers inevitably want to champion their own campaigns. Priorities are pushed to the fore by media coverage and public incidents that provide new opportunities to promote a campaign. Shifting government agendas create new chances to achieve a campaign goal.

A logical approach is to tailor-make a set of criteria against which alternative demands can be assessed. Such criteria are likely to include:

- the importance of the issue
- the potential for making progress
- the unique role of the organization on the issue
- the resources required
- the need to work with other organizations.

When reviewing strategic and operational plans, management and board members can then give each campaign that is competing for resources a rating to make the process of choosing priorities more rigorous. Such an approach does not obviate the need for the board to use its wisdom to make good judgements. It does help to provide a framework within which these critically important judgements can be made.

SUMMARY OF KEY POINTS

Organization life cycles
- Organizations develop in stages: periods of stability are followed by revolutionary change.
- Life cycles for individual organizations differ in detail. The power of the concept is that it helps boards and staff to see their problems in a broader context.

Classifying organizations
- Useful ways to classify organizations so as to gain insights into their management are by:
  — the broad purpose of the organization
  — the main source of funds
  — the composition of the board.
- The purpose of classifying organizations is to determine combinations of purpose, funding source and board membership that fit together well and to identify combinations that cause problems.

Putting the classifications together
- Combinations which are comparatively straightforward to manage include:
  — service organizations funded by sales, contracts or grants and managed by experts
  — mutual-support organizations funded by members and managed by users
  — campaign organizations funded by donations and managed by concerned individuals.
- Organizations that have other combinations are much more challenging to manage.

Managing different types of organization
- Keys to the successful management of **service-delivery** organizations include:
  — clarifying the fundamental purpose

— orientating systems around meeting users' needs
— marketing the service and simultaneously managing demand
— developing the skills needed to survive in the contract economy.
● Managers of **mutual-support** organizations have to work with the values associated with the cause. Tensions between members and staff are common and need to be addressed openly.
● Successful **campaigning** organizations require strong leadership, creative skills and political acumen. They need to avoid the pitfall of paying insufficient attention to the practicalities of management and they need to be ruthless in setting campaign priorities.

15 A Glimpse into the Future

From the turn of the nineteenth century to the end of the Second World War, the third sector was in decline. Ideas and services that emanated mainly from charitable initiatives were gradually being taken over by the state. Provision of housing, schools and health care was increasingly seen as a government responsibility. Many services that historically had been provided or supported by charitable institutions were slowly being incorporated into the public sector. From the end of the Second World War to the early 1970s, the charities that remained in the core of the third sector were seen as playing only a minor and secondary role to the new and rapidly growing public services.

During the early 1970s that situation began to change. It started when charitable organizations began to reassert their influence, often driven by idealistic people who were determined to take action to address the pressing social, health, environmental and educational problems that society faced. A combination of imaginative new ideas and increased funding from donors and the state led to the beginning of a period of explosive growth. For a period, the top two hundred charities were growing ten times faster than the economy as a whole.

From the mid-1980s, there was a more fundamental change. The assumption that large public-sector organizations, funded and managed by the state, were the best way to provide public services began to be challenged. The distinct notions of 'purchasers', who define the services that are required, and 'providers', who concentrate on the delivery of those services, began to emerge. This had a dramatic impact on the third sector as organizations began to compete for work that had previously been undertaken by the public sector. At the same time, a number of public-sector services, such as local authority housing departments and residential homes, left the public sector and became independent third-sector organizations. Despite the misgivings many people had about separating purchasers and providers and making charities compete against one another for contracts, they have undoubtedly led to better services and have become an accepted way of working.

More recently, the agenda for many third-sector organizations has moved on again, as government has indicated that it sees partnerships between the public, private and third sectors as another important development in the provision of more comprehensive and better-integrated services. Joint ventures, loose networks and strategic alliances are becoming the way to take new initiatives and achieve results quickly.

This final chapter takes a glimpse at the future of the third sector. It is a personal view, derived from my experience of working in the sector. It contains a mixture of some predictions and some aspirations for a sector of the economy that I believe will become an increasingly powerful force in years to come.

The sector will become fully established

Until comparatively recently, the third sector was not recognized as a sector at all. It was a group of disparate and unconnected organizations that championed good causes but were generally seen as inefficient and badly managed. It is increasingly seen as an essential part of the fabric of society, because people need organizations that are neither profit-seeking nor part of the public sector. Slowly but steadily, all these organizations are being acknowledged as one group that has a common cause: to take independent action to make the world a better place without personal gain.

In the foreseeable future the third sector will become fully established as a group of organizations that are as essential to post-industrial, democratic and caring societies as the private and public sectors. It will remain smaller in economic terms than the private and public sectors – but it will continue to have disproportionate influence because it champions justice, fairness and morality.

The sector will nevertheless grow larger because:

- it will ride on the back of overall growth in economic activity

- public-sector organizations that are on the boundary of both sectors (such as colleges, schools and parts of the health service) will increasingly become part of the third sector as they diversify their income sources and their independence grows
- ever more sophisticated ways of raising new funds will be created
- businesses will wish to associate more closely with third-sector organizations and will have to pay for the goodwill this generates.

These trends will combine to create a stronger, more vibrant and more effective third sector. Whereas the sector now accounts for less than 5 per cent of GDP in the UK, the new third sector could account for 10 per cent – a figure near the size of the American not-for-profit sector.

Accountability will increase

This much-enlarged sector will have two distinct parts. One part will consist primarily of contract-, grant- and sales-funded service-delivery organizations. It will include contract-funded charities, housing organizations, schools, colleges and hospitals. Their priority will be the delivery of the highest possible quality of services within available funding. Their success will depend on their ability to meet purchasers' specifications for services in the most cost-effective way.

The other part will be donor- and member-funded organizations that exist primarily to champion causes. In these 'pure' charities, there is only a weak connection between the donors and the service users. These organizations have great freedom to allocate their resources as they wish. They will be expected to demonstrate more clearly the results they achieve with their funds, they will be subject to greater public strutiny and will be held more accountable by their stakeholders. Their success will ultimately depend on their entrepreneurial skills.

There will be no clear dividing line between these two broad categories. Many organizations will continue to provide services and simultaneously champion their cause. They will continue to benefit from being able to run campaigns based on their own practical experience. However, they will have to become increasingly clear about how they allocate their 'unrestricted' funds. They will need to take explicit decisions about the extent to which they wish to subsidize their contract services with unrestricted income. Such subsidies are sometimes a valuable way of leveraging extra public funds for their service users, but they can also encourage inefficiency in service provision. Increasingly organizations will be expected to account for their expenditure in ways that make the allocation of donor and contract funding of different activities entirely transparent.

Organizations will be judged by their results

Public confidence and trust in institutions are likely to continue to decline. Third-sector organizations will not be immune from this trend; they will be judged by their results. Those that are seen to deliver the best results will command public respect and receive a greater share of the available funds. Those that are less able to command respect will see a decline in their share of the fund-raising market.

Management attention will therefore have to focus much more sharply on demonstrating tangible results. Objectives, strategies and plans will have to be based on demonstrating positive outcomes for services and campaigns. Funders will set performance standards, and organizations will need to find ways to measure results and report on the impact of their services.

This will require significant investment in systems that allow organizations to follow people up, months (and sometimes years) after the service was provided, in order to pinpoint the difference that the service made. Boards and managers will then be able to adjust their services to focus on approaches that have been shown to have the greatest impact.

Cost effectiveness will be the primary measure of success

The prevalent assumption that reducing costs automatically leads to a reduction in quality will be challenged, as innovative organizations discover imaginative ways of achieving the desired outcomes with fewer material and human inputs. The private sector has demonstrated conclusively that, with effective management, services can be improved and costs reduced at the same time. At present third-sector organizations find it difficult to see how these seemingly contradictory objectives can be achieved.

However, pressure to compete successfully for contracts and to deliver quality services to users will drive organizations to discover ways of increasing their productivity. Managers will increasingly be expected to demonstrate how every person and every expenditure contribute directly to the delivery of a cost-effective service. Activities that do not make a cost-effective contribution will be cut.

Missions will have to motivate people

As more people look for greater meaning in life, and in particular for purposes beyond meeting their own needs, third-sector organizations will provide more opportunities for people to contribute to society in meaningful ways. People will, however, have to be inspired to volunteer and work for these organizations. Those that promote their missions powerfully will have motivated people who have the energy and commitment required to deliver top-quality services. For younger people, the sector will increasingly become a positive career choice, and for older people it will provide many new opportunities for voluntary work in retirement.

In his book *The Hungry Spirit*, Charles Handy talks about accepting responsibility for making the most of oneself by finding a purpose beyond oneself. He calls this being 'properly selfish'. Third-sector organizations offer just that opportunity, provided their management ensures that the organization's mission is strongly promoted and is at the heart of all their work.

Specialization will increase

Mergers do not often occur in the third sector because there is seldom an economic imperative. However, as organizations are driven to focus on those activities in which they have the greatest expertise, they will need to adjust the portfolio of services they manage. This will mean acquiring, divesting and exchanging services with other organizations. This will happen mainly within the sector, but there will also be more movement between all three sectors.

Competition for contracts, donors and sales will force organizations to specialize in those services in which they have most expertise and to withdraw from services in which they have fewer skills. Niche providers will grow faster than generalist organizations that diversify into many services and inevitably develop cumbersome management overheads.

Trading income will grow

It is already possible to buy environmentally friendly washing machines and fridges from Friends of the Earth, furniture from Oxfam, insurance from RSPB, ethical investment plans from Amnesty, photocopy paper from Mencap, and gifts from most of the major charities. These opportunities will grow as third-sector organizations realize that the 'feel-good' factor associated with purchasing a product or service is a competitive advantage that can be exploited to raise unrestricted funds.

New technology will transform the way organizations work

The impact of information technology – and, in particular, communications technology – will dramatically change the way third-sector organizations work. Many organizations are spread around the country and the globe. Until now, their centre or headquarters has been the hub of the organization and of its communications. Email, voice-mail and inexpensive video conferencing will change all that. The furthest parts of the organization will be able to communicate with each other easily and cheaply. This will drive the centres of organizations to define their unique contribution more precisely and give the outposts more freedom to do their work within agreed boundaries.

Management and governance will be streamlined

Internally, organizations with cumbersome management structures, boards and committees will need to streamline themselves to increase their effectiveness. Management structures will become flatter as managers and their staff discover more effective ways of working together. Boards will continue to grow smaller and at the same time more accountable. The notion that committees automatically add value will be challenged.

In future, every level of management and governance will need to focus on purpose, people and performance to justify their existence.

All this will require greatly increased effort to be put into governance and management development. Training courses, mentoring, shadowing and coaching will all play a greater role in the daily lives of managers. Skill-acquisition will become a major objective of ambitious managers. Organizations will have to respond by making time and resources available for board members and managers to become more skilled.

Managers will face many contradictory pressures

Managers will be expected to work with many contradictory pressures. They will be expected to:

- give the organization a strong sense of direction *and* adapt quickly to changing circumstances
- have long-term objectives and strategies *and* meet short-term performance targets
- devolve power to the field *and* maintain a common purpose throughout the organization
- streamline management and governance *and* maintain people's motivation
- expect massive commitment from people *and* offer them less job security
- invest in organizational learning *and* work with fewer spare resources.

These will provide challenges for managers throughout the sector.

Characteristics of successful organizations

To meet these challenges, organizations will need to exhibit many characteristics. They will require:

- **leadership from visionary individuals**
  — ensuring that a clear mission pervades all parts of the organization
  — communicating effectively with all stakeholders

- **a sharp focus on results**
  — understanding what users want

— providing services that exceed users' expectations
— continuously monitoring service quality
— benchmarking against the best in the world

● **investment in people**
— empowering them to deliver results
— learning continuously from each other
— encouraging innovation in all aspects of their work

● **enthusiasm for change**
— embracing new opportunities and ways of working
— relishing the chance to be more effective.

An ambitious list, you may say. But most third-sector organizations want to make a significant impact on the world in which we live. To achieve that ambition will require excellence in all aspects of management.

Appendix:
Compass Partnership

Compass Partnership is a management consultancy that works exclusively with third-sector organizations. It provides consultancy services to chairs, chief executives and senior managers of third-sector organizations. The firm helps organizations and their funders with:

- strategic planning
- governance and management structures
- governance and management processes
- team-building, coaching and facilitation
- benchmarking
- performance management
- reviews and evaluations.

Compass works with all types of third-sector organization, including voluntary organizations, housing organizations, development agencies, arts organizations, trade and professional associations and the organizations that fund them, including government departments, non-departmental public bodies and foundations.

At the time of writing, the firm had twenty full- and part-time consultants and had worked with over 500 organizations.

The leaders are Mike Hudson, Roger Parry and Joy MacKeith. If you would like assistance, please do not hesitate to contact them at Compass Partnership, 203–209 North Gower Street, London NW1 2NJ (Tel.: 0171-391 9911; E-mail: info@compassnet.co.uk).

Further Reading

There are relatively few books focusing on the overall management of third-sector organizations. This further reading section therefore draws on relevant literature from both the public and private sectors. It also includes many books from the USA, since much more has been published about managing not-for-profit organizations in the USA. Books which draw primarily on American experience are marked (USA).

I have deliberately been selective in writing this section, believing that this will be more useful to busy practising managers than a lengthy bibliography of every book, report and article I read in order to produce this book.

Selection criteria included:

- significant works on 'not-for-profit' management
- major private- or public-sector works that are transferable to the third sector
- practical and useful publications for busy managers.

SOME USEFUL NUMBERS FOR OBTAINING THESE PUBLICATIONS

Association of British Insurers	0171-600 3333
Association of Charitable Foundations	0171-404 1338
Centre for Voluntary Organizations, London School of Economics	0171-405 7686
Charities Aid Foundation	

Industrial Society Press	0121-454 6769
Institute of Chartered Secretaries and Administrators	0171-580 4741
Joseph Rowntree Foundation	01904-629241
Jossey–Bass (UK distributor, IBD/Prentice Hall)	01442-881900
London Voluntary Service Council	0171-388 0241
National Council for Voluntary Organizations	0171-713 6161
Open University	01908-654723
Third Sector Magazine	0171-247 0066
VOLPROF, City University Business School	0171-477 8603

SETTING THE CONTEXT

Billis, D., and M. Harris, *Voluntary Agencies – Challenges of Organization and Management*, Macmillan Press, 1996
A valuable collection of articles from the leading British academics in the field on current management issues in the sector.

Leat, D., *Managing Across Sectors – Similarities and Differences Between For-Profit and Voluntary Non-Profit Organizations*, VOLPROF (City University Business School), 1993
An insightful report, comparing business and third-sector organizations.

McCarthy, K., and associates, *The Non-Profit Sector in the Global Community*, Jossey–Bass, 1992
Twenty-eight articles on the role and significance of the non-profit sector in industrialized countries, Eastern Europe, the old Soviet Union and developing countries.

Prochaska, F., *The Voluntary Impulse,* Faber and Faber, 1988
A fascinating book, placing philanthropy in Britain in historical context.

Saxon-Harold, S., J. Kendall *et al.*, *Researching the Voluntary Sector*, Charities Aid Foundation, 1993 (Volume I), 1994 (Volume II)
Thirty articles in two volumes, covering local, national and international research into all aspects of the voluntary sector.

GOVERNING BOARDS

ACENVO, *Planning for Partnership – The Relationship between Chairs and Chief Executives*, ACENVO, 1996

Carver, J., *Boards that Make a Difference*, Jossey–Bass, 1990 (USA)
An interesting and radical view of governance, based on the view that the board's role should be strictly limited to a few key policy issues.

Chait, R., *et al.*, *The Effective Board of Trustees*, American Council on Education, 1993 (USA)
Board-effectiveness guru on the different roles of the board, based on particularly thorough research at the University of Maryland.

Harris, M., *Do We Need Governing Bodies?*, Centre for Voluntary Organizations, London School of Economics, 1994
Article analysing the functions of governing bodies and the gap between intentions and practices.

Ingram, R., and associates, *Governing Independent Colleges and Universities*, Jossey–Bass, 1993 (USA)
Twenty articles to guide trustees and chief executives responsible for managing colleges and universities. Much pertinent material, as UK colleges and universities become financially more independent from government.

Kirkland, K., *The Good Trustee Guide*, NCVO, 1996
The UK guide to the role, responsibilities and workings of effective governing bodies. Packed with valuable advice for trustees and board members.

National Centre for Non-Profit Boards, *Non-Profit Governance Series*, NCNB (USA)
A series of sixteen booklets on key aspects of governance. American in orientation but increasingly relevant to the UK. Available from NCVO.

NCVO, *On Trust – Increasing the Effectiveness of Charity Trustees and Management Committees*, National Council for Voluntary Organizations, 1993
Report of the NCVO – Charity Commission Working Party, which identified the scale of the problem and actions required to improve the effectiveness of management committees.

Palmer, P., and J. Harrow, *Re-thinking Charity Trusteeship*, Institute of Chartered Secretaries and Administrators, 1994
A review of the role and purpose of charity trustees.

MANAGING THIRD-SECTOR ORGANIZATIONS

Adirondack, S. M., *Just About Managing*, London Voluntary Service Council, 1998
A very practical introduction to managing smaller voluntary organizations.

Boléat, M., *Trade Association Strategy and Management*, Association of British Insurers 1996
The book to read on the nature, functions and management of trade associations.

Boutall, T., *The Good Manager's Guide*, Management Charter Initiative, 1997
Immensely useful check-lists on managing people, resources and strategy. Valuable as an *aide-mémoire* and to check that all aspects of a management activity have been considered before taking action.

Bruce, I., *Successful Charity Marketing – Meeting Need*, Institute of Chartered Secretaries and Administrators, 1998
A practical and thorough book on marketing in voluntary organizations. Written by the Director General of the Royal National Institute for the Blind and consequently particularly applicable to UK organizations.

Batsleer, J., et al., *Issues in Voluntary and Non-Profit Management*, Addison Wesley, 1991
The reader for the Open University 'Managing Voluntary and Non-Profit Enterprise' course. Sixteen articles covering a wide range of issues.

Billis, D., *A Theory of the Voluntary Sector*, Working Paper 5, London School of Economics, 1989
An excellent analysis of how the voluntary sector sits between the public, private and personal sectors and why this leads to ambiguity in their management.

Billis, D., *The Roots of Voluntary Agencies: A Question of Choice*, Centre for Voluntary Organizations, London School of Economics
Insightful article analysing the factors underlying management problems in voluntary organizations.

Drucker, P., *Managing the Non-Profit Organizations*, Butterworth–Heinemann, 1990 (USA)

Classic Drucker: a punchy, relevant and practical book, incorporating nine edited interviews with practitioners.

Handy, C., *Understanding Voluntary Organizations*, Penguin, 1988
One of the first books to shed light on the special issues of managing voluntary organizations.

Harmer, M., and J. Champy, *Reengineering the Corporation*, Nicholas Brealey, 1993
The original book on business process re-engineering. The basics of re-engineering, with a certain amount of hype.

Herman, R., *et al.*, *The Jossey–Bass Handbook of Nonprofit Leadership and Management*, Jossey–Bass, 1994 (USA)
Twenty-five articles by American practitioners and academics on most aspects of managing third-sector organizations.

Hind, A., *The Governance and Management of Charities*, Voluntary Sector Press, 1995
Very thorough self-published book on every aspect of charity management.

Kinnell, M., and J. MacDougall, *Marketing in the Not-For-Profit Sector*, Butterworth–Heinemann, 1997
Applies marketing principles to much of the third sector, including schools, social services, churches and voluntary organizations.

Kotler, P., and A. Andreasen, *Strategic Marketing for Non-Profit Organizations*, 1995 (USA)
A wide-ranging and comprehensive book about marketing, now in its fourth edition.

Paton, R., and many others, *Managing Voluntary and Non-Profit Enterprises*, Open University, 1993
Twelve excellent books for the Open University course with the same title, covering most aspects of managing voluntary organizations. Expensive for non-course participants.

Sayer, K., *A Practical Guide to Financial Management for Charities*, Directory of Social Change, 1998
User-friendly, down-to-earth guide, aimed at non-accountants and covering all the most important areas of financial management in charities.

Young, D., *et al.*, *Governing, Leading and Managing Non-Profit Organizations*, Jossey–Bass, 1993 (USA)
Fourteen articles on governance, human and financial resources, man-

agement strategies and public-policy issues, written mainly by academic researchers.

STRATEGIC PERFORMANCE

Ashby, J., *Towards Voluntary Sector Codes of Practice*, Joseph Rowntree Foundation, 1997
Describes how codes of practice can help voluntary organizations improve the management quality.

Barnard, H., and P. Walker, *Strategies for Success*, National Council for Voluntary Organizations, 1994
A self-help guide to strategic planning for voluntary organizations.

Bryson, J., *Strategic Planning for Public and Non-Profit Organizations*, Jossey–Bass, 1988 (USA)
Best-selling introduction to strategic planning.

Campbell, A., *A Sense of Mission*, Hutchinson Business Books, 1990
Although this is a business book, the early chapters (which unpack the idea of mission) are equally relevant to third-sector organizations.

Finnigan J., *The Manager's Guide to Benchmarking*, Jossey–Bass, 1996 (USA)
Blow-by-blow account of how to approach benchmarking, drawing on American business experience.

Johnson, G., and K. Scholes, *Exploring Corporate Strategy*, Prentice Hall, 1993
The highly popular basic text on all aspects of corporate strategy. Primarily aimed at business, it has a few public- and third-sector examples.

Kaplan, R., and D. Norton, *The Balanced Scorecard*, Harvard Business School Press, 1996 (USA)
The original work on using a range of measures to manage the performance of business organizations. A great concept that is proving difficult to apply in the third sector.

Lawrie, A., *Quality of Service – Measuring Performance for Voluntary Organizations*, NCVO/Directory of Social Change
A practical introduction to measuring performance in voluntary organizations.

Manley, K., *Financial Management for Charities and Voluntary Organizations*, Institute of Chartered Secretaries and Administrators, 1994

An introduction to the whole process of planning, budgeting, controlling, and reporting on financial matters, aimed particularly at service-giving charities.

Martin, N., and C. Smith, *Planning for the Future*, NCVO Publications, 1993
A practical introduction to business planning in voluntary organizations.

Mintzberg, H., *The Rise and Fall of Strategic Planning*, Prentice Hall, 1994
A critical reassessment of strategic planning, focusing on the private sector, but the conclusions are transferable.

Mintzberg, H., and B. Quinn, *The Strategy Process*, Prentice Hall, 1992 (USA)
Succinct summaries of forty-eight of the best articles on strategy, organization and the contexts in which strategy is used. A business-orientated book, some of which is relevant to the third sector.

Nutt, P., and R. Bachoff, *Strategic Management of Public and Third Sector Organizations*, Jossey–Bass, 1992 (USA)
A helpful overview and some useful techniques for strategic planners.

Schein, E., *Organizational Culture and Leadership*, Jossey–Bass, 1992 (USA)
A tightly defined introduction to managing organization culture, written by one of the culture gurus.

Williams, A., *et al.*, *Changing Culture – New Organizational Approaches*, Institute of Personnel Management, 1993
A very accessible introduction to culture, illustrated with ten corporate and two public-sector examples.

MANAGING CHANGE

Binney, G., and C. Williams, *Leaning into the Future*, Nicholas Brealey Publishing, 1997
Shows how effective leaders combine top-down leading skills with bottom-up listening skills to bring about major change.

Briner, W., *et al.*, *Project Leadership*, Gower, 1996
Step-by-step approach to managing and leading projects.

Kotter, J., *Leading Change*, Harvard Business School Press, 1996

Harvard guru sets out the eight essential stages for a successful change-management process.

LEADERSHIP

Adair, J., *Not Bosses but Leaders*, Kogan Page, 1990
Adair introduces a new manager to leadership concepts. A quick and easy read.

Bryson, J., and B. Crosby, *Leadership for the Common Good*, Jossey–Bass, 1992
Leadership of public and non-profit organizations in a world where pluralism means 'no one is in charge' of the big public-policy issues.

Green, M., *Leadership for a New Era – Strategies for Higher Education*, American Council on Education, 1988 (USA)
Twelve articles on leading and managing higher education institutions.

Herman, R., and R. Heimovics, *Executive Leadership in Non-Profit Organizations*, Jossey–Bass, 1991
Insights in leadership, focusing particularly on the leadership role of the board, and on chief executive–board relationships and how to make them more effective.

Hesselbein F., *et al.*, *The Leader of the Future*, Jossey–Bass, 1996 (USA)
Thirty-one articles on leadership, put together by the Drucker Foundation.

Kouzes, J., and B. Posner, *The Leadership Challenge*, Jossey–Bass, 1987
Ten commandments for effective leadership, based on research in the USA. Makes compelling reading.

Lynch, R., *LEAD!*, Jossey–Bass, 1993 (USA)
The best book on leadership of public and non-profit organizations. Explains how managers bring out the best in themselves and their organizations.

MANAGING PEOPLE

Blanchard, K., and S. Johnson, *The One Minute Manager*, Fontana, 1983
The famous guide to setting goals, praising and reprimanding people. Packed with insightful advice that needs regular re-reading.

Grummitt, J., *Team Briefing*, The Industrial Society, 1993
  Guide to implementing team briefing, with advice on overcoming objections.
Handy, C., *Understanding Organizations*, Penguin, 1994
  The best-selling book on how to get people working together in different types of organization.
Jenks, J., and J. Kelly, *Don't Do Delegate!*, Kogan Page, 1986
  A very readable book on delegation. Examples are from the private sector, but the messages are equally applicable to third-sector organizations.
Sheal, P., *The Staff Development Handbook*, Kogan Page, 1992
  Practical advice on training, monitoring and coaching staff, including a chapter on conducting performance reviews.

PROMOTING LEARNING

Casey, D., *Managing Learning In Organizations*, Open University Press, 1993
  Insightful guide to managing the chief executive's learning, and managing learning in small groups and management teams.
France, S., *360° Feedback*, The Industrial Society, 1997
  A useful introduction to the subject.
Garratt, B., *The Learning Organization*, HarperCollins, 1994
  Second edition of one of the early insights into learning organizations. An essential part of the learning organization literature.
Garratt, B., *Learning to Lead*, HarperCollins, 1990
  More great reading from Garratt, including material on developing directors, people and organizations, and how to create a learning climate.
Honey, P., and A. Mumford, *Manual of Learning Styles*, McGraw Hill, 1992
  Well-known work on individuals' preferences for different ways of learning.
Megginson, D., and D. Clutterbuck, *Mentoring in Action*, Kogan Page, 1995
  Good introduction to mentoring, with masses of case studies and learning from their experiences.

Senge, P., *The Fifth Discipline*, Century Business, 1990
A much-quoted and insightful book on organization learning.

PERIODICALS

Academic Journals

Non-Profit Management and Leadership, published by Jossey–Bass
The most useful journal for practising managers who want to keep in touch with academic research into the management of not-for-profit organizations.

Non-Profit and Voluntary Sector Quarterly, (USA) published by Jossey–Bass
This journal focuses on policy issues. It is sponsored by a research group which specializes in voluntary action.

Voluntas – International Journal of Voluntary and Non-Profit Organizations, published by Plenum Press
This journal takes an international perspective. It covers policy issues and has less on management than the other journals.

News Magazines

Third Sector, published by Arts Publishing International Ltd (Tel.: 0171-247 0066)
A fortnightly news magazine, focusing mainly on the voluntary sector.

NGO Finance, published by Plaza Publishing Ltd (Tel.: 0171-793 0001)
A monthly, mainly for finance directors and managers, but with a broader range of articles since taking over *Charity* magazine.

Arts business, published by BC Publications (Tel.: 01954 250600)
A fortnightly, free to UK-based arts professionals.

Housing Today, weekly, published by National Housing Federation (Tel.: 0171-843 2278)

Inside Housing, weekly, published by Inside Communications (Tel.: 01732 464154)

Roof, bi-monthly, published by Shelter (Tel.: 0181-289 7957)

Housing, monthly, published by the Chartered Institute of Housing (Tel.: 0171-827 9928)

Index

Abbey National, 11
accountability, 173–4, 225
  for results rather than methods,
    320, 324
  of boards, 41–2, 77
  of cross-departmental group
    members, 230
  of managers, 40, 198, 207, 230, 293,
    301, 304, 309
  of senior management team, 282
  of 'third sector' organizations, 18,
    22
  of workers for their work, 172
  to stakeholders, 172, 192, 203
accrual of costs, 197
achievements
  building on, 252
  celebration of, 316, 323
  measurement of, 386
action learning sets, 289
action plans, 294–5
'activists' in learning, 333
Adam Smith Institute, 8
adaptability, 147, 156, 329
'adult' boards, 45–6
'adult' organizations, 358
advice services, 30; see also Citizens'
  Advice Bureaux

advisory boards, 62–3
advisory panels, 55, 61–2
Age Concern, 369
agendas for boards, 83–4
AIDS, services for people with, 130;
  see also London Lighthouse
aims see objectives
alienation of groups within the
  organization, 243
alignment between jobs and people,
  331
alms-giving, 2–3
altruism, 20
Amnesty International, 8, 378, 388
anarchy, organizational, 324
Anheier, H., 11
anticipation
  of change, 136, 252
  of decisions, 48
  of divisions of opinion, 286
  of future needs, 206
appointment of board members, 36,
  75
appraisals, 338; see also performance
  reviews
Arthritis Care, 74
Arts Council, 11
arts organizations, 17, 115, 362, 364, 368

Ashridge Management College, 104,
308
assessment and rehabilitation centres,
310
Association of Chief Executives of
National Voluntary
Organizations, 346–7
assumptions
challenging of, 349
subconscious, 237
audit committees, 61, 90
authority, use of, 286–7
Automobile Association (AA), 8,
13
'away-days', 88, 312

balanced scorecard, the, 180
Barnardos, 103–4, 368
Belbin team roles, 350
Belbin test, 350
beliefs
changing, 239, 263
see also values
benchmarking, 185–90, 352, 390
'service', 'process' and 'strategic'
types, 187
benefits see costs and benefits
best practice, 186, 190
Beveridge, William, 13
'big bang' changes in management,
220, 231
Billis, D., 1
Binney, G., 268
board composition, classification of
organizations according to, 358,
365–6
board members
advisory, 62–3
definition of, xxii
developing the skills of, 76, 92
motivations of, 20, 70

of federal organizations, 34–5
of mutual-support organizations,
375
recruitment of, 69–75, 91–2
selection of, 36–8, 74
boards
annual meeting cycle for, 82–3
agendas for, 83–4
characteristics of those in 'third
sector', 69
committee discussions repeated at,
84, 92
competencies of, 52
definition of xxi
documentation of procedures of, 87
functions of, xviii, 39–42, 63
improving the working methods of,
80–83, 92, 119
life cycle of, 44–7, 64
of campaigning organizations,
379–80
reasons for ineffectiveness of, 67–9,
91
research into effectiveness of, 81
resources needed for support of,
87–8
reviewing performance of, 78, 88–9
roles of, 47–51, 64, 66–8, 91, 106
size of, 53–4, 64
staff role in relation to, 84–5
bosses, management of, 304–7, 327
'bottom-up' approach to change, 241
brainstorming, 132, 237
branches of organizations, xxii, 23–7,
33–5
'Breaking the Cycle' scheme, 30
British Epilepsy Association, 99
British Hedgehog Preservation
Society, 8
Broadcasting Support Services, 185
budgeting, 164–6, 196, 215, 226–7

building societies, 11
bureaucratic processes, 167–8, 185, 326
burial societies, 2
'buying in', 255–6

campaign teams, 310
campaigning organizations, 4, 100, 139, 151–2, 156, 159, 163–4, 177, 207, 235, 324, 361–2, 367, 369, 373, 378–82
Cancer Research Campaign, 17, 25–6
Care Homes, 200, 202
cause and effect, linking of, 177
centralization *versus* decentralization, 215–16, 231
chairs of boards
    involvement in strategic planning, 137, 156
    role of, 40, 68, 77–81, 92
chairs of committees, 89–90
Chait, Richard, 48, 52
change leaders, 234
    skills needed by, 267–8, 271
change management, 233–71, 325
    and changing people, 263–5
    nature of, 238–41
    stages of, 246–7, 265, 270–71
    ups and down in, 265
change teams, 248–59, 267
    types of, 249
charitable sector
    definition of, 8
    growing importance of, 383
Charities Aid Foundation, 369, 392
charity
    origins and history of, 1–4, 6
    philosophy of, 1
Charity Commission, 37
Charity Organization Society, 4
charters, 34
Cheshire, Leonard, 299, 368

chief executives
    and their boards, 49–50, 57, 66, 68, 275, 281–6, 290
    and their chairs, 78–81, 282–3, 289, 338
    and their divisional directors, 294
    as members of teams, 350
    bad habits of, 283
    definition of, xxii
    deputies to, 216–18, 231
    entrepreneurial and political skills of, 276, 301
    good habits of, 289–90, 329
    involvement in management of change, 224, 249, 263
    involvement in strategic planning, 137, 143–4, 156
    leadership provided by, 284–91, 301
    numbers of people reporting to, 210
    own area of expertise, 282–3, 288
    roles of, xviii, 82, 98, 272–5, 301
    sitting on boards of other organizations, 276
    structuring the work of, 277–84, 301
    titles given to, 273
Christian Aid, 228
churches, 100, 207, 362
Citizens' Advice Bureaux, 13, 24, 369
citizenship, 14, 21
City Housing Association, 306
classification of organizations, 359–65, 381
cliques, 68
coaching, 304, 313, 324, 337, 344–5, 353
    of teams, 314, 327
coalitions
    between organizations, 233
    of people, 19, 39, 93, 96, 110, 113, 120, 164, 243, 280

Codes of Practice initiative, 191, 193–4
collective responsibility, 309
committees
  advisory or decision-making, 40,
    61–3
  definition of, xxii
  functions of, 55–7
  governance through, 60–61, 64
  increasing the effectiveness of,
    89–92
  problems with, 56, 91
  size of, 90
  structure of, 57–61
  communication with stakeholders,
    141, 143–4, 243, 255–6, 268,
    280–81, 288; *see also* internal
    communication
communications departments, 211
communications technology, 388
community drugs agencies, 189
Compass Partnership, xx, 391
competencies
  of boards, 52
  of individuals, 339
  of leaders, 290
  of management, 234, 332, 352
  of organizations, 107, 163
competition with other organizations,
  12, 128, 163
Confederation of British Industry, 377
confidentiality issues, 177, 188, 323, 346
consensus management, 206–7, 277,
  298–9
constitutional arrangements, 23
consultation
  about changes in management
    structure, 220–21, 223, 231
  about performance review
    processes, 340
  about strategic planning, 140,
    144

  by chief executives, 280
  with government, 14
consultative councils, 27
Consumers' Association, 36
continuity of key decision-makers,
  105
continuous adjustments to
  management structures, 205–6,
  231
continuous improvement, 191
continuous learning, 390
contract funding, 15, 17, 96, 372–3
conventional wisdom, challenging of,
  140–41
  co-operative societies, 11
co-option onto boards, 37, 71, 75
co-ordinating bodies, 36
corporate strategy, overall, 161
cost-effectiveness 386–7; *see also* value
  for money
costing of services, 373
costs and benefits, analysis of, 131, 148,
  162–3
counselling, 337
Countryside Commission, 146
creative skills, 379, 382
crisis situations, 138, 156, 322
critical factors for success, 132, 314
cross-departmental groups, 225–32
cultural change, 128, 262
culture, organizational, 191, 234
  characteristics of, 236–7
  diagnosis of, 237–8
  incorporating change into, 262–3
  levels of, 235, 270
culture of learning, 330
cynicism amongst staff, 109, 238

decentralisation 215–216, 231
decision-making processes, 48–9,
  279–80, 290, 316, 318

delegation, 195, 215–16, 228, 291–2, 303, 320–23, 327, 336
  reasons for, 321–2
demand for services
  limitless nature of, 18
  management of, 371, 374
democracy, 'managed', 75
democratic values, 309
demographic changes, 128, 162
departmental and cross-departmental objectives, 116–18
departmentalism, 225
departments, definition of, xxii
departments represented on senior management team, 211–12
deputy directors, 216–18, 231
development agencies, 150–51, 166, 207, 364
developmental change, 239
diagnosis of problems, 237–8, 246, 250–53
'diagonal' teams, 249
dialoguing mode, 348–9
directing skills, 273, 294–6
directors *see* deputy directors; divisional directors
disability organizations, 17, 125, 131, 150–51, 158, 172
disciplinary procedures, 343, 353
dismissal of staff, 300, 343, 353
dispersed organizations, 60, 67, 295, 300, 388
distinctiveness of individual organizations, 135, 163
diversification of services, 151–2, 156
divisional directors
  definition of, xxii
  development of, 294–6
  roles of, 172, 272–3, 291, 301–302
  skills of, 292–3
documentation, 87, 89–91

donors, motivations of, 20
drug-prevention centres, 166, 189

economic viability, 278
économie sociale, 8–9
educational institutions, 10, 17, 96, 152, 172, 364, 368, 371, 383, 385
effectiveness, measures of, 179
efficiency, measures of, 176, 178–9
elder statesmen, 63
election of board members, 36, 41, 74–5
'embedding' of changes, 262
emotive campaigning, 152
employment projects, 152
empowerment, 324–7, 390
  definition of, 320
  timescale for, 325–6
English National Ballet, 8
environmental organizations, 159
equal opportunities, 192
ethical behaviour, 193
ethos of 'third sector' organizations, xv, xvii
evolution or organizations, 355
Excellence Model, 191, 194–5, 234
executive assistants to boards, 87–8
executive committees, 53, 57–60
experts, 69, 365

facilitating, 337
Family Service Units, 25, 153–4
Family Welfare Association, 4
federal institutional structures, 24–8, 31, 37–8
  bringing about change in, 35
  governing of 33–5
feedback, 176–7, 289, 294, 336, 340
finance and general purposes committees, 57
financial contribution, 198–201

financial management systems, 50, 61,
    195–7, 202, 373
financial planning, 147
'forming' stage of team development,
    138, 309
forums, non-executive, 54
forward-looking attitude, 291
founders of organizations, 357
'founding' phase of a board's life
    cycle, 44–5
franchise arrangements, 29–30
'freedom within a framework', 325
friendly societies, 11, 17
Friends of the Earth, 388
frustrations, 306
funding sources
    classification of organizations
        according to, 358, 362–4
    diversity of, 67
    information required by, 172
    linking service users to, 96, 110
    trends in, 127–8, 163
fund-raising, 119, 147, 278
fund-raising charities, 27
fund-raising departments, 211
fund-raising dilemma, 122

Gabarro, John, 304
gap analysis, 130–31, 148
Garratt, Bob, 328
governance, xviii-xix, 388–9
    as distinct from management, 41–4,
        64, 78
    as distinct from representation,
        57–8
    by boards, 40, 63
    chief executives' role in, 82
    through committees, 60–61
Greenpeace, 378–9
group behavioiur, patterns of, 235–7
The Guardian, 13, 369

Guide Association, 102
Guide Dogs for the Blind Association,
    128–9, 253, 257–8
Guinness Trust, 108

hands-on boards, 53–4
hands-on bosses, 293, 298
Handy, Charles, 310, 387
Harvey-Jones, John, 274
hearts and minds, 104, 239
Heimovics, R., 81
'helicopter' view, 293
help lines, 13
Herman, R., 81
hierarchical structures, 206
hobby-horses, 122
homeless people, services for, 150,
    157–8, 369
honesty of leaders, 290
hospices, 375
hospitals, 6, 11, 100, 152, 385
housing associations, 17, 108, 117, 153,
    158, 172, 235, 314–15, 362, 368–9,
    371
Housing 21, 117
human resource development, 119, 212

impact of services provided, 135, 178
    measurement of, 18, 22
independence, 137, 201
induction, 76, 300, 335, 353
information technology, 388
information to support change
    management, 251
innovation, 13–14, 21, 133, 278–9, 390
input indicators, 178
insecurity amongst managers and
    staff, 269
inspirational leadership, 291
institutional structure, choice of,
    23–38

integrated approach to management, 95

integration across departments, 225–7

integrity, 76

interim management, 219–20

intermediary organizations, 377–8

Intermediate Technology, 31, 144–5

internal communication, 86–7, 141, 143, 281, 325–6, 351

internal functions of organizations, 278

International Classification of Non-profit Organizations, 359–61

international organizations, 31–2, 38

International Union for the Conservation of Nature, 31

intervention by senior managers, 298, 293, 302

investment in plant and buildings, 119

Investors in People, 191–3, 195, 234, 352

involvement of people, 109, 111, 161, 238, 251, 325

job descriptions for board members, 71

Johnson, G., 95

Kolb's learning cycle, 334

Kotter, John, 246, 304

Kouzes, J., 291

leadership
  as distinct from management, 284–5
  combined with listening, 241–2
  followers' expectations about, 290–91
  from boards, 39
  from chief executives, 284–91

from committee chairs, 89

of campaigning organizations, 379, 382

of change see change leaders

of cross-departmental groups, 226–8

of federal organizations, 35

leadership skills 285–8

Leadership Trust 101

learning, xviii-xix
  about delegation, 321–3
  about leadership, 285
  about planning, 148, 168
  by chief executives, 289
  by directors, 294–6
  by teams, 328, 348–50, 353–4
  commitment to, 186, 351–2
  encouragement of, 328–33, 348–52, 353–4
  from outside the organization, 352
  from planning, 113, 135
  from relationships with bosses, 306
  from users, 163
  managers' role in promotion of, 333, 353
  motivation towards, 330, 352
  organization-wide, 328, 351–3

learning cycle, 334

learning opportunities, 233, 327–8, 348, 351

'learning organization', 328, 352

learning points, 295

learning styles, 333

legal issues, 23

Lewisham Hospital Trust, 54

life cycle
  of boards, 44–7, 64
  of organizations, 355–9, 381
  of teams, 309

'linear' institutional structures, 24–8, 31–3, 37, 62

listening, 241–2
lobbying, 19
logos, 33
London Business School, 101
London Lighthouse, 103, 167
long-term future of service-providing
    organizations, 369
Long-Term Medical Conditions
    Alliance, 377
loose-tight organization, 215, 231
loyalty, 250
Lynch, Richard, 285

McGregor, Douglas, 286–7
management
    as distinct from governance, 41–4,
        64, 78
    as distinct from leadership, 284–5
    challenges facing, 297–9, 389
    components of, 97–8
    history of, 2–3
    in 'third sector', perceptions about,
        xvii
    levels of, 272, 301
    roles of, 272–3, 302
    skills of, xviii, 296–7
management accounting, 196–7
Management Charter Initiative, 332
management committees, 57
management consultants, 358
management information systems, 119
management of change *see* change
    management
management structure, xviii-xix, 19,
    22
    alternative forms of, 208, 231
    alternatives to making changes in,
        219
    criteria for changing, 224, 231
    definition of, 207
    making changes in, 205, 218–24

related to managers' skills and
    experience, 214, 223, 231
    see also change management;
        organizational change
management theories, application of,
    xvii-xviii
managing performance *see*
    performance management
managing the boss, 304–7, 327
marketing, 372, 374
'mature' boards, 45–6
'mature' organizations, 358
mediation, 49
medical charities, 105–8, 151
medical research advisory panels, 55,
    61, 90
meetings of boards, annual cycle of,
    82–3
membership organizations, 100
Mencap, 119–20, 132, 251, 388
mental models, 239
mentoring, 76, 289, 294, 302, 304,
    345–7, 353
milestones and milestone plans,
    179–80, 227
minutes, 91
mission, sense of, xvii, 100–112
    passim, 387
    for teams, 315
mission statements, 94, 109, 134
mistakes, acknowledgement of, 328
monasteries, medieval, 2–3
motivating vision, 247, 254
motivation
    in the 'third sector', 20–22, 100,
        242, 297, 387
    of board members, 70
    of donors, 20
    towards learning, 330, 352
'mourning' stage of team
    development, 310

multi-input reviews, 340
Mumford, Alan, 295, 333
Murvis, P., 297
mutual societies, 11
mutual-support organizations, 361–2,
    367–8, 374–8, 381–2
    tensions between members and
    staff, 376–7
Myers Briggs test, 350

names of organizations, use of, 32–3,
    38
National Asthma Campaign, 99, 102,
    115
National Council for Voluntary
    Organizations, 7, 76, 191, 194,
    369, 377, 394
National Health Service Trusts,
    85
National Housing Federation, 377
National Society for the Prevention of
    Cruelty toChildren (NSPCC),
    182
National Trust, 8, 36
negotiating with purchasers of
    services, 373
Nepal Water for Health, 32
Nolan Committee, 76
non-governmental organizations
    (NGOs), 8, 36
'norming' stage of team development,
    310
norms, behavioural, 263
not-for-profit sector, definition of, 8–9
Nuffield Nursing Homes Trust, 8

objectives
    checking quality of, 122
    clarification of, 120, 155
    conflict between, 115–16, 120
    definition of, 94

departmental and cross-
    departmental, 117–19
development of, 112
established by service strategies, 164
external and internal, 118
for delegated work, 321
for teams, 313–15, 327
hierarchy of, 113–14, 155
management by, 321
personal, 338, 260, 288
realism of, 122, 172–3, 315, 379
setting of, 121
specificity of, 18, 22, 122
strategic, 115–16, 155
value of having, 120
objectivity, 76
The Observer, 13
observers at board meetings, 85–7
officers, definition of, xxii
'old guard' and 'new guard', 358
one-to-ones, 304, 307, 330, 335–8, 345,
    353
Open University Business School, 331,
    337
openness, 77, 316
operational planning, 160, 164–70
opinion, differences of, 286, 316
opportunism, 133
orchestras, 124, 158
organization, definition of, xxi
organization design
    dilemmas of, 214–18, 231
    reviews of, 222, 231
'organization development', 241
organization-wide learning, 328,
    350–51, 354
organizational change
    commitment to, 252
    characteristics of, 244–6, 271
    obstacles to (and possible
    solutions), 268–71

organizational change – *cont.*
    opposition to, 242–3, 267, 271
    types of, 239–40
    see also change management
organizational culture *see* culture
outcome indicators, 178
outdoor education centres, 166
output indicators, 178
overhead costs, 197, 199
'ownership' of tasks or
        responsibilities, 324; *see also*
        empowerment
Oxfam, 8, 17, 31, 213–14, 370, 388
Oxford University, 368

paradigms, 239
partnerships
    between board and management,
        47
    between organizations, 369
    between sectors, 16, 384
    for benchmarking, 188
pay determination, 342
people, development of, 234, 303–4,
        322, 326, 330–35, 353, 390
people affected by change 264–5
people management, competencies
        for, 332
people-related activities, 337
performance, below-standard, 342–3,
        353
performance indicators, 176–80, 227
    for projects and special initiatives,
        179–80
    for service and overall strategy,
        178–9
    objections to, 177–8
performance management, xviii, 110,
        171–86, 350
    concepts behind, 173–6
    definition of, 94

strengthening of systems for, 181–6
    performance-management cycle,
        173
performance measurement, 50, 147,
        156, 171
performance monitoring, 67, 141, 324,
        371, 373
    strategic and operational, 174–6,
        183–4
performance reviews, 336, 338–40
    for teams, 316
    linked to pay, 342
    360°, 289, 340–42, 353
'performing' stage of team
        development, 310
person specifications, 335
personal development, 294–5, 304, 353
personality conflicts, 305
personality traits, 350
personnel departments, 212
Petronius Arbiter, 313
piloting of change initiatives, 259–60
planning
    commitment to, 140
    of the planning process itself,
        139–41, 156, 161, 169
    strategic or operational, 138
    timescales for, 161–2
    see also operational planning;
        strategic planning
planning architecture, 160, 169
planning guidelines, 165, 170
policies established by boards,
        documentation of, 87
'political' aspects of management, 19,
        123–4, 379, 382
political developments affecting the
        organization, 128, 163–4, 293
Poor Law, 3–4
Posner, B., 291
    power bases, 286

'pragmatists' in learning, 333–4
predictability of the environment, 139
prescriptive approach, xix-xx
Prince's Trust - Action, 261–2
Prince's Youth Business Trust, 101
prioritisation, 173, 259, 269, 298, 320
   in campaigning organizations, 380
private lives of managers, 297
private sector, 15–16
process indicators, 178
professional associations, 125, 362, 374
professional development of
      managers, 226, 282, 352
professional groups, pressure from,
      298
programme management, 240
project management, 229–30, 240
project planning, 229
project teams, 183–4, 308
public sector, 3, 11–12, 16, 383
purchaser-provider relationship, 7, 12,
      374, 383–4
purpose, statements of, 102, 107
purpose of organizations, 277, 372
   classification according to, 361–2

quality standards, 234
quality management, 190–91
quality of services, 177, 277
quality principles, 191–2
quasi-autonomous non-governmental
      organizations (quangos), 11
quick wins, 259, 271, 379

recognition of people's efforts, 285–6
Red Cross, 28–9, 110
redundancy policies, 343, 353
reflection, time for, 267, 339, 349
'reflectors' in learning, 333
're-forming' stage of team
      development, 310

regional managers, 211, 304
Relate, 25, 121, 150–51, 251
religious organizations, 2; see also
      churches
remuneration committees, 60
representation
   as a function of boards, 39–41,
      53–4, 63
   as a function of leaders generally,
      323
   as a role of voluntary action, 13, 21
   as distinct from governance, 57–8
   non-specialist skills of, 72–3
representative teams, 249
reputations of chief executives, 288
research departments, 211
resources
   allocation of, 20, 50, 150–52, 215
   needed to support managers, 300
   strategic review of, 128
results, focus on, 172, 389
risk-aversion of boards, 81
role swapping, 86
Roman Empire, 2
Royal National Institute for the Blind
      (RNIB), 100, 101, 116–17, 175,
      183–4, 369
Royal National Lifeboat Institution, 17
Royal Society for Prevention of
      Cruelty to Animals (RSPCA), 54
Royal Society for the Protection of
      Birds, 388
RPS Rainer, 30
Ryder, Sue, 368

St. Bartholomew's Hospital, 368
Salamon, L., 11
Samaritans, the, 25–6, 54, 151, 166
Save the Children Fund, 62
scenario planning, 144
scheduling of strategic choices, 135

Schein, E., 238
Scholes, K., 95
SCOPE, 100
Scott Trust, 13
self-assessment of quality standards, 194
self-image, 288
self-perpetuating boards, 37, 75
semi-independent organizations, xvi, 7
Senge, Peter, 348
senior management teams, 137–8, 206, 272, 275, 281, 293
  definition of, xxii
  departments represented on, 211–12
  size of, 210–11
  structure of, 282
SENSE, 168, 198, 218, 357
sensitivity analysis, 135, 144
'service', definition of, 157–8
service delivery units, xxii, 118, 158–60, 169
service plans, 169–70
service-providing organizations, 361–2, 368–74, 381
service reviews, 162–3
service strategies, 160–64, 169
service users
  see users of services
shadowing, 346–7, 353
shaping, 49–50, 337, 350
skill base of an organization, 275
skills
  need for, 72–3
  of existing staff, 260, 322, 331–2, 339
'slice' teams, 249
SMART criteria, 116
Social Audit, 191, 193, 195
social events, 87, 312
social exclusion, 30
social franchise model, 30, 38

social service organizations, 150, 154, 166, 276
Solly, Henry, 4
Spastics Society, 100
specialist skills, 72–3
specialization amongst 'third sector' organizations, 387–8
sponsors of projects, 267
sponsorship from alcoholic drink and tobacco companies, 152
sports clubs, 13
staff associations, 223
stakeholders, xxi, 18, 22, 49, 124; *see also* accountability; communication
standard-setting, 6, 33, 61, 191
state intervention in social affairs, 6–7, 11–12
'storming' stage of team development, 309
'straight-line' institutional structure, 24; *see also* 'linear'
strategic choices, 133–5, 143, 148, 155
  weighting and scheduling of, 134–6
strategic dilemmas, 148–53, 156
strategic frameworks, 145, 147
strategic freedom, 138–9, 364
strategic issues, 132–3
strategic management, xviii–xix, 4, 6, 93–9 *passim*, 110–11, 158
  benefits of 96–7
strategic planning, 112–15, 350
  ACENVO survey of, 148
  history and nature of, 112–13
  in campaigning organizations, 380
  in different types or organization, 138–9
  objections to, 136, 140
  preconditions for, 137–40
  timescales for, 140, 143, 147
Strategic Planning Society, 93

strategic plans
    content of, 145–6
    desirable characteristics of, 147,
        156
    preparation of, 141–4
    responsibilities for implementation
        of, 147
strategic position, 130–32, 155
strategic reviews, 125–7, 155, 174
strategic thinking, 147, 161, 292, 301
strategy
    definition of, 94
    development of, 112, 156
    disagreements over, 154–5
    evolution of, 123–4, 155
    frequency of review of, 113
    levels of, 125
    management of, 125–6
structural change in organizations see
        management structure
styles of working 305, 307, 317; see also
        learning styles
sub-committees, 55, 59–61, 314, 327
subconscious assumptions, 237
subsidy requirements, 131, 163, 166
succession planning, 78–9
supervision meetings, 335; see also
        one-to-ones
SWOT, 131–2, 148
    symptoms or causes, dealing with,
        150–51, 156, 268

targets, 172; see also objectives
task groups, 55, 63, 87, 143, 225
task-related activities, 337
teams
    changes in membership of, 312–13,
        327
    characteristic roles of members of,
        350
    creation of, 310–12

    desirable characteristics of, 308–9
    development of, 313–19
    leadership of, 303–4
    learning by, 328, 348–50, 353–4
    members' characteristics in, 311–12
    reviewing work and learning of, 349
    size of, 310, 327
    types of, 308
    useful people in 350
telephone conferencing, 295
tendering, 373
theatres, 154
'theorists' in learning, 333
'third sector'
    boundaries of, 8–12, 21
    characteristics of, xvi, 18, 112–13,
        308–9
    definition of, xv–xvi
    distinctiveness of, 16, 22
    diversity of, 366
    future of, 382–9
    history of, 1–4, 21, 383
    impact on everyday life of, 14–15,
        18, 22
    philosophy of, 1
    rising expectations about, 233
    role of, xvii
    share of GDP of, 385
    size and growth of, 13–15, 21
'third sector' organizations
    'core' and 'peripheral', 10, 363, 368
    selected dates of establishment, 4–6
    successful, 389–90
time budgets, 229–30
time-limited appointments to boards,
        71
time management, 285, 318
time recording by staff, 159
timetables for implementing plans,
        147, 156, 166, 168
timing of initiatives, 280–81

tobacco sponsorship, 152
top-down management, 24, 98, 241, 335
trade unions, 223, 322, 362, 374
Trades Union Congress, 377
trading income, 388
training, 163, 260, 338, 340, 351
  of board members, 76
tranformational change, 239, 246, 249, 263
transactions in different sectors, nature of, 17–18
transitional change, 239–40, 249, 263
Transport and General Workers' Union, 8
trends
  in external environment, 126–7, 210, 293, 301
  in service delivery, 177
trust, 312, 321
trustees, 37
  see also board members

umbrella bodies, 377–8
uncertainty, coping with, 95, 206
United Response, 212
United States, xvi
unrestricted income, 138, 196, 201, 385
user involvement, 72–3, 92, 233
user satisfaction, 179, 370
users of services
  definition of, xxi
  information from, 17–18, 251
  needs of, 130, 162, 370–71, 374
  potential numbers of, 127, 162
  sitting on boards, 365
  views of, 176–7, 299
value added, 48, 192, 388

value for money, 131–2, 172; see also cost-effectiveness
value systems, 275–6
values, xx, 16, 19, 22, 102–3, 107, 111, 145, 152, 154, 156, 207, 236–8, 374
  inappropriate, 276
  of mutual-support organizations, 375, 382
values statements 109
Victim Support, 8
vision, 99–100, 110–11, 288, 291
  creating and refreshing, 105–8, 111
  definition of, 93
  for change initiatives, 254–5
  shared, 96
  see also motivating vision
vision statements, 109
visionary leadership, 389
voluntarism, 19, 22
voluntary sector, 6–8, 11, 13–14, 368
Voluntary Service Overseas (VSO), 102, 103, 146, 209, 240–41, 255
volunteers, 13, 20, 387

waiting lists, 371
WaterAid, 32, 99, 101
welfare dependency, 4
Williams, C., 268
work plans, 298
work programmes, 165
World Blind Union, 32
Worldwide Fund for Nature, 265–6

Young, Ken, 13
Young Men's Christian Association (YMCA), 81
young people, services for, 30–31
'youthful' boards, 45
'youthful' organizations, 358

About the Directory of Social Change

Set up in 1975, the DSC is now one of the largest independent organisations to serve the needs of the voluntary sector. Its aims are to support the voluntary sector by:

- giving voluntary and community groups the information and skills they need to meet their objectives;

- encouraging groups to network and share information, thus developing a sustainable future for UK voluntary activity;

- campaigning to protect and promote the interests of the sector as a whole.

Publications   Tel. 0171 209 5151

We research and publish a comprehensive range of directories, handbooks and journals on many subjects concerning the voluntary sector today. Our reputation rests on our commitment to providing expert information which is accurate, accessible and affordable. Phone us for a free copy of the publications list.

Courses and Conferences   Tel. 0171 209 4949

We run the largest programme of training courses in the UK voluntary sector. Our training courses – like our publications – cover the key skills needed in the sector.

Our conferences and seminars focus on the latest important issues affecting the voluntary sector.

Charityfair   Tel. 0171 209 4949

Charityfair is the biggest annual event for the UK's voluntary sector. Over 10,000 people come each year to benefit from the most extensive selection of training, advice and debate for charities to be found under one roof.

Charityfair takes place at London's Business Design Centre at the end of April every year.

Charity Centre   Tel. 0171 209 1015

The Charity Centre at 24 Stephenson Way, London NW1 2DP provides five training or meeting rooms, a large conference room and a reference library. Also located at the Charity Centre is London's largest charity bookshop, where the entire range of DSC books and many other titles can be bought over the counter.

PENGUIN ONLINE

READ MORE IN PENGUIN

In every corner of the world, on every subject under the sun, Penguin represents quality and variety – the very best in publishing today.

For complete information about books available from Penguin – including Puffins, Penguin Classics and Arkana – and how to order them, write to us at the appropriate address below. Please note that for copyright reasons the selection of books varies from country to country.

In the United Kingdom: Please write to *Dept. EP, Penguin Books Ltd, Bath Road, Harmondsworth, West Drayton, Middlesex UB7 0DA*

In the United States: Please write to *Consumer Sales, Penguin Putnam Inc., P.O. Box 12289 Dept. B, Newark, New Jersey 07101-5289.* VISA and MasterCard holders call 1-800-788-6262 to order Penguin titles

In Canada: Please write to *Penguin Books Canada Ltd, 10 Alcorn Avenue, Suite 300, Toronto, Ontario M4V 3B2*

In Australia: Please write to *Penguin Books Australia Ltd, P.O. Box 257, Ringwood, Victoria 3134*

In New Zealand: Please write to *Penguin Books (NZ) Ltd, Private Bag 102902, North Shore Mail Centre, Auckland 10*

In India: Please write to *Penguin Books India Pvt Ltd, 11 Community Centre, Panchsheel Park, New Delhi 110017*

In the Netherlands: Please write to *Penguin Books Netherlands bv, Postbus 3507, NL-1001 AH Amsterdam*

In Germany: Please write to *Penguin Books Deutschland GmbH, Metzlerstrasse 26, 60594 Frankfurt am Main*

In Spain: Please write to *Penguin Books S. A., Bravo Murillo 19, 1° B, 28015 Madrid*

In Italy: Please write to *Penguin Italia s.r.l., Via Benedetto Croce 2, 20094 Corsico, Milano*

In France: Please write to *Penguin France, Le Carré Wilson, 62 rue Benjamin Baillaud, 31500 Toulouse*

In Japan: Please write to *Penguin Books Japan Ltd, Kaneko Building, 2-3-25 Koraku, Bunkyo-Ku, Tokyo 112*

In South Africa: Please write to *Penguin Books South Africa (Pty) Ltd, Private Bag X14, Parkview, 2122 Johannesburg*

READ MORE IN PENGUIN

BUSINESS AND ECONOMICS

Webonomics Evan I. Schwartz

In *Webonomics*, Evan I. Schwartz defines nine essential principles for growing your business on the Web. Using case studies of corporations such as IBM and Volvo, as well as smaller companies and web-based start-ups, Schwartz documents both the tremendous failures and the successes on the Web in a multitude of industries.

Inside Organizations Charles B. Handy

Whatever we do, whatever our profession, organizing is a part of our lives. This book brings together twenty-one ideas which show you how to work with and through other people. There are also questions at the end of each chapter to get you thinking on your own and in a group.

Lloyds Bank Small Business Guide Sara Williams

This long-running guide to making a success of your small business deals with real issues in a practical way. 'As comprehensive an introduction to setting up a business as anyone could need' *Daily Telegraph*

Teach Yourself to Think Edward de Bono

Edward de Bono's masterly book offers a structure that broadens our ability to respond to and cope with a vast range of situations. *Teach Yourself to Think* is software for the brain, turning it into a successful thinking mechanism, and, as such, will prove of immense value to us all.

The Road Ahead Bill Gates

Bill Gates – the man who built Microsoft – takes us back to when he dropped out of Harvard to start his own software company and discusses how we stand on the brink of a new technology revolution that will for ever change and enhance the way we buy, work, learn and communicate with each other.

READ MORE IN PENGUIN

BUSINESS AND ECONOMICS

Public Spending   Evan Davis

Does a large public sector 'crowd out' innovation and investment? Can we combine the best features of the old 'public service ethos' with a commitment to efficiency and value for money? In this superb new book, leading economic journalist Evan Davis offers a refreshing dose of clear thinking.

The Strength to Change   Peter Pugh

The Strength to Change tells the remarkable story of one of the largest and most successful mergers in business history: of the Halifax and the Leeds, two of the largest building societies in Britain, and their courageous and ambitious decision to convert the combined society into a public company.

Release 2.1   Esther Dyson

In *Release 2.1* Esther Dyson, the most powerful woman in the computer world, explodes the myths and mysteries surrounding the Internet and explores its role in our future, both in business and our everyday lives. 'Will help to demystify the Digital Age for the most oppressed of technophobes' *Guardian*

Faith and Credit   Susan George and Fabrizio Sabelli

In its fifty years of existence, the World Bank has influenced more lives in the Third World than any other institution, yet remains largely unknown, even enigmatic. This richly illuminating and lively overview examines the policies of the Bank, its internal culture and the interests it serves.

The Penguin Companion to European Union   Timothy Bainbridge

A balanced, comprehensive picture of the institutions, personalities, arguments and political pressures that have shaped Europe since the end of the Second World War.

READ MORE IN PENGUIN

BUSINESS

Corporate Strategy	Igor Ansoff
Atlas of Management Thinking	Edward de Bono
The 5-Day Course in Thinking	
Lateral Thinking for Management	
Water Logic	
Opportunities	
Wordpower	
Accidental Empires	Robert Cringely
Offensive Marketing	Hugh Davidson
Even More Offensive Marketing	
Commercial Law	R. M. Goode
Cosmopolitan Guide to Working in Finance	Robert Gray
New Marketing Practice	David Mercer
Understanding Company Financial Statements	R. H. Parker
Cosmopolitan Guide to Working in Retail	Elaine Robertson
An Insight into Management Accounting	John Sizer
Corporate Recovery	Stuart Slatter
The Art of Japanese Management	Richard Tanner Pascale and Anthony Athos
Management and Motivation	Victor H. Vroom and Edward L. Deci
The Manager's Casebook	Woods and Thomas